Cornell Studies in the Philosophy of Religion

EDITED BY WILLIAM P. ALSTON

On a Complex Theory
of a Simple God

Christopher Hughes

ON A COMPLEX THEORY
OF A SIMPLE GOD

An Investigation in Aquinas'
Philosophical Theology

Cornell University Press, Ithaca and London

First published 1989 by Cornell University Press.

International Standard Book Number 0-8014-1759-7
Library of Congress Catalog Card Number 89-42877

Printed in the United States of America

Librarians: Library of Congress cataloging information appears on the last page of the book.

The paper in this book is acid-free and meets the guidelines for permanence and durability of the Committee on Production Guidelines for Book Longevity of the Council on Library Resources.

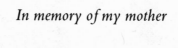

In memory of my mother

Contents

Preface

For Aquinas, one and the same God may be characterized in two very different ways. He is the simplest possible subsistent being, identical to all of His parts, and to His (intrinsic) attributes, His essence, and His existence. At the same time, He is three persons in one nature, one of whom subsists in a human as well as in the divine nature. In the first part of this book, I attempt to explicate Aquinas' conception of divine simplicity; in the second, I attempt to explicate his account of the Trinity and the Incarnation. I also try to determine whether Aquinas' conception of divine simplicity and his accounts of the Trinity and the Incarnation are individually and jointly workable. This involves trying to answer the following questions: Could anything be simple in all the ways Aquinas thinks God is simple? Could any being have the kind of metaphysical structure which for Aquinas makes God triune? Could any being have the kind of relational property which for Aquinas makes God's Word incarnate? Could anything as simple as Aquinas' God be three persons in one nature, one of whom subsists in each of two natures? I argue that Aquinas' full-strength conception of divine simplicity is unworkable, although a weakened and reconstructed conception may not be. Moreover, I argue that because Aquinas' accounts of the Trinity and the Incarnation each presuppose the full-strength conception, they inherit its unworkability. Finally, I address the question whether or not a reconstructed account of divine simplicity will mesh with anything like Aquinas' account of the Trinity and Incarnation—or any other (orthodox) account thereof.

I am grateful to many friends and colleagues for criticism and advice—among them Roy Endersby, Lily Knezevich, Shelly Kagan, Richard Gale, Philip Quinn, Al Martinich, David Kaplan, Marilyn McCord Adams, Eleonore Stump, Sydney Shoemaker, Robert Stalnaker, Richard Boyd, Richard Sorabji, Christopher Peacocke, and Mario Mignucci. I am especially indebted to Gerald Massey, without whose help and encouragement the dissertation that became this book never would have been; to Norman Kretzmann, who—in spite of and because of our disagreements over the distance between Athens and Jerusalem—helped me greatly in turning the dissertation into a book; and to William Alston, whose suggestions about how to turn this book into a better one were very valuable (however well they were implemented). These acknowledgments would be incomplete without mention of David Lewis. Although he has only rarely written on philosophical theology, his ideas have had a considerable influence on this book—and in particular, on those sections in which I attempt to cross-pollinate medieval and contemporary ideas. Finally, I thank my wife, Marcia, for her unfailing and loving support from the time I began to think about Thomas Aquinas to the completion of this book, and my daughters, Laura Kimi and Amanda, for their attempts to "help Dada make book."

CHRISTOPHER HUGHES

Wimbledon, 1989

Abbreviations

CT	*Compendium theologiae*
DE	*De ente et essentia*
DP	"De potentia"
DPN	*De principiis naturae*
DSC	"De spiritualibus creaturis"
DUVI	"De unione verbi incarnati"
DV	"De veritate"
IPH	*In peri hermeneias*
ME	*In duodecim libros metaphysicorum expositio*
PE	*In octo libros physicorum expositio*
QQ	*Quaestiones quodlibetales*
SCG	*Summa contra Gentiles*
SS	*Scriptum super libros sententiarum*
ST	*Summa theologiae*

Unless stated otherwise, the translations provided in the text are my own, although I am indebted to existing translations.

PART I

THE GOD OF THE PHILOSOPHERS

Divine Simplicity:
God and His Existence

Types of Divine Simplicity

Of the properties ascribed to God in Aquinas' natural theology, we may call one sort *ampliative,* and one sort *limitative.* The ampliative properties, which include knowledge, power, and goodness, are familiar: they are the (positive) perfections of God. The limitative properties are less familiar and more problematic. They are properties God is said to have by virtue of not having certain kinds of (putative) imperfections—where Aquinas' conception of imperfection includes many properties that seem essential to any possible being. Among those (putative) imperfections is composition: according to Aquinas, God is incomposite in each of the following ways:

(1) He is not composed of extended parts; hence He is not, and does not have, a body.

(2) He is not composed of substantial form—in virtue of which He is the kind of thing He is—and form-receiving matter—in virtue of which He is the particular thing He is. God is instead pure self-subsistent form, devoid of matter of any kind.

(3) God is not 'composed' of act and potency. There is no distinction in God between an element by virtue of which He has certain potentialities, and an element by virtue of which those potentialities are actualized. Consequently, God is entirely immutable and atemporal.

(4) God is not composed of essence and anything disjoint from that essence. While there is a difference between the individ-

ual, Socrates, and his essence (humanity), there is no difference between God and His essence (Godhead or Deity).

(5) God is not composed of subject and accidents. There are not in God any properties outside of the divine essence which enter into composition with that essence. Instead, His wisdom, His power, His goodness, and the like are all the same as the divine essence (which is to say, the same as God), and hence all the same as one another.

(6) God is not composed of essence and *esse* (existence)—of a what-He-is and a that-He-is. The divine essence (God) is pure subsistent existence, inherent in nothing distinct from it, and having nothing distinct from it inherent in it.[1]

It follows from (1)–(6), on Aquinas' account, that God is altogether simple (*omnino simplex*) and in no way composite.

Some of (1)–(6) are conceptually unproblematic. For example, the claim that God has no extended parts is on the face of it intelligible: there may be a great many things (propositions, sets, geometrical points) which fail to have extended parts. Similarly, there is no evident incoherence in supposing that God lacks composition of form and matter: various possible objects (instants, numbers) lack such composition. (Of course, it does not follow from the fact that God lacks form-matter composition that God may be described as a pure self-subsistent form. As we shall see, there are problems about whether anything could be at once subsistent and a form.)

If (1) and (2) are unobjectionable, then (3) and (4) are worrisome, and (5) and (6) daunting. (6) is perhaps the single most baffling claim Aquinas makes about God. It is also one of the most central: for, Aquinas holds, (1)–(5) all follow from (6) (see, e.g., ST Ia.3.7, *responsio*). This suggests that an exposition of Aquinas' conception of divine simplicity should take the following form: first we would explicate Aquinas' claim that God is *ipsum esse* (pure subsistent existence), and then we would make clear why Aquinas thought anything that was *ipsum esse* would have to have all the sorts of noncomposition ascribed to God in *Quaestio* 3 of the *Prima pars* of the *Summa theologiae*. A defense of Aquinas' conception of divine simplicity would have the same structure: its goal would be to show both that something could be pure subsistent existence, and that any being of that sort would necessarily lack all the sorts of composition discussed in *Quaestio* 3.

[1]This list is culled from ST Ia.3 and DP 7.

Unfortunately, I don't know how to construe Aquinas' claim that God is *ipsum esse* in such a way that it fails to come out necessarily false. Before arguing that God could not be *ipsum esse,* I shall try to explicate what Aquinas means when he says that, although in creatures *esse* is distinct from essence, there is in God nothing distinct from His own *esse.*

Form and Existence

In order to understand Aquinas' conception of *esse,* it is helpful to look at his conception of form, since forms and *esse* have important features in common. Suppose that Socrates is wise. We may ask by virtue of what Socrates is wise, or what it is in Socrates that makes him wise. Aquinas would say that what makes Socrates wise is the accidental form *Socrates' wisdom.* The wisdom in Socrates, for Aquinas, is not to be thought of as the universal, wisdom, present in its entirety in all and only those things that are wise. Rather it is a dependent particular, present only in Socrates (see, e.g., ST Ia.29.1, *responsio*). Just as its existence is parasitic on that of a particular substance (if Socrates had never existed, Socrates' wisdom never could have), so too is its individuation: the distinctness of Socrates' wisdom from Plato's wisdom is grounded in the metaphysically prior distinctness of Socrates and Plato. Aquinas would not deny that one can speak of the universal, wisdom, common to both Socrates and Plato; but he would hold that such an entity has no existence outside the mind: real beings—whether substantial or accidental—are particulars, not found in more than one thing.

Aquinas conceives of the received substantial form of Socrates, *Socrates' humanity,* in much the same way—with this difference: accidental forms are received in the substance Socrates, and realize Socrates' potentiality to be a certain way (*viz.,* wise); the substantial form, *Socrates' humanity,* is received by a particular chunk of matter, and realizes that matter's potentiality to be a certain kind of thing.

Although Aquinas does not take *esse* to be just another form,[2] he thinks of the *esse* or existence of a (created) substance as a dependent particular in much the sense described above. Thus Aquinas believes

[2]For Aquinas, the existence of a thing is not its substantial form: its substantial form, but not its existence, is that by virtue of which it falls under a specific natural kind. Nor is existence for Aquinas an accident in the ordinary sense, although he is willing to call existence an accident, if all this means is that existence is a property not included in a (created) thing's essence: "Et sic dico quod esse substantiale rei non est accidens, sed actualitas cuiuslibet formae existentis . . . dico quod accidens dicitur large omne quod non est pars essentiae; et sic est esse in rebus creatis" (QQ 12.5.1).

that the answer to the question "What is it in Socrates that makes him exist?" ("What is it in virtue of which Socrates exists?") is Socrates' *esse;* he thinks that Socrates' *esse* is distinct from Plato's *esse;* he does not believe that Socrates' *esse* could exist apart from Socrates; and he holds that the distinctness of Socrates' *esse* and Plato's *esse* is grounded in the (logically) prior distinctness of Socrates' and Plato's essences (see, e.g., DP 7.2 *ad* 5). Finally, Aquinas thinks that the *esse* that is common to all entities is a being of reason, having no real existence (see SCG I.26 and ST Ia.76.2, *responsio*).

Socrates' substantial form, his accidental forms, and his *esse* have this in common: they all realize certain potentialities. (His substantial form realizes a potentiality to be this man, his accidental forms a potentiality to be a certain way [for example, wise or white], and his *esse* the potentiality to be at all.) A natural question is whether forms and *esse* themselves have potentialities, which potentialities are realized by (higher-order) entities.

In the case of substantial forms, the answer depends on what sort of substantial form we are considering. Aquinas seems to think that the received substantial forms of material substances do not themselves have potentialities realized by accidents or by *esse,* although the substances having those substantial forms do (DP 7.4, *responsio*). But Aquinas thinks that some substantial forms—for example, angelic forms—are subsistent, and have potentialities realized by accidents and by *esse.* (See ST Ia.50.5, *responsio*. There are worries about how any substantial form could be subsistent; I discuss some of them in Chapter 3.)

Where accidental forms are concerned, things are not so clear. Aquinas sometimes speaks as if accidents had their own esse, which just was *inesse*—that is, inherence. His considered view, however, is that *esse* is strictly speaking (*proprie et vere*) found in substance, and not in accidents. The whiteness in a tooth is said to be, just because something else (namely, the tooth) has a qualified sort of being (namely, being white) on account of it.[3]

---

[3]"Esse enim proprie et vere dicitur de supposito subsistente. Accidentia enim et formae non subsistentes dicuntur esse inquantum eis aliquid subsistit; sicut albedo dicitur ens, inquantum ea est aliquid album" (DUVI 4, *responsio*). See also ST Ia.45.4, *responsio:* "Formae autem et accidentia et alia huiusmodi non dicuntur entia quasi ipsa sint, sed quia eis aliquid est." Despite these general remarks, Aquinas is committed to the view that in one special case *esse* may be properly ascribed to accidents—namely, when some accidents of bread and wine continue existing, although they are in no subject, after transubstantiation (ST 3a.77.1 *ad* 4 and ST 3a.77.2). As Aquinas recognizes, if accidents can go on existing, while inherent in no subject, it cannot be that for them to exist is just for some subject to have a qualified sort of existence on their account.

As to whether accidents can be the subject of (higher-order) accidents, Aquinas thinks that at least in one case they can: in the Eucha-
rist, accidents that were received by bread and wine before transubstantiation are received after transubstantiation by nothing other than
the accident of dimensive quantity which used to be received by the
(no longer existent) bread and wine. In his discussion of this case,
some of Aquinas' remarks suggest that he thinks that even in non-
miraculous cases, one accident can be the subject of another, although
a miracle is necessary for an accident to be an unsupported or ultimate
subject of an accident (cf. ST 3a.77.2 *ad* 1).

Although for Aquinas forms can, as it were, be found at either end
of the receiving relation, the same is not true for *esse*. *Esse* does not
receive higher-order *esse* (the supposition that it did would lead to a
kind of infinite regress Aquinas would not be happy with); and it does
not receive accidents. For it is always the least potential element in a
thing: "Existence is the most perfect of all things, and is related to
everything else as act. Nothing else has actuality except insofar as it
exists, so existence itself is the actuality of all things and even of forms
themselves. For this reason it is not related to anything else as receiver
to received, but rather as received to receiver" (ST 1a.4.1 *ad* 3). *Esse* is
at the other end of the spectrum from prime matter. Prime matter
receives but is never received; forms can either be received or receiving; *esse* is received but never receives.

If *esse* is formlike, it is in one way more like an accidental form, and
in one way more like a substantial form. On the one hand, it is like an
accidental form, on Aquinas' view, in that (except in the case of God)
it is not contained in the essence of a thing (see QQ 12.5.1). Existence
is neither what kind of thing Socrates is nor part of what kind of thing
he is. Indeed, Aquinas often speaks of *esse* as coming to a creature from
without—the way the accident of heat can come to a creature from
without (say, when it is placed next to a fire). On the other hand, it is
the nature of any accidental form to exist in some subject distinct from
it.[4] Substantial forms by contrast come in two varieties—those received in matter, and those that (naturally) subsist on their own. The
same is true of *esse*. For Aquinas, just as there are received and subsistent substantial forms, so too there is received and subsistent *esse;* and
the distinction between received and subsistent *esse* just is the distinction between creaturely *esse* and divine *esse*.

The above sketch of Aquinas' conception of *esse* does not make it
easy to see what it would be like for it to be true that God was nothing

[4]Aquinas holds that in transubstantiation, accidents (miraculously) exist in a way
that is not natural for them.

but subsistent existence, but it does help make evident the links between the view that God is subsistent existence and (1)–(5). In particular, we can see why Aquinas would hold that we could get from (6)—
the claim that God was His own existence—to (5)—the claim that
God was the subject of no accidents. Accidents are found only in a
being with potentialities to be actualized; *esse* has no potentialities;
consequently, any being that is nothing over and above its *esse* must be
accident-free. Likewise, we can see why Aquinas thought there was an
entailment between (6) and (4)—the claim that in God there are no real
potentialities.[5]

Of course, whether we can in fact get from (6) to (5) will depend on
whether *esse* is in fact the subject of no accidents. When we realize,
though, how restrictive Aquinas' notion of accident is, it looks plausible that anything that was just subsistent existence would be accident-
free.

Contemporary analytic philosophers are often generous about what
counts as a property, supposing that for every function from the set of
possible worlds to the set of possible individuals, (or every set of
world-bound *possibilia,* for the counterpart theorist) there is a corresponding property. And someone might think that when Aquinas
speaks of Socrates' accidents, we should understand by this the set of
properties (broadly conceived) that are not essential to Socrates—that
is, the set of properties of Socrates which he lacks in some possible
world in which he exists. This would be a mistake, for two reasons.
First, some (though not all) of the properties inseparable from Socrates
are accidents of him. Although Aquinas would hold that *being a man,
being an animal, being rational, being self-identical, being one,* and *existing*
are not accidents of Socrates, he would say that *being risible* and *being
susceptible of certain kinds of instruction* are Socratic accidents, even
though they follow on his nature, and are consequently inseparable
from him. Second, some of the properties Socrates has in some but not
all of the worlds he inhabits would not be counted as accidents by
Aquinas. Thus neither *being thought of by Plato* nor *lacking sight* would
be recognized by Aquinas as accidents of Socrates.

Under what conditions, then, would Aquinas say that an expression
of the form "the *F*-ness of an *x*" picks out an accident of *x*? Aquinas'

[5]The notion of a real potentiality is an elusive one. As a first approximation we might
say: a subject *s* has a real potentiality to be *F* at a time *t* just in case *s* is not *F* at that time *t*,
s is *F* on some possible future relative to *t*, and it is not the case that *s*'s becoming *F*
would be a mere Cambridge change in *s*. For a discussion of mere Cambridge changes,
see Peter Geach, "God's Relation to the World," in his *Logic Matters* (Berkeley:
University of California Press, 1972), pp. 318–27.

view is something like this: "The *F*-ness of *x*" may pick out either the nature of *x*, or something contained in that nature. In neither case does it pick out an accident of *x*. Consequently, humanity, animality, and rationality are not accidents of Socrates. If the expression does not signify anything contained in the nature of *x*, it may or may not pick out a dependent particular in *x* which makes *x* be a certain way—*viz.*, *F*. Again, if it does not, it does not pick out an accident of *x*. Thus for Aquinas *lacking sight* is not an accident of Homer, because what it is for Homer to lack sight is not for him to have a qualified sort of being, but rather for him to lack a certain kind of being—*being sighted*. (Nor would Aquinas count *being blind*—which he thinks of as different from *lacking sight*—as an accident: privations, like negations, are distinguished from accidental forms [cf. DPN 2].) Similarly, *being thought of by Plato* is not an accident of Socrates; what it is for Socrates to be thought of by Plato is—grammatical appearances to the contrary—for Plato, rather than Socrates, to have a certain kind of being. For a different reason, existence is not (except in a broad sense) an accident of Socrates; it does not make Socrates be a certain way, it just makes him be (see QQ 12.5.1). *Being one thing* is not counted as an accident by Aquinas, on the grounds that it no more makes a thing be in a qualified way than does existence (see ST Ia.11.1, *ad* 1, where Aquinas says that each thing is one by its substance [hence not by dint of any accident in it]). The above is far from a complete specification of the circumstances under which Aquinas would deny that an expression of the form "the *F*-ness of *x*" stands for an accident of *x*, but it should make somewhat clearer what sort of properties Aquinas takes to be accidents. The set of accidents, as conceived by Aquinas, is a proper subset of the set of properties conceived generously—excluding certain properties intimately connected with the natural kind under which an individual falls, certain properties whose exemplification by an individual is derivative (either from the nonexemplification of some other property by that individual, or from the exemplification of some property by some other individual), and certain universally exemplified properties (such as existence) which do not as it were make an individual be any particular way.

All this supports Aquinas' contention that if God is pure subsistent existence, then He must be devoid of accidents. Although pure subsistent existence would presumably have any number of properties in the broad sense (*existing, being self-identical, being one, being immaterial, being thought about often by Aquinas,* and so on), none of these properties is an accident (in Aquinas' sense). Although the obscurity of the notion of pure subsistent existence makes it difficult to say just what properties would be correctly ascribed to such a thing, it is at least far from obvious that among those properties would be any accidents.

Moreover, it would appear that Aquinas is right in thinking that any being that was pure subsistent existence would have to be incomposite in the ways described by (1)–(4). It is hard to see how pure subsistent existence could have spatially extended parts, or be composed of form and matter. And as will become clear in Chapter 3, anything as singular as subsistent existence would have to be the same as its nature. Finally, pure existence does not look like the sort of thing that could have real (as opposed to mere Cambridge) potentialities. A subject cannot have real potentialities unless it can undergo real change, and pure subsistent existence could not undergo any real changes. For such changes would involve the acquisition or the loss of either a substantial or an accidental form, and hence presuppose matter or accidents. Consequently, if God is pure subsistent existence, He will not be act-potency composite. (Actually, as we shall see later, Aquinas has a conception of real potentiality a good bit broader than the one suggested above. For this reason, it is not obvious that we can get from the claim that God is pure subsistent existence to the assertion that God is potentiality-free, as Aquinas understands this last assertion. The most we can say unproblematically is that if God is pure subsistent existence, He lacks composition of act and potency, on one natural way of understanding such composition.)

The identification of God with pure subsistent existence is, then, a hinge on which the better part of Aquinas' conception of divine simplicity turns. If we can make sense of that identification, we can make sense of the conception of divine simplicity. But could God be pure subsistent existence?

Are Properties Individualized Particulars?

A simpleminded argument to the contrary is the following: the existence of any one thing is the existence of any other, since existence is a property shared by all and only existents. Hence God's existence is, for example, the existence of this rock. But God is not the existence of this rock; so God can not be identified with His own existence. And since nothing that has its existence without being its existence is pure subsistent existence, God is not pure subsistent existence.

Aquinas, who considers something like this argument in various places (e.g., ST Ia.3.4 and SCG I.26), is not overly troubled by it. For, as we have seen, Aquinas thinks that whether or not a being is God, the existence of that being is a particular found only in that being, not a universal shared by all beings. (In the case of every being except God, its existence is an *individualized* particular, individualized by something else [the essence that receives it]; in the case of God, His existence is an individual not individualized by anything else, since it subsists.)

How satisfactory is this answer? That depends on whether properties of particulars are themselves particulars. The idea that, where *F*-ness is existence or some other attribute of an individual, the *F*-ness of *a* is distinct from the *F*-ness of *b* strikes me as prima facie less plausible than the idea that the very same property, *F*-ness, is a property of both *a* and *b*. I think that a color is a property, and that two things can have the very same color. On the face of it, this entails that one and the same property can be a property of two things. Perhaps not; perhaps what "two things can have the very same color" means is something like "two things can have individualized colors of the very same kind." But unless I have reason for thinking "two things can have the very same color" means something other than what it appears to, I should suppose that one and the same color can be the property of more than one individual. I do not want to put too much weight on this argument, however, since various attractive metaphysical theories force us to suppose that the logical form of certain propositions is different than it appears to be. So how is the argument about whether properties are individual or shared to be resolved?

For the friend of individualized properties, the expressions "the whiteness of this egg" and "the whiteness of that [distinct] egg" pick out two things of the same kind, just as "this egg" and "that egg" do. For the foe of individualized properties, those expressions pick out the same thing by means of different descriptions, just as "the morning star" and "the evening star" do. (I am assuming that the whiteness of this egg is qualitatively indiscernible from the whiteness of that egg.)

The friend of individualized properties postulates a plurality of entities where, it might be thought, one would do. Hence she owes us an account of why this plurality is needed. Such an account might bring to light (higher-order) properties with respect to which the whiteness of this egg and the whiteness of that egg must be held to be discernible. It is not easy, though, to see what such properties would be. Clearly, it would be pointless to appeal to such properties as *being in this egg* and *being in that egg,* or *being here* and *being there.* For nobody is going to agree that the whiteness in this egg and the whiteness in that egg are discernible with respect to those properties, unless they have already bought in on a view on which properties are not ones-over-many (or as I call them, ones-of-many, since a property is not something over a thing, but something of a thing). But the question at issue is why we should buy in on that view in the first place. Moreover, it is difficult to see what other sorts of properties could be appealed to in order to show that the whiteness of this egg and the whiteness of that egg are discernible.

The kind of thing the friend of individualized properties would need to support her view can be seen by considering a different sort of case. Some philosophers have thought that, for example, a gold ring and the gold it is made of were identical, while others have thought that they were distinct. A piece of evidence in favor of the latter view is that there are (apparently property-ascribing) contexts in which 'this ring' and 'the gold this ring is made of' are (apparently) not intersubstitutable *salva veritate:* for example, '———— existed before this ring did.' This evidence is not by itself conclusive; but it is up to a defender of the identity of this ring and the gold it is made of either to argue for the opacity of such contexts, or to argue that the appearance of nonintersubstitutability is deceptive. Someone who believes in individual properties should, likewise, be able to point to (apparently property-ascribing) contexts in which substitution of, say, "the whiteness of this egg" for "the whiteness of that egg" apparently turns a truth into a falsehood.

As far as I know, Aquinas does not argue for the view that properties are individual in this way. Indeed, one gets the impression that Aquinas thought it obvious enough that properties in distinct subjects must be distinct, that no argument to that effect was needed. For instance, at ST Ia.76.2, *responsio,* Aquinas asserts without argument that it is as impossible for distinct individuals to have one form as it is for them to have one *esse*. In the section on Aquinas in *Three Philosophers,* Peter Geach does offer a number of arguments for what I have been calling individualized properties and he calls individualized forms. A representative one has this structure: suppose that A is red and B is green. Then there is some feature of A which makes A red. But redness is not coloredness plus any distinguishable differentia. Hence in a red thing there are not two features, one of which makes A "barely colored," and the other of which makes A red. Instead one and the same feature of A makes A both colored and red. *Pari ratione,* one and the same feature of B makes B both colored and green. Now, if there is a feature present in both A and B which makes each of them colored (*being colored*), that feature would seem to be one that makes A red and B green. But how could one and the same feature make A red and B green? This difficulty, Geach maintains, can be solved by reference to individualized properties, as follows: there is in A one individualized property that both makes A red and makes A colored; there is in B another individualized property that both makes B green and makes B colored; and this is so even though redness, greenness, and coloredness are distinct attributes. (The attributes of redness and coloredness are like distinct functions that have the same value at the argument A; and the same goes *mutatis mutandis* for the attributes of greenness and coloredness.)[6]

Why are there not two features or properties of A, one by virtue of which A is red, and another by virtue of which A is colored? To be sure, there are not two features or properties of A, one of which is redness (or the redness of A), and the other of which is the color of A; but on anyone's account—whether or not the redness of A is an individualized property—the color of A and redness (or the redness of A) are the same feature, since redness is the property p such that p is a color and p is a property of A. Moreover, there are not two features of A, one by virtue of which A is red, and another by virtue of which A is (in Geach's words) "barely colored." Since nothing is or could be barely colored—that is, colored without also being some particular color—there is no feature by virtue of which anything is barely colored. But the opponent of individualized properties need not hold that any feature "makes" a thing just colored, but only that some (determinable) feature just "makes" a thing colored (without also making it any particular color). Is it implausible to suppose there are two properties of a green thing, one by virtue of which that thing is green, and another by virtue of which that thing is colored? I don't see why. If the green thing is a chameleon, I might truly say that this thing has always had the property of being colored, but has not always had the property of being green. True enough, there is a sense in which one and the same feature of a green thing both makes that thing green and makes it colored. But we can understand this as follows: there is a feature of a green thing—*being green*—whose presence both (as a matter of broadly logical necessity) guarantees that the thing is green, and (as a matter of broadly logical necessity) guarantees that the thing is colored. This last claim is consistent with the idea that there is also a feature of a green thing whose presence guarantees that the thing is colored, but not that the thing is any particular color.

Suppose, though, that there are not two features of a green thing, one by virtue of which it is green, and another by virtue it is colored. It follows that *being colored* is not a universal present in all green and red things. But it does not follow (in any obvious way) that *being this*

---

[6]See Peter Geach, "Aquinas," in *Three Philosophers,* ed. G. E. M. Anscombe and P. Geach (Ithaca: Cornell University Press, 1962), p. 81.

determinate shade of green is not a universal present in things this determinate shade of green. As far as I can see, Geach's argument at most
calls into question the supposition that there are determinable properties found in more than one subject. Someone who accepts Geach's
claim that there is no feature of a green thing distinct from its greenness whereby it is colored might accordingly say: there are not determinable features or properties found in more than one subject. But
that is not because determinable properties are individualized forms,
found in just one subject. It is because not every predicate picks out a
property, and, in particular, determinable predicates do not pick out
(determinable) properties. For a determinate predicate to be true of
something is, or at least may be, for a determinate property—a universal—to be present in that thing; but for a determinable predicate to
be true of something is just for some member of a certain family of
determinate properties or universals to be present in that thing. Thus,
for the predicate 'is colored' to be true of a thing is for this maximally
determinate shade of redness, or that maximally determinate shade of
redness, or this maximally determinate shade of blueness . . . to be
present in that thing (and every other thing that is exactly the same
color). Someone might say: granted that someone who accepts the
"no two features" premiss might take this line, why should he? Because, again, there is no reason to think that the determinate shade of
greenness in this bottle is in any way different from (the qualitatively
indiscernible) determinate shade of greenness in that bottle.[7]

Geach has other arguments for what I have been calling individualized properties, and what he calls individualized forms; but (for
different reasons) they look no more conclusive than the one just
considered. He argues that a wave is both a form (that by which a body
of water is in a certain shape over part of its surface) and an individual;
and in a similar vein, that a surface is both a form (that by which an
individual has a certain shape) and an individual.[8]

I am inclined to agree that (water) waves are individuals and deny
that they are individualized forms. Water waves, as I conceive of
them, are (moving) things made of water, rather than things by virtue
of which a body of water is a certain way. This way of thinking of
waves is recognized by the *Oxford English Dictionary,* which lists
among the meanings of "wave," "a moving ridge or swell of water

[7]A philosopher who actually believes in determinate but not in determinable universals is D. M. Armstrong; see his *A Theory of Universals* (Cambridge: Cambridge
University Press, 1978).

[8]Cf. Peter Geach, "Form and Existence," in his *God and the Soul* (London: Routledge
and Kegan Paul, 1969), p. 53, and "Aquinas," p. 81.

between two depressions." A moving ridge of water is an individual, but not an individualized form: instead it is a material object—an individual that, in Aristotelian language, has both matter and form. (A ridge of water has a certain mass, is made of a certain kind of stuff, can crash into houses, and has any number of other properties that may be ascribed to material objects, but not to the forms of those objects.) Admittedly, the *OED* lists other meanings of "wave" relevant here, including "a movement in . . . water by which a portion of the water rises above the normal level and then subsides." A movement in a portion of water will not be a material object, but it will once again be an individual, without being a form, since it will be a particular event. As far as I can tell, none of the senses of "wave" mentioned in the *OED* picks out anything that is both an individual and a property, and I don't see why we should think any sense of "wave" does.

"Surface," like "wave," can apparently be used to pick out a number of different kinds of things. As Avrum Stroll has pointed out, some of our talk about surfaces makes it sound as though the surface of a material object is a physical part thereof, constituted at a time by the atoms that at that time make up the outermost layer of that object.[9] (Naturally, it is often vague and context-dependent how thick this outermost layer of that object is.) For example, Stroll notes, we say that the surface of a frying pan is made of Teflon, describe surfaces as chipped or pitted, speak of removing the surface of a thing, and so on. Other sorts of talk about surfaces makes it sound as though the surface of a material object is an abstract entity—an outermost layer or boundary of that object having zero thickness. If the surface of a material object is thought of as a physical part of that object, it is an individual, but not an individualized form. If the surface of a material object is thought of as a (zero-thickness) outermost boundary of a thing, I'm not sure whether it is an actual individual, or what W. V. O Quine would call a *virtual individual*. That is, I don't know whether or not talk about surfaces abstractly construed really involves reference to surfaces abstractly construed, any more than talk in number theory about ∞ involves reference to ∞.[10] Suppose that surfaces abstractly construed are actual individuals. Are they forms? Well, that depends on how much ground the notion of 'form' covers—on how many things that can be described as that-by-whiches are forms. Even if

[9]See Avrum Stroll, "Two Conceptions of Surfaces," *Midwest Studies in Philosophy* 4 (1979): 227–91.
[10]The example is taken from Dana Scott, "Advice on Modal Logic," in Karel Lambert, *Philosophical Problems in Logic* (Dordrecht: D. Reidel, 1970) pp. 244–73.

surfaces abstractly construed are forms, it needs to be shown that they are properties of the things whose surfaces they are. Otherwise from the fact that surfaces are not found in more than one subject, nothing follows about whether or not properties are. And while it is clear that *having a surface* is a property of the subject that has the surface, it is not clear that a surface is a property of the subject that has that surface. The surface of an object abstractly construed may be thought of as a degenerately thin outermost layer of a thing. Whatever sort of object that might be (a set of points in space? a function from a set of times to a set of points in space?) it does not obviously look like a property of that thing. Moreover, it looks as though, if the subjects of surfaces are ordinary continuants, then surfaces could not be subject-individual-ized properties. In various circumstances, two distinct material things can occupy the same region of space throughout an interval of time. As we have already seen, a now ring-shaped bit of gold is distinct from the ring now constituted of that gold, since the former (we may suppose) will survive a deformation that the latter will not, and noth-ing can survive its own demise; but the (sometimes) ring-shaped bit of gold and the ring will occupy exactly the same region of space throughout a temporal interval. To take Burge's example, a hammock made from a single (length of) rope and that rope are distinct, since the rope antedated the hammock; but the rope and the hammock will occupy the same region of space throughout the interval in which the rope is 'behammocked'.[11] Suppose that a ring-shaped bit of gold and a gold ring occupy the same region of space at a time. The ring-shaped bit of gold now has a surface, and likewise the ring. Whether or not a surface is construed abstractly, the surface the ring now has is the surface the ring-shaped bit of gold now has; there are not two different (but completely overlapping) surfaces, one of which belongs to the ring and one of which belongs to the ring-shaped bit of gold. (Again, with respect to what properties would these surfaces be discernible? It is dialectically out of bounds to answer that one is the surface of the ring and the other is the surface of the ring-shaped bit of gold.) If surfaces were individualized by their subjects, however, there would have to be two such surfaces, since the ring and the bit of gold are

[11]Aquinas would not concede that these examples show that two distinct material objects can occupy the same region of space for a time. For he believes that all artefactual forms are accidental (DPN 1). Because he thinks that a gold ring just is a piece of gold which has acquired an annular accidental form, he would say that the ring-shaped bit of gold and the ring are no more distinct individuals sharing a region of space for a time than a sapling and a tree are. Some of the (powerful) considerations against supposing that all artefactual forms are accidental are set out in Chapter 6.

distinct subjects. To put the point in Geach's terms: the surface of a ring is not that by which exactly one thing is (now) ring-shaped; it is both that by which the ring is (now) ring-shaped, and that by which the bit of gold is (now) ring-shaped. Hence it is not an individualized property or form of any one enduring continuant.[12]

In sum, Geach's arguments fail to make the case for individualized properties, either because they fail to show that certain properties (*being green, being colored*) are individualized properties, or because they fail to show that certain individuals (waves, surfaces) are properties.[13]

I have been arguing that positing many individualized properties of the same kind, rather than a single property of many individuals, involves ontological cost but no explanatory benefit. The reader may suspect that matters are not that cut-and-dried. I think that something like this is right. For it might be that we cannot think of individuals as bundles of compresent properties if we think of properties as ones-of-many, but we can think of individuals in this way if we think of the properties of individuals as themselves individuals.[14] (If properties are

[12]Geach might object to the supposition made here to the effect that the ring and the gold, or the rope and the net, are distinct *things*, on the grounds that identity is sortal-relative. The (familiar) reasons for thinking that identity is not sortal-relative are canvassed in Chapter 5. Though Geach would have nothing to do with this kind of reply, a friend of time-slices who thought of surfaces as subject-individuated properties might argue that when we say—loosely speaking—that a continuant has an intrinsic property at a time *t*, this should be understood as follows: the continuant (which is an aggregate of time-slices) has a *t*-slice that has the intrinsic property in question. (See David Lewis, *On the Plurality of Worlds* [Oxford: Basil Blackwell, 1984], chap. 4, for a defense of this view.) Then she could say that the surface the ring has at *t* is the surface the gold has at *t*, because that surface is an intrinsic property individuated by its subject—a *t*-slice that is both a *t*-slice of the ring and a *t*-slice of the gold. If surfaces are properties of time-slices of things, and if time-slices occupy the same region of space-time only if they are identical, then our argument to the effect that more than one thing can have a given surface does not go through. Of course, the view that continuants are aggregates of temporal parts is quite alien to Aquinas.

[13]Geach also argues that if goodness is thought of as a genuine property (as it should be), and if the attribute of goodness is held to be distinct from any particular good-making attribute (as it should be), then if goodness is thought of as a one-over-many, the goodness of a thing stands in a logically queer relation to the good-making features of that thing ("Aquinas," p. 82). But why is the relation that holds between a thing's goodness and its good-making characteristics—supervenience—logically queer? For more on supervenience, see Chapter 2.

[14]Armstrong and Lewis have also considered the possibility that property-having-particulars may be thought of as constituted solely of properties if but only if the properties of those particulars are themselves particulars. Armstrong denies the possibility, arguing that there must be something more to a particular than its properties; Lewis does not. See D. M. Armstrong, *A Theory of Universals*, 2 vols. (Cambridge: Cambridge University Press, 1978), vol. 1, esp. chaps. 8 and 9; and Lewis, *On the Plurality of Worlds*, pp. 59–65.

repeatables, it may be that two particulars—two indiscernible toma-
toes in a symmetrical universe, two qualitatively indiscernible angels—can have all the same properties; it depends, among other
things, on how sparse the set of properties is. Evidently, if two
particulars can have all the same properties, then particulars cannot be
bundles of compresent properties. If, however, properties are particulars, just like their subjects, this problem need not arise, since numerically distinct particulars may be thought of as bundles of numerically
distinct—even if conspecific—properties.)

I have doubts about whether a bundle theory of individuals is
workable, given a conception of properties as nonrepeatable, and
unworkable, given a conception of properties as repeatable. But I
know of no knock-down argument to show that this is not so. Suppose it is. Then we cannot say that distinguishing this redness from
that redness could do no explanatory work. For it would figure essentially in an account of what individual substances are, and of the
conditions under which individual substances are distinct, thus: individual substances are just mereological aggregates of individual (compresent) properties; for individual substances to be different is just for
them to not have all the same parts.[15] Perhaps this is not the—or even
a—best account of what individual substances are, or of what it is for
individual substances to be distinct. Perhaps we would do better to
think of substances as composed of universals and a particularizing
element (as D. M. Armstrong does); perhaps we would do better to
think of substances as not composed of properties at all (if, say,
properties are best thought of as sets of *possibilia* or functions from

[15]A mereological aggregate is individuated by reference to its parts, and cannot gain
or lose parts over time. This suggests that individual substances may not be identified
with mereological aggregates of (compresent) individual properties. Suppose that an
individual substance has the individual property F-ness for only the first half of its
lifetime; thereafter, that property ceases to exist, although the substance to which it
belonged continues to exist for a time. The aggregate of individual properties with
which the substance is identified cannot have F-ness as a part (throughout its existence), because any such aggregate stopped existing when the substance ceased to be F
(and its F-ness perished), though that substance did not stop existing then. Neither can
the aggregate of individual properties with which the substance is identified lack F-ness
as a part (throughout its existence). So it looks as though the substance cannot be
identified with any aggregate of individual properties. The bundle theorist can get
round this difficulty by supposing that a persisting individual substance is an aggregate
of momentary individuals (the thinnest temporal slices or stages of that individual),
which momentary individuals are themselves aggregates of momentary individual
properties. Alternatively, she may say that substances are constructs from individual
properties and times, rather than bundles of individual properties—say, partial functions from times to aggregates or sets of individual properties, or partial functions from
worlds to functions of the kind just described.

worlds to functions from individuals to truth-values). But we can hardly know whether this is so without doing a lot of metaphysics: so there is no quick and clean argument for the otiosity of distinct but conspecific properties.

Where Q is a philosophical assertion, "there is no quick and clean argument for (or against) Q" is usually true, and this is no exception. I don't have any such argument for the claim that distinct but conspecific properties do not pull their ontological weight. But it does seem tolerably clear that individual*ized* properties (as opposed to individual properties) do not pull their ontological weight. The crucial point about individualized properties, as conceived by Aquinas, is that they are individuated by reference to their recipients; this whiteness is this whiteness because it is received in this subject, and this petreity is this petreity because it is received in this matter. Consequently, something that is white or a stone cannot be thought of as just an aggregate of individualized properties; it must have an unreceived element or elements to receive and individualize those properties. (A hylomorphically composite thing is not its substantial form; a subject is not [the aggregate of] its accidental forms.) Since this is so, we can see that the just considered defense of the utility of positing many conspecific properties of many individuals, rather than one property of many individuals, is not a defense of the utility of positing a plurality of individualized but conspecific properties, rather than a one-of-many. The defender of a conception of individual substances as bundles of individual properties may say to the advocate of properties as ones-of-many:

> Granted, I make an ontological outlay which you consider unnecessary, since I posit a set of whitenesses where you posit the one-of-many, whiteness. But I effect ontological economies elsewhere, since I can say that all there is, is properties and aggregates of properties—while you must maintain that there are not just properties and aggregates thereof but also individual substances, complete with some particularizing element that does not fall under the genus of property.[16]

[16]Someone who holds that individual substances are constructed from individual properties without being aggregates thereof (for example, someone who thinks that individual substances are functions from times to sets of individual properties) could offer the same argument, at least as long as her opponent believes in times and functions, as well as properties and aggregates thereof. So could someone who believes that individual substances are made only of properties, although they are not aggregates of properties. (Someone can hold that a broom or a horse is made only of physical

Aquinas, by contrast, cannot point to any ontological economies effected by the postulation of a set of individualized whitenesses, rather than a one-of-many, whiteness. So we may say to Aquinas:

> Consider a metaphysic very like your own, on which (created) individual substances have properties (received forms) as constituents, but not as their sole constituents. The only difference between this metaphysic and your own is that any two properties that you would think of as conspecific are identified. The proposed metaphysic has a leaner ontology than your own: what have we trimmed from your ontology except fat?

I don't know what sort of answer Aquinas could give. As I indicated, Aquinas sometimes makes it sound as though he thinks it obvious enough that nothing real could be a one-of-many, that no arguments to that effect are needed. But that is surely not the case: much of our ordinary talk of properties at least apparently entails that one and the same property can be a property of more than one thing. Unless there is a reason not to take such talk at face value, we should do just that.

The moral is that Aquinas' un-bundle-ish conception of substances does not assort with his conception of divine simplicity. If we start out supposing with Aquinas, plausibly, that there is more to an individual substance than its properties—that in individual substances there is a particularizing element that enters into some sort of union with, or stands in some sort of relation to, properties but does not itself fall under the genus of property—then we ought to suppose that properties are not unrepeatable particulars, but ones-of-many. (Occam's Razor counsels against building particularity into particular substances twice over.) So if we start out with Aquinas' un-bundle-ish conception of individual substances, we should conclude that, where F-ness is existence or any other property, the F-ness of any one thing that is F is the F-ness of any other thing that is F. But as we saw, if we make this assumption, we can no longer maintain that God is His own existence (since He will not be, and His existence will be, a one-of-many), or maintain that God is pure subsistent existence (since nothing that has existence, without being the existence it has, is pure subsistent existence).

---

parts, even though it is not a mereological aggregate of any physical parts, since mereological aggregates do not undergo compositional change. Analogously, someone can hold that substances are made only of properties, although they are not aggregates thereof.)

Varieties of *Esse*

Suppose, however, we grant Aquinas that properties are individualized constituents of a (created) individual substance, but not the sole constituents thereof. And suppose we grant that among the individualized constituents of a being is an existence, which (in any created being) is something distinct both from the essence of that being (its form and/or its matter) and from all its (predicamental) accidents. Does this enable us to see how it could be true that God was pure subsistent existence? I don't think so. Why not? I am tempted to argue in peremptory fashion, as follows: if God were pure subsistent existence, then He would be identical with His existence. In that case— since God is not the existence of anything distinct from Himself— God would be an existence, which was not the existence of anything but that existence. But supposing that something could be an existence, without being the existence of anything but that existence, is like supposing that something could be a shape, without being the shape of anything but that shape, or be a shadow, without being the shadow of anything but that shadow. It is like supposing that something could be the whiteness of itself, and nothing but itself. Aquinas himself, though, admits that nothing could be the whiteness of itself and nothing but itself; as he says at SCG I.22, whiteness just is the sort of thing that exists in another. Surely, though, existence is no different from whiteness on this score, in which case neither God nor anything else could be just its own existence. Someone might object, however, that it is not evident that nothing could be just its own existence; so perhaps we should proceed more slowly.

For Aquinas, there is in Socrates a constituent by virtue of which he exists (his existence, or *esse*), another constituent by virtue of which he is wise (his wisdom), yet another by virtue of which he is virtuous (his virtue), and so on. But there is in God just one maximal part or constituent—His existence. Although there is something more to Socrates than Socrates' existence, there is nothing more to God than His existence. In that case, it looks as though God will just exist, because there will not be anything else in Him over and above His existence, by virtue of which He could be anything over and above existent. Since there will not be anything in God but existence, and the existence of a thing does not make it anything but existent, God will be nothing more than existent. But it seems clear that nothing subsistent could be just existent: a merely existent substance is too thin to be possible. Moreover, even if some substance could be simply existent, God could not be, since He is any number of other ways than just existent—good, wise, and just, as well as omnipotent, omniscient, and the like.

Aquinas would answer that although there is nothing more to God than His existence, God's existence is not simply that by which He exists. His existence is also that by which He is good, wise, just, omnipotent, omniscient, and so on; in other words, His existence is also His goodness, wisdom, justice, omnipotence, and so on. Consequently God is not just existent, but also good, wise, just, omnipotent, omniscient, and so on.

The difficulty is in seeing how the requisite identities between individual divine attributes (for example, "God's omnipotence is His existence") could hold. To see this, consider two different sorts of cases in which individual attributes are distinct from each other. Suppose there are two spheres, of exactly the same shape, size, and color (say, orange). Then—presuming that the sphericality of a sphere is an individual property of that sphere—each sphere will have its own sphericality, and those two sphericalities will be distinct individuals of the very same kind. Now consider the shape of the first sphere, and the color of that same sphere. Presuming that the color of a sphere is an individual property thereof, its color will be a different individual property from its shape. The sphericality of the sphere and the orangeness of the sphere are individual properties of different kinds belonging to the same individual, just as the sphericality of the first sphere and the sphericality of the second are individual properties of the same kind, belonging to different individuals.

Now (if we suppose that God's existence and God's omnipotence are individual properties), the existence of God and the omnipotence of God will not be properties of the same kind belonging to different individuals; but, one should think, neither will they be properties of the same kind belonging to the same individual.[17] Instead, they will be properties of different kinds belonging to the same individual. Why should one think so? Well, why should one think that the first sphere's roundness and its orangeness are different kinds of individual property? There is something odd about the question. Surely anyone who knows what kind of thing the roundness of this sphere is, and what kind of thing the orangeness of the sphere is, knows that the roundness of the sphere and the orangeness of the sphere are not the very same

[17]When I say that God's omnipotence is an individual property belonging to God, I do not mean to imply God's omnipotence is necessarily anything different from, or a proper part of, God; I mean to leave open the possibility that an individual can be both a property and a substance, and belong to itself (as a maximal rather than a proper part).

property. But clearly, no one individual can have two individual properties of the very same kind (that would involve being one way twice over); so the roundness of the sphere must be a different kind of individual property from the orangeness of the sphere. But how do we know that the roundness of the sphere is different from the orangeness of the sphere? We know, because we know that being round is different from being orange—as is attested to by the fact that things can be round without being orange, or vice versa.[18] So (assuming that divine omnipotence and existence are individual properties) how do we know that they are individual properties of different kinds? Again, we know that existing is different from being omnipotent—as is attested to by the fact that things can exist, without being omnipotent. But if existing is different from being omnipotent, then God's existence is a different kind of individual property from God's omnipotence (just as, if being orange is different from being round, the sphere's roundness is a different kind of individual property from its orangeness).[19]

Aquinas acknowledges that things can exist without being omnipotent, but he denies that this fact entails the distinctness of God's existence from His omnipotence. For he thinks that things can exist without having every perfection (including omnipotence) only in-

[18]If the question of whether a sphere's orangeness is the same as that sphere's roundness is not settled by the fact that being round is different from being orange—so that we could sensibly say, "Granted that being orange is different from being round, is this particular sphere's roundness the same as or different from this particular sphere's orangeness?"—I can't begin to imagine how we would settle the question of whether this sphere's orangeness is the same as or different from its roundness. It might be suggested that two individual properties of an individual are identical if and only if at any time and in any world, an individual has the one just in case it has the other. As I argue in note 19, below, this proposal leads us to identify what intuitively look like distinct properties.

[19]In "Form and Existence," Geach discusses a case similar to the one of the round orange sphere, and argues that we know that the redness of a red square is distinct from its squareness because they may undergo different sorts of changes, and have different persistence conditions. If the appeal to mutability were essential in arguing for the distinctness of individualized forms of the same individual, then there would be no such distinctness in an entirely immutable God. But it does not seem to be. On anyone's view, if size and shape are thought of as individual properties, the size of a material object and the shape of that material object will be distinct individual properties of it (it might remain the same shape while increasing or decreasing in size). But if the size of a material object is a distinct individual property from the shape of that object, then surely the size of a region of space is a distinct individual property from the shape of that region of space, even though a region of space is immutable with respect to both its size and shape. So the size and shape of a region of space will be distinct individual properties of that region of space, neither of which could be unstuck from the other, or from that region.

asmuch as they have a limited and imperfect kind of existence. Thus at
SCG I.28 he avers that things that merely exist (without being, say,
alive or wise) are imperfect not because existence (*esse*), considered as
such, is imperfect, and needs to be supplemented by such perfections
as life and wisdom, but because such beings do not have existence
according to its full power, and participate in existence in a particular
and imperfect way.[20] God, on the other hand, has unlimited and full-
strength existence. And, Aquinas would say, although there is certainly a difference between being omnipotent and existing-in-a-con-
tracted-way, there is no difference between being omnipotent and
existing-in-an-unlimited-and-full-strength-way. If there is no difference between being omnipotent, omniscient, and the like and exist-
ing-in-a-full-strength-way, there is no bar to maintaining the identity
of God's full-strength existence with His omnipotence, or any other of
His perfections.

Why does Aquinas think that having existence according to its full
power intrinsically involves having every perfection? At ST Ia.4.2 he
offers the following (compressed and difficult) argument to that effect:
all perfections pertain to the perfection of existing, because things are
perfect in a certain way insofar as they have existence (*esse*) in a certain
way.[21]

The idea that things are perfect in a certain way insofar as they have
esse in a certain way goes over better in English if we translate 'esse' as
'being' rather than existence. Aquinas appears to be thinking of things
in this way: a (created) individual (*ens*) has both substantial being (*esse
substantiale*) and accidental being (*esse accidentale*). The substantial being
of a thing makes it be in an unqualified sense (*esse simpliciter*), while the
accidental being of a thing makes it be in a qualified sense, or in a
certain respect (*esse secundum quid;* ST Ia.5.1, *ad* 1). Socrates' substantial *esse* makes him be, while Socrates' accidental *esses* make him be
certain ways. Although there is just one substantial *esse* in Socrates,
there are many different accidental *esses*: as Aquinas says at ST 3a.17.2,
the *esse* by which Socrates is white is different from the *esse* by which
Socrates is musical.[22] Just as each substantial form has a corresponding

---

[20]"Illa vero quae tantum sunt, non sunt imperfecta propter imperfectionem ipsius
esse absoluti: non enim ipsa habent esse secundum suum totum posse, sed participant
esse per quendam particularem modum et imperfectissimum."
[21]"Omnium autem perfectiones pertinent ad perfectionem essendi, secundum hoc
enim aliqualiter perfecta sunt quod aliquo modo esse habent."
[22]"Si aliqua forma vel natura est quae non pertineat ad esse personale hypostasis
subsistentis, illud esse non dicitur esse illius personae simpliciter, sed secundum quid:

substantial *esse,* each accidental form has a corresponding accidental *esse.* And just as the substantial form of Socrates is distinct from his (substantial) *esse,* each accidental form of Socrates is distinct from its corresponding (accidental) *esse.* That is why Aquinas says at SCG II. 54 that form is not existence, but is related to existence as whiteness (*albedo*) is related to being white, or (translating more literally) white being (*album esse*).

We can see now why Aquinas thinks that to be perfect in a certain respect is to have a certain kind of *esse,* and that conversely to be imperfect in a certain respect is to lack a certain kind of *esse.* What makes a wise being perfect is not so much its form (wisdom), as its being wise—which is a certain kind of *esse.* What makes a bad man imperfect is his lack of a certain kind of being—being virtuous, or as Aquinas sometimes puts it, the being of virtue (*esse virtutis*); what makes a bad eye imperfect is its lack of a certain kind of being—the being of sight (*esse visus;* ST Ia. 5. 3 *ad* 2 and 5. 5 *ad* 3). What is perfect or desirable or desired is in each case *esse* of some kind or another; when it is said that life, or wisdom, or anything of that sort is desired, what is really desired *per se* is a certain kind of *esse.* So, Aquinas maintains, even when nonexistence is desired, it is desired *per accidens,* inasmuch as nonexistence removes an evil, which evil consists in the privation of a certain kind of *esse:* "That which is desirable *per se* is being (*esse*); nonbeing is desirable *per accidens,* only inasmuch as some kind of being (*quoddam esse*) is desired, which a man cannot bear to be without" (ST Ia. 5. 2 *ad* 3).

So an individual is perfect inasmuch as it has a certain kind of *esse.* If *esse* is understood to have among its instances being good, being wise, and so on, this is unexceptionable. But how we get from there to the supposition that there is a simple, unlimited, full-strength *esse* that includes every perfection is not clear. Although I find Aquinas' thought exceptionally difficult to follow here, I think he has something like this in mind: for a creature to have a given (creaturely, limited) perfection is for that creature to have some kind of (substantial or accidental) *esse.* Alternatively, we may say, it is for a creature to have *esse* in a certain way. Moreover (Aquinas thinks) we may say, it is for a creature to have *esse* that is 'limited' or 'contracted' in a certain

---

sicut esse album est esse Socratis non inquantum est Socrates, sed inquantum est albus. Et huiusmodi esse nihil prohibet muliplicari in una hypostasi vel persona: aliud enim est esse quo Socrates est albus et quo Socrates est musicus."

way, by a certain nature or form. For Aquinas, any *esse* received by a given nature, in virtue of being received by that nature, has some but not all of the "full power" or full perfection of *esse,* considered absolutely. In attempting to explicate this opaque notion at SCG I.28, he offers the following analogy: something may be white, without having whiteness "according to its full power," because, due to some defect, it receives whiteness not according to its full power (*non secundum totum posse albedinis*). In such a case it will have a limited or imperfect sort of whiteness, which has some but not all the perfection or power that belongs to whiteness, considered absolutely or as such: whiteness as such will so to speak exceed the capacity of that white thing to receive it, and that white thing will participate in whiteness, but not fully or perfectly, because it is at once receptive of whiteness (to a degree) and irreceptive of whiteness (to a degree). In such a case, it will be white in an imperfect way, insofar as it receives a whiteness contracted by some underlying defect: it will have (some of) the perfection of whiteness, insofar as it is receives whiteness, and will lack (some of) the perfection of whiteness, inasmuch as it is irreceptive of whiteness. Apparently Aquinas thinks that any created form or nature is at once receptive and irreceptive of *esse,* in something like the way that an imperfectly white thing is receptive and irreceptive of whiteness. *Esse,* considered as such, far exceeds the capacity of any creaturely form or nature to receive it, just as whiteness as such exceeds the capacity of imperfectly white things to receive it. A thing will have a creaturely or limited perfection (say, being wise or being virtuous) inasmuch as it has *esse* of a limited or contracted sort (bounded by some substantial or accidental form); it is perfect insofar as it has *esse,* and limited or imperfect insofar as it is irreceptive of *esse,* on account of the inability of its nature or form to receive *esse* according to its full power. Different sorts of *esses* will be limited to varying extents by different sorts of forms: hence Aquinas says at SCG I.28 that a thing is more or less excellent insofar as its *esse* is contracted to a greater or lesser special mode of excellence. If a thing had *esse,* without any contracting or limiting factor—as would have to be the case, if a being were unreceived, subsistent *esse*—it would be most perfect, because it would have all of what is perfect in any limited or contracted perfection, without any of the limiting or contracting factor.[23]

---

[23]As John Wippel notes, Aquinas is assuming here that if *esse* is not limited by anything else, it is unlimited, because *esse* could not be self-limiting (see *Metaphysical Themes in Thomas Aquinas* [Washington, D.C.: Catholic University of America Press, 1984], chap. 6).

There is a difficulty, though, about the intelligibility of the account just sketched. What could it mean to say that while creatures have *esse* in a limited or imperfect way, God has *esse* according to its full power? It should be clear at the outset that when Aquinas makes this claim, he is not asserting that God, unlike creatures, has a particular kind of accidental *esse* according to its full power. He is not saying that God, and only God, has this particular kind of accidental being, or that particular kind of accidental being according to its full power. Instead, he is saying that God has being "as such," or "absolutely considered," according to its full power. But if the being God has is not any particular kind of accidental being, I don't see how it could be anything other than existence—the existence whereby a being is an entity, which Aquinas calls *esse substantiale*.[24] If what God has according to its full power is not, say, *being white,* or *being square, vel cetera,* but just *being,* then it would seem that what God has according to its full power is just *existence.* And if there is any intelligible content to the idea that there is a difference between having existence according to its full power, and having existence according to something less than its full power, I cannot grasp it.

To put the point in terms of the analogy Aquinas offers: I think I can understand the difference between having whiteness according to its full power and having whiteness according to something less than its full power, because, I take it, it is the difference between being less than perfectly white and being perfectly white. By contrast, there does not seem to be a difference between being perfectly existent and being less than perfectly existent. Existence is an on/off property: either you're there or you're not. Because existence is on/off, it would seem, either you have it according to its full power or you don't have it all.

In short, although Aquinas holds that *esse* or existence fails to include every perfection only insofar as it is 'filtered,' the distinction this presupposes—between having filtered existence, and having "the entire fullness of existence" (DSC 1, *responsio*)—is on the face of it unintelligible. If there is no such distinction to be drawn, we are led back to the conclusion that nothing can be omnipotent, omniscient, omnibenevolent, and the like simply by virtue of its existence, and that accordingly, God cannot be His existence, since He has inter alia omni-properties that may not be identified with His existence.

To leave matters here, though, would not be fair to Aquinas. Aquinas admits that the kind of existence with which he identifies God—an existence that is not the existence of anything else, an exis-

---

[24]See ST Ia.5 *ad* 1.

tence that includes every perfection—is in a certain sense inconceivable. Existence, insofar as we can conceive of it, is inherent in, and limited by, some nature.[25] Even so, Aquinas thinks, we can know that there must be a subsistent and universally perfect existence, although we cannot understand how such a being is possible.

As Aquinas thinks of it, the inconceivable is demonstrable in this way: if a being exists, or is good, knowing, or powerful, there must in each case be something by virtue of which it is existent, or good, or knowing, or powerful (its existence, goodness, *vel cetera*). Now, it can be shown that there is a first, uncaused being, whom all men call God (ST Ia.2.3). Moreover, it can be shown by various *reductiones* that this being could not be different from His own existence (ST Ia.3.4). We might object that even if there is a first being who is the same as His existence, that being could not be God. But, Aquinas would reply, it can be shown that this first being has all the divine perfections (omnipotence, omniscience, perfect goodness, and so on)—in each case as a maximal part; so there is no doubt that this first being is God (ST Ia.3.6 and 7, and *quaestiones* 4.6.14 and 25). If all this is true, it can be shown that God is His own existence, and also His own goodness, knowledge, power, and the like. Consequently, (5) and (6) (see p. 4) are demonstrably true, and a fortiori coherent.

But how can it be shown that God could not be different from His existence? Aquinas sets out a variety of complex and interconnected arguments for that conclusion. In the rest of this chapter, I examine and evaluate those arguments.

Five Arguments for the Identity of God with His Existence

There are in Aquinas at least five sorts of argument for the identity of God's essence with His existence. They are:

(A) The argument from the nature of composites: If God's essence is distinct from His existence, then He is a composite being, resulting from a union of essence and existence. But every composite being (i) has some element that is in potentiality, and some element that actualizes that potentiality; (ii) is subsequent to and dependent on its components; (iii) is potentially dissoluble, and hence capable of perishing; (iv) presupposes a compounder as efficient cause; and (v) has parts less perfect than itself. But God could not have any of these properties. So God's essence is identical to His existence.[26]

---

[25]See, e.g., DP 7.2 *ad* 7.
[26]For this argument, see SCG I.18 and 22; DP 7.1 and 2; CT 9 and 11.

(B) The argument from act and potency: If God's essence is distinct from His existence, then His essence is related to His existence as potency to act, and God is in some way in potentiality. In that case, however, God is neither immutable nor *per se* necessary. Moreover, whatever is in potentiality passes from potentiality to actuality only through the agency of something that is in actuality. It follows that if God is in any way in potentiality, He depends on some being to actualize His potentiality, and so is posterior to and dependent on something else. Since God is an immutable and *per se* necessary first being, then He is in no way in potentiality, and His essence is identical with His existence.[27]

(C) The argument from participation: If God's essence is distinct from His existence, He will exist by participating in existence. In other words, he will be a being by participation *(ens per participationem)* rather than a being through His essence *(ens per essentiam)*. But in that case He will not be the first being. So God's essence is identical with His existence.[28]

(D) The argument from God's uncausedness: If God's essence is distinct from His existence, then His existence must be (a) externally caused, or (b) consequent on—and hence caused by—the divine essence. But God's existence could be caused neither by anything else (since He is the first being) nor by His essence (since nothing can cause itself to exist). So God's essence is identical with His existence.[29]

(E) The argument from the nature of causation: Whenever a number of causes have an effect in common, that effect is the proper effect of a superior cause, by virtue of which they have the common effect. Now, created causes have existence *(esse)* as their common effect, although different causes have different proper effects. For all causes make something *be* a certain way (for example, hot, or a house), although different causes make things be different ways. So existence must be the proper effect of some superior cause, by virtue of which created causes have existence as their (common) effect. This superior cause is God. But the proper effect of any cause bears a likeness to its nature. Hence existence is the nature of God.[30]

I argue that none of these arguments is cogent. The first one splits into three assertions: (a) if God's essence is distinct from His existence, then God is composite; (b) if anything is composite, it has the features specified by (i)–(v); and (c) God could not have any of those features.

[27]See SCG I.16 and 22; ST Ia.3.1 and 4; CT 9 and 10.
[28]See ST Ia.3.4; SCG I.22.
[29]See, again, ST Ia.3.4; SCG I.22.
[30]See DP 7.2, *responsio*.

Someone might want to take issue with (a), on the grounds that it is confused to think of existence as in any way a part or constituent of an existent individual. (The same might be held for essence.) It is certainly true that if there is a composition of existence and essence in an existent individual, that composition will be very unlike more familiar kinds of composition; just how unlike will come out shortly. But Aquinas is well aware that the relation essence and existence bear to an existent individual is quite unlike, say, the relation bricks and mortar bear to a house. He thinks, however, that there is enough similarity between these two relations to warrant describing both in compositional terms. Whether it is ultimately illuminating, or unilluminating but harmless, or perniciously misleading to use compositional language to characterize the relation of essence and existence to an existent individual is a complicated question. But for the purposes of evaluating the argument under consideration, we need not settle it. Even if we grant that the distinction of essence and existence in an individual makes that individual composite, argument (A) does not succeed. This is because (b) and (c) are unconvincing.

Types of Priority

Assertion (b) depends on five universal generalizations. The first of these is that every composite involves an element in potentiality, and an element that actualizes that potentiality. Since argument (B) is devoted to showing that God must be free of potentiality, I won't consider this claim until the section, "From God's Nonpotentiality to the Identity of God with His Existence."

The second universal generalization on which (b) depends is the claim that every composite being is posterior to its components, and dependent on them. How is posteriority to be understood here? At SCG I.18 Aquinas asserts that any composite is posterior to its components, without saying what sort of posteriority he has in mind; at ST Ia.3.7, *responsio,* he says that what is composite is posterior to and dependent on its components, without further explicating either notion. The linkage of posteriority and dependence suggests that posteriority might be a matter of one-way ontological dependence—so that *a* would be posterior to *b* just in case it was impossible for *a* to exist without *b*, but possible for *b* to exist without *a*. This type of posteriority is discussed by Aristotle in a number of passages in the *Categories* and the *Metaphysics* with which Aquinas was familiar. In fact, Aquinas concludes his treatment of Aristotle's discussion of the types of priority and posteriority in the *Metaphysics* by saying that, since the posterior depends on the prior, but not vice versa, anything prior can exist without what is posterior to it, though nothing posterior can exist without what is prior to it (cf. *Commentary on the Metaphysics* 5.13.953).

On the other hand, Aquinas often characterizes priority and posteriority in ways that do not on the face of it make reference to ontological dependence. Thus in the same lesson from the *Commentary on the Metaphysics* as the one just cited, he notes that substance is prior, and accidents are posterior, because substances are in the primary sense, and accidents are only derivatively and secondarily. Presumably Aquinas' idea here is one we've already touched on—namely, that for an accident to be (insofar as an accident can be said to be) is for something else (*viz.*, the subject of the accident), to have a qualified sort of actual being. What it is for a particular stone's roundness to be is for that stone to have a qualified sort of actual being—to wit, being round. On the other hand, it is not the case that what it is for a stone to be is for *something else* to have any kind of actual being. True, for a particular stone to be is for a parcel of matter to receive and individuate a petrean substantial form. Actual existence (*esse*), however, is ascribed to the composite of matter and form, not to the matter, or to the form.[31] Received forms—whether accidental or substantial—are not called beings because they themselves have being, but rather because they make subjects have (accidental or substantial) being; substances are called beings because they have being (*esse*), or—in the case of God— are *esse*. Thus hylomorphically composite substances are prior in being to both their substantial and their accidental forms. Last, hylomorphically composite substances are prior in being to their matter: for the matter of a thing exists only in potentiality, and not actually.[32] Let's call this last sort of priority *existential priority* (since it belongs to those things that may most properly be said to exist), and the first sort *ontological priority*.[33] These two notions will not in general coincide. For example, Socrates will be existentially prior to Socrates' risibility,

[31]"Unde in compositis ex materia et forma, nec materia nec forma potest dici ipsum quod est, nec etiam ipsum esse. Forma tamen potest dici quo est, secundum quod est essendi principium. Ipsa autem tota substantia est ipsum quod est; et ipsum esse est quo substantia denominatur ens" (SCG II.54). See also DSC I *ad* 8; ST Ia.45.4.

[32]"Materia non proprie potest dici quod est, cum non sit nisi in potentia" (DSC I *ad* 8). See also DSC 2 *ad* 15.

[33]I have said that *a* is ontologically prior to *b* if *a* could exist without *b*, but not vice versa. This could be understood in two ways. More weakly, it could mean that *a* is ontologically prior to *b* just in case it is possible that *a* sometimes exists and *b* never exists, but not possible that *b* sometimes exists and *a* never exists. More strongly, it could mean that *a* is ontologically prior to *b* just in case it is possible that at some time *a*

since the latter is an accident of the individual substance Socrates. But he will not be (for Aquinas) ontologically prior to his risibility, since Socrates without Socrates' risibility is (Aquinas supposes) just as impossible as Socrates' risibility without Socrates. Similarly, a tree will be existentially prior but not ontologically prior to its matter and its substantial form (since that very tree could not have existed had its matter and its form not existed).

Existential and ontological priority by no means exhaust the types of priority Aquinas recognizes. In other contexts, Aquinas links priority with causality. For example, in *De principiis naturae* 4, he writes that each cause, insofar as it is a cause, is prior to what it causes. Hence a received substantial form—say, an equinity—is causally prior to the parcel of matter that receives that equinity, because the equinity is what causes or makes the matter receiving it to be an actual individual of the natural kind, horse. Now, for Aquinas there is a very intimate connection between being an individual of a certain natural kind, being an individual, and being: everything that is, is an individual, every created individual falls under some natural kind, and for an individual to start (or stop) being an individual of its (most determinate) natural kind is for it to start (or stop) existing. Consequently, it is not surprising that he speaks (e.g., at DPN 1; DSC 1, *responsio* and *ad* 5; and ST Ia.29.2 *ad* 5) of the form of a composite individual as making the matter of that individual exist, or as giving that matter actual existence.[34] Since he holds that what makes or causes something to exist is prior to the thing caused to exist (whether the causation in question is efficient, final, or as in the case under consideration, formal), he takes the form of a material substance to be prior both to the matter of a composite substance and to that substance itself. This sort of priority—call it *causal priority*—does not coincide with either ontological or existential priority. The form of a stone is ontologically prior to neither the stone nor the stone's matter. Nor is that form existentially prior to the stone itself, since it is existentially posterior to it.

---

exists while *b* does not, and impossible that at some time *b* exists while *a* does not. Given his views on the individuation of accidents, Aquinas would say that accidents are ontologically dependent on their subjects in the weak sense; given his views on transubstantiation, Aquinas would deny that accidents are ontologically dependent on their subjects in the strong sense. However ontological priority is understood, it will fail to coincide with existential priority; I intend it in the weaker way.

[34]See for example, "(Forma) dat esse actuale materiae, ut sic individuum subsistere possit" (ST Ia.29.2 *ad* 5). See also DE 2 ("Per formam enim quae est actus materiae materia efficitur ens actu et hoc aliquid") and DSC 1 *ad* 6.

Aquinas may also recognize a kind of priority distinct from all the ones yet mentioned—a kind we may call *mereological priority*. In various places, Aquinas seems to take the fact that one thing is a proper part of another to be a sufficient reason for supposing that the first thing is (in one way) prior to the second. If Aquinas did think that proper parts were always (mereologically) prior to the wholes to which they belonged, this would explain why at SCG I. 18 he says that in every whole, the parts are prior to that whole, without ever specifying the kind of priority he has in mind, or providing or making reference to any argument for the priority of the parts to the whole. (No argument would be needed, if mereological priority were intended.) More evidence that Aquinas conceives of priority mereologically is found in Aquinas' explication of Aristotle's claim that certain parts of an animal—such as its fingers—are in one sense prior to that animal, and in another sense not prior to it. Aquinas says that the sense in which a finger of an animal is not prior to that animal is that the finger is ontologically posterior to that animal: the animal can go on existing if it loses the finger, which belonged to it, but the finger cannot go on existing if it gets lost by the animal to which it belonged. In what sense, though, is the finger prior to the animal? It is prior, Aquinas answers, in that an animal is a composite entity, one of whose constituents is a finger (see ME 7.10). This passage gives the impression that Aquinas has a notion of priority which is analytically tied to the part-whole relation. The impression is reinforced by Aquinas' assertion in chapter 9 of the *Compendium theologiae* that for every composite entity, there is something prior to it, since components are by their very nature prior to the composita to which they belong. Again, the idea seems to be that proper parts *qua* proper parts are prior to wholes. I'm not sure why Aquinas thinks this is so. Certainly given the wide range of things Aquinas counts as the proper parts of a whole, proper parts will not in general be either ontologically or existentially prior to wholes. Perhaps at some level Aquinas is drawn to this kind of picture: wholes just are the sums of their parts; so facts about wholes just are facts about their proper parts and how those proper parts are put together; so facts about wholes are posterior to facts about their proper parts.

From the Posteriority of Composita
to Divine Incomposition

We may return at long last to the structure of Aquinas' first argument for divine noncomposition. Aquinas intends to show that God is in no way composite, from which (he thinks) it follows that God's essence is His existence. He tries to do this by showing that everything composite has features God could not have. The first such feature is *having an admixture of potentiality;* the second is *being posterior to its components.* If the argument from the posteriority of composita to divine incomposition is to succeed, there must be a way of being posterior to one's parts such that (i) every composite being is posterior to its parts in that way; and (ii) God could not be posterior to His parts in that way. The flaw in the argument is that although there are ways in which every composite must be posterior to its components, and ways in which God clearly could not be posterior to His components, the ways are different. Clearly, God could not be existentially posterior to any of His components; if He were, it would be some component of God, rather than God Himself, which could most properly be said to exist. Nor does it look as if God could be ontologically posterior to any of His parts. If He were, He would be ontologically posterior either to some integral part, or to some metaphysical part. But (Aquinas thinks he can show) God has no (nonmaximal) integral parts.[35] And if God had metaphysical parts, none of those parts (the divine essence, divine existence, the divine subject, and divine accidents) would be ontologically independent of the whole to which it belonged (God). It is not true, however, even on Aquinas' account, that every composite being is existentially posterior to some of its parts, or that every composite being is ontologically posterior to some of its parts. For example, Aquinas supposes that angels are existentially posterior to none of their parts. Indeed, the only composite beings that are for Aquinas existentially posterior to their parts are nonsubstances (such as heaps, or houses). A pile of rocks is existentially posterior to the rocks that make up the pile, in that what it is for the pile to exist is just for a bunch of (actual) individuals to exist, and be arranged in a certain way. But just because the pile of rocks is existentially posterior to its parts, it has no substantial form, and is not a substance. (Indeed, the pile of rocks is not even one thing, save in a qualified sense; see ST 3a.2.1, *responsio.*)

Although no material substances are existentially posterior to any of their parts, generated and corrupted substances will presumably be ontologically posterior to some of their parts. This tree could not have

---

[35]An integral part of a being is a part of that being that is a particular substance (though not necessarily a hypostasis; see pp. 242–43, below). Actually, I shall raise some doubts (especially in Chapter 7) about whether Aquinas should hold that God is without (proper) integral parts.

been this tree—and hence could not have existed—unless this parcel of matter had been there to receive and individuate the tree's substantial form, although the matter of that tree (which did not used to be arboreally informed, and will cease to be so informed) might never have been so informed, and so might have existed even though this tree never did. Aquinas would not, however, maintain that incorruptible material substances—celestial bodies—are ontologically posterior to their matter. Because he thinks that the matter of a celestial body could not exist without receiving the very substantial form it in fact has (DSC 6 *ad* 2; DSC 8, *responsio*), and because he thinks that two created substances can be distinct only if they have different matters or different forms (cf. ST Ia.40.2), he would deny that the matter of this celestial body could have existed, without this celestial body's existing. Nor is a celestial body ontologically posterior to any other of its parts (subject and accidents, essence and existence). And immaterial substances (such as angels) are not ontologically posterior to their matter, because they don't have any, or to any of the parts they do have.

Although some composite beings will be ontologically or existentially posterior to none of their parts, it may be that every composite being will be causally posterior to some part of it distinct from it. That is, composite beings will be a certain way because they have a (proper) part that actualizes their potentiality to be that way. Socrates is a man because he has a part (a substantial form) which actualizes his potentiality to have a certain kind of substantial being; Gabriel is existent because he has a part (an *esse*) which actualizes his potentiality to be. In each case, we may say that the composite being is in one sense posterior to one of its parts: it is actual in a certain way, because it has as a proper part a certain kind of actuator (substantial form, *esse*), and as a proper part something fit to be actuated (matter, essence).

Let us assume, then, that every composite being is causally posterior to something distinct from it, which is a part of it. Why should we suppose that God could not be causally posterior to some (proper) part of Him? If it seems obvious that He could not, this is probably because we have in mind a much narrower conception of cause than the one relevant here. All it means to say that God is causally posterior to one of His parts is that there is some constituent of God (distinct from God) whereby God is a certain way (existent, divine, wise, *vel cetera*). How do we know this is false? I think Aquinas would answer that if God existed or was a certain way, because He had a certain kind of proper part, He would have composition of act and potency; and if He had composition of act and potency, he would be causally dependent on something outside of Him. Since I examine these claims below, I have nothing more to say about the idea that God could not be causally posterior to any of His proper parts, except that it stands in need of support from other arguments.

Similarly, it does not look as though the (trivial) premiss that every composite being is mereologically posterior to some of its parts will be of much use in arguing for divine noncomposition. Again, how do we know that God is not mereologically posterior to some of His parts? "If He were, He would not be a basic entity—there would be a God only because there are divine parts, put together in the right way." But if the notion of "part" is understood broadly enough to cover such things as essence and existence, subject and accident, then it is a distinct possibility that nothing (not even God) could be subsistent (could have independent existence) without being mereologically posterior to some of its parts (broadly construed). In that case it is an open question whether or not God is mereologically posterior to any of His parts.

Aquinas' presentations of the argument from the posteriority of composita are very compressed: in both the *Summa theologiae* and the *Summa contra Gentiles* he lays out the argument in just two sentences (SCG I.18; ST Ia.3.7, *responsio*). In each instance, the supposition that God is composite is said to be incompatible with the (antecedently established) fact that God is a first being (*primum ens*). Now, if we keep in mind what sort of thing Aquinas thinks is *proprie et vere* called *ens,* it does seem problematic to suppose that any *ens* is prior to God. As we have seen, those things that are properly and truly called *entia* are individual substances; and it may be that no individual substance could be prior to God, however priority is understood. Even if this is so, it is still up for grabs whether God is in some sense posterior to some of His constituents, since any constituents of God would not be individual substances distinct from God, and hence would not be (in the strict sense) *entia* prior to God. Examining the argument from the posteriority of composita in isolation makes it clear that for Aquinas God could not have the sorts of priority He has relative to creatures, or be the sort of explanatory terminus He is with respect to creaturely existence and change, if He had any proper parts at all—whether they were integral or metaphysical. But in order to see why Aquinas has this view, we need to look elsewhere.

Other Arguments for Divine Incomposition

The third feature Aquinas thinks is found in everything composite and incompatible with the divine nature is dissolubility and, consequently, perishability. He tells us in SCG I. 18 that composite entities, by their nature as composite, are potentially dissoluble (although some composita have another element that resists dissolution—a metaphysical stabilizer, as it were). But when a composite entity undergoes dissolution, it ceases to exist. So God is composite only if God potentially does not exist; but God lacks any potentiality for nonexistence.

The obvious rejoinder to this argument is: why suppose that every composite is potentially dissoluble? If dissolution is understood in the most natural way, there are in fact good Thomistic reasons to deny that every composite is potentially dissoluble. One would think that what distinguishes the dissolution of a composite being from its annihilation is that only in the former case do the parts of the composite survive its demise. In dissolution, a composite thing is reduced to its elements; in annihilation, it is reduced to nothing. If this is so, it is hard to see how an angel can undergo dissolution. It is not as if an angel has matter that can survive the departure of an angelic substantial form; an angel is an unreceived form, whose only parts are a subject, (subject-individuated) accidents, an essence, and an (essence-individuated) existence. And it is plausible that none of these parts could still exist if the angel to which it had belonged no longer did.[36]

But suppose that we understand dissolution in such a way that it need not involve the survival of any of a thing's parts. Then the argument under consideration reduces to the following: since any composite being can cease to exist, and God cannot, God is not composite. The difficulty here is reminiscent of that encountered with the argument from posteriority. If we construe composition narrowly, so that only material beings composed of integral parts count as composite, it is very plausible that any composite being could cease existing: it would be at least surprising if any composite material object turned out to be incapable of passing away. For it is always imaginable—and hence apparently logically possible—that such an object be broken up into small enough bits that it ceases to exist.[37] If we construe composition narrowly, however, nobody would think

[36]I am assuming here (with Aquinas) that forms, rather than being ones-of-many, are individuated by their bearers. Otherwise, forms would outlast their bearers. As we have seen, Aquinas believes that the (subject-individuated) accidents now in a certain subject may—through the exercise of divine power—outlast that subject. So perhaps he could hold that it is within God's power to bring it about that some of the parts of an angel survive the demise of that angel. But (although I shall not argue the point here) I think that within the context of Aquinas' more or less Aristotelian conception of accidents, it is incoherent to suppose they could outlast their subjects.

[37]This will be so for ordinary sorts of composite material objects, but not for aggregates of incomposite material objects. I don't know whether it is so for very large material objects like the universe.

that whatever lacks composition in that sense must be identical with its existence, nature, and attributes: if we construe composition more broadly, it is no longer evident that only dissoluble things are composite.

Aquinas' presentation of this argument is once again quite brief. At SCG I. 18 he defends the claim that all composite beings are potentially dissoluble by saying that the dissolubility of composite beings follows from the nature or concept of composition (*ex ratione compositionis*). It is not clear what he has in mind here, but it may be something like this: it follows from the nature of identity that whatever stands in the relation of identity to a thing stands in the relation of identity to that thing (and just that thing) as long as it exists. By contrast, it does not follow from the nature of the part–whole relation that whatever stands in the part-of relation to a whole stands in that relation to that whole throughout the part's existence. The nature of the part–whole relation, as it were, leaves room for something to become or cease to be a part of a whole, without coming to be or ceasing to be, whereas the nature of the identity relation leaves no room for a thing to become or cease to be identical to a thing, without coming to be or ceasing to be. Now, whenever a part ceases to be a part of a whole, without ceasing to be, that whole undergoes dissolution. In a sense, then, the possibility of dissolution follows from the nature of the part–whole relation. But this does not entail that every composite being can undergo dissolution. To use an example of Aquinas', it does not follow from the nature of form that forms are received in some matter (otherwise there could not be subsistent forms). So the possibility of separate existence can in a sense be said to follow from the nature of form. All the same, many particular substantial forms (such as the petreity of a particular stone) are incapable of separate existence. Similarly, it could be that although the part–whole relation leaves room for dissolution of wholes, some wholes are incapable of dissolution. The above construal of what Aquinas means when he says that the dissolubility of composita follows from the nature of composition may be off base. Perhaps he just means that it is a truth about composition that all composita *qua* composita are dissoluble. If so, it remains puzzling that Aquinas takes this to be an evident truth about composition.

The next feature Aquinas takes to be present in all composita and absent from God is dependence on some prior agent. He argues that "since composition is only from diverse things, those diverse things are in need of some agent to unite them. For diverse things are not, as such, united. But every composite thing has being insofar as those things from which it is composed are united. Every composite being, then, must depend on some prior agent. Consequently the first being, who is God . . . cannot be composite" (DP 7.1, *responsio*).

The limitations of this argument are again reminiscent of those of the one considered just before it. To put it crudely, Aquinas' idea is that composite objects (as essentially composite) exist only because their parts are, as it were, stuck together;[38] their parts are stuck together because of a prior agent; so composite objects exist only because a prior agent exists. It does seem true that an ordinary material object, composed of material parts, exists because some material parts or other exist (quarks, molecules, or what have you), and are "stuck together" (in the right way to constitute a material object of that kind). Those material parts are not by their very nature (or even always) stuck together (in such a way to constitute a material object of that kind); so we may ask why it is that those parts not only exist but are stuck together (that way). Moreover, the fact that those parts are stuck together (in the right way) may depend not just on the causal powers of parts of that thing but on the causal powers of some external and prior agent. (An icicle in my freezer exists only because some water molecules or other exist, and are put together so as to constitute an icicle; that the water molecules are put together in that way is causally dependent on the action of the cooling unit in my freezer.) But it is not clear that for *every* materially composite being there is a prior agent causally responsible for the fact that its material parts are stuck together. The universe is, I suppose, the largest materially composite being there is, and there may be no prior agent responsible for the fact that its material parts are "stuck together."[39] In any case, since Aquinas deploys the above argument in order to show that God is free from any kind of composition (material or metaphysical), he must be supposing that even immaterial beings stand in need of a causal agent to unite their (metaphysical) parts. But the relation of metaphysical parts to their wholes is quite different from the relation of, say, molecular parts to their wholes in a respect crucial to this argument. Take any two molecules that are in fact "united" as constituents of a particular

---

[38]This might mean, more weakly, that each composite object is essentially composed of some (proper) parts or other, or, more strongly, that for each composite object, there is a set of (proper) parts of which that object is essentially composed. Aquinas would endorse the stronger as well as the weaker thesis; whether or not composition is construed broadly, each thesis is plausible.

[39]Defenders of the cosmological argument might say the fact that all actual creatures are parts of the same universe does demand an explanation in terms of a prior and external agent; considerations of space prevent me from discussing why I think cosmological arguments fail.

midsized material object. As we have seen, those two molecules might both have existed (perhaps did both exist, or will both exist), without being united to each other as constituents of that object. But (for Aquinas), any two metaphysical parts of, say, the angel Gabriel could not have both existed, without being united to each other as constituents of Gabriel. For example, Gabriel's *esse* and any one of his accidents could not have both existed, without being united as constituents of Gabriel. (That is because Gabriel's *esse* and his accidents are individuated by reference to Gabriel, and hence could not have been there except as [sometime] parts of him.)[40] So there is no room for the question "Given that these parts exist, why are they united as constituents of Gabriel?" and no obvious need for a prior causal agent to unite any of those parts, at least as long as their existence is assumed. (Compare: "Given that these subregions of space exist, why are they 'united' [adjoined] in such a way as to constitute this larger region of space?")

It is open to Aquinas to reply that it is a contingent fact that there are any parts of Gabriel to be united as constituents of him, even if all of Gabriel's parts are in every possible world in which they exist united with other parts of him. (Gabriel might not have existed, and if he had not, none of his parts would have existed either.) Now, if it is a contingent fact that Gabriel's parts are there at all, it is likewise a contingent fact that they are united to one another as parts of Gabriel. So, Aquinas could maintain, we need a causal explanation of this last contingent fact, and such an explanation will always lead us back to a prior cause.

Let us suppose that every case of contingent composition of metaphysical parts is to be explained by reference to a prior cause. How does this help us show that God is incomposite? For all we have said, there could be two kinds of composite immaterial beings: one kind all of whose parts only contingently exist, and hence are only contingently bundled together, and another kind all of whose parts necessarily exist, and are necessarily bundled together. Aquinas appears to discount this possibility on the grounds that diverse things as such (*inquantum huiusmodi*) are not united. But this will not do. The necessarily bundled together parts of a necessary being would be diverse things that are not united *qua* diverse things, or *qua* parts; but they could very well be united *qua* the particular parts they are. Once again,

---

[40]Here I am ignoring complications about the sense in which, according to Aquinas, the metaphysical parts of an immaterial being may be said to exist. These complications would raise new difficulties for the argument under consideration.

Aquinas' argument appears to fall short of establishing that God lacks every kind of composition (metaphysical as well as material).

The last argument for God's noncomposition stands apart from the ones considered because it is axiological. As presented at SCG I.18, it has the following structure:

> Every composite has parts less perfect than itself.
> Thus if God is composite, He has parts less perfect than Himself.
> If so, the goodness and perfection that are proper to God will not be in Him purely (*pure*). There will be something in God which is not perfectly good; God will not be, as it were, perfectly good all the way down.
> But in that case God will be less than maximally perfect—He will not be the first and highest good.
> So, God is incomposite.

This argument cannot do the job alone, even if it is conceded that God is maximally perfect, and that the proper parts of a whole are less perfect than that whole. If it is sound, it must be that something can be the first and highest good, and that *being perfectly good all the way down* is a necessary component of *being the first and highest good*. (If *being perfectly good all the way down* is an unexemplifiable property, and *being the first and highest good* is an exemplifiable one, the former cannot be necessarily connected with the latter.) But the argument gives us no reason to think it is possible for anything to be perfectly good all the way down, since it offers us no reason to think that anything could be (in Aquinas' sense) entirely incomposite. It was precisely because there are real doubts about whether anything could be entirely incomposite that we have been examining Aquinas' arguments for divine noncomposition. And those arguments no more demonstrate the possibility of radical noncomposition than they do its actuality. In conclusion, then, argument (A)—the argument from divine noncomposition to the identity of God with His existence—fails because Aquinas does not succeed in showing that anything materially or metaphysically composite must have properties God could not have.

From God's Nonpotentiality to the Identity of God with His Existence

I have not said much about Aquinas' second argument for divine noncomposition, to the effect that since composition always involves potentiality, and God is free from potentiality, God is not composite. I have postponed considering this argument because argument (B) (see p. 28) is meant to show that since there is no potentiality in God, His essence must be identical to His existence. The reader will probably anticipate the sort of objections I make to argument (B). In brief, I argue that if potentiality is conceived broadly enough that whatever is essence-existence or subject-accident composite has potentialities, then there is no good reason to suppose that God could not have them. I have argued that the properties Aquinas takes to be entailed by composition and incompatible with the divine nature turn out either to follow upon composition construed narrowly rather than broadly, or to be (for all Aquinas has shown) compatible with the divine nature. Similarly, I argue that of the properties Aquinas takes to be entailed by potentiality and incompatible with the divine nature, none is both entailed by potentiality in Aquinas' broad sense and clearly incompatible with God's nature.

It may be helpful at this point to introduce the notion of a real potentiality. A subject has a *real potentiality* to be *F* at a time just in case *F*-ness is a genuine or intrinsic one-place property,[41] the subject actually exists at that time, the subject is not *F* at that time, and the subject could become *F* at some later time. (By "the subject could become *F* at some later time" I mean: there is a future compossible with the history of the world up until the present moment, on which future the subject comes to be *F*.) A cold thing, for example, has a real potentiality to become hot, and a puddle of water has a real potentiality to evaporate. A subject has real potentialities at a time just in case for some *F*, the subject then has a real potentiality to be *F*. More weakly, a subject has a *Cambridge potentiality* to be *F* at a time just in case *F*-ness is a one-place property, the subject actually exists at that time, the subject is not *F* at that time, and the subject could become *F* at some later time. A subject has Cambridge potentialities at a time just in case for some *F*, the subject then has a Cambridge potentiality to be *F*. Finally, a subject has a *mere Cambridge potentiality* to be *F* if and only if it has a Cambridge potentiality to be *F*, but not a real potentiality to be *F*. (The number 2000, for instance, now has a mere Cambridge potentiality to number

---

[41]By 'genuine or intrinsic' I mean to exclude such one-place properties as *being an individual such that it is now raining* and *being the number of the planets*. I mean to include such one-place properties as *being round, being human, accelerating, existing, ceasing to exist*, and *crashing into a wall*. (As the last example indicates, I am supposing that what might be called a relational predicate—'crashing into a wall'—may pick out a one-place property, as long as what the predicate is true of is a set of individuals, rather than a set of ordered *n*-tuples.) A genuine or intrinsic one-place property (I think) will be one whose acquisition or loss by a subject constitutes a genuine change in that subject (or the demise or origin of that subject).

a year in which the Red Sox win the pennant, and the largest oak on Wimbledon Common now has a mere Cambridge potentiality to be such that Bill Bradley is the next president of the United States.) A subject has only Cambridge potentialities just in case for some F it has a Cambridge potentiality to be F, but for no F does it have a real potentiality to be F. Anything will have Cambridge potentialities at any moment it exists, except for its last moment of existence, should that moment also be the last moment of time. All and only those things that are either (really) mutable or impermanent will have real potentialities whenever they exist (unless they exist at the last instant of time).

When Aquinas says that God is in no way in potentiality, how should this be understood? Judging from Aquinas' examples, it does not look as if his notion of potentiality is the (very weak) notion of a Cambridge potentiality, since he ties the notion of potentiality to the acquisition, reception, or loss of form or existence by a subject, and there are all sorts of (mere) Cambridge potentialities which are not linked to the acquisition or loss by a subject of any form or existence. So we might think that Aquinas means to deny that God has any real potentialities. Certainly Aquinas would agree that whatever is (in his sense) in no way in potentiality is also free from real potentialities. Moreover, Aquinas would say that whatever is free from real potentialities is (in his sense) in no way in potentiality, since whatever (always) lacks real potentialities is immutable, and he believes that God's being really immutable entails His being potentiality-free (SCG I.15 and 16; CT 9). It follows that lacking real potentialities is for Aquinas a necessary and sufficient condition for being in no way in potentiality. But this does not by itself entail that Aquinas' notion of potentiality is the notion of real potentiality sketched above.

Some of the things Aquinas says about potentiality do make it sound like real potentiality. He opens chapter 1 of *De principiis naturae* by saying that things that can be but are not are in potentiality, while things that are are in actuality. For example, some preexistent matter is in potentiality with respect to being a man before the generation of the same from that matter, and a man is in potentiality with respect to being white before becoming white. Aquinas' characterization of the difference between actuality and potentiality makes it sound as if a thing is in potentiality only if it is not (now) a certain way, and may (yet) be that way;[42] his examples make it sound as if potentialities are potentialities to (later) acquire or lose genuine properties. This is just

[42]In this connection, see also ST Ia.2.3, *responsio*, and SCG I.13, where Aquinas says that it is impossible for one and the same thing to be in actuality and potentiality in the

what we should expect, if by potentiality Aquinas understood something more or less like real potentiality.

On the other hand, there are indications that potentiality as conceived by Aquinas is quite different from real potentiality. For Aquinas, matter is in potentiality with respect to the substantial form it
receives, a subject is in potentiality with respect to whatever accidents
it receives, and an essence is in potentiality with respect to the existence it receives (*vide* ST Ia.3, articles 2, 4, and 6; SCG 17.22 and 23;
DP 7.1 and 2 *ad* 9). In each case, it is hard to see how Aquinas could
make this claim, if he took potentiality to be real potentiality.

It might appear easy to reconcile the claim that matter is in potentiality with respect to substantial form and the idea that potentiality is
real potentiality (as described above). Doesn't the matter that ante-
dates the generation of a man (then) have a real potentiality to become
the matter of a man? Yes; but Aquinas thinks that the matter of some
things is always and could not but be the matter of those things. He
believes that the matter of a celestial body was always the matter of
that body, and that that matter could not receive any other substantial
form than the one it has had throughout its existence. (As he puts it at
ST Ia.9.2, the substantial form of a celestial body perfects [actualizes]
the entire potentiality of that body's matter [to be some kind of actual
individual or other].) So if the matter of a heavenly body is in potentiality with respect to receiving substantial form, that potentiality
cannot be real potentiality as understood above. Also, Aquinas apparently thinks of the world as the largest actual hylomorphically composite object (see ST Ia.47, obj. 3 and *ad* 3). But the matter of the world
could never have had a real potentiality to be world-formed, since the
matter of the world was never anything but the matter of the world. In
short, if what Aquinas meant by 'potentiality' is what I have been
calling real potentiality, it looks as if he could not say (as he does) that
matter—just because of the kind of thing it is—is in potentiality with
respect to substantial form, but only that some matter is always in
potentiality with respect to substantial form, that is, always in potentiality with respect to some substantial form or other.

As a matter of fact, Aquinas at times shows some ambivalence about
whether the matter of a celestial body is in potentiality with respect to
substantial form or substantial being.[43] For this reason, we might not

---

same way, and numerous passages in which he says that whatever is sometimes in
potentiality and sometimes in actuality is in potentiality before it is in actuality. Putting
these passages together, we get a picture of potentiality as incompatible with present
actuality, and tied to future possibility.

[43]See especially DSC 6 *ad* 2, where Aquinas seems not to want to choose between (i)

want to infer from what Aquinas says about the relation of matter to substantial form in general, and about the relation of celestial matter to celestial substantial forms in particular, that Aquinas understands potentiality as something quite different from what I have been calling real potentiality. But if we suppose that a subject is in each case in potentiality with respect to the accidental forms it receives, and that an essence is in each case in potentiality with respect to the essence it receives, we are again led to conclude that the sort of potentiality involved cannot be real potentiality.

To be sure, it will sometimes be true that an individual subject is in real potentiality with respect to acquiring an accidental form: something may exist at a time when it is not actually white, and possibly be white at some later time. But Aquinas holds that some accidents are inseparable from their subjects, since they follow upon their subjects' nature. For example, he thinks that whiteness is inseparable from the subject snow, because it follows from snow's nature (ST Ia.9.2, *responsio*). Whenever an accident is inseparable from its subject, that subject will never have a real potentiality to have that accident, since it will never be true of that subject that it exists, does not now have that accident, and may yet come to have it. Once again, if what Aquinas meant by 'potentiality' is real potentiality, then he could not say that a subject is—just because of the kind of thing it is—in potentiality with respect to all the accidents it receives, but only that a subject is sometimes in potentiality with respect to some of the accidents it will come to receive. In fact, though, he does say in many places that any subject is related to any accident it receives as potentiality is related to act (see ST Ia.3.6, *responsio;* and DP 7.4, *responsio*).[44]

Finally, it is easy to see that if an essence is in potentiality with

the (apparently un-Thomistic) view that the matter of a celestial body is an actual being that needs no form to give it substantial being, but needs form only to give it motion (so that the matter of a celestial body is in potentiality with respect to place but not substantial being), and (ii) the view that the matter of a celestial body does need a substantial form to actualize its potentiality for substantial being, but that the potentiality of the matter of a celestial body is a limited kind of potentiality for substantial being (to be this kind of substance, rather than this kind, or that kind, or . . .) which is entirely actuated by the only substantial form that matter could receive, so that 'after' the reception of substantial form by matter, no unactualized potentiality with respect to being remains, but only potentiality with respect to place. At ST Ia.66.2 Aquinas inclines to the latter view: he says there that the matter of heavenly bodies—considered in itself—is in potentiality with respect to just one substantial form (the one it actually has). And at ST Ia.79.2 he says that the matter of heavenly bodies has a potentiality always perfected by the act that is its substantial form.

44"Subjectum comparatur ad accidens, sicut potentia ad actum: subjectum enim secundum accidens est aliquo modo in actu" (ST Ia.3.6, *responsio*).

respect to the existence it receives, potentiality cannot be real potentiality. Neither an essence nor anything else can ever have a real
potentiality to exist: that would involve a thing's actually existing at a
time when it was not existent, but might yet come to be.[45]

Given that, for Aquinas, matter is to form, subject is to accident,
and essence is to existence as potentiality is to actuality, it looks as
though Aquinas conceives of potentiality in something like this way:
consider any being that is actually a certain way (say, white, or a man,
or existent). There will always be something in that being by virtue of
which that being is that way. That something may or may not be
something distinct from the being itself. That thing in God by virtue
of which God is wise, or a God, or existent is nothing less than God
Himself; but that thing in a man by virtue of which the man is wise, or
a man, or existent is in each case something distinct from that man (a
received accidental form, a received substantial form, a received *esse*).
In any case in which a thing is a certain way by virtue of receiving
something else, we may say that the receiver, as such, is in potentiality
with respect to the received. Thus matter, as such, is in potentiality
with respect to receiving substantial form, a subject as such is in
potentiality with respect to receiving accidents, and an essence as such
is in potentiality with respect to receiving existence. For a received
form of existence to actualize a potentiality it is sufficient that it make a
thing be a certain kind of thing, or be a certain way, or be; for a
receiver to be in potentiality with respect to received form or existence
it is sufficient that something be the kind of thing that can be made to
be a certain kind of individual, or be a certain way, or be. And a thing
is in some way in potentiality if and only if it can be as it were
'factored' into a receiving element and a (distinct) received element.

If potentiality is understood in this very broad way, that God's
essence is distinct from His existence will entail that God is in some
way in potentiality. (At least, it will do so if we concede that any
existence distinct from a subject is received by that subject.) But, one
might ask, why suppose that God is—in this very generous sense of
potentiality—potentiality-free? Aquinas advances a number of arguments for doing so. They include:

(a) Whatever is eternal and immutable is in no way in potentiality;
     but God is eternal and immutable; so God is potentiality-free
     (SCG I.16; CT 9 and 11).

[45]At DSC 1, *responsio,* Aquinas says that a subsistent form is related to its existence as
potentiality to act, not as a potentiality separable from act, but as a potentiality that is
always accompanied by its act. The notion of an always actuated potentiality makes no
sense unless potentiality is construed in some way other than as real potentiality.

(b) Potentiality is not self-actuating; what is in potentiality must be raised to actuality by something else that is in actuality. So what is in any way in potentiality is posterior to and dependent on some other actual being. But God—as the First Being—is not posterior to or dependent on anything else. Hence God is in no way in potentiality (SCG I.16; ST Ia.3.1, *responsio;* DP 7.1, *responsio*).

Each of these arguments either depends on premises at least as doubtful as that argument's conclusion, or else has premises too weak to yield that conclusion.

Argument (a) would be unproblematic if "being in some way in potentiality" meant "having some real potentialities," since nothing that is immutable and eternal can have any real potentialities. But Aquinas' notion of being in some way in potentiality is on the face of it broader than the notion of having a real potentiality. (If there are numbers, presumably they lack real potentialities; but they will not be the same as their properties or existence, and so will be [in Aquinas' sense] in some way in potentiality.) For this reason, (a) stands in need of a lemma to the effect that real potentiality and potentiality as construed by Aquinas coincide. I have been unable to find any good arguments for that lemma in Aquinas.

Argument (b) relies on a principle Aquinas introduces and explicates in the First Way, to the effect that nothing can move from potentiality to actuality, save by something (else) in actuality. There he illustrates the point by saying that wood, which is potentially (and hence not actually) hot, is made actually hot by fire, which is already actually hot. In this example, the potentiality had by the subject is a real potentiality; and the being said to raise the subject's potentiality to actuality is an actual being—fire. And the being that causes the wood to exchange being potentially hot for being actually hot is not just actual, but actually hot.

Aquinas has in mind here this sort of picture: a subject that makes the transition from having a real potentiality to be F to being actually F is in making that transition causally indebted to some actual being that is already actually F.[46] (It cannot just happen to become actually F; it must be made actually F by something that is already actually F.) But any being that is already actually F at the time of the transition must be

---

[46]In putting things this crudely, I ignore complications involving pure and mixed perfections, privations, the difference between being formally, eminently, and virtually F, the distinction between univocal and equivocal causation, and the relation of atemporally actual causes to temporally potential effects. The criticism of (c) set out here will (I think) stand or fall independently of how these fine points are worked out.

distinct from the being that undergoes the transition, since nothing is ever in potentiality and actuality at the same time in the same respect. Consequently, a subject that goes from having a real potentiality to be *F* to being actually *F* is causally indebted to or dependent on another actual being.

So Aquinas thinks that (1) necessarily, whatever exchanges a real potentiality for a corresponding actuality is causally dependent on some other actual being for the exchange. He also thinks that (2) necessarily, God is not causally dependent on any other actual being. (By (2) I mean not just that God's existence could not depend on the existence of any other actual being, but also that God could not be causally affected by any other actual being.) It follows from (1) and (2) that God has no real potentialities. If He did have a real potentiality, that potentiality could be raised to actuality. But necessarily, if it were raised to actuality, God would be causally dependent on some other actual being to raise that potentiality to actuality. So if God could have real potentialities, He could be causally dependent on other actual beings; but God could not be dependent in that way.

It is evident from ST Ia.3.1, *responsio,* and SCG I.16 that Aquinas has in mind an argument that leads from premises something like (1) and (2) to the much stronger conclusion that God is in no way in potentiality (in the Thomistic sense). In the first passage, he argues that God is not a body, because every body is in potentiality, and God is in no way in potentiality. How do we know that this last claim is true?

> It is necessary for that which is a first being to be in actuality, and in no way in potentiality. Although in a thing that moves from potentiality to actuality, potentiality is prior in time to actuality, nevertheless actuality is prior *simpliciter* to potentiality: for whatever is in potentiality is not reduced to actuality except through an actual being [*quia quod est in potentia, non reducitur in actum nisi per ens actu*]. But it has been shown above that God is the first being. Therefore it is impossible for there to be any potentiality in God. (ST Ia.3.1, *responsio*)

Aquinas' appeals to this argument later on in *Quaestio* 3, in the context of establishing that God has neither accidents nor received *esse,* leave no doubt that he takes the argument to have established that God is potentiality-free in the sense of being entirely 'unfactorable' into a receiving and a received element. But it is obscure just how the argument could do that.

Suppose we grant that nothing in potentiality could be reduced to actuality, except by some other actual being, and that God could never be at the far end of the causal relation. It follows that there is in God no reduction of potentiality to actuality. What does this conclusion amount to? Well, Aquinas' examples of the reduction of potentiality to actuality involve the successive exchange of a potentiality for a corresponding actuality in a subject. So we might think that the reduction of potentiality to actuality essentially involves the subject's first being only potentially F, and then becoming actually F (where F-ness is an intrinsic or genuine one-place property). But if that is the way to construe the reduction of potentiality to actuality, there is a lot of daylight between the assertion that there is in God no reduction of potentiality to actuality, and Aquinas' conclusion—that God is in no way in potentiality (that is, that God can in no way be factored into a receiving and a received element). Again, if numbers are atemporal abstract objects, they will not exchange real potentialities for corresponding actualities, but neither will they be what Aquinas calls pure acts. This suggests that we should construe the reduction of potentiality to actuality much more generously, so that whenever something is received (whether substantial form, accidental form, or *esse*) a potentiality of the receiver (matter, subject, or essence) is reduced to actuality. Then we can get from Aquinas' premises to Aquinas' conclusion. But that is only because the key premiss—that a thing's potentiality must be reduced to actuality by some other actual thing— turns out to mean something like: unless something is entirely 'unfactorable', whenever it is a certain way (has a certain accidental form, or substantial form, or *esse*), it is that way through the causal influence of some other actual being—that is, through the causal influence of some other individual substance.[47] Understood this way, the premiss entails that only something with an entirely simple metaphysical constitution could be causally independent from all other individuals. From that premiss, and the premiss that God is causally independent, it follows that God is—in the relevant sense—in no way in potentiality. But this invites the question "Why should anyone think that only what is entirely simple could be causally independent from any other individuals?" As long as we construe the reduction of potentiality to actuality narrowly—as the replacement in a subject of a real potentiality by its corresponding actuality—it is plausible that any being that undergoes the reduction of potentiality to actuality is causally dependent on some other actual individual. (But what if the being is the universe?) Once the reduction of potentiality to actuality is construed broadly enough

[47]As we have seen, for Aquinas what has *esse* or is an actual being (*ens actu*) is an individual substance, rather than anything received by an individual substance (cf. for instance DUVI, 4 *responsio*). So if a being whose potentiality to be F is reduced to actuality depends for that reduction on some other *actual* being, it depends on some other substance (and not just on the received item by virtue of which the being is F).

to coincide with composition (in Aquinas' broad sense), however, all bets are off. Then it needs to be shown that the reduction of potentiality to actuality construed that broadly is not a feature of every possible substance, including ones that no other substance causally affects.

Someone might reply on Aquinas' behalf that if God exists by virtue of having an existence distinct from Him, then He is a dependent being, whether or not He is causally dependent on any other individual substances. Fair enough; if God's *esse* is distinct from God, then there is something distinct from God (divine *esse*) without which He could not exist. Now, how do we know that God does not in existing depend on something distinct from Him? It might be answered that God's dependence on anything distinct from Him is incompatible with His aseity. This will be so, if with Aquinas we suppose that a being has aseity just in case its existence is independent of the existence of everything distinct from it; it will not obviously be so, if we suppose that a being has aseity just in case its existence is independent of the existence of every individual substance distinct from it, or that a being has aseity just in case its existence is independent of everything that is not a (proper or maximal) part of it. If we knew that God has aseity strongly characterized, then we would know that God's existence is nothing real and distinct from God; if we also knew that God's existence is something real, we would know that God is the same as His existence. But is is dialectically out of bounds for someone to appeal to God's aseity strongly characterized in arguing that God's existence is nothing distinct from God which actualizes God's potentiality to exist. For if it is an open question whether or not anything could fail to be related to its existence as receiver to received, it is likewise an open question whether anything possible has aseity strongly characterized, and whether accordingly aseity should be strongly or weakly characterized.

Arguments (a) and (b) do not exhaust Aquinas' arguments for the absence of potentiality in God. Because, however, the other arguments rely on notions to be discussed in subsequent sections, and because my criticism of those arguments runs along the same lines as my criticism of (a) and (b), I will move on to Aquinas' *arguments from participation*.

The Argument from Participation

Each thing exists because it has existence [*esse*]. Therefore nothing whose essence is not its existence exists through its essence, but rather by participation in something—to wit, existence itself [*ipsius esse*].

Now, what exists through participation in something cannot be the first being: because what a thing participates in in order to exist is prior to it. But God is the First Being, to whom nothing is prior. God's essence is consequently His existence. (SCG I.22)

This argument looks at first sight too Platonic to mesh with Aquinas' more or less Aristotelian metaphysics. It appears to move from particulars that exist (but are not their own existence) to a universal, existence itself, by virtue of participating in which those particulars exist. But it would be a mistake to construe existence itself as a universal, and participation as a relation linking particulars and universals. As we have seen, Aquinas thinks that different existents have different existences, and that the existence shared by all (finite) existents has being only in thought. So different existents exist by having different existences, not by having the same one. Moreover, Aquinas says that all existents participate in *ipsum esse,* and he usually means by 'ipsum esse' not any kind of property, but rather an unreceived, particular existence (namely, God).

In fact, Aquinas thinks of an existent-by-participation as bearing two different relations to two different sorts of things, each of which may be called existence. First, an existent-by-participation participates in (its own) existence: "Every substance that is posterior to the first simple substance participates in existence. Moreover, everything that participates is composed of the participant and the participated, and the participant is in potentiality to the participated" (PE 8.21).

Here participation is a relation between a thing and an (individualized) property that is a constituent of that thing. But an existent only participates in its own existence because it stands in a certain causal relation to the first agent, existence itself: "Everything that is not its own existence participates in existence from the first cause, which is its own existence" (PE 8,21). To be an existent-by-participation is to stand in a three-place relation: that is, to participate *in* (one's own) existence *from* existence (itself).

Aquinas often compares being an existent-by-participation to being hot by participation, as in the following passage: "Existence itself belongs to the first agent according to His own nature: for God's existence is His substance, as was shown earlier. What belongs to something according to its own nature is not found in other things except by way of participation; as heat is in other bodies from fire. Therefore existence itself belongs to everything else from the first agent by a certain participation" (SCG II.52). The analogy Aquinas draws here can be better understood with the help of a sketch of his metaphysics of heat transfer. According to Aquinas, the question

"Why is (this) fire hot?" can be answered by reference to the kind of thing fire is, since heat is a quality that follows upon the substantial form of fire (ST Ia.67.3, *responsio*). The question "Why is this water hot?" must instead be answered by reference to the causal activity of some fire. Water only becomes hot because fire makes water hot. The way fire does this is by causing (the matter of) water to (imperfectly and inchoately) take on a substantial form of fire, which form gives rise to the quality of heat. If fire causes (the matter of) an individual substance to perfectly receive a substantial form of fire, then that substance turns into fire; if it causes it to imperfectly receive that form, the substance only becomes hot. If the form has been received only imperfectly by the water's matter, it will not take; consequently, once the fire has been removed, the hot water will in time grow cold as the substantial form of fire imperfectly received by it departs (ST Ia.67.3 *ad* 1). Since fire makes other things hot by making them, as it were, imperfectly fire, hot things distinct from fire become hot by participating (imperfectly) in the nature of fire. To put this slightly differently: hot water gets hot from fire by participating (less than perfectly) in the nature of fire.

The way that heat is in things other than fire is for Aquinas both like and unlike the way that existence is in things other than God. The obvious similarity is that in order to explain the presence of heat in anything besides fire, we must appeal to the causal agency of fire; and in order to explain the presence of existence in anything besides God, we must appeal to the causal agency of God. The obvious difference is that, for Aquinas, no creature participates in existence by (even inchoately, or imperfectly) receiving a divine substantial form. For this reason, Aquinas thinks of light as providing a better model for existence than heat. Just as heat is a quality following upon the substantial form of fire, light is a quality following upon the substantial form of the sun. And just as heat is in hot water by participation in heat from fire, light is in air by participation in light from the sun. But air does not participate in light by imperfectly receiving a solar substantial form: while heated water is on the way to being fire, illuminated air is not on its way to being a sun. Hence although hot water participates in heat by participating in the nature of fire, illuminated air does not participate in light by participating in the nature of the sun. As Aquinas puts it, the light in the air (unlike the light in the sun) has no root in its subject, since it follows upon no substantial form in that subject.[48]

---

[48]That is why—Aquinas thinks—illuminated air ceases to be luminous once the source of its light is taken away, while heated water remains hot after the source of its heat has been taken away—for as long as it can keep even a tenuous and imperfect hold

Hence, Aquinas concludes, although heat is in fire and hot water in the same way—namely, as a quality consequent upon a (perfectly or imperfectly received) substantial form—light is not in the sun and in the air in the same way: light in the sun follows from the sun's substantial form, whereas light in the air does not follow from any substantial form in the air, whether that form is perfectly or imperfectly received. All the more is existence found in God and in creatures differently: the existence in God just is the divine substance, while the existence in creatures is an accident in the broad sense.

The argument from participation at SCG I.22 may now be seen to have this structure:

> Whatever has an essence distinct from its existence exists by participation in (its own) existence from something else— existence itself.
> No such being can be the first being, since there will be some being prior to it—the existence itself from which it exists.
> But God is the first being.
> Therefore, God's essence is not distinct from His existence.

The priority alluded to in the second premiss is of a robust, causal sort: that from which an existent-by-participation participates in existence will be an efficient cause of that existent. Consequently, this argument cannot be blocked by maintaining that for all we know some being could be (in the sense at issue) prior to God. That would be tantamount to saying that for all we know God could be a creature. The sticking point of the argument is, of course, its first premiss. If having an essence distinct from your existence is taken to be a sufficient condition for participating in existence, then it needs to be shown that whatever participates in existence gets existence from something else. If participation is so defined that nothing can participate in existence without getting that existence from somewhere, then it needs to be shown that whatever has an essence distinct from its existence participates in existence. If we have an argument establishing that everything but existence itself is caused to exist by existence itself, we can conclude that God could not be distinct from existence itself; just as, if we have an argument establishing that everything changeable is (ulti-

---

on the substantial form of fire. Since existence resembles light rather than heat in this respect, Aquinas maintains, any creature whose existence ceased to be sustained by divine agency would immediately fall into nothingness: God is the source of existence, and creatures are, as it were, only existence reflectors. A discussion of these matters is found at ST Ia.104.1, *responsio*.

mately) caused to change by some changeless being (as the first way purports to do), we can conclude that God could not be distinct from that changeless being. However, in neither his presentation of the argument from participation at SCG I.22, nor his more compressed presentation of that argument at ST Ia.3.4, does Aquinas deploy or make reference to an argument supporting the claim that existence itself is the cause of all other existents. The argument from participation is for that reason at best an enthymeme. Since the missing premisses concern the link between receiving existence and the property of being caused, a natural place to look for them is in the last two arguments (each of which are causal) for the identity of God and His existence.

The Argument from God's Uncausedness

Unfortunately, Aquinas' argument from the uncausedness of divine existence appears incomplete in much the way the argument just considered was. Perhaps the clearest version of the argument from the uncausedness of divine existence is found at ST Ia.3.4:

> Whatever is in a thing over and above its essence must be caused either by the principles of that essence, the way proper accidents follow upon a thing's species (as *being risible* follows upon *being a man* and is caused by the essential principles of the species), or by something external (the way heat in water is caused by fire). So if the existence of a thing is other than its essence, that existence must be caused either by something external or by the essential principles of that thing. Now, it is impossible for an existence to be caused by the essential principles of a thing alone, because nothing has the wherewithal to cause its own existence (if its existence is caused). Consequently, a thing whose existence is distinct from its essence has its existence caused by another being. But this cannot be said of God, since we call God the first efficient cause. Therefore it is impossible for essence and existence to be distinct in God.

There is, no doubt, something peculiar about the supposition that God could be the cause of His own existence: if God were the cause of His own existence, it would have to be true not just that He exists, and nothing else made Him exist, but also that He made Himself exist.[49]

---

[49]Is it impossible for a thing to cause its own existence? Perhaps not. There is no evident incoherence in the notion of circular time. But if time can be circular, maybe something a being does at a later time could cause its generation at an earlier time (since its generation will occur after as well as before the being's action). A being of this

And there is something more than peculiar about the supposition that something else could be the cause of God's existence. But why are these the only options available to someone who denies that God's essence is His existence? After all, by Aquinas' own reckoning God's existence is an uncaused maximal part of the divine essence. If God's existence can be an uncaused maximal part of the divine essence, why couldn't it be an uncaused proper part of the divine essence?

In the version of the argument from God's uncausedness at SCG I.22, Aquinas makes it clear how he would meet this objection, when he says that if God's existence is not identical to God's essence, it cannot be a part of it, since God's essence has been shown to be incomposite. The reference is apparently to SCG I.18, where Aquinas lays out the arguments for God's noncomposition examined earlier. (Aquinas is supposing that everything is at least as composite as its essence, since its essence is a [proper or maximal] part of it.) So the argument under consideration presupposes that God is in no way composite. I have already argued that Aquinas has shown no such thing: he has at most shown that certain kinds of composition— composition out of material parts, composition caused by another agent, and composition of contingently compounded things—are not found in God. And to say that God's essence is (necessarily) composed of a quidditative component and an existence is not to ascribe any of those kinds of composition to God. (Nor is it to ascribe to God an element of potentiality, in any sense of potentiality which has been shown to be incompatible with the divine nature.) Even if it is granted, then, that God could not have an existence disjoint from His essence (because whatever has such an existence is caused to exist, and the causing-to-exist relation is a finite linear ordering), it does not follow that there is nothing more to God's essence than His existence.

Suppose, though, that (an) existence is not the sort of thing that can be a proper part of an essence. (It is hard to imagine what an argument establishing this would look like, which did not also show *contra* Aquinas that existence could not be a maximal part of a thing's essence; but suppose there is some such argument.) It remains difficult to see how Aquinas can get from the distinctness of a thing's essence and

---

kind—which might either be a denizen of the universe, or the whole universe—might be said to be the cause of its own existence. For a defense of the possibility of circular time, see Richard Sorabji, "Closed Space and Closed Time," in *Oxford Studies in Ancient Philosophy*, vol. 4, ed. Julia Annas, (Oxford: Clarendon Press, 1986), pp. 215–31; for some related issues, see David Lewis, "The Paradoxes of Time Travel," *American Philosophical Quarterly* 13, no. 2 (1976): 145–52.

its existence, to its being caused, without relying on considerations appealed to in the arguments from the nature of composition and potentiality. On Aquinas' view, "God exists" is a truth not to be explained in terms of the activity of any other causal agent: God does not get existence from anywhere else. Nor does He get His existence from Himself—as if He caused Himself to exist. Why couldn't all this be true if what it was for God to exist was for an existence disjoint from God's essence to be (necessarily, uncausedly) welded to that essence?[50] In his presentation of the argument at SCG I.22, Aquinas says that if God's essence were joined to an existence disjoint from it, there would have to be some cause of the joining of divine essence and divine existence, because whenever things that are not *per se* one are joined, they are joined through some cause. Once more we are led back to the argument from composition and to the conclusion that the argument from God's uncausedness can be no more successful than the first two arguments we examined.

The Argument from Characteristic Effects

The last argument for the identity of the divine essence and divine existence we shall consider is also causal:

> When causes producing different effects jointly produce a common effect, as well as different ones, they must produce that common effect by virtue of some superior cause that has the common effect as its own characteristic effect. . . . All created causes have existence [*esse*] as a common effect, though different causes have different characteristic effects. . . . There must, then, be a cause superior to all others, by virtue of which they all cause things to be, and existence [*esse*] will be its characteristic effect. This cause is God. Now, the characteristic effect of any cause proceeds from it according to a likeness of its nature. Existence, therefore, must be the substance or nature of God. (DP 7.2, *responsio*)

The conclusion appears to depend on ancillary unstated premisses. Suppose that created causes, which produce existence as their common effect, do so by virtue of the agency of God, whose characteristic

---

[50]Someone might think that the existence of a thing should not be thought of as a constituent of that thing disjoint from its essence, on the grounds that for an individual to exist is not for it to have an essence, (predicamental) accidents, and an extra constituent—existence; it is just for it to have an essence and the predicamental accidents that follow upon that essence. But this line of thought is obviously of no help to Aquinas.

effect is existence; and suppose also that the characteristic effect of a cause bears a likeness to the nature of its cause. What follows? That existence bears a likeness to the divine nature—but not, in any obvious way, that (divine) existence *is* the divine nature. This can be seen when we consider that although heat is a characteristic effect of fire, the heat in fire is not for Aquinas identical to—or even part of—the nature of fire; instead it is a quality consequent upon the nature of fire (cf. again ST Ia.67.3, *responsio*). Why, then, couldn't divine existence follow upon the divine nature (as heat follows upon the nature of fire), or be a proper part of that nature? Answering that question takes us back to the argument from God's uncausedness, and ultimately to the argument from the nature of composition.

Conclusion

I have examined Aquinas' arguments for the identity of God and His existence at length, because they are crucial to Aquinas' defense of the possibility of subsistent existence (and also because they illuminate various features of Aquinas' metaphysics). If the arguments do not work, the question of why we should suppose that a subsistent existence is even possible is a vexed one for Aquinas. To reiterate: Aquinas holds that although we can know *that* subsistent existence is actual, we cannot know *how* it is possible. For us to see how subsistent existence is possible would be for us to see how something could be at once completely simple and subsistent. But, Aquinas holds, in our understanding what is most simple is not a subsistent whole but rather a part of a subsistent whole (cf. SCG I.26). Accordingly, Aquinas grants that subsistent existence is inconceivable for us: "Our understanding conceives of existence in the way it is found in the inferior beings from which it takes its knowledge—and in such beings existence is not subsistent, but inherent. Reason, however, finds that some existence is subsistent" (DP 7.2 *ad* 7). For Aquinas, then, we know that subsistent existence (unlike subsistent whiteness, or subsistent heat) is possible, only because we know that unless there were such a thing, there could be no existents at all. As a result, Aquinas' defense of the possibility of pure subsistent existence stands or falls with his defense of its actuality. If a quite different sort of defense could be provided of the possibility of pure subsistent existence, we could still defend the idea that God is pure subsistent existence. But as I have already argued, the prospects for such a defense are dim: a subsistent individual constituted of existence, and nothing but existence is too thin to be possible.

Some readers may wonder why I have made no mention of Aquinas' view that neither existence nor anything else is predicated univocally of God and creatures. (That view might be thought crucial to the explication and defense of the idea that God is pure subsistent existence.) The reason is that Aquinas' arguments for the nonunivocality of creaturely and divine predication depend on the claim that divine existence, divine wisdom, divine goodness, and so on are all just the divine substance.[51]

As we have seen, Aquinas' starting point is that whenever it is true that this K exists, it is true that there is something—namely, the existence of this K—which is proper to this K, and which must be appealed to in saying what this K's existing consists in. This principle, Aquinas thinks, applies equally to God and creatures: that is why he is sure that the expression "the existence of God" refers to something—in particular, to something proper to God which is that by which God exists. (Similarly, Aquinas does not doubt that the expressions "the essence of God" and "the wisdom of God" have as their referents, respectively, something proper to God by which God is divine, and something proper to God by which God is wise.) For Aquinas, when we do metaphysics we discover that divine existence is nothing less than God, and accordingly that the relation divine existence bears to God is not the (irreflexive) inherence relation, but the identity relation; we likewise discover that the divine essence, divine goodness, and the like are all identical to God. Only at this point may we conclude that existence, goodness, and so on are not predicated univocally of God and creatures.[52] Consequently, if the coherence of Aquinas' conception of divine simplicity is at issue, it is no use defending that conception by reference to Aquinas' views on the nonunivocality of creaturely and divine predication.

If we can't make a go of the idea that God is a pure subsistent existence, or His own existence, and we want to save something like Aquinas' conception of the relation of God to His existence, it is

[51]For example, at ST Ia.13.5, *responsio,* Aquinas says that wisdom is not predicated univocally of God and creatures, because although when wisdom is predicated of a man, the term "wise" signifies a perfection distinct from that man's essence, existence, and so on, the term *wise* predicated of God signifies nothing less than the divine essence or existence. At DP 7.7, *responsio,* he argues that nothing can be predicated univocally of God and creatures, because God and creatures are related differently to *esse* (in that God is His *esse,* while creatures only have their *esse*). And at CT 27 Aquinas says that terms are not applied to God and creatures univocally, because the definition of what is predicated of the creature is not a definition of what is predicated of God. It is not, because a definition makes reference to a genus and *differentia,* and God, as existence itself, has no *differentia* and falls under no genus.

[52]This point is also made by Geach; see "Aquinas," p. 122.

natural to look for some weaker, defensible analogue of the idea that God is His very existence. Granting that the most intimate relation of all—identity—fails to hold between God and His existence, might it be that God is intimately related to His existence, and more intimately related to His existence than creatures are to their existence? If we suppose with Aquinas that existences are proper to their subjects, it is hard to see how this could be. For whether a being is God or a creature, that being's existence will exist at all the same times and in all the same worlds as that being. On the other hand, if we think of existence as a one-of-many, we could maintain that God stands in an especially intimate relation to existence. For—if all creatures are contingent, at any rate—then it will be true of any creature that the existence of that creature could have existed, even if that creature had not;[53] but—if God is a necessary being—it will not be true that God's existence could have existed, if God had not. A creature and (its) existence are not found in all of the same worlds; God and (His) existence are.

All the same, the claim that God is more intimately related to His existence than creatures are to their existence—as construed above—has to do with divine ubiquity and creaturely nonubiquity, rather than with divine simplicity and creaturely composition. It comes to the claim that God, unlike creatures, is in every world, just as He is (after a fashion) present at every time and in every place. This feature is, no doubt, crucial to Aquinas' conception of God; but it has little to do with divine simplicity.

In sum, neither the claim that God is pure subsistent existence, nor anything very like it, could be true. In the next chapter, I ask whether the same holds for the claim that God is the same as His goodness, wisdom, and all His other intrinsic attributes.

---

[53]The expression "the existence of creature c" picks out the property of existence by reference to a higher-order property that existence only contingently has. So the existence of c would have existed, even if c had not—although the existence of c would not have been the existence of c; just as the color of this jacket would still have existed, even if this jacket had not—although the color of this jacket would not have been the color of this jacket. (I'm assuming here that properties are ones-of-many.)

2

Divine Simplicity:
God and His Attributes

The Identity of Divine Attributes

> The perfections that preexist in God in a simple and unified way are in creatures received as many and divided. Just as to the different perfections of creatures there corresponds one simple source represented by the different perfections of creatures in many and varied ways, so to the many and varied concepts of our intellect there corresponds something entirely simple, imperfectly understood through those concepts. And so the terms applied to God, although they signify just one thing, are not synonomous, because they signify it under many different concepts [*sub rationibus multis et diversis*]. (ST Ia.13.4, *responsio*)

In this passage, Aquinas indicates his awareness that expressions such as "God's knowledge" and "God's goodness" no more have the same sense than "the temperature of x" and "the mean molecular kinetic energy of x" do.[1] Because expressions picking out divine attributes have different senses, he thinks, one may have partial knowledge of the divine attributes, without realizing that those attributes are all the same—just as one may have partial knowledge of temperature and mean molecular kinetic energy, without realizing that temperature and mean molecular kinetic energy are one and the same. In the latter case, the discovery that we are dealing with one property under two descriptions is a matter of empirically finding out

---

[1]The example is taken from Hilary Putnam; see "The Nature of Mental States," in his *Mind, Language, and Reality* (Cambridge: Cambridge University Press, 1975), pp. 429–41.

something metaphysically exciting about the nature of a property, and not a matter of discerning hitherto unnoticed relations among concepts. Likewise, Aquinas would say, we do not discover that divine goodness is divine wisdom by conceptual analysis, but by doing metaphysics, and finding out that composite existents are possible only if there is something absolutely simple, in which there is no room for a distinction between goodness and power.

But can we make sense of Aquinas' idea that "God's wisdom" and "God's goodness," for example, are nonsynonymous but co-referential terms? Apparently not, if we suppose that goodness and wisdom are what I have called ones-of-many. For in that case, the logical form of

(1) God's goodness is God's wisdom.

would seem to be

(A) Goodness, which is had by God, is the same property as wisdom, which is had by God.

Statement (A) says that goodness and wisdom are the same property, and that this property is had by God; and it is false. Manifestly, properties are not the same if they are not properties of all the same things. Goodness and wisdom, though, are not properties of all the same things (since any number of things are good but not wise). Besides, even if (A) were true, it would not capture anything like Aquinas' picture of the relation of divine goodness to divine wisdom. That is because (A) makes no surprising claim *about God*. It makes the unsurprising claim about God that He has goodness and wisdom, together with the surprising claim about the properties, goodness and wisdom, that they are identical. Aquinas, of course, holds that it is a surprising fact *about God* that His goodness and wisdom are identical, which holds by virtue of God's supreme simplicity. To put this another way, since Socrates is both good and wise, (A) will be true if and only if

(B) Goodness, which is had by Socrates, is the same property as wisdom, which is had by Socrates.

or, more succinctly,

(2) Socrates' goodness is Socrates' wisdom.

But on any remotely Thomistic account of the different ways that perfections are found in God and creatures, (1) and (2) will have different truth-values: the perfections of creatures are many and divided, though the perfections of God are one.

The obvious (and Thomistic) way to try to get (1) without (2) is by recourse to individual properties. But for the reasons touched on in Chapter 1, the appeal to individual properties does not obviously help. Given that being orange is different from being round, the roundness of an orange sphere is different from the orangeness of that sphere, even if both the roundness and the orangeness are proper to that sphere. By the same token, given that being good is different from being wise, the wisdom of God is different from His goodness, even if each one is proper to God.

At this point, a defender of Aquinas might appeal to the idea that God has a very special kind of goodness, perfect goodness, and a very special kind of wisdom, perfect wisdom. As Eleonore Stump and Norman Kretzmann have argued,[2] it might be true that perfect wisdom is perfect goodness, even if goodness is not wisdom, since it does not in general follow from the fact that F-ness is different from G-ness, that perfect F-ness is different from perfect G-ness. This suggests the following way of understanding (5): God's attributes are perfections—such things as perfect goodness, perfect wisdom, perfect power, and the like. Those attributes are all the same as one another, and the same as God, even if their imperfect creaturely counterparts—goodness, wisdom, power, and the like—are distinct. (If I have not misunderstood them, Stump and Kretzmann take this line.)

If this defense of (5) is workable, it makes the appeal to individual properties unnecessary. If being perfectly good is the same as being perfectly wise, then there is no reason why we cannot suppose that "God's perfect goodness is His perfect wisdom" is equivalent to "Perfect goodness, which is had by God, is the same as perfect wisdom, which is had by God." I take this to be a welcome result, since (I have argued) the only way of motivating an ontology of individual properties is by reference to a conception of substances (as bundles of properties) to which Aquinas is firmly opposed.

Still, even if we can make a case for the idea that God's (perfect) goodness is the same as God's (perfect) wisdom, can we defend the idea that each of those in turn is nothing other than God? The following line of thought makes one think not: suppose God's perfect good-

[2]See Eleonore Stump and Norman Kretzmann, "Absolute Simplicity," *Faith and Philosophy* 2, no. 4 (1985): 353–81.

ness is the same as God. Since God could not be a property of anything else, neither could God's perfect goodness. So there is some property—God's perfect goodness—which is a property of itself (since it is a property of God, and God is identical to His perfect goodness), and is not a property of anything else. But the idea of a property that is its own and only its own property certainly looks incoherent.

Insular Attributes

Surprisingly, though, it looks like we can make sense of this possibility, at least within a metaphysical framework significantly different from Aquinas'. For Aquinas, individual substances are constituted (inter alia) of properties. We might, however, think of properties in a very different way, as "constituted"—or better, built up out of—individual substances. On the simplest version of this idea, we think of a property as just the extension of a predicate that designates that property. (Having a property is thought of as being a certain kind of thing—that is, belonging to a certain kind; and kinds are construed as sets of actual individuals.) A one-place property, like *being red,* is thought of as the set of red things; a two–place property, like *being the sister of,* is thought of as the set of ordered pairs such that the first member of the pair is the sister of the second, and so on. There are, however, well-known objections to thinking of properties as the sets of things actually having those properties. If the property *being F* is the same as the property *being F',* then *being F* and *being F'* could not fail to be properties of all the same things. (After all, *being F* could not but be a property of exactly the same things as itself.) But if the property *being F* is just the set of actual F-things, and likewise the property *being F',* this conditional will be false. For in some cases F-ness and F'-ness will be true of exactly the same objects, but would not have been true of exactly the same objects had the world been a different way. (Where S is the largest size the universe ever actually attains [I assume that S is finite], let F be *being twice as large as S,* and F' be *being thrice as large as S.*) In this type of case, if properties are identified with extensions, then *being F* gets identified with *being F',* even though it might have been that not all the same things were F and F'.

These difficulties suggest that if we want to entify properties as things built up out of individual substances, we should extend our horizons beyond the actual world. A standard way to do this is to entify a property as a function that assigns to each world a (possibly empty) extension: redness turns out to be a function that assigns to each world the (possibly empty) set of things that are red at that world.

Then *being twice as large as* S and *being thrice as large as* S turn out to be different properties, since they are different functions from worlds to individuals.[3]

Someone might wonder: why not take the simpler tack of thinking of a property as a set of possible individuals? If we think that individuals are found in a plurality of worlds, we will not in general want to think of a property as a set of possible individuals—*viz,* the set of possible individuals which has the property in question at some world or other. As long as possible individuals inhabit more than one world, it appears, it will sometimes happen that *F*-ness is distinct from *G*-ness, even though the set of possible individuals that has *F*-ness at some world or other is the set of possible individuals that has *G*-ness at some world or other.[4] Suppose, on the other hand, we thought that nothing was found in more than one world. Then we could think of a property as a set of (world-bound) possible individuals: for example, redness would be the set of (world-bound) red individuals scattered throughout logical space.

Why should individuals be thought of as world-bound? David Lewis has argued that at least some should in this way: if we say that a tomato is a trans-world individual, then we shall have to say that one and the same thing—the tomato—has this shape at this world, and that (different) shape at that (different) world. If the shape of a tomato varies from world to world, then its shape is a relational rather than an intrinsic property: it will not be, say, round *simpliciter,* but round-at-this-world, and pear-shaped-at-that-one.[5] This, Lewis thinks, is unac-

---

[3]Some will think that this way of thinking of properties is still too coarse-grained, even though it is finer-grained than the extensionalist one. In conversation Marcia Mayeda has offered the following argument to that effect: *having a top half* is a different property from *having a bottom half,* even though the function from worlds to things that have top halves is the function from worlds to things that have bottom halves (since, necessarily, something has a top half if and only if it has a bottom half). The standard rejoinder to this kind of objection grants that the predicates 'having a top half' and 'having a bottom half' have different meanings, while holding that the predicates nevertheless pick out the same property. How effective the rejoinder is, I'm not sure.

[4]An artificial example: if this tomato is a trans-world individual, then the set of possible individuals which has the conjunctive property of being both red and the same as this tomato at some world or other is the set of individuals which has the conjunctive property of being both green and the same as this tomato at some world or other. (That set is just {this tomato}.) Less artificial examples could be constructed.

[5]"But the roundness of a tomato (or at least, a temporal stage thereof) is one of its intrinsic properties; a tomato (or tomato stage) which is red in the actual world is red *simpliciter,* not relative to this or that. How then can a red tomato or tomato stage fail to be red at some other world? Because other worlds are special kinds of stories; what it is for a tomato to be non-red in some other world is for it to be non-red according to

ceptable: shape is an intrinsic rather than a relational property. We should conclude that one and the same tomato is not found in different worlds—or at least, not in different worlds at which that tomato's intrinsic properties vary.

Suppose there is something whose intrinsic properties vary neither over time nor across worlds. Then, as Lewis notes, there is no bar to supposing that this individual inhabits a plurality of worlds (or all worlds, in the case of a necessary being of this kind). So, even if we should take the tomato in my crisper to be limited to this world, there is no reason to suppose that such individuals as the number 7 are world-bound.

For Lewis, then, properties are sets of possible individuals—some or all or none of which may be world-bound.[6] The property *being an oak or a horse chestnut* will be a set of world-bound possible individuals; the property *being an even integer* will be the set $\{ \ldots -2, 0, 2 \ldots \}$, none of whose members is world-bound.[7] Some properties will be singleton sets of numbers—for example, *being an even prime,* or *being the same as 2* will be $\{2\}$. Now, it is usual in set theory to distinguish an individual from the singleton set containing that individual. Usual but not mandatory: following Quine, one may in set theory identify individuals and their singletons.[8] If we do, we get a surprising result: the property *being an even prime* turns out to be a property of itself and nothing but itself! The property of being an even prime is just the set $\{2\}$; the individual that has that property is the number 2; but (we are supposing) $2 = \{2\}$.[9]

---

some story, which is perfectly compatible with that tomato's being red *simpliciter."* Lewis is unsatisfied with this response, because he thinks that worlds are not stories, but large, concrete individuals. Whether or not he is right about this is a matter that would take us too far afield.

[6]This is an oversimplification: Lewis is neutral on the question of whether there are things quite different from sets of world-bound individuals (universals or tropes) which could be called properties. (See *On the Plurality of Worlds,* pp. 50–69.)

[7]Lewis believes that an individual may fail to be world-bound because it inhabits less than one world, or—perhaps—because it inhabits more than one. Thus he holds that the number 7 exists from the standpoint of all worlds, while inhabiting none (*Counterfactuals* [Cambridge, Mass.: Harvard University Press, 1973], p. 40, and *On the Plurality of Worlds,* p. 96), and that universals—if there are such things—inhabit more than one world (*On the Plurality of Worlds,* p. 205).

[8]See W. V. O. Quine, *Set Theory and Its Logic* (Cambridge, Mass.: Harvard University Press, 1963).

[9]Of course, someone might object that individuals just could not be the same as their singletons, even if we can perfectly well do set theory on the supposition that they are. On this view, we have knowledge about what kind of things sets could and could not

In short, if we make certain not obviously crazy assumptions, it
turns out that there are properties that are properties of something, but
not properties of anything else—subsistent properties. (Actually, I
don't like the locution 'subsistent property', since as some understand
'subsistence', a property could both be a subsistent entity, and a
property of something besides itself. So I will call a property that is its
own and only its own property an *insular* property, since such a
property cannot as it were hook up with anything else.)

The possible theological application of all this should be evident.
Suppose we think that God, as a necessary being who has all His
intrinsic properties essentially, is not limited to any one world, but
inhabits them all.[10] Then any property necessarily had by God and
only God will turn out, on the current assumptions, to be God. For
example, *being God* will be {God}, and hence God. Likewise, if *being
omnipotent* is necessarily a property of God and of God alone, then
God's omnipotence (which is to say {God}) just is God.

The upshot is that we cannot simply and quickly dismiss the idea
that God is His goodness, His wisdom, and all His other perfections
on the grounds that if it were true, there would be insular attributes,
and nothing could be an insular attribute. Given certain assumptions
about what attributes, sets, and possible worlds are—assumptions
that seem neither (in any obvious way) individually incoherent nor (in
any obvious way) jointly inconsistent—*being an even prime* turns out to
be insular. (To take a different case, so does *being this very world-bound
individual* or *being this very trans-world individual*.) Consequently, the
prospects for defending the coherence of the idea that God is His
goodness, wisdom, power, and the like suddenly look brighter. Suppose someone has been arguing that this claim could not be true,
because God's goodness and the like are attributes, and no attribute
could be its own and only its own attribute. Someone attempting to

---

be which is not captured by that which is common to all axiomatizations of set theory:
knowledge that rules out certain hypotheses about sets and individuals consistent with
some or perhaps all current axiomatizations of set theory. I tend to believe that we do
have knowledge about what kind of things sets could and could not be which is not
captured by any axiomatizations of set theory, although I don't know how I would
defend this claim. That our knowledge rules out the identification of individuals with
their singleton sets is not something I have any inclination to believe—though I don't
have a strong inclination to disbelieve it either.

[10]I argue in Chapter 4 that God could not have all His intrinsic properties essentially;
but it is not obvious that this is so, since some things (for example, sets) do have all their
intrinsic properties essentially.

defeat this argument need not actually subscribe to the conception of worlds and properties just sketched. She can say: this is one not obviously incoherent conception of attributes on which something could be its own and only its own attribute. Perhaps there are others; but the existence of this one is enough to show that insular attributes may not be dismissed out of hand as impossible objects. To put this slightly differently: as long as an attribute is (actually or possibly) an attribute of more than one thing, there is no hope for identifying that attribute with anything that is not (actually or possibly) the attribute of anything but itself. But—as the Lewis-Quine account shows—if an attribute is necessarily only an attribute of this very being, then there is conceptual room for the identification of that attribute with the being that has it. Hence there is conceptual room for the identification of God with His wisdom, goodness, power, and so on.

The Problem of Shared Attributes

At this point, the objector may counter: perhaps some attributes are insular. And perhaps some attributes of God are insular. If so, some attributes of God are just the God whose attributes they are. All the same, not every intrinsic attribute of God could be insular (just as not every attribute of the number 2 could be insular). In particular, God's goodness and wisdom could not be.

This is just the point where a defender of Aquinas might want to reintroduce the idea that while creatures are good, wise, and so on, God and God alone is perfectly good, wise, and so on. If perfect goodness and perfect wisdom are necessarily attributes of God and God alone, then we can tell the same story about how there might be no difference between God's perfect goodness (or wisdom) and God as we told about how there might be no difference between God's Deity (or omnipotence) and God.

The problem is that if God has the attribute of perfect goodness (or perfect wisdom), then a fortiori God has the attribute of goodness (or wisdom). (Nothing can be perfectly good without being good, or perfectly wise without being wise.) And even if the attributes of perfect goodness and perfect wisdom are had by God alone, the attributes of goodness and wisdom are shared by God and creatures. If goodness were had only by God or had only by creatures, then it would either strictly speaking be false that God is good, or strictly speaking be false that creatures are good. For the attribute of goodness just is the kind of thing that is had by a thing if and only if that thing is good.[11] Likewise, if wisdom were not shared by God and creatures, it would be false that God is wise, or false that creatures are wise. The principle is the same: where *F*-ness is any attribute, if *F*-ness is an attribute of *x* and not of *y*, then *x* is *F* and *y* is not, since the attribute of *F*-ness just is the kind of thing whose possession by an entity is (necessarily) biconditionally linked to that entity's being *F*.

If God's goodness is an attribute He shares with creatures, then it cannot be an insular attribute, and thus cannot be identical to God. Moreover, if God's goodness and God's wisdom are shared attributes, then (as we have seen) they will not be shared with exactly the same creatures, and will accordingly be distinct from each other, as well as distinct from any unshared attribute of God (such as omnipotence). There will be a distinction, not just between God and His perfections, but also between different divine perfections—some of which are, and some of which are not, shared with creatures, and different ones of which are shared with different creatures.[12]

"But if God has the attribute of perfect goodness, perfect wisdom, and so on, this fact by itself entails that He is good, is wise, and so on. . . . So 'God is good', 'God is wise', and so on all come out true, but we needn't suppose that God has the (shared) attributes of goodness, wisdom, and so on; all He has is the (insular) attribute which is perfect goodness, perfect wisdom, and the like." Granted, having the attribute of perfect goodness or perfect wisdom is a logically sufficient condition for being good, or being wise. Even so, if we countenance the attributes of goodness and wisdom, having those attributes will be a necessary condition for being good and being wise; it is just that having the unshared attribute of perfect goodness or perfect wisdom is a sufficient condition for having the shared attribute of goodness or wisdom.

---

[11]"If one and the same attribute is both the goodness of creatures and the goodness of God, then the goodness of creatures is the goodness of God. But the goodness of creatures is limited, noneternal, and so on; while the existence of God is unlimited, eternal, and so on. Hence the goodness of creatures is not the goodness of God; no attribute of goodness is had by each." That argument is no more successful than: "If (having a) shape is an attribute of both this penny and this football, then the shape of this penny is the shape of this football. But the penny and the football have different shapes, so . . ."

[12]Someone might also argue that God cannot be the same as His omnipotence, omniscience, and so on, on the grounds that these attributes, too, are shared—not by God and any other actual individual, but by God and some otherworldly divine individual distinct from God. This argument, however, depends on the controversial premiss that someone else (someone other than the actual individual who is God) might have been divine. For more on that premiss, see Chapter 3.

It is open to a defender of Aquinas to reply here that because attributes are not universals, there are no such things as shared attributes, and accordingly there is no distinction between those attributes shared by God and creatures and those attributes had by God alone. But this response does not get to the heart of the difficulty, which is independent of whether or not properties are ones-of-many. The friend of individual properties needs an equivalence relation that will do for her the work that identity does for the friend of ones-of-many—a relation we may call *conspecificity*. (Two individual roundnesses will be conspecific, but an individual roundness and an individual squareness will not.) Now, if it should turn out, for example, that God's wisdom is, and God's omnipotence is not, conspecific with, say, Socrates' wisdom, then God's wisdom will be distinct from His omnipotence, and at least one of them will be distinct from God. So the friend of individual properties must maintain either that God's omnipotence is conspecific with the Socrates' wisdom (which is absurd), or maintain that no more is God's wisdom conspecific with Socrates' than God's omnipotence is. This last view presents much the same difficulty as the view that God's wisdom no more is shared with Socrates than His omnipotence is.

Here some readers may protest in exasperation:

> What about analogical predication? To say that "God is good" and "Creatures are good" (or "God is wise" and "Creatures are wise") are both true only if the attribute of goodness (or wisdom) is had by God and creatures is to presuppose that goodness (and wisdom) are predicated univocally of God and creatures. That is just what Aquinas takes pains to deny! He holds that, although "is good," "is wise," and the like are not predicated purely equivocally of God and creatures (the way the Latin *canis* is predicated of dogs and dogfish), neither can they be predicated univocally of God and creatures (the way *canis* is predicated of this dog and that dog). Instead, "is good," "is wise," and the like are predicated analogically of God and creatures, just as "is healthy" is predicated analogically of animals and medicines, or "being" is predicated analogically of substances and accidents. (See ST Ia.13.5; SCG I.32–34)

Guilty as charged: I am assuming that "is good" and "is wise" are predicated univocally of God and creatures. To deny that "is good" and "is wise" can be predicated univocally of God and creatures is, I take it, to contend that God and creatures cannot be said to be good (or wise) in just the same sense. Since this contention is less than obvious, it needs some support.

As I indicated in Chapter 1, Aquinas attempts to support the contention by showing that it follows from the fact that God is the same as His existence and all His other perfections. For instance, Aquinas' argument at ST Ia.13.5 for the impossibility of predicating anything univocally of God and creatures employs the premiss that while the perfections found in creatures are distinct from one another and their receiver, all the divine perfections are the same as God. A related argument at SCG I.32 makes use of that same premiss, and a different sort of argument offered in that same chapter rests on the premiss that nothing is predicated of God as a genus, species, difference, accident, or *proprium*—which premiss Aquinas would defend by reference to the identity of God with His existence and other perfections. (For more instances of arguments from divine simplicity to nonunivo-cality, see note 51 of Chapter 1.)

Suppose we could move from the claim that God is identical to His existence, goodness, and all His other perfections to the claim that nothing is predicated univocally of God and creatures. Would this provide the needed support for the claim that nothing is predicated univocally of God and creatures? That depends on whether there is any reason to think it is true that God is identical to His existence, His goodness, and so on. Aquinas thinks there is; but as I have tried to show in Chapter 1, his attempts to make this out fail. Since I don't think there are any good reasons to believe what I shall call (for brevity) the identity thesis, I don't think the identity thesis can provide support for the nonunivocality thesis.

So, putting considerations of divine simplicity to one side, how might one support the contention that God and creatures cannot be said to be good (or wise) in just the same sense? Well, how might one support the contention that medicines and animals cannot be said to be healthy in just the same sense? Presumably, along the following lines: "This medicine is healthy" (on its natural and true reading) means "This medicine is conducive to good health." But "This animal is healthy" (on its natural and true reading) does not mean "This animal is conducive to good health"; it means "This animal is in a state of good health." So, although the medicine and the animal may each be said to be healthy, the medicine is not healthy in the same sense as the animal. Now, it is hard to see how we could provide a similar defense of the idea that God and creatures cannot be said to be good in just the same sense. To do so, we would need an F such that "God is good" is synonomous with "God is F," while "This creature is good" is not synonomous with "This creature is F." What could F be? Note that F

could not be "supremely good," or "the source of all goodness," or "goodness itself, unreceived and unlimited by any factor." For if F were, say, "goodness itself," then "Not only is God good, He is also goodness itself" would be deviant in just the way that "Not only is this medicine healthy, it is also conducive to health" is. In short, it appears that the kind of considerations that can be appealed to in favor of the idea that healthiness is not predicated univocally of medicines and animals, cannot be appealed to in order to support the idea that goodness is not predicated univocally of God and creatures. Since I don't know of any other considerations that make plausible the idea that God and creatures cannot be said to be good in exactly the same sense, I think we should conclude that goodness, wisdom, and the like are predicated univocally of God and creatures. (To paraphrase Occam, equivocality should not be posited without necessity.) Accordingly, I don't think one can effectively block the argument at issue for the nonidentity of God with His perfections by appeal to the idea that nothing can be predicated univocally of God and creatures. Also, as best I can see, there is no other effective way of blocking that argument.

So the prospects for making sense of the idea that God is His goodness, wisdom, and His other perfections once again dim. At this point it is natural to ask whether there is some weakening of the identity thesis that captures at least some of what Aquinas holds about the relation of God to His perfections, and at the same time avoids the difficulties that beset the identity thesis. Even if God's perfections do not stand in the most intimate relation of all to one another, they might be especially intimately related to one another, and perhaps to the God whose perfections they were. In that case, we could see how it might be that (as Aquinas says in the passage cited at the beginning of this chapter) divine perfections are found in God in an especially unified way, even if we had to resile from the claim that each of the divine perfections is identical to God. It will be useful in this context to look at a rather intimate relation between attributes which falls short of identity.

Identity and Supervenience

As Jaegwon Kim has pointed out, *being a table* is not identical to any natural property recognized by physics.[13] Tables come in all sorts of

___

[13]See Jaegwon Kim, "Causality, Identity, and Supervenience in the Mind-Body Problem," *Midwest Studies in Philosophy* 4 (1979): 31–51. By 'natural property' I mean to exclude a gerrymandered infinitely disjunctive property that is "built up" from

shapes and sizes, and are made of all sorts of stuff. But even though no natural property in the ontology of physics stands in the relation to *being a table* that *having a particular molecular energy* stands to *having a certain temperature*, it would be a mistake to think that *being a table* floats entirely free from physical properties. Facts about tables seem to be intimately connected with and determined by microphysical facts; something that is a table is a table because it has certain physical properties.

Kim suggests we characterize the dependency in this way: the property of being a table supervenes upon some set of microphysical properties. Kim's formal definition of (strong) supervenience, given in terms of families of properties, is:

> A family of properties M is *strongly supervenient upon* a family of properties N just in case necessarily, for each x and each property F-ness in M, if x is F, there is a property G-ness in N such that x is G and necessarily, if any y is G, it is F.[14]

(Here M and N are closed under complementation, disjunction, conjunction, and so on.) If G-ness is a subvenient property whose possession by any thing (at any possible world) is a sufficient condition for that thing's being F (at that world), and G-ness is a property of x, we may call G-ness a *supervenience base property* of x's being F.[15] In Kim's view, the notion of supervenience is useful in giving us a way of understanding certain reductive claims to the effect that token-identities hold between properties (or events) in the absence of corresponding type-identities. Consider tabularity: we have seen that *being a table* is not the same as any (natural) physical property. Nevertheless, there is a strong temptation to say—if Sam is a particular table—that Sam's being a table is not really any different from, or is nothing over and above, or consists in, Sam's having some conjunctive microphysical property P_1 and P_2 and . . . and P_n. (As Kim points out, P_1 . . . P_n

---

ultimate properties recognized by physics, and which is a property of an individual at a world if and only if that individual is a table at that world. Whether that gerrymandered infinitely disjunctive property just is the property of being a table is an interesting question, which I shall not pursue here.

[14] The definition is taken from Jaegwon Kim, "Concepts of Supervenience," *Philosophy and Phenomenological Research* 3 (1984): 151–63.

[15] I am not offering quite the definition of 'supervenience base' that Kim offered in "Causality, Identity, and Supervenience in the Mind-Body Problem," since that definition is too weak for our purposes; see his "Concepts of Supervenience" for a discussion of these matters.

may have to include certain relational properties to capture the functional, purpose-related component of being a table.) The idea is that Sam's being a table is somehow not a *further* determination added to Sam's having the properties $P1 \ldots Pn$; Sam's way of being a table is by exemplifying properties $P1 \ldots Pn$. So, if we want to say things like "Even though being a table is not the same as having microphysical properties $P1 \ldots Pn$, still *Sam's* being a table consists in (or amounts to) its having properties $P1 \ldots Pn$," Kim suggests we take this to mean, roughly, that the conjunctive property $P1$ and . . . and Pn is a supervenience base property of Sam's being a table.[16] Then we can give an account of how both (i) and (ii) can be true:

(i) *Being a table* is different from having the microphysical property $P1$ and . . . and Pn.

(ii) *Sam's being a table* is no different from (that is, amounts to or consists in) Sam's having the microphysical property $P1$ and . . . and Pn.

We can also use the relation of supervenience to give an account of how it can be that, for example,

(c) Understanding is different from will.

but

(d) God's understanding is no different from God's will.

Suppose that (d) is equivalent to the claim that God's understanding and God's will share a supervenience base property in God. Then there is at least no *formal* problem about both (c) and (d) being true, since distinct properties may share a supervenience base in an individual.

---

[16]Note that where x is an individual and F-ness is a supervenient property, there will be more than one (microphysical) supervenience base property of x's being F. For instance, if Bob is a hammer made of magnetized iron, then one supervenience base of Bob's being a tool will be a (conjunctive) microphysical property whereby Bob is a hammer, and another will be a (conjunctive) microphysical property whereby Bob is a magnet. (Magnets are tools, aren't they?) If an individual has a supervenient property P, and there are a number of supervenience base properties of its having P, I suppose we should say that the individual's having P consists in its having each of the supervenience bases in question. Since Bob is a tool many times over, Bob's being a tool consists in having the right kind of shape-*cum*-rigidity, and in being composed of magnetized iron, and . . . If Bob becomes demagnetized, it will still be a tool, but what its toolhood consists in will have changed.

If we read (d) and its congeners in the way just suggested, the following picture of the difference between creaturely and divine attributes emerges: in both God and creatures, there is a multiplicity of supervenient properties. In creatures, this multiplicity corresponds to a multiplicity of supervenience bases. Take, for instance, abilities. If an opera singer is both able to squeeze an orange and to hit high C, those abilities will have different (microphysical) supervenience bases in the singer. On the view advanced, however, any two abilities God has have the same supervenience base. There is in God one ability-under-lying state, which stands in the sort of relation to all the divine abilities that a certain chemical structure stands in to the ability (or abilities) of a substance to dissolve in a variety of liquids. [17]

To take a different case, if I both understand and will that my writing this book will not drive my wife to distraction, my understanding and willing of that proposition have different (microphysical) supervenience bases. But if God both understands that gravity falls off in accordance with the inverse square law and wills that it so fall off, His understanding and will have a common supervenience base property. Fix all the facts about what God wills nature to be like, and you have fixed all the facts about what God understands nature to be like; God's way of understanding that facts about nature obtain is not by finding out after the fact that they do, but rather by willing that they actually hold. As Aquinas would put it, God's knowledge of nature is fabricative.

Examples of this kind could be multiplied. Thus *judging something to be good* and *loving that thing* need not have a common base in creatures, but always do in God; similarly, *judging an action to be evil* and *failing to perform that action*. Perhaps, though, we have said enough to establish the point: it is not just that the logic of the supervenience relation allows us to say that properties that do not share a base in creatures do share a base in God; it is also true that there are good Thomistic reasons to suppose the situation often obtains.

Indeed, some things Aquinas says sound not unlike the view that in God many supervenient properties have a common base. Consider this passage:

> Although God is existence alone, one should not conclude that He lacks any other perfections or excellences. Rather He has the perfections found in any genus . . . but He has them in a more excellent way than

[17]At present, I have in mind only abilities essential to God. "Accidental abilities"—such as God's ability to destroy this very (contingently existing) thing—pose special problems, to be dealt with later.

other things do, because in Him they are one, and in others they are diverse [*habent diversitatem*]. And this is because all these perfections belong to Him according to His simple existence. Just as if someone through one quality could perform the operations of all the qualities, he would have every quality in that one quality; so, too, God has every perfection in His very existence. (DE 5)

Here Aquinas is pulled in two directions. He wants to say that, in a tough sense, there aren't any properties in God outside of or beyond His existence, but he emphatically does not want to stop at saying that God is His altogether simple existence. To do so would be to neglect that all the perfections found in any genus really are in God. His attempt to resolve this tension involves saying that all of the perfections in question really are in God, but "according to His simple existence." God's way of getting to have those perfections is by "simply existing." The last sentence of the passage reinforces the impression that, at least in this context, Aquinas thinks of God's perfections as amounting to nothing more than, or consisting in, His 'simple existence'. It is just such a picture the relation of supervenience can be used to capture.

So, as a first attempt at a construal-*cum*-reconstruction of

God's goodness is God's wisdom.

we could try:

Goodness and wisdom have the same supervenience base property in God.

Or equivalently, if we want to construe "God's goodness is God's wisdom" as an identity statement:

The supervenience base property of goodness in God is the same as the supervenience base property of wisdom in God.

The difficulty here is that the construal-*cum*-reconstruction presupposes that each divine attribute has exactly one supervenience base property in God, and this will not be the case. (Given the definition of supervenience base property, every property will [trivially] be its own supervenience base property.) So we might try the weaker

Goodness and wisdom share a supervience base property in God.

More generally, we could offer the following as a reconstruction of Aquinas' account of God's relation to His perfections:

(1) There is a property P in God such that for any divine perfection F-ness, P is a supervenience base property of God's being F.

On this account, *being loving, knowing all the truths there are to be known, being omnipotent,* and a host of other properties share a supervenience base property in God—the one Aquinas calls "simple existence." The same way that when we have Sam (the table) with microphysical properties $P_1 \ldots P_n$, nothing new needs to be added to logically guarantee that Sam exemplifies tabularity, so (Aquinas thinks) when we have a Being with divine existence, nothing new needs to be added to guarantee that that Being exemplifies goodness, or power, or understanding. Just as anything with microphysical properties $P_1 \ldots P_n$ must be a table, so (for Aquinas) anything that is pure act must have all the above-mentioned divine properties. Facts about God's perfections are all determined by, supervenient upon, the fact that God has the incredibly rich property of divine existence. That is why Aquinas can say that the most appropriate name for God is "He who is." Small wonder that Aquinas holds that in a sense we cannot know what is meant by the claim that God exists, given that His existence stands in so many determinative relations to other properties. In this respect, divine existence is at the opposite end of the spectrum from the existence found in creatures.[18] The existence in creatures is compatible with being many different ways (as the variety of creatures attests); while some properties supervene on creaturely existence, the ones that do are either "thin" in the way existence is (like *being one*), or relational (like *being such that arithmetic is incomplete*). By contrast, in God, *an sit* (that He is) completely determines *quomodo sit* (how He is [intrinsically]).

---

[18]Of course, the existence found in creatures will on this view be present in God as well, as an attribute supervenient upon divine (superrich) existence. Moreover, one might wonder why the superrich attribute should be called *existence* at all. For the reference of "existence" (a term of *our* language, not God's) gets originally fixed in a creaturely setting, where it picks out a very thin property of things, on which relatively few interesting properties supervene. How does that term also get to pick out the superrich attribute of God, as well as (presumably) the thin attribute of God? Still, whether or not the superrich attribute could properly be called "existence," if there could be such a thing, it would help us see how something like Aquinas' account of God's relation to His perfections might be true.

But there is a problem here: (1) is not strong enough to characterize God in an interesting way. Let P be a property such that Socrates has that property and necessarily, if Socrates has that property, then Socrates has P', where P' is any property of Socrates. (We could think of P as an "infinitely conjunctive" property—*being wise and risible and the teacher of Plato and . . .*) For any property F-ness that is had by Socrates, P will (trivially) be a supervenience base of Socrates' being F. Accordingly, the fact that God satisfies (1) fails to single God out in any interesting way. This argument presupposes that a supervenience base property for a thing's being F may be a property that is logically stronger than it needs to be in order to guarantee that a thing is F. But as Kim himself notes, this possibility is not ruled out by the definition of a supervenience base property.

Someone might respond as follows: call MBP a *minimal supervenience base property* of an individual i's being F if and only if MBP is a property in the subvenient family N such that i has MBP, necessarily whatever is MBP is F, and there is no logically weaker property P' in N such that i has P', and necessarily whatever has P' is F. When an individual has two supervenient properties—say, *being brown* and *being a table*—there will be a conjunctive microphysical property that is both a supervenience base of the table's being a table, and a supervenience base of its being brown. That property will not, however, be a minimal supervenience base property of the table's being a table, or of the table's being brown. So, we might say, (1) should be restated as the claim that that there is a property P in God such that, for any divine perfection F-ness, P is a minimal supervenience base of God's being F. But if the last condition offered was too easy for God to satisfy, this one is too hard. A minimal supervenience base property of a thing's having a supervenient property F-ness is a weakest property in the subvenient family N had by that thing whose possession by a thing at a world guarantees that the thing will be F at that world. If MBP is a minimal supervenience base property of an individual i's being F, then MBP and F-ness will hold of all the same things in all the same worlds. (Suppose this is not so. Then either some individual i' has MBP without being F—in which case MBP is not after all a supervenience base property for i's being F—or some individual i' is F without having MBP. If i' does not have MBP, it must have some other minimal supervenience base property MBP'. In that case the disjunctive property of *having MBP or MBP'* will be a supervenience base property of the individual i's being F, and a logically weaker property than MBP [since i' has that disjunctive property, but does not have

MBP]. This contradicts the assumption that *MBP* was a minimal supervenience base of *i*'s being *F*.)[19]

Now, we know that, for example, *being alive* and *being loving* do not hold of all the same things in all the same worlds, because they do not even hold of all the same things in this world. Let *MBPA* be a minimal supervenience base of God's being alive, and *MBPL* be a minimal supervenience base of God's being loving. By the reasoning of the last paragraph, *MBPA* and *MBPL* are true respectively of just those things that are alive, and just those things that are loving. Therefore *MBPA* and *MBPL* are distinct attributes. In that case, it is false that *being alive* and *being loving* share a minimal supervenience base in God. (We could also have run the same argument with the pair of attributes [*being good, being omniscient*]: all that is needed is a pair of perfections not had by all the same things).

The claim that all the divine perfections share a supervenience base in God, though possibly (indeed, necessarily!) true, is not strong enough to be interesting; the claim that all the divine perfections share a minimal supervenience base in God is too strong to be possibly true. (We may say that one claim is stronger than another just in case the set of worlds in which the first claim is true is a proper subset of the set of worlds in which the second is true: in that case, the claim that any two divine perfections share a supervenience base in God is one no weaker than which may be conceived, while the claim that any two divine perfections share a minimal supervenience base property in God is one no stronger than which may be conceived.) Is there a way to steer a middle course between triviality and impossibility?

There are at any rate a number of possibilities. We want to say that

---

[19]On various conceptions of properties, *F*-ness and *MBP* will be the very same property. For the argument at hand, however, it does not matter whether or not properties that hold of all the same things in all the same worlds are identified, as long as properties that do not hold of all the same things at all the same worlds are distinct. (In fact, for the argument at hand, we need only the premiss that properties that don't actually hold of all of the same actual individuals are distinct.)

If I am not mistaken, Kim does not see that the minimal supervenience base of a thing's being *F* could not be any property stronger than *F*-ness itself. In "The Concepts of Supervenience" he contrasts minimal with nonminimal supervenience bases, and goes on to say both that (i) it might be that Saint Francis was good by virtue of being honest and benevolent, while Socrates was good by virtue of being courageous and honest, and (ii) *being honest and benevolent* might be a minimal supervenience base property for a person's goodness. If Socrates could be good by virtue of being both honest and courageous (though not benevolent), then *being honest and benevolent* will not be a minimal supervenience base property of any person's being good, since *being honest and benevolent or courageous* will be a weaker supervenience base property of that person's being good.

the divine perfections not only share a supervenience base property in God, but also share a ——— supervenience base property in God. Since putting 'minimal' in the blank does not work, we might try 'nonconjunctive.' There is a property of a brown table which is a supervenience base property of its being brown, and also a supervenience base property of its being a table; but that property is a conjunctive supervenience base property, whose conjunct properties are a supervenience base property of the table's being a table, and a supervenience base property of the table's being brown. On the other hand, there might be a simple, nonconjunctive property of God which is a supervenience base property of His being good, and a supervenience base property of His being wise, and so on.

This suggestion, as formulated, invites the charge that predicates and properties are being conflated. It is predicates (linguistic items) that may be conjoined, disjoined, and the like—not the properties to which predicates refer. Nor could one say that a conjunctive property is one picked out by a conjunctive predicate, except at the cost of trivializing the notion of a conjunctive property, since the property of being F is picked out not just by the predicate "being F," but also by the predicate "being both F and F."

The suggestion under review, however, does not obviously depend on confusing predicates with properties, even if its formulation did. It might be that certain properties are simple, and that other properties are molecular or complex, and built up out of simpler ones. The idea that the property of being both gray and round is a complex one, built up from simpler ones in a way partially mirrored by the way that the predicate "is both gray and round" is built up from simpler predicates, does not on the face of it depend on confusing predicates with properties, is apparently workable, and is not without intuitive plausibility.[20] If there are complex properties, it is quite plausible that any supervenience base property that is both a supervenience base property of the table's being brown, and a supervenience base property of the table's being a table, will be a complex property. (Consider scenarios on which the brown table ceases to be brown, while going on being a table.) But it might be that some simple property of God is at once a supervenience base property of His being good, and a supervenience base property of His being wise. So, we could exchange (1) for

---

[20]For a theory on which complex properties are constituted from simpler ones, see D. M. Armstrong, *A Theory of Universals*, 2 vols. (Cambridge: Cambridge University Press, 1978).

(1+) There is a simple but superrich property in God (the one Aquinas calls God's "simple existence") such that for any divine perfection F-ness, that simple and superrich property is a supervenience base property of God's being F.[21]

If, however, we don't think of the class of properties as having the sort of structure just adumbrated—for example, because we think that properties are sets of *possibilia,* and sets of *possibilia* cannot be sorted into the more complex and the less complex in the way relevant here—there is another way to rescue (1) from triviality. Suppose, for instance, that properties are sets of *possibilia.* Following Lewis, we may say that certain properties (sets of *possibilia*) are more natural than others.[22] While it is obviously no easy matter to give a contentful and general characterization of naturalness, the basic idea is that sets of *possibilia* are more natural insofar as their boundaries trace the contours of similarity and difference in the world, and less natural insofar as their boundaries do not. Thus the set of *possibilia* which is the property *being a quark* is a highly natural set. The set of *possibilia* which is the property *being a quark or something once thought of by Julius Caesar* is much less natural, because it contains very dissimilar sorts of things.[23]

Consider again our brown table. We saw that brownness and tabularity share a (nonminimal) microphysical supervenience base in that table—the property of having both this microphysical supervenience base property of this table's being brown (call it *SBB*), and this micro-

---

[21]Presumably, the superrich attribute of "simple existence" will necessarily be had by God and God alone. So if we can make sense of the idea that those attributes necessarily proper to God are the God whose attributes they are, we can move from
    (1+) to the stronger
    (1++) God is a simple supervenience base of all His intrinsic attributes.
    (1++) says that none of God's attributes is anything over and above the God whose attribute it is.

[22]See Lewis, "New Work for a Theory of Universals," *Australasian Journal of Philosophy* 61, no. 4 (1983): 343–77.

[23]If properties are sets of *possibilia,* then the union of two properties may be a less natural property than either or both of the original properties. (It also may be more natural: the union of the not very natural *being red or green or yellow or blue* . . . and the even less natural *being not green and not yellow and not blue* . . . is the more natural *being red.*) Can the intersection of two properties be less natural than either property? Lewis seems to suggest that it could not ("New Work," p. 347). But someone might think that the property that is the intersection of *being a quark* with *inhabiting a possible world in which an even number of people have thought of Methuselah* is less natural than the property of *being a quark,* not on the grounds that the intersection property groups together very dissimilar things, in a way that *being a quark* does not, but on the grounds that it "groups apart" very similar (intrinsically indiscernible) things (in different worlds), in a way that *being a quark* does not.

physical supervenience base property of this table's being a table (*SBT*). *Having SBB and SBT* is certainly a no more natural supervenience base property of this table's being brown than is *SBB*. Note, however, that a stronger microphysical supervenience base property of a thing's having a property is sometimes more natural than a weaker one. *SBB* is a supervenience base not just of our table's being brown, but of our table's being colored. There is a weaker microphysical supervenience base property of our table's being colored—a (disjunctive) microphysical property had by this brown table and any other colored thing, whose possession guarantees being colored. But that weaker microphysical supervenience base property of the table's being colored is a less natural property than *SBB* (since it groups together more dissimilar things).

It should be clear how we can use naturalness to move from the trivial (1) to something more interesting. We may rank supervenience base properties of an individual's having a supervenient property according to their naturalness. Then we restate (1) as

(1*) There is a property *SBP* such that, for any divine perfection *F*-ness, *SBP* is a supervenience base property of God's being *F*, and any weaker supervenience base property of God's being *F* is less natural than *SBP*.[24]

Statement (1*) says that there is a property that, for any divine perfection *F*-ness, is both a supervenience base property of God's being *F*, and more natural than any weaker supervenience base property of God's being *F*. That super-natural, superrich property would bear something like the relation to God's wisdom, goodness, and so on that a highly natural structural property would bear to a variety of dispositional properties grounded in that structural property.

In Chapter 1, I argued that it could not be true that

(6) God is not composed of essence and *esse:* the divine essence (God) is pure subsistent existence, inherent in nothing distinct from it, and having nothing distinct from it inhering in it.

Also, I argued that nothing very like (6) could be true.

Now, for the reasons set out in this chapter, it does not look as though it could it be true that

[24]Again, if we can identify an attribute necessarily had by God and God alone with God, then we can say that the supernatural base property described in (1*) is just God Himself. The strengthened version of (1*) will say that all of God's (intrinsic) attributes are "nothing over and above" God Himself.

(5) God is not composed of subject and accidents. There are not in God any properties outside of the divine essence which enter into composition with that essence. Instead, His power, wisdom, goodness, and the like are all the same as the divine essence (God), and thus all the same as one another.

(Again, God's wisdom will be shared with, or at least conspecific with, some attribute had by creatures; God's essence and God will not be.) But this leaves open the possibility that something rather like (5) could be true—namely, a reconstrual of (5) in terms of supervenience rather than identity. That reconstrual might take either of two forms, *viz.*:

(5+) Wisdom, power, goodness, and all the rest of God's intrinsic attributes are "nothing over and above," or "consist in"—that is, have as a supervenience base—the simple but superrich attribute that is the divine essence.

or

(5*) Wisdom, power, goodness, and all the rest of God's intrinsic attributes are "nothing over and above" or "consist in"—that is, have as a supervenience base—the divine essence, an attribute more natural than any weaker supervenience base property of God's being F, for any divine intrinsic attribute F-ness. [25]

(Why speak of God's intrinsic attributes, rather than of His attributes *simpliciter?* If we have a generous conception of attributes, then we'll countenance such attributes as *being such that Boston won the 1988 American League East title*. But that extrinsic attribute, which is had by God in some but not all of the worlds in which He exists, could not have as its supervenience base property the essence God has in every world in which He exists.)

If we can make a go of the idea that the simple or super-natural attribute that is God's essence is insular, we can replace "the divine essence" in each of the above by "the divine essence, which is to say God"—bringing our reconstruals a bit closer to (5). In either case, we

---

[25] In moving from (5)—an identity claim—to a supervenience claim, we are of course making just the move that Kim and others have suggested we make in giving an account of the relation of mental properties and events to physical properties and events.

give up the problematic Thomistic identification of God with (all) His intrinsic attributes, while retaining the Thomistic idea that God has His intrinsic attributes in an especially unified way, simply by virtue of being the kind of thing He is.

Against either (5+) or (5*) the following objection might be advanced:

> Suppose some property is both a supervenience base property of God's being omniscient and a supervenience base property of His being loving. A supervenience base property that was a supervenience base of God's having each of such such dissimilar properties could not be a simple supervenience base property, or a maximally natural one: there would have to be a simpler (or more natural) supervenience base property of God's being omniscient, and likewise a simpler (or more natural) supervenience base property of God's being loving.

This objection is not without force: it is hard to see how any maximally natural or completely simple state in God could underlie every one of God's intrinsic attributes. Perhaps the best we can do in answering the objection involves drawing a distinction between what is clearly not possible and what is not clearly possible. That is, we might grant that it is impossible for us to see how any state satisfying (5+) or (5*) could underlie all of God's intrinsic attributes: if we try to imagine a property underlying all of God's perfections, we either draw a blank, or come up with some property that can be factored into more natural subproperties. For all that, we might insist, perhaps there could be an attribute of the kind described in (5+) or (5*) underlying all of God's intrinsic attributes. We can't see how there could be; but we can't see that there could not be. After all, there is no obvious logical contradiction in the idea that there is such an attribute.

I have doubts about how effective this defense is: it certainly does not entirely eliminate worries about how either (5+) or (5*) could be true. Perhaps the best we can say in their favor is that it is not immediately or entirely evident that neither one could be true.

Supervenience and Simplicity

Someone might point out that as long as we understand such notions as "is nothing over and above" or "consists in" in terms of supervenience, the assertion that each one of God's intrinsic attributes is nothing over and above God's simple essence (or even God Himself) has less to do with (5) than its verbal formulation suggests. It amounts to the thesis that there is a simple (or super-natural) essence in God the possession of which guarantees having all the divine perfections. This last thesis does not have all that much to do with (5), since it is compatible not only with the claim that God is distinct from His intrinsic attributes, but also with the claim that God's intrinsic attributes are proper parts of Him, disjoint from His essence.

True, the claim that all of God's intrinsic attributes supervene on His (simple or super-natural) essence does not entail that none of God's attributes is a proper part of Him, or even that none of God's attributes is a part of Him disjoint from His essence. If we want to capture this idea (one that is central to (5)), we need to explicitly add it to our reconstruction. But if we give up Aquinas' idea that properties are (proper or maximal) parts of their subjects, nothing stands in the way of our doing so. If, say, we think that properties are not constituents of individuals, but sets of (actual or merely possible) individuals (or functions from worlds to functions from individuals to truth-values), a plurality of divine attributes will not entail any form of composition within God, and we shall be able to maintain that God has His attributes in a unified way that involves no composition. It will no longer be true of God *alone* that He lacks composition of subject and attribute, but it will be true of God and true of God alone that He has all His intrinsic attributes in an especially unified way. Naturally, taking this line involves saving some of Aquinas' conception of divine simplicity at the cost of sacrificing his conception of properties as constituents of their subjects.

This approach to reconstruction may be contrasted with one that preserves Aquinas' compositional account of the inherence relation, but modifies his account of just what sorts of things are intrinsic properties of God. For Aquinas, whenever an individual satisfies a given predicate, it does so in virtue of having and/or lacking some constituent properties (whether insular or noninsular). But, by his lights, it is not in general true that when an individual satisfies the predicate "is F" (that is, when it is true of that individual that it is F), it satisfies that predicate in virtue of having a constituent property of F-ness. For example, as we saw in Chapter 1, although Homer satisfied the predicate "is blind," Aquinas holds, he did not do so by virtue of having a constituent property of blindness, but rather by (i) being an individual of a species whose members are meant to see, and (ii) lacking sight. Moreover, Aquinas would say that although Socrates satisfied the predicate "is wise or spherical," he did not do so by virtue of having a constituent property of wise-or-spherical-ity, distinct from both wisdom and sphericality. Things satisfy the predicate "is wise or spherical" insofar as they have a constituent property of wisdom, or a constituent property of sphericality; Socrates satisfied that predicate by having a constituent property of wisdom.[26]

To retrace our steps: I argued earlier that it could not be true both that God's intrinsic properties include *being good, living, existing,* and so on, and that all of God's intrinsic properties are identical to God and to one another. For the property of living found in God would be identical to, or at least conspecific with, the property of living found in, say, the angel Gabriel, while the property of omnipotence found in God would be neither identical to nor conspecific with any property found in Gabriel.

If we think that something can satisfy the predicate "is *F*" without having a property or attribute of *F*-ness, we will also think that it in no obvious way follows from the fact that God and creatures each satisfy various predicates, that God and creatures share the same attributes (or have conspecific attributes). Unlike Aquinas, we might suppose that whenever "is *F*" was a predicate satisfied by both God and creatures ("is wise," "lives," "exists," and so on), "God is *F*" was true not by virtue of God's having a constituent attribute of *F*-ness. Thus "God is good" would be true not by virtue of God's having goodness among His constituents, but by virtue of God's having the one and only attribute He has—that simple and superrich property Aquinas calls "simple existence"—while "Socrates is good" was true by virtue of Socrates' having some quite different attributes on the having of which the fact that Socrates was good supervened. (Compare: a cube and a sphere are each spherical or cubical, but it is true that the sphere is spherical or cubical because the sphere has the constituent attribute of sphericality, and true that the cube is spherical or cubical because the cube has the constituent attribute of cubicality.) If this line is feasible, then the problem of shared attributes is dissolved, since it turns out that no divine attribute is identical to or conspecific with any attribute of any creature, even though various predicates are satisfied both by God and by creatures. At the same time, we apparently dissolve that problem without making God a noumenon, utterly indescribable and

---

[26]I don't know of any place where Aquinas explicitly repudiates disjunctive properties. However (to oversimplify in ways irrelevant to the present point) he tells us that two things resemble each other insofar as they have forms of the same kind (ST Ia.4.3, *responsio*). If whenever an individual had a constituent property of *F*-ness, it had an additional property of *F*-or-*G*-ness, then it would be too easy for things to resemble each other. (Whenever one was *F*, and the other was *G*, they would resemble each other by virtue of each having a constituent property of *F*-or-*G*-ness.)

unthinkable, since we can know that He satisfies various predicates, without knowing how it is He satisfies them (because of our inability to conceive of His simple and superrich attribute). And we capture the idea that God has His perfections in an especially unified way by supposing that it is in virtue of His one attribute that God satisfies the perfection predicates "is omniscient," "is omnipotent," and so on. Moreover, if we can make sense of the idea that God's simple and superrich attribute is the same as God, it looks as though we can get much closer to (5) than on the previous reconstruction. We save the idea that all the intrinsic divine attributes are maximal parts of God,[27] and jettison only the notion that those attributes include goodness, existence, wisdom, and the like.[28] We end up with something along the lines of:

> No intrinsic divine attribute is a proper part of God, disjoint from His essence; instead, each one is just the divine essence—which is to say, God.

In fact, though, we may be able to get closer to (5) than this. Even if "goodness," "power," "wisdom," and so on are not predicates that pick out attributes, it might be that the predicates "perfect goodness," "perfect power," "perfect wisdom," and the like do pick out attributes. (I don't see just how one would argue for this asymmetry, although one might try to rely on the idea that perfect wisdom is to wisdom as determinate is to determinable, and the idea that there are determinate universals, but no determinable universals.) If that were so, we could offer the following reconstrual of (5):

(5++) Neither God's (perfect) wisdom, nor His (perfect) goodness, nor any other of His intrinsic attributes are proper parts of God disjoint from His essence; instead each one is just the divine essence—which is to say, God.[29]

[27]Wouldn't divine attributes need to be anchored in something else? Suppose that we thought of the properties of individuals as themselves individual, and thought of ordinary individuals as bundles of individual properties. (This is, as I have argued, the only promising way of defending an individualistic conception of properties against the charge of otiosity.) Then we might hold that God was (in the mathematician's sense of 'degenerate') a degenerate bundle of properties—that is, a one-membered bundle of properties: and all the divine attributes would turn out to be identical not just to each other, but also to the God to which they belonged.

[28]For the sorts of reasons offered by Armstrong in *A Theory of Universals,* I think that if there are constituent attributes, it is quite unlikely that existence, goodness, or wisdom are among them. This provides some independent philosophical motivation for the envisaged reconstruction.

[29]Alternatively, we might suppose that two very different sorts of things may be

Both (5++) and (5*) entail that all of God's intrinsic attributes are
essential to Him. This should be immediately clear in the case of
(5++): if God has an intrinsic attribute inessentially, that attribute
cannot be the same as any intrinsic attribute God has essentially. (After
all, one and the same attribute cannot be both essential and inessential
to God.) But if God has at least two intrinsic attributes distinct from
each other, He must have at least one intrinsic attribute distinct from
Himself, since no two things that are distinct from each other can both
be identical to a third. Likewise, if (5*) is true, then every intrinsic
attribute of God has God's superrich, super-natural essence as its
divine supervenience base: but an attribute inessential to God could
not have the super-natural one (which is essential to Him) as its divine
supervenience base.

Should it turn out that we have to countenance inessential intrinsic
properties of God, we would have to retreat to a weaker version of
(5++) or (5*), according to which God's *essential* intrinsic attributes
were all identical with one another, or all had the same supernatural
divine supervenience base. If we conceive of intrinsic attributes as
(proper or maximal) parts of their subjects, and accept that God has
some intrinsic attributes inessentially, then we shall have to concede
(very un-Thomistically) that there is composition of subject and attribute in God. Suppose, on the other hand, we conceive of attributes
quite differently (for example, as sets of possible individuals, or the
like). Then even if God has inessential intrinsic attributes, we can still
maintain that everything *in* God (as a part) is God, although not
everything *of* God is God (since at least some intrinsic attributes of
God are distinct from Him). This suggests that, if we can't make a go
of the idea that all of God's intrinsic properties are essential to Him,
and we want to get as close as we can to Aquinas' conception of divine
simplicity, we are better off with a reconstruction along the lines of a
weakened version of (5*) than we are with one along the lines of a
weakened version of (5++). In fact, in Chapter 4 I argue that we
should recognize inessential intrinsic attributes of God.

---

called attributes: constituent attributes and, say, sets of possible individuals, or functions from worlds to individuals. (For a discussion of why we might want to suppose
something like this, see Lewis, "New Work.") Then we could construe (5) as the claim
that every constituent attribute of God is God, and we wouldn't have to deny that a
statement like "Wisdom is an attribute" is a truism.

3

Divine Simplicity:
God and His Nature

Immateriality and the Relation of a
Thing to Its Essence

> It seems that God is not the same as His essence or nature. Nothing is in itself, but the essence or nature of God, which is Deity, is said to be in God. It seems, then, that God is not the same as His essence or nature.
>
> Moreover, an effect resembles its cause, because what an agent does is similar to what it is. But in the created realm, the *suppositum* is not the same as its nature: a man is not the same as his humanity. Neither, then, is God the same as His Deity. (ST Ia.3.3, objs. 1 and 2)

Each of these objections draws on the intuition that a thing's nature, like its whiteness, or its existence, is something categorically different than the subject or *suppositum* of that nature. We would expect Aquinas to answer in the *responsio* by arguing that since God must be incomposite in certain ways, and since any being distinct from its essence is composite in those ways, God is no different from His essence. Aquinas does respond along these lines, but he does so in a very surprising way. The type of divine incomposition he appeals to in arguing for the identity of God with His essence is not one of the exotic forms of incomposition proper to God, but the more familiar sort God shares with souls and angels—immateriality:

> God is the same as His essence or nature. To see this, it should be noted that in things composed of matter and form the *suppositum* must differ from the nature or essence. For the essence or nature includes only such things as fall under the definition of the species: thus humanity includes

only those things that fall under the definition of man, by which a man is a man, for 'humanity' signifies that by which a man is a man. But individual matter, together with all individuating accidents, does not fall under the definition of the species; neither this flesh and these bones, nor whiteness, blackness, or anything of that sort, falls under the definition of man. Hence this flesh and these bones and the accidents designating this matter do not belong to humanity, but do belong to that which is a man. So that which is a man has something that humanity does not, and on account of this a man and humanity are not entirely the same. . . . In those things not composed of matter and form, individuation is not by reference to individual matter—that is, *this* matter— but the forms themselves are individuated *per se*. Consequently, the forms themselves must be subsistent *supposita*. So in such things the *suppositum* does not differ from the nature. (ST 1a.3.3, *responsio*)

This passage splits into two parts. First Aquinas explains why a (materially) composite individual is not the same as its essence or nature; then he explains why an immaterial individual is the same as its essence or nature.

Why is an individual man different from his nature (humanity)? Aquinas seems to be thinking along these lines:

> There is more to being a particular individual man (for example, Socrates) than there is to being human: for an individual man is made of this flesh and these bones, is white or black, and so on, even though being human does not (*per se*) involve or include having this flesh and these bones, being white or black, *vel cetera*. Therefore, an individual man is not the same as his essence.

On the face of it, what is crucial to the argument is that, for some genuine property F-ness, an individual man is F, even though F-ness does not fall under the definition of the species humanity, and hence does not belong to *being human*. On this account, *being black, being white,* and *being made of this flesh and these bones* are the instances of such F's Aquinas happens to fasten on: he could equally well have appealed to *being sunburned,* or any number of other accidental F's. For as long as an individual had some such property F-ness, it would be true that that individual had a property that did not belong to its specific nature, and accordingly that the individual was not the same as its specific nature.

As will become clear later on, I think that Aquinas accepts something like this argument, and may even have it (partially) in mind here. If this is the way the argument is meant to work, however, then

Aquinas should conclude (as he does conclude) that immaterial beings are the same as their essences or natures only if he believes that every genuine property of an immaterial being belongs to its specific nature. Evidently, Aquinas believes that this condition holds for one immaterial being—God. But he does not believe that it holds for angels. For example, he believes that the angel Lucifer sinned, but not that sinning is connatural to the kind of angel Lucifer is (see ST Ia.63.4, *responsio*). And although Aquinas believes that some angelic knowledge is connatural to an angel (so that an angel could not be deprived of it), he believes that angels who fall suffer a diminished knowledge of the divine mysteries (ST Ia.64.1, *responsio*). So neither *having an undiminished knowledge of the divine mysteries* nor *having a diminished knowledge of the divine mysteries*—each of which is at some time a property of Lucifer—could belong to the kind Luciferity, since Lucifer, while remaining the same kind of being, exchanged the first property for the second.[1] In fact, Aquinas so much as says that some accidents of angels float free of angels' being the kind of being they are: "A simple form that is not its own existence, but is related to its existence as potentiality to act, can be the subject of accidents, *especially* of those that follow upon the species" (italics mine, ST Ia.54.3, *ad* 2). The occurrence of 'especially' indicates that Aquinas thinks that some accidents of angels are neither included in nor follow upon the specific essence of that angel. In such a case, Aquinas must think, an angel will have a certain accident, even though that accident does not belong to that angel's specific essence. Moreover, even if an accident follows upon an angelic essence, it remains on Aquinas' account extraessential: so the existence of accidents following upon an angel's specific essence is sufficient to show that angels have certain properties that do not belong to their essence.

If Aquinas is arguing for the distinctness of Socrates from his essence on the grounds that Socrates has something not included in his essence, why doesn't he conclude in that passage that only one immaterial being (God) is the same as his essence? It may help to say something here about how Aquinas thinks essence, form, and matter are interrelated. In *De ente et essentia* 2, Aquinas begins by arguing that the essence of a material substance (say, the humanity that is the essence of an individual man) is not just matter, and is not just form: it includes both matter and form. It must include matter as well as form, Aquinas tells us, because the essence of a thing is what is signified by

---

[1]We know that *having an undiminished knowledge of the divine mysteries* was at some time a property of Lucifer because (on Aquinas' account) Lucifer could not have fallen at the first moment of his existence (see ST Ia.63.5).

the definition of that thing, and the definition of a material substance makes reference not just to form, but also to matter. (In this respect, the definition of material things differs from that of mathematical or geometrical entities. The definition of the latter does not make reference to matter, and accordingly those entities can be understood without matter, even though [for Aquinas] they cannot exist apart from matter.)

At this point, Aquinas notes that if the essence of a thing contains both form and matter, it may appear that the essence of a thing will be particular, and not universal. But, Aquinas maintains, this impression arises from a failure to see the way in which matter is included in the (specific) essence of a thing. Although the essence of a material substance includes both form and matter, it does not include designated matter (*this* matter)—as something particular would—but only matter, considered absolutely. For designated matter is not included in the definition of a man insofar as he is a man, although it would be included in the definition of a particular man (say, Socrates) were there such a thing (DE 2). To prevent a misunderstanding: Aquinas does not deny that there is something that is an essence of Socrates, and includes this form and this matter. He accepts that there is such a thing (call it Socrates' *individual essence*), and maintains that it differs from Socrates' individual essence just in that the individual essence includes this form and this matter, whereas the specific essence includes a form of this kind and matter.[2]

The idea that the (specific) essence of a material substance could 'contain' or 'include' matter without including any particular matter is somewhat puzzling. We might, however, think about it this way: what it is for Socrates to have the essence, humanity, is not just for him to have a certain kind of substantial form. (The essence is the what-it-is-to-be [*quod quid erat esse*] of a substance; what it is to be human is not just to have a certain kind of substantial form, but also to have a substantial form received in matter.) Now although having the essence humanity is not just a matter of having a substantial form of a certain kind, neither is it a matter of having this substantial form and

---

[2]"Sic ergo patet quod essentia Socratis et essentia hominis non differunt nisi secundum signatum et non signatum" (DE 2). There is or at least appears to be a tension between Aquinas' view that the essence of Socrates includes this form and this matter, and his recognition that an individual like Socrates undergoes compositional change. (For Aquinas' recognition of compositional change in humans, see SCG IV.81.) If Socrates' essence includes this form and this matter, but different parcels of matter constitute Socrates at different times, it is not clear what sort of thing 'this matter' is meant to refer to in this context. I don't know of any place in which Aquinas discusses these issues.

this matter (where this form and this matter are the form and matter of Socrates): otherwise humanity could not be the essence of Plato, who has a numerically different substantial form, received and individuated by a different chunk of designated matter. So for Socrates to have the essence humanity is for him to have a substantial form of this kind, together with form-receiving matter (not *this* matter, but "common matter," as Aquinas sometimes calls it).

Now, suppose that Gabriel is an angelic immaterial substance. For him to have a certain specific essence is not for him to have a certain kind of substantial form, together with matter: it is just for him to have a certain kind of substantial form. We might suppose that just as there is a difference between Socrates' individual essence (which includes this substantial form and this matter) and Socrates' specific essence (which includes a substantial form of this kind and matter), there would be a difference between Gabriel's specific essence (which would include a substantial form of Gabriel's natural kind) and Gabriel's individual essence (which would include this very substantial form). But Aquinas would acknowledge no such difference, since he thinks that two forms (whether substantial or accidental) can be distinct forms of the same kind only if they are received and individuated by distinct things—parcels of matter, or subjects. (Why Aquinas holds this view will be discussed later.) For Aquinas, then, what it is for Gabriel to have a specific essence of a certain kind is just what it is for Gabriel to have an individual essence of a certain kind—namely, for him to have a certain substantial form, which is (necessarily) the only one of its kind. To put this another way, Gabriel's specific essence and his individual essence are one and the same—but why is that essence the same as Gabriel? Aquinas appears to be thinking along these lines: unlike the received substantial forms of hylomorphically composite substances, angelic substantial forms are not individuated by any receiving matter. So, he infers, they must be individuated *per se*. And, Aquinas thinks, whatever is individuated *per se* subsists *per se,* and is accordingly a *suppositum* or first substance. Doubtless, though, a particular angel (say, Gabriel) is a first substance. It follows that if Gabriel is distinct from his substantial form or essence, then Gabriel and his substantial form are distinct individual substances. Since Aquinas regards this as impossible, he concludes that an angel is no different from his substantial form or essence: "an angel is a subsisting form" (ST Ia. 50. 5, *responsio*).[3] Given the premiss that an immaterial substance is a

---

[3]See also SCG II. 54: "In substantiis autem intellectualibus, quae non sunt ex materia et forma compositae ut ostensum est, sed in eis ipsa forma est substantia subsistens, forma est quod est."

form that subsists *per se,* and the premiss that the (substantial) form of an immaterial thing is its essence, we can move from its immateriality to its identity with its own essence or nature.

But there is a catch: the form of Gabriel could not be at once the first substance, Gabriel, and the essence of Gabriel. As we saw, Gabriel has various (intrinsic or genuine) properties contingently—for example, *having an undiminished understanding of the divine mysteries.* Since for Aquinas such properties belong to Gabriel, if Gabriel is (the same as) a subsistent form, those properties must belong to that form. Hence the subsistent form that is Gabriel must be what I call a *thick form,* in which are found accidents following upon Gabriel's intellect and will, accidents following upon Gabriel's specific nature, and also the *esse* whereby Gabriel is an *ens.*

If a form is the same as Gabriel's essence (Gabrielity), however, it will not include such properties as *having an undiminished understanding of the divine mysteries,* since Gabriel's essence includes only that whereby Gabriel is the kind of being he is (what is included in the definition of the kind of being Gabriel is), and *having an undiminished understanding of the divine mysteries* floats free from Gabriel's being the kind of being he is (is not included in the definition of the kind of being Gabriel is). Neither (Aquinas should suppose) will the form that is Gabriel's essence include the accidents that follow upon Gabriel's specific essence, since (he thinks) even those accidents are extranatural.[4] *Pari ratione* (Aquinas should suppose) it will not include Gabriel's *esse,* since the *esse* of a created thing is again something extranatural that comes into composition with Gabriel's essence. In short, the form that is Gabriel's essence (Gabrielity) will be a *thin form,* and will not be entirely the same as the thick form that is Gabriel. Instead, the thin form or essence, Gabrielity, will be related to the thick form of Gabriel as part to whole, just as humanity is related to an individual man as part to whole.[5]

Our original puzzlement about Aquinas' argument for the identity of God with His essence at ST Ia.3.3 had the following form: the

---

[4]"Accidens neque rationem completae essentiae habet neque pars completae essentiae est" (DE 6; see also CT 23).

[5]If the essence of a man is only part of him, why does Aquinas often say (e.g., at ST Ia.3.3) that the essence of an individual man and that man are not *entirely* the same? Aquinas says that things are entirely the same just in case they have all the same (metaphysical) constituents, entirely diverse if they have none of the same constituents, and are neither entirely the same nor entirely diverse if they have some but not all of the same constituents. See, e.g., DP 9.1, *responsio,* where Aquinas says that the essence of a composite substance is neither entirely the same as it, nor entirely diverse from it, because it is related to that composite substance as a formal part.

argument Aquinas deploys to show that an individual man is not the same as his essence seems equally to show that any immaterial being besides God is not the same as its essence. (Just as any material creature will have properties that do not belong to its essence, so too will any immaterial creature.) Yet Aquinas appears to think of the argument he offers for the distinctness of an individual man from his essence as leaving room for the identity of immaterial substances and their essences. Why? I am inclined to think that Aquinas simply fails to see the implications of his own argument, perhaps because he conflates the notion of an immaterial substance's thin form (which may be identified with its essence) with the notion of a thick form (which may be identified with the individual substance, but is something more than that substance's essence).[6]

It is always dangerous to suppose that a philosopher of Aquinas' acumen failed to see where his own argument leads. In this case, however, we may invoke his own authority to support the charge. In the *Summa theologiae,* the *De ente et essentia* (4), "De potentia" (9.1, *responsio*), and *De spiritualibus creaturis* (5 ad 9) Aquinas asserts that any immaterial substance and its essence are the same. But in *Quaestiones quodlibetales* 2.2.2 he takes a very different (and better) line. There he answers the question of whether in an angel the *suppositum* and the nature differ as follows:

> In God alone . . . is no accident found outside of His essence, because His existence is His essence, as we said. So in God the *suppositum* and nature are entirely the same. In an angel, however, they are not entirely the same, because something is an accident of that angel, which is outside of that which belongs to the *ratio* of its species [*In angelo autem non est omnino idem: quia aliquid accidit ei praeter id quod est de ratione suae specie*]. The existence of an angel is outside of his essence or nature, as are other things that belong entirely to the *suppositum* but not to the nature.

We have here an argument quite similar to the one offered in ST Ia.3.3 for the distinctness of a man from his nature, purporting to

---

[6]At DSC 1 Aquinas says that it is all right to say that there is a composition of form and matter in spiritual substances, if this means only that there is composition of act and potency in those substances. But, Aquinas thinks, this way of talking is apt to mislead, since the matter of a thing is not usually understood simply as the potential element in that thing. Similarly, I think it is all right to say that a spiritual substance is a subsistent form, as long as we understand by 'form', 'thick form'—where it is understood that a thick form is just an individual substance, which has a thin form, but is not identical to it. Again, though, this way of talking may mislead, since the form of a being is usually and naturally understood as the thin form of that being.

show that because there is more to an angel than there is to its nature, the *suppositum* that is that angel and its nature are not entirely the same. So Aquinas himself (some of the time) sees that if the considerations appealed to at ST Ia.3.3 establish that a man and his nature are not entirely the same, they likewise establish that an angel and his nature are not entirely the same. Nor is the second *Quodlibet* the only place where Aquinas sees this. In the "De unione verbi incarnati" he avers that if there is something in a thing over and above its specific essence, then—whether that something extra is individual matter or an accident—the *suppositum* will not be entirely the same as its nature, as is *especially* apparent in the case of creatures composed of form and matter.[7] In fact, Aquinas' answer to objection 2 at ST Ia.3.3 suggests that even there he is at some level inclined to think that only one immaterial being is the same as its essence. The gist of that objection (cited at the beginning of this chapter) was that, because creaturely effects resemble their uncreated cause, and because created essences are distinct from their subjects, God's essence is distinct from its subject. The objection apparently presupposes that subject/essence composition is a feature of every creature. Aquinas answers that because God's effects resemble Him imperfectly and compositely, in those effects there is a distinction between subject and nature. What is interesting is that in his reply to objection 2, Aquinas does not deny, and apparently accepts, that subject/essence composition is found in all creatures, since he says quite generally (without any qualifiers concerning materiality) of the created effects of God that they cannot be identified with their natures. But if Aquinas in some way saw that on his views no creature should be identified with its essence, he did not see this clearly when he wrote *Quaestio* 3 of the *Summa;* otherwise the *responsio* of *Quaestio* 3 would not have the structure it does. It is interesting in this connection to note that in the (late) *Compendium theologiae* Aquinas does not try to move from the premiss that God is immaterial to the conclusion that God is the same as His essence. Instead he argues that because whatever is distinct from its essence has composition of the *per se* and the *per accidens,* and composition of act and potency, and because God could have neither form of composition, God must be the same as His essence. Why does the argument here depend on features proper to God, rather than on the immateriality shared by God, angels, and

---

[7]"Si vero aliqua res sit intra quam praeter essentiam speciei, quam significat definitio, sit aliquid aliud, vel accidens vel materia individualis; tunc suppositum non erit omnino idem quod natura; sed habebit se per additionem ad naturam; sicut apparet *praecipue* in his quae sunt ex materia et forma composita" (italics mine). See ST 3a.2.2 for much the same point.

souls? It may be that when Aquinas wrote the *Compendium theologiae,* he saw that the argument for the identity of God with His essence set out at ST Ia.3.3 was flawed, for the reasons just specified.

God and His Essence

If I am right, neither the argument for the identity of God with His essence set out at ST Ia.3.3, nor the one offered in the *Compendium theologiae,* is successful. (The *Compendium theologiae* argument presupposes that we can show that God lacks composition of act and potency in the idiosyncratically broad Thomistic sense; I have argued in Chapter 1 that Aquinas has not made this out.) Be that as it may, it is an open question whether a Thomistic defense of this claim, or any other kind, can be provided.

Clearly, if God's (specific) essence is something that could be had by some other individual—as Socrates' (specific) essence is—then that essence cannot be identified with God. So we may begin by asking whether—on the assumption that something has the divine nature— anything else might have; or, to put it another way, whether there is any distinction between God's individual essence and His specific essence. Aquinas thinks that this condition is met just in virtue of God's immateriality. As we have seen, he argues that because immaterial beings are pure forms, albeit subsistent ones, there could no more be two immaterial beings of the same species than there could be two subsistent whitenesses, or two subsistent humanities (see ST Ia.50.4 and DSC 8 for the application of the argument to the case of angels, and CT 15 for its application to the case of God). The principle Aquinas is appealing to is that conspecific forms cannot be multiplied or diversified, save by being received (either by matter or by a subject). If the form at issue is whiteness, or humanity, it does seem unexceptionable that there is no multiplication in a species without reception (leaving open the question of whether there is multiplication even when there is reception). If there were two unreceived whitenesses (that is, two whitenesses that were not the whiteness of anything else), they would either have to be the whitenesses of nothing at all, or (as Aquinas envisions in the relevant passages) their own and only their own whitenesses. It is more than plausible that there could not be a plurality of unexemplified whitenesses, or a plurality of insular whitenesses. *Mutatis mutandis,* the same holds for humanity. If, however, the forms at issue are not properties, like whiteness and humanity, but thick unreceived forms and individual substances—like angels—it is not clear why reception should be thought a precondition of multiplication within a species. After all, even though angels and whiteness each lack matter, an angel is a very different sort of thing from a whiteness, or a humanity. To put this another way, even if angels and whitenesses are both forms, they are forms in very different senses, and the difference is not obviously irrelevant to the possibility of multiplication within a species. Nor does it help to say that an angel is rather like a subsistent or substantial whiteness—or what a whiteness would be like, were it subsistent—since, by Aquinas' admission, a subsistent whiteness is an impossible object, and it is not clear what else the *possibile* Gabriel and the *impossibile* subsistent whiteness have in common besides immateriality. Why, then, should we think that distinct conspecific angels are impossible?

Aquinas seems to be thinking of things in this way: when two individuals are distinct, there must be an answer to the following question: "How is it the case that (in virtue of what is it true that, what grounds the fact that) they are distinct individuals?" One sort of answer is: "They are just different kinds of things." If this answer cannot be given, because the individuals in question are of the same kind, there are two possibilities. If the individuals are forms, the answer will be: "These individuals are distinct, by virtue of the fact that they are received by distinct subjects." If the individuals are hylomorphically composite, the answer will be: "These individuals are distinct, by virtue of the fact that they have different matter(s)." As far as I can see, Aquinas supposes these are the only possible sorts of answer to an inescapable question. From this it follows that different angels are of different species, since there could be no answer to the compulsory question "How is it that these angels are distinct individuals?" were the angels of the same species.

This does not really help, though. The difficulty is in seeing why we should accept that whenever two individuals are distinct, they either are of different kinds, or have different recipients, or have different matter. Distinct points in space, or instants in time, are different things of the same kind which do not differ in any of the ways just mentioned. If Aquinas thought that the only things that existed were hylomorphically composite substances, matter, and received and individualized forms, then we could see why he would conclude that any two things are discernible with respect to kind, recipient, or matter.[8] Precisely because he does not think so, it is hard to see why he should accept this condition.

---

[8]If matter is conceived of as that which can survive substantial change, however, this condition will not be met. Suppose that the matter that composed an oak tree at its first

This is not to say that I have anything illuminating to offer about what it would be like for immaterial beings of the same species to differ from one another. With respect to what sort of properties must any two conspecific immaterial beings be discernible? Perhaps all that can be said is that they must be numerically different selves—with numerically different thoughts, experiences, and so on. Perhaps any two conspecific immaterial beings are discernible not just in this way, but also with respect to some unknown family of relational properties which is in some way a counterpart of the family of spatial relations. My inability to tell any sort of illuminating story about what it would be like for conspecific immaterial beings to differ from one another, together with my uneasiness about accepting such difference as intelligible in itself, leads me to worry about whether distinct immaterial beings of the same kind are a real possibility. (I have more to say about this a bit later.) But I have been unable to convert this worry into anything as decisive as a good argument, and I don't think Aquinas has been able to either.[9]

Is there a reason to think that, even if different possible angels fall under the same species, only one possible being falls under the God-kind? One might try something like this: perhaps there is actually an uncreated individual—God—who necessarily exists, so that

(1) There is an individual substance who actually has the nature, Deity, and who exists in every possible world.

It is plausible that certain natural kinds are tied to certain kinds of causal powers, in that nothing could belong to a certain natural kind

---

moment of existence a thousand years ago comes to compose a duplicate oak at its first moment of existence now; suppose further that for any j, the duplicate oak is made of just the matter at the jth moment of its existence which the original oak was made of at its jth moment of existence. The first oak and the second oak (I am pretty confident) will be distinct throughout their existences, but—as long as matter is conceived of as the stuff that can survive substantial change—they will not differ with respect to matter, or recipient, or kind. Examples of this sort suggest that discernibility with respect to location in space or time, rather than discernibility with respect to matter, is a precondition for the distinctness of material substances of the same kind. I think this is right, though I won't defend the view here.

[9]If there were an argument showing that immaterial substances are conspecific only if identical, it would be bad news for Aquinas' metaphysic of the Trinity. For Aquinas holds that the Father and the Son are individuals, that they are distinct from each other, and that the Father and the Son are not different kinds of individual; there is at least a prima facie problem about how each of these claims could be true if the conspecificity of immaterial beings entailed their identity. But consideration of these difficulties will have to be deferred to Chapter 6.

(have a certain specific nature) unless it had certain kinds of causal powers. For example, it is plausible that nothing actual or possible could belong to the natural kind electron (have the specific nature of an electron) if it had causal powers radically different from the causal powers electrons actually have.[10] Similarly, it could be that nothing actual or possible could have the specific nature Deity unless it had unlimited causal powers: just as the electron nature is tied to a limited set of causal powers, the divine nature is tied to an unlimited set.[11] In particular, it might be that anything that has the divine nature is such that any other individual substance exists only at its sufferance, so that:

(2) For any possible world w, and any individual x, if x has the specific nature Deity at w, then for any individual y, if y exists in w, and y is an individual substance distinct from x, then (i) for some world w', in w' x wills that y not exist, and (ii) at every world w' in which x wills that y not exist, y does not exist.[12]

Suppose that (1) and (2) are both true, and that some being B at some world w has the nature Deity. By (2), any individual substance in world w distinct from B exists there only at the sufferance of B, and would not have existed if B had exercised its will in a way it might have. By (1), we know there is an individual substance—the individual in our world which is (a) God—which exists in w, and does not exist at the sufferance of B, that is, could not have failed to exist through any possible exercise of B's will. It follows that the individual who is a God in our world is identical to B. Since B and w were chosen arbitrarily, we may conclude that nothing actual or possible could have the specific nature Deity without also being the very same individual as God. In other words, God's individual essence is no different from His specific essence.[13]

[10]For a view on which all the causal potentialities of a (real) property of a (concrete) individual are essential to that property, see Sydney Shoemaker, "Causality and Properties," in Peter van Inwagen, ed., *Time and Cause* (Dordrecht: D. Reidel, 1980). Less extreme versions of this view are also considered by Shoemaker.

[11]"Unlimited" must be unpacked carefully. In one sense, God might be said to have limitations that creatures do not have, if He does not have the power to bring about His own destruction, or the power to sin. If these are genuine limitations, then talk of "unlimited power" is a place holder for a notion that needs to be explicated.

[12]Here "individual substance" is to be construed narrowly enough to exclude, say, numbers, which do not obviously exist only at God's sufferance.

[13]The argument would, I think, still go through, if (1) were replaced by the weaker premiss that there is some individual substance that exists in every possible world. (2)

While this argument has a flavor more Leibnizian than Thomistic, it draws on premises Aquinas accepts. He would agree that nothing could have the nature Deity without being unlimited in power in a sense that entails (2), since he thinks that unlimited power is tied to God's nature by the most intimate relation of all (identity). And he would agree that something in this world (God) exists necessarily, since, he thinks, the Third Way shows that contingent existence is possible only because some existence is necessary.

Still, how much of an improvement is it on the argument from immateriality? I don't find the new argument convincing, since I don't believe (1). That is because I follow Hume in thinking that, necessarily, no individual substance exists necessarily. (Again, I am construing "individual substance" here so that it applies only to beings with causal powers, and not to such things as numbers, which presumably are necessary existents.) It seems very clear to me that there might have been nothing at all with causal powers. Of course, not everyone will share this Humean intuition. Someone may maintain that she can no more imagine a possible world free from causally empowered individuals than I can imagine a world where arithmetic is not true. If she does, I don't know how to convince her that there is such a world (although, symmetrically, I doubt she could convince me that there is not). It might be thought that the burden of proof is on the party to the dispute who maintains that a world without causally empowered individuals is impossible. It is not in general true, however, that the burden of proof falls on the disputant maintaining that something is impossible. If we are inclined to think that in this case it does, it is probably because we are supposing that each party to the dispute agrees that there is some prima facie reason to believe a world without causal agents is possible—since each party agrees that we can at least apparently imagine a possible world where nothing at all with causal powers exists. If someone denies that she can even apparently imagine this, and denies that it is even prima facie plausible that there might have been nothing with causal powers, then she and I will end up in a dialectical standoff, championing our (inconsistent) intuitions. [14]

---

says that if any being in any world has the nature Deity at that world, then that being has (at that world) the ability to exist unaccompanied by any other individual substance. But as long as there is some necessarily existing individual substance S, it is impossible for anything but S to have the ability in question.

[14] Of course, Aquinas would say there is countervailing evidence against the Humean intuition, since he believes it can be shown that contingently existing individual

So, although I don't know any way to convince a determined defender of the new argument that it is unsound, I don't find the new line of argument for the identity of God's individual with His specific essence any more persuasive than the Thomistic one first considered. Moreover, there is some intuitive plausibility to the idea that if something could have the nature Diety, then so might something else have had it (although, presumably, no two things in the same world could have that nature). Against this, it is considerably more difficult to establish by appeal to intuition that—assuming there is a God—there might have been something else of the same kind than it is to establish that, for example, there might have been something else of the boson-kind, in addition to or instead of the bosons there actually are. To support the latter claim, we need only point to possible worlds with more bosons than this one; in such a world at least one thing of the boson-kind must be distinct from any actual boson. No such argument can be used in the theological case, since, presumably, there is at most one individual of the God-kind in any given world. (Recall the connection between Deity and unlimited power over one's world-mates.) Nor do I know of any other argument that would convince a doubter that a being of the same kind as God in another world was really a different being of the same kind, rather than the same being of the same kind. Appeals to stipulation ("I simply stipulate that we are talking about *another* individual of the God-kind") do not help, since we cannot stipulate possibilities into or out of existence, although we can stipulate which sorts of possibilities are included or excluded—and what is at issue is whether there is a genuine possibility that something else might have fallen under the God-kind.[15] Someone who wanted to establish that the putative possibility at issue is genuine would need to point to a clear case of a property that was essential to God, but not essential to God *qua* the kind of being He is. What would one be? The property in question would have to be an essential property that did not follow from the specific nature of its subject. In the case of material

---

substances presuppose a necessarily existing one. For reasons of space, I can't go into why I find this line of argument unconvincing, except to say that, with Hume, I lack the sort of antipathy to contingent brute facts which is grist for the mill of a certain sort of cosmological argument.

[15]If the reader is unconvinced: suppose someone held the decidedly odd view that there might have been a different point in space (distinct from all actual points) exactly where this one was. We might well ask, "What makes you think this otherworldly point in space is any different from the one actually there?" It would be to no purpose if he replied, "I simply stipulate that I am talking about *another* point in space just where this one is."

objects, it is easy to find clear cases of such properties—they might be compositional, or locational, or have to do with a thing's origin. But God has no material parts, or origin, or spatio-temporal location. Someone who thinks that there might have been a different God than there actually is could take at least three approaches here. He might hold that the different God would be discernible from the actual one with respect to a particular batch of known nonhaecceitistic[16] properties had essentially by just one of those individuals. I can't think what these properties would be, though this might just be a failure of imagination on my part. Alternatively, he might hold that the different God would be discernible from the actual one with respect to some unknown (nonhaecceitistic) properties had essentially by just one of those individuals. But if the defense of the putative possibility in question turns on unknown properties, it will certainly fall short of establishing that possibility. Finally, he might argue that we can make sense of the possibility that a different being had the nature Deity, even if that being was indiscernible from the actual being with that nature in every nonhaecceitistic way; that being would be just like the actual God, but He would be a different God, with different experiences, thoughts, and so on.[17] I am simply unsure about whether or not this sort of move is legitimate. On the one hand, I am inclined to think that any distinction between qualitatively indiscernible, doppelganger Gods is a distinction without a difference; on the other, the belief that there are such doppelganger Gods seems somehow less crazy than, say, the belief that there are distinct but nonhaecceitistically indiscernible points in space, or distinct but nonhaecceitistically indiscernible propositions, or truth-values. In short, I am in something of a quandary about whether or not there is a distinction between God's individual and specific essence: I know of no knockdown arguments either for or against the proposition. But, as we shall see in Chapter 4, it will not be necessary to resolve this quandary in order to answer the main question addressed in this chapter—whether or not God could be the same as His essence.

---

[16]By 'nonhaecceitistic' I mean to rule out such properties as *being the same as this very individual* or *being both something of the God-kind and this very individual*.

[17]Compare: "An electron different from any actual electron might have had the same world line, qualitative properties, and causal properties as this very electron. It would be just like this electron, but not the same one." "But why wouldn't it be the same electron?" "There's nothing more I can tell you; it's just a primitively intelligible, intuitively plausible idea that some electron besides all the ones there actually are might have had the same world line and all the same qualitative and causal properties as this one." Is this response legitimate? I'm pulled both ways.

Putting aside for the moment the question of the relation between God's individual and His specific essence, we may ask whether God could be the same as His individual essence. Obviously, how we construe this question will depend on what sort of thing we take an individual essence to be. Although Aquinas and contemporary analytic philosophers would agree that an individual essence is something an individual could not be without, in virtue of which that individual is the very individual it is, Aquinas and those philosophers would probably conceive of individual essences rather differently. The latter are likely to think of an individual essence as a property of a certain kind—say, the strongest property had by an individual in every world it inhabits.[18] For someone thinking of individual essences in this way, the question of whether God is His individual essence is just the question of whether God is the same as the strongest property He has in every world He inhabits.[19] Aquinas would answer this last question affirmatively, but he would take it to be a different question from the one about whether God and His individual essence are the same. As we have seen, Aquinas thinks of a created individual as constituted from an individual essence—which will be a composite of individuating matter and individuated substantial form, in the case of a material creature, or a subsistent substantial form, in the case of an immaterial creature—together with a plurality of accidents, some of which will float free from the individual's essence (in the way *having an undiminished understanding of the divine mysteries* floats free from Gabriel's

[18]Actually, the counterpart theorist will not characterize individual essences in this way, since on his account, a world-bound individual has nothing but properties it (vacuously) has in every world it inhabits. He would conceive of an individual essence as something more like the strongest property had by an individual and all its counterparts. (I ignore complications arising from the fact that the counterpart theorist may not suppose that each individual has just one set of counterparts; see Lewis, "Counterparts of Persons and Their Bodies," *Journal of Philosophy* 68 [1971]: 203–11.)

[19]Again, the counterpart theorist would say, "Whether God is the same as the strongest property He and all His counterparts have" (leaving open whether or not God's counterparts are distinct from Him). Note that if God is a trans-world individual (identical to all His counterparts), an individual essence is the strongest property had by that individual and all its counterparts, properties are sets of *possibilia,* and singleton sets are their members, then God turns out to be identical to His essence, even if He turns out to be distinct from some of His (intrinsic) properties. This suggests that, although Aquinas would say that God could not be the same as His essence unless He were the same as all His intrinsic properties, one could endorse the former claim, and abandon the latter, given an un-Thomistic way of construing both properties and essences, and the assumption that God does not have different intrinsic properties at different worlds. (As we saw in Chapter 2, one would have to invoke the modal constancy of God's intrinsic properties to explain why God's counterparts are God, though my counterparts are not me.)

essence), and others of which will "follow upon" or be "caused by" that essence (in the way the cognitive powers of Gabriel follow upon his essence [see DSC 11]). Consequently, Aquinas would think that "Is God the same as His individual essence?" means: "Is there in God a subsistent substantial form, or a composite of individuating matter and individuated form, together with some accidents, disjoint from that form or form–matter composite?" If the answer is yes, then God is composed of essence and accidents, and cannot be identified with that part of Him that is His individual essence; if the answer is no, then God's essence (the divine form or, as Aquinas sometimes calls it, quasi-form) can be identified with God. It should be clear that there will not be any composition of essence and accident in God if (as Aquinas supposes), necessarily, God is identical to each of the intrinsic attributes constituting Him. Accordingly, nothing stands in the way of identifying God with His essence if God turns out to be a "minimal bundle" of attributes, of the sort alluded to in note 27 of Chapter 2.

So there is a way of moving from the identity of God with each of His intrinsic attributes, to the identity of God with His individual essence. By contrast, there is no obvious route from the claim that, necessarily, God is the same as each of His intrinsic attributes, to the claim that God is the same as His specific essence. For we haven't ruled out the possibility that there could be two different divine individuals, inhabiting different worlds, each of which was constituted of just one, superrich individual attribute. (The individual attributes would be conspecific but distinct.) If this were the case, then God's individual essence (which He shares with nothing else) would be distinct from His specific essence (which He would share with the otherworldly divine being).

Suppose we gave up the claim that God is the same as His specific essence, and contented ourselves with the weaker claim that God is the same as His individual essence. Would this involve sacrificing anything essential to Aquinas' conception of divine simplicity? Not obviously. It would if God's specific essence had to be either a proper or a maximal part of God. There is, however, no immediately evident reason to suppose that if God's specific essence is different from God, then it must be a (real) part of Him.[20] Indeed, within a Thomistic

[20]Of course, if we suppose that God's specific essence is a universal, present in different individuals in different worlds, and we suppose that no individual can have any universals among its constituents unless that individual also has among its constituents some "particularizing element," then God's specific essence will be a proper part of God. But these suppositions are no more compulsory than they are Thomistic.

framework, there are good reasons to deny this supposition. If God's specific essence were distinct from His individual essence, it would—on Aquinas' account—differ from the individual essence in being a form (or quasi-form) which might have been a constituent of some other individual than the individual of which it is actually a constituent. But as we have seen, Aquinas holds that there is really no such thing as a shareable form: forms are either intrinsically individual and subsistent, or else individualized by, and hence necessarily limited to, just one subject. (See ST Ia.76.2, *responsio*, where Aquinas says that it is impossible for many individuals to have one form, just as it is impossible for many individuals to have one *esse*.)[21] It follows that if God's specific essence is not identical to God, it is not a real proper part of God.[22] Hence, as long as we suppose with Aquinas that forms are individual constituents of their subjects, and that the essence of an immaterial individual is a form, there is no direct route from the premiss that God's specific essence is not His individual essence to the conclusion that God is in any way composite.

Given ancillary Thomistic premises, there is an indirect route from that premiss to that conclusion. The crucial ancillary premiss is that one can distinguish a substance's individual essence from its specific essence only if that substance is hylomorphically composite. I have already argued, though, that Aquinas has not made this out. One might still think that—assuming properties are constituents of their subjects—it can be shown that any individual substance whose individual essence is not its specific essence is composed of a plurality of properties. But if there is an argument to that effect, which does not also show that any individual substance is composed of a plurality of properties, I don't know how it goes. Again, one can presumably distinguish the individual essence of a point in space from its specific essence, but I don't know that points in space are composed of a

---

[21]I am ignoring Trinitarian complications here. At ST Ia.39.3 Aquinas says that in Cicero, Plato, and Socrates—three *supposita* of human nature—there are three humanities; whereas in the three *supposita* of the Trinity, there is but one divine nature.

[22]As we have seen (cf. DE 2), Aquinas says that the essence of (a) man—that is, the specific essence of Socrates or any other man—and the essence of Socrates—that is, his individual essence—differ only in that the latter includes designated matter and the former does not. In one sense this talk of Socrates' individual essence as differing from his (or any other human's) specific essence is misleading. For, on pain of giving up his individualism, Aquinas would have to say that the specific essence of a man is nothing really distinct from the individual essence of that man. The specific essence of a man, as Aquinas conceives of it, is, as it were, a real thing—a form-matter composite—with the unshareability that is really inseparable from it abstracted away. Hence it is nothing both real and distinct from the individual essence of that man.

plurality of properties. To take a more Thomistic example, if there are such things as individual roundnesses, we can distinguish the individual essence of an individual roundness from its specific essence. (All individual roundnesses are the same kind of thing, but they are not the very same thing.) But Aquinas himself would say that individual roundnesses are not themselves composed of a plurality of individual properties. (Besides, suppose they were so composed. We could distinguish those component individual properties' individual essence from their specific essence, and run the same argument again.) So Aquinas accepts, and—given his ontology of individual properties—ought to accept, that individuals of the same kind can differ, even though neither has any property other than itself as constituent. Why should we suppose that individual substances cannot differ in this way—unless it is because individual substances cannot fail to have a plurality of component properties? If there is an argument for doing so, it is not a straightforward one.

In sum: if we can defend the view that God is the same as each of the intrinsic attributes constituting Him, we can also defend the view that God is the same as His individual essence. While this leaves open the possibility that God and His specific essence are distinct, leaving that possibility open does not entail opening the door to any form of composition in God. Moreover, if the view that God is the same as each of His intrinsic attributes is defensible, then at least there is no compelling argument against the Thomistic claim that God is the same as His (specific as well as individual) essence. For as we have seen, it is by no means clear that there is any difference between God's individual essence and His specific essence, since it is less than evident that both God and someone else might have been divine.

We have already seen, though, that God could not be the same as all His intrinsic attributes unless God has all the same intrinsic attributes in every world He inhabits (cf. the end of Chapter 2). There presumably are beings whose intrinsic attributes do not vary from world to world: sets, numbers, and (I think) regions of space. But, as I indicate in Chapter 4, there are worries about whether *God*'s intrinsic properties could be constant from world to world, given that He is omniscient. If these worries are well founded, we shall have to give up not just the identity of God with all His intrinsic attributes, but also the identity of God with His essence: if God has properties that are neither included in nor follow upon that essence, He cannot very well be the same as His essence. In the next chapter, I consider some of these worries and Aquinas' response to them.

[4]

Knowledge, Contingency, and Change in God

Intrinsic and Extrinsic

We may distinguish, among the properties things have, the intrinsic properties from the extrinsic.[1] An intrinsic property is, intuitively, one that a thing has just in virtue of the way that thing is: roundness and existence are intrinsic properties. An extrinsic property is one that a thing has at least in part because of the way other things are: proximity to Colle D'Oggia and namelessness are extrinsic properties. Following Lewis, we may connect the notion of intrinsicality with the idea of perfect duplication as follows: a property is intrinsic if for any actual or possible perfect duplicates of each other, either both of them have that property, or neither of them do.[2] A property is extrinsic otherwise. Extrinsic properties may be purely extrinsic, if they divide every class of duplicates; or impurely extrinsic, if they divide some classes of duplicates, but include or exclude others. *Having a name* is a purely extrinsic property; *being round and such that Wimbledon Common is larger than Hampstead Heath* and *being square or such that Wimbledon Common borders on Richmond Park* are impurely extrinsic properties that, as it were, have a purely intrinsic component and a purely extrinsic component.

An individual may have an intrinsic property either essentially or inessentially: for example, a lump of clay has the (determinable) prop-

---

[1]Here I am construing 'property' quite generously, since we want to count extrinsic properties as properties.

[2]See Lewis, "Extrinsic Properties," *Philosophical Studies* 44 (1983): 197–200.

erty of shape essentially, and the particular shape it has (say, round-ness) inessentially.[3] Why might one suppose that God must have some intrinsic properties inessentially? An argument to that effect would go like this: since God is essentially omniscient, at every possible world, He knows whatever is true at that world. Because different things are true at different worlds, what God knows must vary from world to world. Knowledge, whatever else it involves, involves belief: so God's beliefs vary from world to world. But if God's beliefs vary from world to world, so too must His intrinsic properties.

One way to meet this argument would be to deny that if God could not but be omniscient, then His beliefs vary from world to world. The most obvious way to support this denial might be called the Avicen-nan strategy: this would involve holding that the only genuinely possible world is the actual one, and maintaining that our feeling that there are myriad ways things might have been is an illusion based on incomplete understanding. Alternatively, one might argue against the view that God's beliefs vary from world to world by maintaining that although there are many possible worlds, God's knowledge does not vary from world to world: what He knows at each world is just the totality of truths of the form P is true at world w, P is true at world w', P is true at some world or other, and so on (all of whose truth-values are constant from world to world). The natural objection here is that if all God knows is these truths, then He is not omniscient; for it is not only (necessarily) true-in-world-w that the Red Sox won the 1986 pennant, and (necessarily) true that in some world or other the Red Sox won the 1986 pennant, but also (contingently) actually true that they won that pennant. If at every world, God knows at that world only the propositions whose truth-values are modally constant, then it would seem that God is necessarily unomniscient. Someone who thought that possible worlds were large, concrete individuals, and that they all existed, and that what we call the actual world was just the one inhabited by us, could answer as follows: if we knew all the true propositions of the form event E is happening at place p, we would not know all there was for us to know about the location of events, if we didn't also know whether or not, for example, event E was happening *here* (equivalently, whether or not place p was *here*). So for us to know all the locatively invariant propositions about events (that is, all the

---

[3]Here and elsewhere in this chapter, I use 'essential' in the standard contemporary sense, according to which a property is essential to an individual just in case the individual has that property in every world in which it exists (or, for counterpart theorists, that individual and all its counterparts have that property).

propositions whose truth-values are constant from place to place) is not for us to know all there is to know about the location of events. Suppose, on the other hand, there was a being who, unlike us, had no spatial location. Then, plausibly, if that being knew all the locatively invariant propositions about events, it would not also need to know any locatively variant ones. For that sort of being, there is no here or there, and if it knows that E happened at p, E' happened at p', and so on, it knows all there is for it to know about the location of events.

Now, suppose actuality were a locational property; that is, suppose that what we call the actual world is just the one and only world we inhabit. And suppose that God had no particular 'modal location'— either because He inhabited no world at all, or because He inhabited all of them. Then, we might say, it would be true of God (though not of us world-bound individuals) that if He knew all the propositions true at every modal location, then He would know all there was for Him to know, and would accordingly be omniscient.[4] In that case, nothing would preclude God's being essentially and intrinsically invariantly omniscient.

Neither the Avicennan nor the "Lewisian" way of defending the proposition that God is both essentially omniscient and intrinsically invariant looks particularly promising. The Avicennan view that the actual and the necessary are one and the same is, on the face of it, massively implausible. And even if we can make plausible the (very surprising, at least) Lewisian view that possible worlds are concrete particulars, the supposition that all of God's beliefs exist necessarily seems to preclude God's beliefs having the sort of causal-explanatory role that is constitutive of belief states. In any case, neither the Avicennan nor the Lewisian strategy is remotely Thomistic. Unlike the Avicennan, Aquinas holds that there are many different ways the world might have been (cf. ST Ia.25.5 and 6); unlike Lewis, he holds that there is but one world (ST Ia.47.3).

Accordingly, the only Thomistic way to block the just considered argument from God's essential omniscience to His intrinsic inconstancy is to deny that God's having different beliefs at different worlds entails His being different ways intrinsically at those worlds. In fact, there is something be to said for this denial. In two recent articles,[5]

---

[4]At present, I am putting the point impressionistically; more detail will be provided in the next section on the account of propositional attitudes which goes along with this picture.

[5]Tyler Burge, "Individualism and the Mental," *Midwest Studies in Philosophy* 4 (1979): 31–55, and "Other Bodies," in *Thought and Object: Essays on Intentionality*, ed. A. Woodfield (Oxford: Oxford University Press, 1982), pp. 97–121.

Tyler Burge has discussed in detail two cases in which there appears to be variation at the level of beliefs, and constancy at the level of internal states and intrinsic properties:

(A) Suppose someone has the notion of arthritis, but incorrectly believes that arthritis can occur not just in the joints, but in other areas, such as the thigh. (He has acquired the notion of arthritis from causal conversation or reading, in which it was never specified whether arthritis can occur anywhere but in the joints.) Suppose that this person believes that he has arthritis in his thigh. Now consider a counterfactual situation, in which that person has the same physical history, and has all the same nonintentional mental phenomena. In the counterfactual situation, however, the person is part of a linguistic community in which the word *arthritis* is (correctly) used in such a way that it can apply not just to inflammatory ailments of the joints, but to such ailments in other parts of the body. In the actual situation, the person believes (falsely) that he has arthritis in his thigh. In the counterfactual situation, he lacks that belief. For he could only believe that he had arthritis in his thigh if he had the concept or notion of arthritis; and he could not have acquired that notion in the counterfactual community. (In that community, 'arthritis' does not mean *arthritis*.) It follows that differences in the social environment of the believer can make a difference to what his beliefs are, even if they make no difference to his internal states (or, more broadly, his intrinsic properties).

(B) Following Putnam, let us suppose that there is a planet, Twin-Earth, which is in almost every respect a perfect duplicate of Earth: for each inhabitant of Earth, there is a duplicate inhabitant of Twin-Earth, with the same physical and experiential history as his earthly counterpart. Suppose further that Twin-Earth differs from Earth in that, instead of containing water, it contains a different liquid, twater. Twater has a different chemical composition than water, but looks, tastes, and so on just like water. Assume that on Earth, Adam has the belief that water is a liquid. He has a counterpart, $Adam_{te}$, on Twin-Earth, who is in all of the same internal states as Adam. (Actually, as Burge notes, this is inconsistent with certain physiological facts, but this is irrelevant to the philosophical point, which could be made by reference to aluminum and twaluminum, or elms and twelms, instead of water and twater.) But although $Adam_{te}$ has the same physical and experiential history as Adam, he does not have the same beliefs, for while Adam has the belief that water is a liquid, and lacks the belief that twater is a liquid, Adam$_{te}$ has the belief that twater is a liquid, and lacks the belief that water is liquid. (Again, if we fill in the story the right way, it will seem incredible that Adam could have the concept of twater, or that Adam$_{te}$ could have the concept of water.) So, differences in the physical environment of the believer can make a difference to what his beliefs are, even if they make no difference to his internal states, or intrinsic properties.

These examples make it plausible that someone's beliefs may vary from one world to another, even though his intrinsic properties do not.[6] In that case, a defender of Aquinas might say, it could be that although God's beliefs always varied from world to world (in such a way as to preserve His omniscience at every world), His intrinsic properties never did. So, for example, the difference between God's believing (in the actual world) that Pluto exists, and His disbelieving (in a Plutoless world) that Pluto exists, would be a purely extrinsic difference, even if *believing that Pluto exists* and *disbelieving that Pluto exists* are not purely extrinsic properties (that is, properties that divide every class of duplicates). The same would go for every case in which God had different beliefs at different worlds.

The difficulty here is in making sense of the role that, on the Thomistic picture, purely extrinsic properties play in fixing what God believes. We are meant to suppose that God's believing that Pluto exists does not consist in His having any (purely) intrinsic property; rather, it consists in His being in the one internal state He is essentially "locked into," together with His having a purely extrinsic or relational property R. And God's believing that Pluto does not exist consists in His being in that same internal state, together with a different purely extrinsic or relational property R'. But just what could these properties R and R' be, and just *how* would their exemplification by a God locked into all His internal states respectively constitute God's believing and disbelieving that Pluto exists? It should be clear that neither of the Burge stories is much help in answering this

[6] I say 'plausible', instead of 'certain', because one response to (A) and (B) is to say they show not that two intrinsically indiscernible believers may yet have different beliefs, but only that one and the same belief sentence may be true of one believer in one environment, and false of an intrinsically indiscernible believer in another. (On this line, belief sentences do a good deal more than ascribe beliefs.) For the present purposes, we needn't decide whether this response is a good one.

question. In those stories, the person's having a certain belief (that he has arthritis in his thigh, that water is a liquid) consists in his being a certain way intrinsically (the way that each of the counterpart believers is), together with his having a certain purely extrinsic property, and the person's having the other belief (that he has tharthritis in his thigh, that twater is a liquid) consists in his being that same way intrinsically, and having a different purely extrinsic property; but in each case, the extrinsic properties are ones that involve being causally affected in the right sort of way, either by what the belief is about, or else at least by other members of the believer's linguistic community. But Aquinas would maintain—as anyone should who holds that God has all of His intrinsic attributes necessarily—that God could never be on the far end of the causal relation. It follows that He could not have extrinsic properties of the type that together with the internal states of the believer fix belief in the Burge-type cases. So, once again, what are the purely extrinsic properties R and R' such that God's having R (and being in a certain internal state) is what God's belief that Pluto exists consists in, while God's having R' (and being in that state) is what God's belief that Pluto does not exist consists in? Well, someone might say, the properties are just the paradigmatically extrinsic properties *inhabiting a world in which Pluto exists* and *inhabiting a world in which Pluto does not exist*. After all, God's being in His necessary internal state and inhabiting a Pluto-inhabited world is a logically necessary and sufficient condition for His believing that Pluto exists; and God's being in His necessary internal state and inhabiting a Plutoless world is a logically necessary and sufficient condition for His believing that Pluto does not exist. So why not say that God's believing that Pluto exists consists in His being in His necessary internal state, together with His inhabiting a Pluto-inhabited world, while God's believing Pluto does not exist consists in His being in that state, together with His inhabiting a Plutoless world? Well, if God is necessarily omniscient, then Pluto's existing is a logically necessary and sufficient condition for God's believing that Pluto exists. But it would be mad to suppose that God's believing that Pluto exists (simply) consists in Pluto's existing. On anyone's view, there has to be more to God's believing that Pluto exists than that. Now—presuming that God is infallible and omniscient—there is no problem about supposing that for some internal state God is necessarily in, God's being in that state, together with His having the extrinsic property of inhabiting a Pluto-inhabited world, is a logically necessary and sufficient condition for His believing that Pluto exists; and, likewise, that His being in that internal state, together with His having the extrinsic property of inhabiting a Plutoless world, is a logically necessary and sufficient condition for His believing that Pluto does not exist. But this does not mean that we can make sense of the idea that God's believing that Pluto exists consists in His being in His necessary internal state, together with His inhabiting a Pluto-inhabited world, while His believing that Pluto does not exist consists of His being in that same internal state, together with His inhabiting a Plutoless world. If we start with an internal state God is necessarily in—a state that is entirely neutral with respect to believing or disbelieving that Pluto exists—how can it be that God's being in that state, together with Pluto's existing, is enough to constitute His believing that Pluto exists, while God's being in that state, together with Pluto's not existing, is enough to constitute His believing it does not? The constituting states of affairs, as it were, do not sum to the constituted ones.

Someone might suggest that God's believing that Pluto exists consists in His necessarily being a certain way intrinsically, plus a certain state of affairs (*Pluto's existing*) being caused by Him; while God's believing that Pluto does not exist consists in His being that same way intrinsically, plus the state of affairs *Pluto's not existing* being caused by Him. In fact, I think that if we suppose that God has all His intrinsic properties necessarily, we encounter problems similar to the ones under discussion about what God's causing contingent states of affairs could consist in. Be that as it may, how could God's believing that Pluto exists consist in God's being in a certain necessary state—which state is completely neutral with respect to believing or disbelieving in Pluto—plus God's causing Pluto to exist, while God's believing that Pluto does not exist consists in His being in that same internal state, together with His causing Pluto not to exist? Again, things do not seem to add up.

At this point, the defender of Aquinas might draw on the Thomistic idea that God's knowledge is fabricative (ST Ia.14.8), and say that God's believing that Pluto exists consists in God's being in His necessary state and causing Pluto to exist in a particular way—*viz.*, by willing that Pluto exists—while God's believing that Pluto does not exist consists in His being in that state and causing it not to exist. Bracketing worries about whether we can apply this account to God's knowledge of such things as creaturely sins, this suggestion only seems to push the problem back a bit. Given the necessary efficaciousness of the divine will, and the contingent existence of Pluto, God's willing that Pluto exists will (on the view under consideration) be a matter of His necessarily having an intrinsic property, together with His having an inessential extrinsic one, while His willing that Pluto not exist will be a matter of His having that same intrinsic property, and a different inessential extrinsic one. We can then ask what the extrinsic properties in question could be, and how they could do what they are supposed to do; and we're back to our original problem.

Now, I have not shown that there is no pair of purely extrinsic or relational properties R and R' such that God's believing that Pluto exists consists in His being in the internal state He's locked into, together with His having R, while God's believing that Pluto does not exist consists in His being in that same state, together with His having R'. In the nature of the case, it is hard to see how one would go about proving that sort of negative existential. The idea, however, that a being locked into all of its internal states could be necessarily omniscient is, I take it, bizarre enough to be at least prima facie implausible. If someone holds that such a being could be necessarily omniscient, after all, on account of the different purely extrinsic properties it had at different worlds, then she owes us some kind of account of what the extrinsic properties in question might be, and how they could play their belief-fixing role. Until something in the way of an account is provided, the presumption stands against the view that a being incapable of different internal states could be an essentially omniscient being.[7]

So it looks as though an omniscient God could not be the same as His essence, or the same as all His intrinsic attributes.[8] In the section "Omniscience and Immutability," I consider whether an omniscient God could be, as Aquinas supposes, atemporal and immutable. Before doing so, I explicate the Thomistic conception of eternity, since Aquinas relies on that conception in his attempt to show the compatibility of God's omniscience with His immutability.

Eternity

For Aquinas, God and His knowledge are eternal, where eternity has the following features:

    (i) Eternity is incomposite: it has no earlier or later parts. (In this respect, eternity resembles the present moment; cf. ST Ia.10.1, *responsio* and *ad* 3.)

---

[7]This point was suggested to me by Robert Stalnaker; his conversations with me on the issues under discussion were very helpful.

[8]If some intrinsic attributes of God are had by God in every world in which He exists, and others are had by God in only some of the worlds in which He exists, then those attributes cannot be the same as one another, and cannot both be the same as God; so it must be false that whatever is an intrinsic attribute of God, just is God.

    (ii) Eternity is not, however, like the present moment, evanescent: it is a kind of boundless duration, lacking a beginning and an end (cf. ST Ia.10.1, *responsio*).

   (iii) Eternity lacks temporal location: it is neither earlier nor later than any instant of time, since it is altogether outside of time (cf. SCG I.66).

   (iv) Nevertheless, eternity is not entirely unrelated to time. Each moment of time—and each event—coexists with eternity, and is quasi-present to eternity (cf. SCG I.66).

Features (ii) and (iv) are meant respectively to prevent misunderstandings of (i) and (iii): (ii) blocks the identification of eternity with any instant, while (iv) specifies that eternity is not to be understood as insulated atemporality. In order to see that the conjunction of (iii) and (iv) is not obviously incoherent, it is important to note that—when he is careful—Aquinas says not that everything existing in time is present to eternity, but rather that everything existing in time is 'as it were' present to eternity (*quasi praesens,* as he puts it at SCG I.66). Hence Aquinas is not committed to the view that there is something extratemporal with which every event is literally simultaneous, and he can maintain that the relation of quasi-presence holding between temporal events and eternity is neither symmetric nor Euclidean.

Of course, the relation of being quasi-present to should bear some similarity to the relation of being present to, if the former relation is happily described as quasi-presence. In fact, two such similarities immediately come to mind. First, for Aquinas, God has the sort of epistemic access to events quasi-present to Him that we have—under ideal conditions—to events present to us: He has a certain and intuitive knowledge of all the events quasi-present to Him, knowing them nonconjecturally, and not merely in their causes. Second, all the events quasi-present to God depend causally on Him in a way analogous to the way present effects depend on their present causes. For example, according to Newtonian physics, there are facts about the way the earth is being gravitationally attracted right now which depend causally on the sun's having the mass it does right now. (I owe this example to Calvin Normore.) Or, to take a medieval example, Aquinas thinks of the fact that the moon is now illuminated as causally dependent on the fact that the sun is now luminous. Analogously, Aquinas holds, the fact that any creature now exists is causally dependent on God's willing in eternity that it exist.

Features (iii) and (iv) jointly say that each instant of time stands in a relation to eternity which is both like and unlike the relation of simultaneity. Likewise, (i) and (ii) jointly say that eternity is both like and unlike the present instant. It is like the present instant in being incomposite, and unlike it in being a species of duration without beginning or end.

It might be thought that the conjunction of (i) and (ii) is manifestly unintelligible, on the grounds that, while we may suppose that eternity is punctile, and we may suppose that it is a kind of duration, we cannot coherently make both suppositions at once. For on any ordinary understanding of duration, it is constitutive of duration that it involve earlier and later parts. True, Aquinas warns us that we should not think of eternal duration as stretched out through before and after—the way temporal duration is—but rather as *tota simul*. But how does this help? The idea of duration, which is *tota simul*, is on the face of it like the idea of (nonzero) length, which is *tota hic*.

It would, however, be premature to conclude that Aquinas incoherently takes eternity both to be atemporal, and to have a feature (boundless duration) which entails omnitemporality. For it might be that Aquinas has a broader notion of duration than our own, and one that is consistent with atemporality. In fact, I think this is so.

At ST Ia.10.1 Aquinas endorses Boethius' definition of eternity as the perfect possession all at once of a life that cannot end. In that article's *responsio* he remarks that, just as we understand simple things by reference to composite ones, so we understand eternity by reference to time. That is, we understand eternity as that mode of existence which both lacks a beginning and an end (unlike the now of time), and lacks the succession of before and after (unlike extended parts of time).[9]

Note that Boethius' definition makes no explicit reference to duration, although it does make reference to endlessness. Nor does Aquinas' concluding characterization of eternity at the end of the *responsio* of ST Ia.10.1 make any explicit reference to duration, although it again mentions endlessness. Now, it might be objected that Boethius' definition and Aquinas' characterization both make implicit reference to duration, on the grounds that to say that eternity is endless (and beginningless) is just to say that eternity is everlastingness—that is, unlimited temporal duration. But something could be endless either because it was everlasting or because it was atemporal: atemporal objects do not start or stop existing any more than everlasting ones do.

Why might one want to stress that atemporal existence is endless?

---

[9]"Sic ergo ex duobus notificatur aeternitas. Primo, ex hoc quod id quod est in aeternitate est interminabile, idest principio et fine carens. . . . Secundo, ex hoc quod ipsa aeternitas successione caret tota simul existens" (ST Ia.10.1, *responsio*).

One motivation would be to contrast eternal existence with instanteous existence (thus preventing a certain misunderstanding of the claim that eternity is *tota simul*). Something that fails to be temporally extended, because it is instantaneous, is a fleeting or transient being: it can be said of such a thing that very soon it will be no more. The same cannot be said of an eternal being. Similarly, the present instant *is* (where we understand 'is' as present-tensed) only now; the present instant immediately gives way, as it were, to instants yet to be. Eternity, by contrast, could not give way to anything. Boethius draws attention to this fact, saying that while time is constituted by the transient now (*nunc fluens*), eternity is constituted by the permanent now (*nunc stans*).[10] Aquinas cites this remark approvingly, and explicates it as follows: just as our apprehension of time is based on our apprehension of the flux of the now, our understanding of eternity is based on our grasp of the idea of a permanent or fixed now (cf. ST Ia.10.2 *ad* 1).

What is noteworthy, then, is that nothing in Aquinas' discussion of eternity in ST Ia.10.1, *responsio,* commits him to the view that eternity has some features proper to atemporality, and some features proper to omnitemporality. While some of his remarks there about the endlessness of eternity could be interpreted as expressing the view that eternity is everlasting (in the sense mentioned above), none of his remarks needs to be so interpreted.

Much the same could be said about Aquinas' discussion of eternity at chapter 15 of the *Summa contra Gentiles.* There Aquinas argues from the Aristotelian idea that time is the measure of things movable, and the claim that God is immovable, to the conclusion that God is not measured by time, and hence is free from any before or after. Hence, Aquinas goes on, "[God] does not exist after having not existed, nor can He not exist after having existed, nor can any succession be found in His existence: for none of these things can be understood without time. Consequently, He lacks both a beginning and an end, having all

[10]In *Time, Creation, and the Continuum* (London: Duckworth, 1983), chap. 8, Richard Sorabji argues that although Boethius ascribes permanence and endlessness to eternity, he nevertheless conceives of eternity as timelessness, and in ascribing the aforementioned properties to eternity, means only to deny that eternity is changeable. On Sorabji's view, Boethius conceived of eternity as both permanent and durationless. Sorabji's reading of Boethius led me to reconsider my view that Aquinas' conception of eternity conflated everlastingness with atemporality. As will emerge, I think that Aquinas conceived of eternity in much the way Sorabji thinks Boethius did; but in light of the fact that Aquinas explicitly says that eternity is a kind of duration (cf., e.g., SS 19.2.1), one cannot say that Aquinas thought of eternity as durationless, without employing a notion of duration narrower than the one with which Aquinas worked.

of His existence at once [*Est igitur carens principio et fine, totum esse suum simul habens*]. In this consists the concept [*ratio*] of eternity" (SCG I. 15). Note that the definition of eternity offered here is said to follow straightforwardly from a twofold denial that succession applies to divine existence. First, it is denied that there are any successive moments such that at just one of those moments does God exist. Second, it is denied that there are any successive moments such that God exists at each of those moments. To put this another way, there is no successiveness about God's existence, and there is no successiveness within God's existence. From the former claim, Aquinas concludes that God lacks a beginning and an end; from the latter claim, he concludes that God has His existence all at once. The penultimate sentence of the above passage, taken out of context, might be thought to ascribe everlasting existence to God. In context, however, it is clear that the account of eternity Aquinas offers here specifies neither that eternity is everlasting, nor that it is a kind of duration—in anything like the ordinary sense of the word. For the claim that God's existence lacks a beginning and an end is taken to follow simply from the claim that God neither starts nor stops existing. And it will be true of anything atemporal that it neither starts nor stops existing, even if we think of it as free from anything like duration ordinarily conceived.

There is much, then, to suggest that Aquinas does not incoherently try to combine everlastingness and atemporality in his conception of eternity. Rather, he thinks of eternal existence as existence, with the (interconnected) imperfections of changeability, potentiality, and successiveness subtracted. When those imperfections are subtracted, what is left is atemporal existence—on the one hand endless and permanent (which is to say nonephemeral), and on the other indivisible. If we ignore his views on the relations holding between time and eternity, Aquinas' conception of eternity is in no way richer than the notion of atemporality. That is why Aquinas thinks we can move straightaway from the claim that what is beyond change is beyond time, and the claim that God is entirely unchangeable, to the conclusion that God is eternal (cf. ST Ia. 10. 1 and 3).

It may make things clearer to contrast the interpretation I have been offering with an alternative one. According to Stump and Kretzmann, it is at best misleading to say that either Boethius or Aquinas thought of eternity as punctile.[11] For Boethius and Aquinas, the eternal present "is not instantaneous but extended, because eternity entails duration. The temporal present is a durationless instant. . . . The eternal pres-

---

[11]See Eleonore Stump and Norman Kretzmann, "Eternity," *Journal of Philosophy* 78, no. 8 (1981): 429–58, esp. p. 422 and n. 10.

ent, on the other hand, is by definition an infinitely extended, pastless, futureless duration" ("Eternity," p. 435).

The obvious drawback of this interpretation is that it attributes to Aquinas a view whose intelligibility is very much in doubt, since it is at best unclear whether we can make sense of the idea of extended, but nontemporally extended, duration. I think I can make sense of the idea that something lacks temporally extended duration (that is, is atemporal); and I can make sense of the idea that something has temporally extended duration; but I don't know what it could mean to say that something's duration was literally extended, but not in a temporal way. (It is not as if, for example, there is any illuminating way of completing the following sentence: "Eternal duration is not extended through *time;* it is extended through ————." Although "eternity" completes the sentence, it fails to do so in an illuminating way.) If eternity is a nontemporally extended mode of existence, it is far from obvious that it follows from there being no successiveness either about or within divine existence, that God is eternal. But we have seen that Aquinas takes this entailment to be entirely straightforward (cf. not just SCG I.15, but also SCG I.66). Moreover, the idea that eternity is extended (never mind that it is not *temporally* extended) does not mesh well with Aquinas' remarks at SCG I.66 about the relation of eternity to time. There he says that eternity is related to the whole of time in the way an indivisible outside of a continuum is related to that continuum. If Aquinas had thought of eternity as in any way extended, this would be an unhappy analogy for him: whatever is (in any way) extended is (in some way) divisible. (Otherwise, what is meant by "extended"?)

The obvious advantage of the Stump-Kretzmann interpretation is that it provides an explanation of the fact that Aquinas describes eternity as a kind of duration. It should be clear, however, that it is not the only explanation. An alternative explanation is that Aquinas thinks of duration as permanent—that is, nonevanescent—existence. Then it will turn out that any temporal continuant and any atemporal being has duration, although no instantaneous being does. And it will turn out that there is no inconsistency in saying that God's duration is nonsuccessive. Also—if the arguments offered above are on the mark—this supposition about what Aquinas means by "duration" is not an ad hoc attempt to defend Aquinas from the charge that his notion of eternity is inconsistent.

Finally, when we consider Aquinas' belief that all times are quasi-present to God, we can see why it would have been more natural for Aquinas to speak of God's eternal existence as having (atemporal) duration than, for example, it would be for Quine to speak of sets as having atemporal duration. As we have seen, for Aquinas even events nonsimultaneous with one another are (each) quasi-simultaneous with divine eternity. Now—on the ordinary understanding of duration— the existence of a being involves duration just in case some events nonsimultaneous with one another are (each) simultaneous with some part of the existence of that being. Thus, from the fact that something like simultaneity can be said to hold between any two nonsimultaneous events and divine existence, it follows that something like boundless duration (in the ordinary sense of the word) can be attributed to divine existence.[12] True, this line of thought only takes us from quasi-simultaneity to quasi-duration. Why would Aquinas want to hold that God's existence has duration, and not just quasi-duration? Because he thinks that duration is a perfection, and thinks that temporal duration presupposes the imperfections of potentiality and change. Accordingly, it is theologically incumbent upon Aquinas to construe duration as something other than a straightforward negative property (cf. ST Ia.10.1 ad 1), and at the same time to construe duration broadly enough that something atemporal could have it. This he does, by construing duration as nonephemeral existence.

Given that Aquinas speaks of all times as present to eternity, and describes eternity as a kind of duration, it may appear that his conception of eternity inconsistently combines temporal and atemporal elements twice over. The appearances deceive: Aquinas consistently thinks of God's eternity as atemporal existence, hooked up causally and epistemically (in the right sort of way) with time. If Aquinas' way of thinking about eternity is after all internally consistent,[13] we may go on to ask whether—as Aquinas supposes—it in fact gives us the wherewithal to reconcile God's immutability with His omniscience.

Omniscience and Immutability

The intuition behind arguments for the incompatibility of omniscience and immutability is—crudely put—that since the world is

---

[12]I was made aware of this point by Gerald Massey.

[13]Of course, I haven't considered every worry one might have about the internal consistency of Aquinas' notion of eternity. One such concerns the question of whether an atemporal being could be said to know, act, or be alive (cf. William Kneale, "Time and Eternity in Theology," *Proceedings of the Aristotelian Society* 61 [1960]). I share the intuition that there is something very puzzling about the idea of an atemporal being's knowing, acting, or living: but it is quite difficult to show that outright inconsistency is involved in the claim that an atemporal being does any or all of those things. Similarly, it is not clear that it is metaphysically possible for something atemporal to have effects in time (or for that matter outside of it); but I don't know of any good argument showing that atemporality is incompatible with causal efficacy.

always changing, an (always) omniscient mind must change in order to keep up with it. Such arguments usually rely on temporal indexicals or tensed verbs, as does this one, considered by Aquinas: "God knew that Christ would be born. But He does not know now that Christ will be born, because it is not the case that Christ will be born. Therefore God does not know whatever He knew. So God's knowledge would seem to be changeable" (ST Ia.14.15, obj. 3). A natural way of trying to escape the above conclusion is to argue that although some of the time it can be said truly that God knows Christ will be born, and some of the time it cannot be said truly, no change in God's knowledge corresponds to this fact. This could be so, if the objects of knowledge were propositions, and the propositions expressed by tensed sentences were tenseless. Suppose, for example, the sentence "Christ will be born," uttered at 12:01 A.M., January 1, 500 B.C., expressed a proposition with this sort of form:

> For some time t later than 12:01, January 1, 500 B.C., Christ is born at t.

Then we could say that God (either omnitemporally or atemporally) has invariant knowledge of the proposition expressed in 500 B.C. by "Christ will be born," since the proposition expressed by that sentence would have a temporally invariant truth-value. (I ignore complications about future contingents.) If the objects of divine knowledge are propositions, and propositions all have temporally invariant truth-values, nothing stops us from saying that God always knows anything He ever knows, even though whether a sentence saying what God knows expresses a truth may depend on what time it is.

The difficulties with the just sketched view of the relation of sentences with tensed verbs to propositions are well known. Someone could believe at 12:01, January 1, 500 B.C., that Christ will be born, without then believing that at some time t later than 500 B.C. Christ is born at t; just as someone could at that time believe that at some time t later than 500 B.C. Christ is born at t, without then believing that Christ will be born. (Both of these cases are possible when the believer does not know what time it is.) It follows that if believing at a time t that Christ will be born is a matter of then standing in the believing relation to the proposition expressed at that time by the sentence "Christ will be born," the proposition then expressed by "Christ will be born" is not of the form "Christ is born at some time t' later than t."

Aquinas considers and rejects an attempt like the one just sketched to block the argument of ST Ia.14.15, obj. 3. He remarks that according to the ancient nominalists, to say (at the respectively appropriate times, presumably) that Christ was born, that Christ is born, and that Christ will be born was to make the same statement, because in each case the same thing was referred to—namely, the birth of Christ. From this, Aquinas says, the ancient nominalists concluded that whatever God knew, He knows (ST Ia. 14. 15 *ad* 3). Although Aquinas puts the nominalists' view rather briefly and crudely, that view would seem to be one on which different tensed sentences (uttered at different times) can nevertheless make the same statement, or express the same proposition, because the proposition expressed by the tensed sentences is not itself tensed.[14]

The trouble with the nominalsits' view, Aquinas thinks, is precisely that it takes propositions to have invariant truth-values: "[From the nominalists' position] it would follow that a proposition that was once true would always be true, which goes against the Philosopher, who says that this statement, *Socrates is sitting,* is true when he is sitting, and false when he stands up" (ST Ia. 14. 15 *ad* 3). Aquinas does not here defend Aristotle's belief that (some) propositions have different truth-values at different times, but we have seen that there is this to be said for it: straightforward theories of propositions as tenseless and invariant in truth-value do not square well with the idea that belief is a relation between a person and a proposition.[15]

If Aquinas concedes that (some) propositions vary in truth-value over time, must he not concede the variability of divine knowledge? He does concede that the statement 'Whatever God knew, He knows' is not true, if it is taken as a universal conditional about propositions. He maintains, however, it does not follow thence that God's knowledge is variable. For "just as it is without any change in divine knowledge that God knows one and the same thing sometimes to exist and

---

[14]In summarizing Aquinas' description of the ancient nominalists' view, I have used 'proposition' for the Latin *enuntiabile.* Perhaps 'statement' would be a better translation, since Aquinas speaks of an *enuntiabile* both as existing *in voce,* and as existing *in intellectu.* In the present context, Aquinas is thinking of *enuntiabilia* as both objects of judgment and bearers of truth, so 'proposition' seemed a fair translation.

[15]It might be argued that a more complicated construal of the propositions expressed by tensed sentences as tenseless and constant in truth-value can be made to mesh with an account of belief as a relation to a proposition. (J. J. C. Smart and Hans Reichenbach have attempted to offer construals of this type.) Any such construal I know of either fails to assign the right truth-conditions to some statements, or else covertly helps itself to temporal indexicals. Moreover, propositions do not in general have world-invariant truth-values. Given the strong formal similarities between modal operators and temporal operators, it is difficult to see the motivation for giving an account of propositions which allows them to be, as David Kaplan puts it, modally neutral, without also allowing them to be temporally neutral (see Kaplan, "Demonstratives," unpublished manuscript).

sometimes not to exist, so without any change in divine knowledge
God knows a proposition [*enuntiabile*] sometimes to be true, and
sometimes false" (ST Ia.14.15 *ad* 3). Aquinas' reply to the same objection in *De veritate* 2.13 provides a bit more detail on God's knowledge
of propositions:

> [God] knows of different propositions when they are true and when
> they are false; because He knows each one to be true at that time at
> which it is true. For He knows, say, the proposition that Peter is
> running to be true at at that time at which it is true; and similarly for the
> proposition that Peter will run, and the like. Consequently, even
> though it is not true that Peter is running, but rather that he ran, God
> nevertheless knows both of these things; because He at once sees each
> time at which each proposition is true. (DV 2.13 *ad* 7)

In explaining how God has this kind of time-indexed knowledge,
Aquinas compares God's knowledge of singular propositions to our
knowledge of propositions concerning species. In knowing the essence of a species, Aquinas says, we know all the properties that are the
per se accidents of that species. And, Aquinas holds, God knows not
only the specific essence (*essentiam universalem speciei*) of each individual, but also the particular essence (*essentiam singularem*) of each individual. (This applies to merely possible as well as actual individuals.)
But the individual essence of an individual is related to all of its
accidents (including existence at a time) in the way that the species
essence of an individual is related to its *per se* accidents. Hence, Aquinas concludes, in knowing the individual essence of each thing, God
immediately knows all the facts about when it exists, and what properties it has when it exists (cf. DV 2.7, *responsio*).[16] To put it in
Leibnizian terms, God knows (all) time-indexed truths by (atemporally) having a complete and nonsuccessive grasp of every individual concept.

Clearly, if God's knowledge is like that, it does not involve mutability. But have we saved divine omniscience as well as divine immutability? Aquinas obviously thinks so: that is, he supposes that if for
every (actual or possible) individual and every time, God knows what
properties that individual has at that time, and if for every (tensed)
proposition and every time, God knows the truth-value of that proposition at that time, then God is ignorant of nothing.

There are, however, familiar arguments purporting to show that

---

[16]There are interesting questions here about how to put this passage together with
passages highlighted in Chapter 3 on the relation of essence to accidents; for reasons of
space I don't pursue them here.

there is information about the world which could not be the object of the kind of knowledge Aquinas attributes to God. Suppose I know that the Red Sox game starts at 2:15, but don't know what time it is. I walk over to my television set, turn it on, and see Bruce Hurst delivering the first pitch of the game. Clearly, I have gotten hold of new information: that the Red Sox game is starting now, that it is now approximately 2:15, and so on. This new information, it appears, is not of a kind that could be captured by any proposition or set of propositions free from temporal indexicality.[17] Consequently, it appears to be information of a kind that an atemporal God must be ignorant of.

A defender of Aquinas could try to fend off this conclusion in a number of ways. He might argue that our belief that there are facts about what time it is, and about what is happening now, is an illusory one. This position is not a very attractive one, and is certainly un-Thomistic. Second, a defender of Aquinas might try to show that only our inability to understand how rich the set of temporal-indexicality-free propositions is leads us to suppose that there is information we could not get hold of by getting hold of all the propositions free from such indexicality. The difficulty is in seeing why we should think this is so. Third, he could argue that even though temporal beings are ignorant of something, if they don't know what time it is, or what is happening now, the same does not hold for God, just because He is not in time. This defense fits well with Aquinas' views, and has a greater degree of intuitive plausibility than the other two. Again, we may appeal to the analogous case of locatively indexical propositions. Knowledge about where I am, or about whether something is happening here, is not to be captured by propositions free from locative indexicality. (As John Perry notes, if I had no beliefs at all about where I was, no amount of looking at atlases would help me find out.) Thus I would have to be ignorant of something, if I had no access to locatively indexical propositions. It does not obviously follow that a being who lacked spatial location, but knew all the true nonlocatively indexical propositions, would be less than omniscient, if he did not know any propositions featuring such indexicals. Somehow, I feel, if such a being knew all the true locative propositions that did not feature locative indexicals, there would be no more locative facts *for him* to

---

[17]For arguments to this effect, see Richard Gale, *The Language of Time* (London: Routledge & Kegan Paul, 1968); Arthur Prior, "Thank Goodness That's Over," *Philosophy* (1959); and John Perry, "The Problem of the Essential Indexical," *Nous* 13 (1979): 3–23.

know. If that is so, couldn't it work for temporal location the way it does for spatial location? I argue that it does; in order to do so I need to provide a sketch David Lewis' theory of *de se* belief.[18]

The tradition in California Semantics (as Putnam calls it) is to treat belief as a relation between a person and a proposition, and to reify a proposition as the set of possible worlds in which the proposition holds (or, equivalently, the characteristic function of that set). On this picture, someone who believes that there are pigs is of the opinion that the actual world is a member of a certain set—*viz.*, the set of worlds in which there are pigs. We could think of this in a slightly different way: someone who believes that there are pigs takes the world he inhabits— that is, the actual world—to be a pig-inhabited world. In his thought, he locates himself in a pig-inhabited region of logical space. This is equivalent to saying that he takes himself to have a certain property— namely, the property of inhabiting some pig-inhabited world. So there is an alternative to saying that what it is for Jones to believe that there are pigs is for him to stand in a certain relation to the set of pig-inhabited worlds; we may say that what it is for Jones to have that belief is for him to stand in a relation—which Lewis calls *self-ascription*—to the property *inhabiting a world in which there are pigs*. Whenever one can construe the object of a belief as a set of worlds, one can also construe it as a property, since for every set of worlds there is the corresponding property of inhabiting some member of that set of worlds.

The advantage of taking properties rather than California propositions to be the objects of belief is that we get a better account of indexical beliefs—one on which we see how certain indexical beliefs can float free from certain nonindexical ones. For example, even if I am Jones, I can believe that I am six feet tall, without believing that Jones is six feet tall, or vice versa (as long as I don't believe I am Jones). Hence the object of my belief that Jones is six feet tall is not the object of my belief that I am six feet tall, even though I am Jones. This raises a problem for the California propositional account of belief, since (given that I am Jones) the set of worlds in which Jones is six feet tall is just the set of worlds in which I am six feet tall.[19]

---

[18]Lewis' theory is set out in "Attitudes De Dicto and De Se," *Philosophical Review* 88 (1979): 513–43; see also his "Individuation by Acquaintance and Stipulation," *Philosophical Review* 92 (1983): 3–32.

[19]Actually, one can give a *subtilior* California propositional account of belief which allows for the possibility that Jones believes that he is six feet tall, without believing that Jones is six feet tall, or vice versa; Stalnaker offers that kind of account in "Indexical Belief," *Synthese* 49 (1981): 129–51. I think the defense of the compatibility

Lewis' approach faces no such problem: even if I am in fact Jones, I can self-ascribe the property of *being six feet tall* without self-ascribing the (extensionally inequivalent) property, *living in a world where Jones is six feet tall*. Or to take another case that is problematic for the (standard) California propositional account, if I don't know that I am Jones, I can believe that Jones is Jones, without believing that I am: for I can self-ascribe *inhabiting a world where Jones is Jones,* without self-ascribing *being Jones*.

Just as I can believe that Jones is Jones, without believing that I am Jones (even if I am), I can also believe that 2:15 is 2:15, without believing that 2:15 is now (even if it is). Lewis' theory handles this as follows: for me to believe at 2:15 that 2:15 is 2:15 is for my 2:15 slice to self-ascribe the (uninteresting) property of *inhabiting a world in which 2:15 is 2:15;* for me to believe at 2:15 that 2:15 is now is for my 2:15 slice to self-ascribe the more interesting property of *being at 2:15*. We may extend Lewis' treatment in the obvious way to explain how I can believe at 2:15 that the Sox game starts at 2:15, without believing that it starts now (or vice versa). In the first case, my 2:15 slice self-ascribes *inhabiting a world where the Sox game starts at 2:15;* in the second, that slice self-ascribes *being when the Sox game starts*.

Lewis concludes that the basic category of belief is *de se* belief or self-ascription of a property: *de dicto* belief is a special case of *de se* belief, in which the property self-ascribed is exemplified by all of one's world-mates or none, and *de re* belief is another special case of *de se* belief.

If Lewis' theory is adopted, omniscience will not longer be defined in terms of knowing all and only true propositions. Instead, it will be defined along these lines:

> X is omniscient if and only if X knowingly (that is, in such a way as to satisfy the conditions for knowledge) self-ascribes all and only those properties that X exemplifies.

Surely any being who satisfies the *definiens* will be omniscient: such a being will knowingly self-ascribe every property it has, and were it to self-ascribe any other properties, would have false beliefs!

If, like Aquinas, we hold that God is outside of time, we can now give a satisfying explanation of why, although a temporal being all of whose information about the world is nontemporally indexical is

---

of omniscience and immutability I provide presupposing Lewis' account of belief has a counterpart presupposing Stalnaker's; considerations of space prevent me from saying here how it would go.

ignorant of something, the same is not true of God. When I learn that it is now 3:00, my 3:00 slice comes to self-ascribe a property it has—to wit, *being at 3:00*. And when I learn that the Red Sox game is starting now, my current slice comes to self-ascribe another such property—*being when the Sox game starts*. By contrast, were an atemporal God to believe that it is now 3:00, or believe that the Sox game is starting now, He would have false beliefs: for in that case, God would self-ascribe a property (*being at 3:00, being when the Sox game starts*) which He does not have. Again, once we have taken properties to be the objects of knowledge and belief, we can ask no more of an omniscient God than that He knowingly self-ascribe all and only the properties He exemplifies; and the prima facie plausible claim that if *we* know that it is now 3:00, so must an omniscient God, turns out to be the absurd claim that God must knowingly self-ascribe the same properties we do, even if we exemplify them, and He does not.

This may be a good time to take stock. Against arguments purporting to show that an omniscient being must change to keep track of a changing world, Aquinas maintains that there is no inconsistency in the idea of an omniscient but timeless and changeless God. If we grant that a timeless knower is possible—and I don't know of any conclusive argument to the contrary—then it seems that such a being could be both changeless and omniscient. So there is no straight and short path from the assertion that God is omniscient (and change exists) to the denial of God's immutability or atemporality.

Timelessness and Openness

Following Boethius, Aquinas thinks that the notion of eternity is crucial, not just in reconciling God's omniscience with His immutability, but also in squaring His infallibility and omniscience with the genuine openness of the future. Before trying to make out whether this is so, I shall try to say why there is a problem about supposing that God has infallible foreknowledge of future contingents, and why Aquinas thinks that problem can be resolved if, but only if, we maintain that God's knowledge is eternal rather than temporal.

Let us begin—in Thomistic fashion—by thinking of propositions as (possibly) having different truth-values at different times. (In the following, for the sake of familiarity and expositional simplicity, I take propositions rather than properties to be the objects of knowledge and belief.) For example, we may think of the proposition *it is raining* as true at all and only those times when it is raining, and we may think of the proposition *it was raining* as true at all and only those times later than some time at which the proposition *it is raining* is true. We may call a proposition *inevitably true* or *settled* at a time just in case it will turn out to have been true at that time, no matter which future compossible with the history of the world up to and including that time is realized; we may call a proposition *contingent* at a time just in case neither it nor its negation is inevitable then. If a proposition P is contingent at a time, I shall say that it is not (then) settled whether P, or that it is (then) *open* whether P. Following John Burgess,[20] I call a possible future that is compossible with the history of the world up to and including a certain time a *then-possible* future, and a possible future that is compossible with the history of the world up to and including the present a *now-possible* history. The proposition that Julius Caesar crossed the Rubicon is now inevitably true, as in the proposition that I am in London now: no matter which now-possible future is realized, it will be true in the future that it was true now that Caesar crossed the Rubicon, and that I'm in London now. The proposition that I shall be in London in three years time is, or at least appears to be, contingent: it is (apparently) neither the case that, whatever now-possible future is realized, it will be true in the future that it was true now that I would be in London in three years time, nor the case that whatever now-possible future is realized, it will be true in the future that it was true now that I wouldn't be in London in three years time.

Now, suppose that we think that God is temporal, and now has infallible knowledge of some proposition about the future—say, that there will be a sea battle in the South Atlantic in 1999. If God now knows that there will be a 1999 South Atlantic sea battle, then God now believes there will be such a sea battle. And if it is true now that God now believes there will be a 1999 South Atlantic sea battle, then, it would seem, it is inevitably true now. The facts about what someone believes now are what they are, however the openness of the future gets filled in; they are not up for grabs, depending on which now-possible future turns out to be actual. (How can what happens tomorrow, or ten thousand years from now, make any difference to what God or anyone else believes right now? Compare this to the case of the correctness of what someone believes now: whether or not someone's current belief about the occurrence of a South Atlantic sea battle in 1999 turns out to have been correct is up for grabs, depending on which now-possible future turns out to be actual.) So it is inevitably true now that God now believes there will be a sea battle in the South Atlantic in 1999. And assuming divine infallibility, it is inevitably true now that if God now believes that there will be a South

[20]See his "The Unreal Future," *Theoria* 44 (1978): 157–74.

Atlantic sea battle in 1999, then there will be such a sea battle. (Were this condition not met, it could turn out that something God now believes was false, which is inconsistent with God's infallibility.) From this it follows that it is inevitably true now that there will be a South Atlantic sea battle in 1999, since any inevitably true conditional whose antecedent is inevitably true has an inevitably true consequent. We have moved from the premiss that God now has infallible knowledge of an arbitrary proposition, to the conclusion that that proposition is now inevitably true. If God's foreknowledge is in each case infallible, then the object of God's current foreknowledge is never a contingent proposition: if there are contingent propositions about the future, not even God can now have (infallible) foreknowledge of them. Nor is this just a fact about the present: we can use the same argument to show that whatever was or is or will be contingent at a time cannot have been or be (infallibly) foreknown by God at such time as it was or is or will be contingent.[21]

Aquinas is familiar with an argument essentially like this one,[22] and accepts its conclusion. At DV 2.12 he says that, just because future contingents may or may not happen, may or may not be precluded, they cannot be foreknown with certainty; and he explicitly draws the conclusion that not even God could have (certain) knowledge of future contingents as future.[23] In his commentary on Aristotle's *De interpreta-*

---

[21]Here of course 'contingent' does not mean 'true at some possible worlds and false at others', but rather, 'true on some now-possible ways of filling in the future, and false on others'.

[22]Although the argument Aquinas considers at ST Ia.14.13 and DP 2.12 has the same structure as the one set out here, it relies on the premiss that if it is true that God knew that such-and-such would happen, then it is inevitably true that God knew it would, rather than the premiss that if it is true that God believed that such-and-such would happen, then it is inevitably true that God believed it would. The former claim is more controversial than the latter; perhaps we can retrospectively credit someone with knowledge of a proposition that was then evitable, if we can say retrospectively that the belief "came true," and that person had the right sort of reasons for having that belief. Consequently, I have substituted a less dubitable premiss for a more dubitable one.

[23]"Contingens, ut futurum est, per nullam cognitionem sciri, cui falsitas subesse non possit; unde cum divinae scientiae non subsit falsitas nec subesse possit, impossibile esset quod de contingentibus futuris scientiam haberet Deus, si cognosceret ea ut futura sunt" (DP 2.12, *responsio*). There is, however, a problem reconciling this view of Aquinas' with his beliefs about prophecy. In the *Summa contra Gentiles,* Aquinas avers that God has revealed to prophets how future contingents will turn out: "The gift of prophecy would not provide sufficient testimony to the truth of the faith, if prophecy were not of those things that can be known only by God. These are . . . things hidden in our hearts, and future contingents" (SCG III.154). Moreover, Aquinas thinks, when God has revealed to a prophet that a future contingent matter will turn out a certain way, the prophet knows with perfect certainty that it will turn out that way, because what the prophet believes about the future could not possibly turn out to be false. ("Oportet igitur eandem esse veritatem propheticae cognitionis et enuntiationis quae

tione, he discusses the unknowability of future contingents in somewhat more detail. There he says that, since future states of affairs do
not yet exist, they cannot be known directly, but only in their causes,
which already exist. If the future state of affairs has a present cause
upon which it will inevitably follow, it may be known with certainty;
if the future state of affairs has a present inclining, but not necessitating

---

est cognitionis divinae, cui impossibile est subesse falsum. Unde prophetiae non potest
subesse falsum" [ST II.II.171.6, *responsio*].) If a prophet can have before-the-fact
infallible knowledge of his open future, just as God can have timeless knowledge of it,
what becomes of Aquinas' claim that future contingents cannot be (infallibly) known *as*
future and contingent? I think Aquinas would say that, *via* divine revelation, a prophet
knows future contingents in the way God knows them—as present (as they are in
themselves), rather than as future (as they are in their causes) (cf. ST II.II.171.6, esp. *ad*
1). Knowing future contingents as future is not the same thing as knowing future
contingents before the fact, although, in any case not involving divine revelation, one
can only know future contingents before the fact, by knowing them as future.

So, for Aquinas, a prophet can have infallible knowledge of how his open future will
turn out, but only by "tapping into" God's timeless infallible knowledge of his open
future. If a being has infallible foreknowledge of how his open future will turn out, that
knowledge must be derivative. It follows that if God's beliefs could not possibly turn
out to be false, then God could not have before-the-fact knowledge of future contingents, since His knowledge could not be derivative, any more than it could be
fallible.

Given that Aquinas supposes that in the special case of divine revelation a prophet
can have infallible foreknowledge of how the open future will turn out, should he make
that supposition? I don't think so. As I argue at pages 133–34, Aquinas can consistently
maintain that, inevitably, what God (timelessly) believes about whether it will turn out
that Q will not turn out to be false, even though it is now open whether it will turn out
that Q, only if he supposes that it is likewise (now) open what God (timelessly) believes
about whether Q is true at some time in our future. Similarly, Aquinas can coherently
maintain that in some cases, when God has revealed to a prophet whether it will turn
out that Q,

> (i) it is inevitable at the time the revelation is made that what the prophet
> believes about whether it will turn out that Q will not turn out to be false,
> and open at that time whether it will turn out that Q.

only if he maintains that, in such cases,

> (ii) it is open, then, what the prophet believes about whether it will turn out
> that Q.

But if, for example, the prophet's belief that it will turn out that Q has already led him
to prophesy that it will come to pass that Q—if the prophet's belief has already left its
mark on the world—how can it not be settled that the prophet believes that it will turn
out that Q? More generally, how could the way the open future goes make any
difference to what the prophet believes concerning the open future? (Some argumenta-
tive backing for this appeal to the reader's intuitions is provided on pages 134–35.)
Because I don't think that the way the open future turns out could make any difference
to what the prophet then believes about it, I think Aquinas would be better off
maintaining that God could no more give someone infallible foreknowledge of future
contingents than He could present them with a round square.

cause, it may be known conjecturally (*per conjecturam*); and if that future state of affairs has no present cause that is any more inclined to its futurition than its nonfuturition, it cannot be known in any way (IPH I.1.14). It follows that God could at best have conjectural foreknowledge of future contingent states of affairs, and could not have even that sort of knowledge about future contingent states of affairs that lack inclining as well as necessitating causes.

Aquinas is not perturbed by this result, since he holds that God, as eternal, is not the kind of being who could have foreknowledge of anything. Foreknowledge involves knowing before the fact, and hence existing before the fact; and God does not exist before, or after, or at the same time as anything else. Events and states of affairs are never future for Him, or past, or temporally present, although they are all quasi-present to His eternity.

The notion of quasi-presence, Aquinas thinks, gives us some insight into how it is that if God's knowledge is not temporally located, it can be at once infallible and of what is (for us) future and contingent. For, Aquinas says, there is no problem about how one can have infallible knowledge of an event that has come about contingently, when it is present. I see Socrates sitting in front of me, and judge that he is sitting there. My judgment is infallible—in the sense that it will not turn out to have been wrong, no matter which now-possible future is realized—and yet Socrates' sitting there came about contingently, unlike, say, an eclipse of the sun, whose prior causes made its occurrence inevitable even before it took place (cf. DV 2.12, *responsio*). In the same way, God has infallible knowledge of all the states of affairs that are "present" to His eternity, including all the ones that are contingent and future with respect to us:

> What God sees is future with respect to another thing that it succeeds in time; but to God's sight, which is not in time, but outside it, it is not future, but present. . . . Just as our sight is infallible when we see contingents as they are present, and yet this does not take away from the fact that they come about contingently; so God infallibly sees all contingents, whether they are present to us, or past, or future, because to Him they are not future. (DV 2.12, *responsio*)

In the same way that we can now see, all at once, the present temporal segment of an ongoing event, God can "see," from outside of time, "all at once," the maximal temporal event that has every other event as a part. And in the same way that our seeing the present segment of an ongoing event is consistent with its having been contingent, or "open" whether or not that event would occur, God's timelessly "seeing" a particular event take place is consistent with its being open now whether or not that event will take place.[24]

It may help to elucidate Aquinas' thought here if we draw an analogy with our descendants' knowledge of now-contingent future states of affairs and propositions about the future. As long as we suppose that there is contingency about how the future will turn out, there is no problem about supposing that our descendants will have certain and infallible knowledge of events or states of affairs that have not yet come about, and will come about contingently (that is, take place on some but not all now-possible futures). To put the point in terms of propositions: there is no problem about supposing that our descendants will have certain and infallible knowledge of some propositions that are now contingent (that is, such that neither they nor their negations are inevitably true).[25] Of course, if Aquinas is right, we cannot know for certain which now-contingent future states of affairs and which now-contingent propositions our descendants will have certain and infallible knowledge of; otherwise, we could have certain knowledge of future contingents.[26] Be that as it may, we may and should suppose that our descendants will have certain and infallible knowledge of some batch or other of now-contingent propositions about the future—or, to put matters more Thomistically, certain and infallible knowledge of some future states of affairs or others whose futurition is contingent.[27]

[24]If God "sees" the maximal temporal event, it is—as Aquinas thinks of it—a kind of seeing quite unlike the ordinary kind, since the ordinary kind involves being caused to be in a certain state by what one is seeing. For Aquinas, God's relation to what He "sees" is in some ways less like our relation to what we see than it is like our relation to what we "see" in a dream. (We are not causally affected by the winged horses we "see" in a dream.) Of course, what the dreamer "sees" in a dream matches his environment by chance, if at all; what God "sees" could not but match His actual environment (because, Aquinas would say, it is His "seeing" it that makes that environment actual).

[25]We might suppose, for example, that although each of the propositions *there is or there will be a sea battle in the South Atlantic* and *there is not and there will not be a sea battle in the South Atlantic* is now-contingent, our descendants in the South Atlantic at the last moment of time will have certain and infallible knowledge of one or the other of those propositions.

[26]Suppose I know for certain that some of my descendants will know a particular now-contingent proposition—say, the proposition that a sea battle is taking place or will take place in the South Atlantic. If I have certain knowledge that there is no sea battle going on in the South Atlantic now, and a minimum of logical acumen, I can move from my certain knowledge that a sea battle is taking place or will take place in the South Atlantic to certain knowledge that a sea battle will take place in the South Atlantic. But, as we have seen, Aquinas thinks this is the sort of thing we can know at best *per conjecturam* (except in the special [and, I think, problematic] case of divine revelation).

[27]Aquinas' view on future contingents is consistent with the idea that even we right now could in some cases have a pretty good hunch—*per conjecturam* knowledge—that

The reason our descendants can have infallible knowledge of some now-contingent states of affairs, and infallibly know some now-contingent propositions, Aquinas would say, is that those states of affairs belong not to the future of our descendants, but to their present (or perhaps their past); and those propositions are about our descendants' present (or past), although they are about our future. But, Aquinas thinks, just as some future contingent events and states of affairs are present for our descendants, all future contingent events (together with all other events, whether or not they came about contingently) are "present" to God's eternity. So God can have infallible knowledge of (what are for us) future contingents. Just as we may suppose that our descendants will have infallible knowledge of some future contingent states of affairs or other, we may suppose that God eternally has knowledge of all such states of affairs—whatever they turn out to be. The sort of knowledge God has of those states of affairs would more aptly be called simul-knowledge than foreknowledge.

Does Aquinas' attempt to reconcile God's knowledge of future contingents with the openness of the future succeed? As I try to show below, it avoids at least one (pressing) difficulty besetting any attempt at reconciliation on which God's knowledge is temporal.

Whether God's knowledge is temporal or timeless, *God believes that Q* will be contingent at a time if and only if Q is contingent at that time. Whether we construe "God believes that Q" as meaning "God now believes that Q," or as meaning "God timelessly believes that Q," we shall have to say, on the theological assumptions in play, that Q and *God believes that Q* are necessarily equivalent. And if two propositions are necessarily equivalent, then for any time t, both of them or neither of them are contingent at t. (If the reader is puzzled about what it could mean to say, for example, that it is *now* contingent whether God *timelessly* believes that Q, she may think of it as meaning: it is neither the case that, no matter which now-possible future is realized, it will turn out to have been true then that God timelessly believes that Q, nor the case that, no matter which now-possible future is realized, it will turn out to have been true now that God does not timelessly believe that Q. This condition will be satisfied if Q is now contingent.) By the same reasoning, if Q was contingent at some past time, then it was contingent at that time whether God (then, or timelessly) believed that Q.[28]

---

our descendants will have certain and infallible knowledge of a particular now-contingent proposition *P*.

[28]Unfortunately, Aquinas never says this clearly; in fact, he says some very puzzling things that sound inconsistent with it (see, e.g., ST 1a.14.13 *ad* 2).

Suppose it was contingent, or "open," up until 1982 whether a sea battle in the South Atlantic would take place that year. By the considerations just advanced, someone who thinks God has always had infallible foreknowledge of future contingents will have to say:

(i) Ten thousand years ago, it was not inevitably true that God then believed a South Atlantic sea battle would take place in 1982, and ten thousand years ago, it was not inevitably true that God then believed no South Atlantic sea battle would take place in 1982.

Someone who holds that God has timeless knowledge of future contingents will have to say:

(ii) Ten thousand years ago, it was not inevitably true that God timelessly believes that the tensed proposition *a sea battle takes place in the South Atlantic* is true in 1982, and ten thousand years ago, it was not inevitably true that God timelessly believes that the tensed proposition *a sea battle takes place in the South Atlantic* is false in 1982.[29]

Someone might suppose that these claims are equally defensible (or indefensible). But (ii) is vulnerable to the following line of argument:

Suppose God had believed ten thousand years ago that no South Atlantic sea battle would take place in 1982. Would God have been just the same then intrinsically as He actually was? If so, the difference between God's having believed ten thousand years ago that there would be a sea battle in the South Atlantic in 1982, and His having believed then that there would be no such sea battle, would be a purely extrinsic difference. Since a purely extrinsic property could not make all the difference between believing and disbelieving in the occurrence of a 1982 South Atlantic sea battle (cf. the first section of this chapter), if God had believed ten thousand years ago that there would not be a South Atlantic sea battle in 1982, He would have had some intrinsic property that He in fact lacked. So, if it was open ten thousand years ago whether God believed then—or ten thousand years earlier—that there would be a sea battle in the South Atlantic in 1982, it was also open ten thousand years ago

[29]I put matters this way because for Aquinas what God knows (timelessly) is that tensed propositions are true at some times, and false at others (see ST Ia.14.15 *ad* 3).

whether God had a certain intrinsic property then (and open then whether He had had that intrinsic property, twenty thousand years ago). But there cannot be openness at a time about what intrinsic properties a being has at that time, or had at any time earlier than that time. Equivalently: how the openness of the future relative to a certain time gets filled in could not make any difference to what *intrinsic* properties anything has at that time, or has had at any time prior to that time. (If it could, then the past and the present would not be fixed; but they are.)[30]

The above is, I think, a cogent argument against (i). Because, however, my focus is on Aquinas' theory of God's knowledge of future contingents, I won't defend its cogency against various possible objections.) Suppose we try to advance a parallel argument against (ii). That argument will depend on the premiss that there was no contingency or openness ten thousand years ago about what intrinsic properties God *timelessly* has.

I used to think this premiss was obviously true.[31] Certainly, for most timeless entities one is likely to think of (say, pure sets, or numbers) there could never be any openness about what intrinsic properties those entities timelessly have. If there were, then the history of the world up to a certain time would be compossible with a pure set or a number's having a certain intrinsic property, and compossible with that pure set or number's lacking that property. To put this another way, there would be two possible histories or worlds, with the same initial segment (or duplicate initial segments, if no two worlds overlap), in just one of which it would be true that the pure set or the number had a certain intrinsic property. Since the intrinsic properties of numbers, pure sets, and the like do not vary between worlds a fortiori they do not vary between worlds sharing an initial segment. By contrast, if God is a timeless entity, He will be one whose intrinsic properties vary from world to world (see the first section of this chapter). If His intrinsic properties can vary between worlds, it is not clear why they could not vary between worlds that have the same initial segment (or duplicate initial segments). And if they could, there can be openness about what intrinsic properties God timelessly has.

Because the argument offered above against (i) does not go through against (ii), I'm inclined to agree with Aquinas that the prospects for

---

[30]John Martin Fischer discusses an argument of this kind in "Freedom and Foreknowledge," *Philosophical Review* 92 (1983): 67–79.
[31]I was made to by see that it is not by William Alston.

reconciling God's omniscience with the openness of the future are brighter if we maintain that He has timeless rather than temporal knowledge of future contingents. I used to think, though, that a different sort of argument showed the unworkability of Aquinas' attempt at reconciliation.

The following story seemed possibly true to me:

> Ten years ago, a creature on another planet built a very power-ful bomb—one that would destroy our entire galaxy if deto-nated. He attached a detonator to the bomb and flipped the detonator's switch. Before the creature flipped the switch, it was open whether or not he would; but once he had flipped it, it was and forever would be settled that he had. The creature did not realize that it was an indeterministic or chancy matter whether, once the switch had been flipped, the bomb would go off. But it was a chancy matter (the detonator had a ran-domizer inside it) and the bomb did not go off. As we know now, God allowed the switch to be flipped, and He believed (then, or timelessly) that the flipping of the switch would not cause the galaxy to be destroyed. After the alien had flipped the switch—but before he realized that the detonator had failed—he saw for the first time what a monstrous thing he had done; he dismantled the bomb, repented, and was reconciled with God. Again, God believed (then, or timelessly) that the flip-ping of the switch would harm no one, and would lead to the creature's repenting. He allowed the creature to flip the switch, because (i) He believed that the flipping would harm no one and would lead the flipper to repent, and (ii) He had an (on-balance) desire to allow any action that would harm no-body and lead a sinner to repent. Now, God also had an (on-balance) desire to prevent acts that cause the galaxy to be destroyed. So, unless God had thought that the flipping of the switch would not cause the destruction of the galaxy, He never would have allowed the switch to be flipped. More awkwardly, but equivalently: if God had not believed that the flipping of the switch would not cause the destruction of the galaxy, He would not have allowed the switch to be flipped.

Now, consider the precise time at which the switch was flipped—call it t. At t it was settled that the switch was being flipped, but it was open whether or not the flipping of the switch would cause the de-struction of the galaxy. A counterfactual is true at a time if it is open at that time whether the antecedent is true, and settled at that time that the consequent is true.[32] Hence it was true at t that

> (a) (Even) if the flipping of the switch were to cause the destruction of the galaxy, it would (still) be true that the switch was being flipped right now.

If at t it is open whether the flipping of the switch will cause the destruction of the galaxy, and if (as Aquinas supposes) God is infallibly omniscient, then at t it is open whether God believes the flipping of the switch will cause the destruction of the galaxy, and likewise open whether God *does not* believe the flipping of the switch *will not* cause the destruction of the galaxy. (There is a then-possible world [one whose history up to and including then matches that of the actual world] in which God does not believe that the flipping of the switch will not cause the destruction of the galaxy, and a then-possible world in which God does believe that the flipping of the switch will not cause the destruction of the galaxy.) Accordingly, it is true at t that

> (b) (Even) if God did not believe that the flipping of the switch would not cause the destruction of the galaxy, it would (still) be true that the switch was being flipped right now.

But, Aquinas would suppose, it is a necessary truth that nothing takes place unless God allows it to take place. If it is true that if it were that A, then it would be that B, and it is true that, necessarily, if B then C, it must also be true that if it were that A, then it would be that C.[33]

---

[32]See Bas van Fraassen, "Report on Tense Logic," in *Modern Logic: A Survey*, ed. Evandro Agazzi (Dordrecht: D. Reidel, 1981), for a discussion of the validity of the inference from "It is not settled that not-A" and "It is settled that B" to "(Even) if it were that A, it would be that B." Clearly, if that inference is valid, so is the inference from "It is open whether A" and "It is settled that B" to "(Even) if it were that A, it would be that B," since "It is open whether A" entails "It is not settled that not-A." For some related issues involving the interplay of settledness, openness, and counterfactuals, see Richmond Thomason and Anil Gupta, "A Theory of Conditionals in the Context of Branching Time," in *Ifs*, ed. William Harper, Robert Stalnaker, and Glenn Pearce (Dordrecht: D. Reidel, 1980).

[33]Those who do not find the validity of this inference evident, and are familiar with the Stalnaker-Thomason semantics for counterfactual conditionals, may find this explanation of its validity helpful: if it is true that if it were that A, then it would be that B, then the closest A-world is a B-world. But if as a matter of broadly logical or metaphysical necessity, if B, then C, then every B-world is a C-world. In that case, the closest A-world to the actual world is a C-world, and the counterfactual, if it were that A, it would be that C, is true.

So, Aquinas would have to say, (b) entails

    (c) (Even) if God did not believe that the flipping of the switch
        would not cause the destruction of the galaxy, He (still) would
        allow the switch to be flipped.

But if (c) was true at *t,* then, it would seem, it is true now that

    (d) (Even) if God had not believed that the flipping of the switch
        would not cause the destruction of the galaxy, He (still) would
        have allowed the switch to be flipped.

If it was already settled at *t* that God allowed the switch to be flipped,
and it was open at *t* whether God did not believe that the flipping of the
switch would not cause the destruction of the galaxy, then it is true
now that even if God had not had the belief in question, He would
have allowed the switch to be flipped. (Compare: if it was settled at
9:00 that I was betting this coin would come up heads, and open
whether it would not come up heads, then—just as it was true *then*
that, even if it did not come up heads, I [still] would be betting on its
coming up heads now—it is true *now* that, even if it had not come up
heads, I [still] would have bet on its coming up heads then. Both
counterfactuals come out true, because of the counterfactual indepen-
dence of what is then settled from what is then up for grabs.)
    If, however, (d) is true now, it looks as if it cannot after all be true
that

    (e) If God had not believed the flipping of the switch would cause
        the destruction of the galaxy, He would not have allowed the
        switch to be flipped.

It cannot be true both that (even) if it had been that *A,* it (still) would
have been that *B,* and that if it had been that *A,* it would not have been
that *B,* unless the antecedent *A* is unentertainable; and in this case it
clearly is not.
    So it looks as though Aquinas would have to say that the story just
told could not possibly be true in its entirety. He would have to insist
that, as a matter of logical necessity, either there was not after all a time
when it was settled that the switch was flipped, and open whether the
galaxy would be destroyed; or God did not actually have all the on-
balance desires ascribed to Him in the story; or—in spite of the fact
that He had those on-balance desires—it was not true that if God had

not timelessly believed the flipping of the switch would not cause the bomb to go off, He would not have allowed the switch to be flipped.

At one time, I thought this showed the unacceptability of Aquinas' account of God's knowledge; it seemed to me much more plausible that there was something wrong with Aquinas' account, than that the apparently coherent bomb story was necessarily false. But a defender of Aquinas could say that our inclination to think that the bomb story is true in its entirety is based on an understandable failure to keep in mind the logical peculiarities of an infallible believer. She might defend this view as follows:

> We are willing to say that the following sort of thing is possible: when Jones put his money on Alipede in the fifth at Belmont, it was settled that he was putting his money on Alipede, but open whether doing so would make him any richer. He bet on Alipede, because he thought betting on Alipede would make him richer, and he had an (on-balance) desire to be richer; but if he had not believed betting on Alipede would make him any richer, he would not have bet on Alipede.[34] So we are tempted to think that, similarly, it could

[34]Some may object here that, if Jones is free to bet and free not to bet, then there is no fact of the matter about whether he would have bet had his beliefs been different than they actually were (cf. Robert Adams, "Middle Knowledge and the Problem of Evil," *American Philosophical Quarterly* 14 [1977] pp. 109–17). Someone of this persuasion might also object to the bomb story on the grounds that there is no fact of the matter about whether God would have allowed the switch to be flipped, if He had not believed that the flipping of the switch would not cause the destruction of the galaxy. In fact, I find it intuitively very plausible that counterfactuals involving what free agents would freely do in counterfactual circumstances are sometimes true; and I think that this intuition can be squared with the idea that a free agent *might* have done more than one thing in a counterfactual circumstance. (For a discussion of cases in which we are pretheoretically disposed to say that counterfactuals involving what free agents would freely do in counterfactual circumstances are true, see the last section of Adams' paper; for a view of "might" counterfactuals which allows us to square the claim that the agent *would* have done this in such-and-such a counterfactual circumstance, with the claim that the agent *might* have done something else in that circumstance, see Lewis, Postscript D to "Counterfactual Dependence and Time's Arrow," in *Philosophical Papers,* vol. 2 (Oxford: Oxford University Press, 1986), pp. 63–66. For present purposes, though, it is not necessary to resolve this issue. We could tell a version of the bomb story in which, rather than saying it was true that had God not believed that the flipping of the switch would not cause the destruction of the galaxy, He would not have allowed the switch to be flipped, we said only that it was *not* true that had God not believed that the flipping of the switch would not cause the destruction of the galaxy, He (still) would have allowed the switch to be flipped. If Aquinas has to deny that the original story could be true in its entirety, he also has to deny that the modified story could be.

be true that if God had not had certain beliefs about the (then) open future, He would not have allowed (or made) the (then) settled past or present be a certain way. But this temptation must be resisted, because there is a crucial difference between the two cases. If the story is filled in the right way, we are willing to say that Jones would not have bet on Alipede, unless he had thought doing so would make him richer, because we believe that

(A) If Jones had not believed that betting on Alipede would make him richer, and had had an on-balance desire to be richer, he would not have bet on Alipede.

and

(B) If Jones had not believed that betting on Alipede would make him richer, he (still) would have had an on-balance desire to be richer.

Similarly, we should hold that if God had not believed that the flipping of the switch would not cause the destruction of the galaxy, he would not have allowed the switch to be flipped, if we think that

(C) If God had not believed that the flipping of the switch would not cause the destruction of the galaxy, and God had had an on-balance desire to prevent acts causing the destruction of the galaxy, then God would not have al-lowed the switch to be flipped.

and

(D) If God had not believed that the flipping of the switch would not cause the destruction of the galaxy, then God (still) would have had an on-balance desire to prevent acts causing the destruction of the galaxy.

There is no problem about (C)'s being true; but why should we think that (D) is true? Perhaps someone will say:

In terms of the Robert Stalnaker–Richard Thomason ac-count of counterfactuals: (D) will be true, if at the "clos-est" (most similar) world to the actual one in which its antecedent is true, its consequent is also true. This condi-

tion is satisfied. For a possible world in which God lacks
the belief that the flipping of the switch will not cause the
destruction of the galaxy, but still has the on-balance
desire to prevent galaxy-destroying acts, is closer to the
actual world than any world in which God lacks both the
belief that the galaxy will not be destroyed and the desire
to prevent galaxy-destroying acts. (It is more of a departure from actuality to change both God's beliefs about
the switch flipping, and His on-balance desire to prevent
galaxy-destroying acts, than it is to change God's beliefs
about the switch-flipping, but keep His on-balance desire
to prevent galaxy-destroying acts.)

We have been supposing, however, that (even) if God had
not believed that the flipping of the switch would not cause the
destruction of the galaxy, He (still) would have allowed the
switch to be flipped. That is because, in terms of the Stalnaker-
Thomason account, we have been supposing that the closest
world to the actual one in which God did not have the relevant
belief is a world whose history does not diverge from the
actual one until after the switch is flipped. If the closest world
to the actual one in which God did not believe that the flipping
of the switch would not cause the destruction of the galaxy is
one whose history does not diverge from the actual history of
the world until after the switch is flipped, can it be true at that
world that God has an on-balance desire to prevent galaxy-
destroying acts? No. At that world it is true that the switch is
flipped, and true that God does not believe that the flipping of
the switch will not cause the galaxy to be destroyed. From this
(together with the premiss that God could never be ignorant
or mistaken) it follows that at that world it is true that God
allows the switch to be flipped, believing that the flipping of
the switch causes the galaxy to be destroyed. If we suppose
that at that world God has an on-balance desire to prevent acts
causing the destruction of the galaxy, then we are supposing
that at that world God has an on-balance desire to prevent acts
causing the destruction of the galaxy, and yet allows the
switch to be flipped, even though He believes that the flipping
of the switch will cause the destruction of the galaxy. In other
words, we are supposing that at the closest world in which the
antecedent of our counterfactual is true, God is imperfectly
free or imperfectly rational. This is absurd. Accordingly, (D)
is now false. In fact, it is now true that

(E) If God had not believed that the flipping of the switch would not cause the destruction of the galaxy, He would not have had an on-balance desire to prevent acts causing the destruction of the galaxy.

Once we see that this is so, we shall no longer be tempted to say that if God had not believed that the flipping of the switch would not cause the destruction of the galaxy, He would not have allowed the switch to be flipped; and we shall see how it can be true that, on the contrary,

(F) (Even) if God had not believed that the flipping of the switch would not cause the destruction of the galaxy, He (still) would have allowed the switch to be flipped.

This defense of Aquinas relies on the assumption that the closest world to the actual one in which God does not have the relevant belief is one whose history diverges from the history of the actual one only after the switch is flipped. This assumption might be contested; but someone arguing from the possible truth of the bomb story to the falsity of Aquinas' position is not in a good position to contest it. If he does not make that assumption, it is hard to see how he will get the counterfactual,

(Even) if God had not believed that the flipping of the switch would not cause the destruction of the galaxy, He still would have allowed the switch to be flipped.

Without this last counterfactual, he cannot argue that, given Aquinas' beliefs about God's knowledge, Aquinas would have to deny that the bomb story is even possibly true.

The point is that the opponent of Aquinas cannot have it both ways. He can maintain that when we ask what would have been the case if God had not believed that flipping the switch would not cause the destruction of the galaxy, we must hold fixed the actual history of the world up to and including the time at which the switch was flipped. If he does, he gives the defender of Aquinas the materials for the just provided explanation of why the counterfactual in the bomb story could not possibly be true, even though similar ones involving fallible creaturely believers could be.[35] If he does not make that assumption,

---

[35]Of course, the opponent of Aquinas may not find the explanation satisfying. Aquinas' defender says: since it is impossible that (i) what is settled at a time is

he no longer has the resources to argue that Aquinas' account of God's knowledge compels him to deny that the bomb story is possibly true.

(C) is rather similar to the counterfactual, if God hadn't believed that the flipping of the switch would not cause the destruction of the galaxy, He would not have allowed the switch to be flipped. For this reason, someone might suspect that there are the same sort of difficulties about about how (C) could be true, on Thomistic assumptions, as there are about how it could be true on those assumptions that if God had not believed that the flipping of the switch would not cause the destruction of the galaxy, He would not have allowed the switch to be flipped. In fact, though, the defender of Aquinas can accept the truth of (C) with equanimity, because she can (and should) deny that (even) if God had not believed that the flipping of the switch would not cause the destruction of the galaxy, and had desired on-balance to prevent acts causing the destruction of the galaxy, He (still) would have allowed the switch to be flipped. There is no problem about her denying this last, "even-if" counterfactual, because she can hold that the closest world to our own in which God lacks the belief that the flipping of the switch will not cause the destruction of the galaxy, and has the (on-balance) desire to prevent acts causing the destruction of the galaxy, is a world that diverges from our own before the switch is flipped, and is a world in which God does not allow the switch to be flipped. (To put this another way: although it was open at the time the switch was flipped whether or not God did not believe that the flipping of the switch would not cause the destruction of the galaxy, it was already settled then that either God did not have the relevant belief, or God did not have an on-balance desire to prevent acts causing the destruction of the galaxy.)

There is a second sort of worry about the defense of Aquinas just provided. As long as we make the usual assumptions about God's goodness, there appear to be desires that God could not but have—for example, the desire to prevent pointless suffering (that is, suffering devoid of any salvific, retributive, *vel cetera* point). Suppose that at

---

counterfactually independent of what is open at that time, (ii) it is impossible for God to be ignorant or mistaken, (iii) it is impossible for God to be less than perfectly free and rational, and (iv) the bomb story could be true, we should conclude that the bomb story could not be true. The opponent may counter: the bomb story is at least on the face of it coherent; so we should hold on to (i) and (iv), and jettison (ii) or (iii). I doubt, however, that someone taking this line will get anything better than a dialectical standoff here; the defender of Aquinas can reply that it is on the face of it coherent to suppose that there is, or at any rate could be, a God who could not possibly be mistaken or ignorant, or less than perfectly free and rational.

some past time it was settled that a bit of suffering was taking place, and open whether or not that suffering would turn out to have been pointful. In that case, it seems, Aquinas would have to endorse not only

(1) If God had not believed this suffering was pointful, and had had an on-balance desire to prevent pointless suffering, He would not have allowed it.

but also

(2) If God had not believed this suffering was pointful, He would still have had an on-balance desire to prevent pointless suffering.

From (1) and (2) we can get to

(3) If God had not believed this suffering was pointful, He would not have allowed it.

And (3) is inconsistent with something we know (by the reasoning set out earlier) to be true in the hypothetical case described—*viz.*,

(4) Even if God had not believed this suffering was pointful, He would have allowed it.

(Again, at the time the suffering took place, it was settled that it was taking place, and open whether it would turn out to have been pointful.)

The trouble with this argument is that if we suppose that God essentially has an on-balance desire to prevent pointless suffering—and make the usual assumptions about God's knowledge and rationality—we cannot also (consistently) suppose that at some past time it was settled that a bit of suffering was taking place, and open whether or not that suffering would turn out to have been pointful. If we make all these suppositions at once, we are supposing that at some past time there was a then-possible world in which God allowed suffering to take place, in the belief that the suffering was pointless, even though He had an on-balance desire to prevent pointless suffering.

In sum, the bomb argument fails to show that God could not timelessly have infallible knowledge of our open future, as well as our fixed past and present. Nor do I know of another argument that succeeds where the bomb argument fails. At some level, I remain worried about whether we really can coherently suppose both that the past and present are fixed and the future is open, and that God time-lessly has infallible knowledge of exactly how the future will turn out. But if there is an incoherence here, I have been unable to put my finger on it.

Suppose it is true that we can have a fixed past and present, and an open future, together with a God who could not possibly be ignorant or mistaken, *if* we suppose that God is outside of time. Could the 'if' in this last clause be replaced by an 'if and only if'? It would be interesting if it could: for in that case, given the plausible premiss that the past and present are fixed, and the future is open, we could move from the claim that God could not possibly be ignorant or mistaken, to the claim that if God exists, He is outside of time.

It may seem obvious that the only way to reconcile the thesis that God could not possibly be ignorant or mistaken with the fixity of the past and present, and the openness of the future, is to suppose that God is extratemporal. If God exists now, and the future is open, then either God has beliefs about how the now–open future will turn out, or He does not. If He does, and if the present is fixed, then He has beliefs that could turn out to be false (by the argument of pages 128–29); if He does not, then He is ignorant of how the future will turn out.

But does it follow from the fact that God has no beliefs one way or the other about how the open future will turn out, that God is igno-rant? It does, if there are facts right now about how the now-open future will turn out. Suppose, though, that whenever it is open whether it will be that Q, it is neither true that it will be that Q nor true that it will not be that Q.[36] Then we could say something like this:

---

[36]Here "It will not be that Q" should be understood as equivalent to "It will be that not-Q," rather than "It is not the case that it will be that Q." Where it is now open whether Q, we might suppose either that both "It will be that Q" and "It will not be that Q" are indeterminate (undefined, neither true nor false), or that "It will be that Q" and "It will not be that Q" are both false. Putting Burgess' terminology to slightly different use, we may call the view that when Q is open, both "It will be that Q" and "It will not be that Q" are false, *hard* or *Peircean antactualism,* and the view that when Q is open, "It will be that Q" and "It will not be that Q" are indeterminate, *soft* or *Aristotelian antactualism.* Thomason has argued convincingly that hard antactualism has some very counterintuitive consequences—not least the very one at issue—*viz.,* that if it is open whether or not it will rain next week, it is false now that it will, and false now that it will not. (Another counterintuitive consequence is that, if it is now inevitably true that it is raining, but it was open yesterday whether it would be raining today, we can truly say "It is raining today, but yesterday it was false that it would be raining today.") But either hard or soft antactualism would enable us to fit God's infallible omniscience together with an open future. For a very helpful discussion of actualist and antactualist approaches to temporal logic, see John Burgess, "The Unreal Future," *Theoria* 44 (1978).

God is omniscient at a time just in case He knows everything
that is true *at that time;* God is infallible at a time just in case
none of the beliefs God has then could ever turn out to have
been false. It is perfectly possible that God always has been and
always will be omniscient and infallible, even though the future was or is or always will be open. Even if whenever it was
open whether or not it would be that Q, God neither knew it
would be that Q, nor knew that it would not be that Q, God
has always infallibly known whatever was *then* true, and will
always infallibly know whatever is *then* true—which is the
most we could reasonably ask of an infallible and omniscient
being.

We might call the picture of God's knowledge which naturally goes
along with this account the *Priorian* picture.[37] On the Boethian-
Thomistic picture, God, from His extratemporal vantage point, sees
all the possible histories of the world branch out from the first moment
of time, and sees one of those histories, as it were, lit up by the glow of
actuality. On the Priorian picture, God, from the vantage point of the
particular time at which He exists, sees all the possible histories of the
world branch out from the first moment of time, and sees *one part* of
history—the actual history of the world up to then—lit up by the
glow of actuality. God sees only part of history as actual not because
His vision is limited, but because only part of history is (then) actual.
Everything that is true then—and, hence, everything that God knows
then—is a necessary consequence of facts about the history of the
world up to and including then.

If there were no way to make sense of the view that the openness of
the future gives rise to truth-value gaps, then the Priorian picture of
God's knowledge would not be an alternative to the Boethian-Thom-
istic one. But it appears that formal sense at any rate can be made of
that view: Richmond Thomason has provided us with an account that
does just that.[38] To give a quick and impressionistic account of how
this works: in order to capture the Aristotelian idea that the past and
present are fixed, and the future is open, we start with a set of complete
possible histories of the world, branching toward the future.[39] That

[37]After Arthur Prior, who indicates his attraction to this sort of picture in "On the
Formalities of Omniscience," in *Papers on Time and Tense* (London: Oxford University
Press, 1968), pp. 26–44.

[38]See Richmond Thomason, "Indeterminist Time and Truth-Value Gaps," *Theoria*
36 (1970): 23–42. The account of future contingents Thomason offers is what I've
called a soft or Aristotelian antactualist account.

[39]This is done by taking the set of times to be ordered by the earlier-than relation,

way, times will belong to a plurality of possible histories, and any time will have exactly one past, but a plurality of possible futures. Any particular proposition—future-tensed or otherwise—comes out either true or false at a time relative to a choice of then-possible history (that is, relative to a choice of a particular then-possible future to complete the history of the world from that time on). But truth-at-a-time-relative-to-a-particular-possible-history is not truth *simpliciter* at a time. Instead, we define truth *simpliciter* at a time thus:

> *P* is true at a time just in case for every then-possible history (that is, every possible history to which that time belongs), *P* is true-at-that-time-on-that-history.
>
> *P* is false at a time just in case for every then-possible history, *P* is false-at-that-time-on-that-history.
>
> *P* is indeterminate (neither true nor false) otherwise.

Then it will turn out that a proposition about the future is true at a time if and only if it is inevitably true then (that is, true whichever then-possible history turns out to be actual), false at that time if and only if it is inevitably false (false whichever then-possible history turns out to be actual), and indeterminate otherwise. Moreover, we can say—as Aristotle may have wanted to say in *De interpretatione* 9—that although it is not true now that there will be a sea battle, and is not true now that there will not be, it is still true now that either there will be a sea battle or there will not be. If there is a now-possible history *h* such that it is true now on *h* that there will be a sea battle, and a now-possible history *h′* such that it is false now on *h′* that there will be a sea battle, then, on this account, it is neither true now that there will be a sea battle, nor true now that there will not be one. The disjunction, there will be a sea battle or there will not be, however, comes out true now, because on every now-possible history it comes out true-now-on-that-history (since on every now-possible history, one or the other of its disjuncts comes out true-now-on-that-history).

Although Thomason provides a very pretty semantics for the view of future contingents often attributed to Aristotle, it might be that the view that truth-value gaps follow upon the openness of the future is still at some level incoherent or at least implausible. Although I won't argue the matter here, I don't think this is so. It is not that I find the

---

where that relation is irreflexive, transitive, and treelike. (A relation *R* is treelike just in case, whenever *bRa* and *cRa*, then either *bRc*, or *cRb*, or *b* = *c*.)

view that future contingents now lack truth-value compelling. Quite the other way: I strongly incline to the belief that, however much or little we might know about the future portion of it, there is a unique (complete) actual history of the world, and any future contingent proposition is either true right now or false right now, depending on whether it is true now or false now on the one and only history among the now-possible ones which is the actual history of the world. Nevertheless, after years of arguments with scores of people, I have come to the conclusion that I have no conclusive, or even compelling, arguments to make those not originally well disposed to my view come to share it. My attempts to show those people that their view has unacceptable consequences always end in failure, because whatever consequences I bring out they deem acceptable. Of course, it is more than possible that this is a reflection of my inability to come up with clever arguments. But because I have not been clever enough to find the right arguments, don't know of any in the literature, and am hard pressed to see what they might look like, I must judge that there are no conclusive arguments against the notion that truth extends only so far as inevitability (although, symmetrically, there are no conclusive arguments for it either).[40]

So, contra Aquinas, in order to believe in a fixed past and present, and an open future, together with a God whose nature excludes ignorance or error, we needn't suppose that God is outside of time. But, as far as I can tell, we can. In the preceding section, I argued that the changing universe is compatible with a timeless and omniscient God; so too, it appears, is a fixed past and an open future.

---

[40]In conversation, Allan Gibbard has suggested to me that there might be no fact of the matter about whether actualism or antactualism offers a correct account of the truth-conditions of contingent propositions about the future: we may sort propositions into those that are now inevitably true, those that are now inevitably false, and those that are neither, but perhaps whether we give an actualist or an antactualist account of those propositions in the third category is a matter of convention. I don't know whether or not this is true; perhaps there are a bunch of arguments unknown to me that show my pretheoretical preference for actualism is justified (or that the preference of others for antactualism is). If it should turn out that there is no fact of the matter about whether truth outruns inevitability, this would have the curious result that, should God be temporal, there would be a fact of the matter about His being infallible, but no fact of the matter about His being omniscient.

It is interesting to note that if the Priorian picture of God's knowledge is the right one, then the bomb story could not be true, because a God whose nature excludes ignorance or error could not have beliefs about whether the flipping of the switch will cause the destruction of the galaxy early enough for His having such a belief to make a difference to whether or not He allows the switch to be flipped.

Looking Back

At the beginning of Chapter 1, I noted that for Aquinas, since God is completely simple, He is incomposite in each of these ways:

(1) He lacks composition of extended parts.

(2) He lacks composition of form and matter.

(3) He lacks 'composition' of act and potency, and is accordingly atemporal and immutable.

(4) He lacks composition of essence and individuating principles or accidents; instead, He is the same as His essence.

(5) He lacks composition of attributes: instead, His goodness, wisdom, power, knowledge, and all His other intrinsic attributes are the same as Him.

(6) He lacks composition of essence and existence: He is His own existence, just as He is His own essence.

The aim of Part I has been to explicate (1)–(6), and to see whether each one could be true. In the first three chapters, I argued that, while it might well be true that God's existence, goodness, wisdom, and so on are not proper parts of Him, those attributes—which are either shared by creatures, or at least conspecific with properties had by creatures—could not be identical to Him, as (5) and (6) maintain. But I left open the question of whether, if we conceive of attributes restrictively enough that goodness, wisdom, existence, and so on do not count as attributes, God might be identical to some or even all of His intrinsic attributes (as (5) maintains). Also, I left open the question whether God might be the same as His (individual or specific) essence (as (4) maintains). In this chapter, I have argued that as long as we suppose that God is necessarily omniscient, we should suppose that He has some of His intrinsic attributes inessentially. If we make that supposition, then we can't maintain either that God is the same as all of His intrinsic attributes, or that God is the same as His essence. So (5) and (4) go the way of (6).

What about (3)? As we saw in Chapter 1, Aquinas construes potentiality broadly enough that only something that is the same as its existence and all its other attributes could fail to be in some way in potentiality, and fail to have composition of act and potency. If we construe potentiality in this idiosyncratically broad way, then (3) will

entail each of (4)–(6),[41] and will have to be given up if they are given
up. We might, however, (re)construe potentiality more narrowly
(and, I think, more naturally) in such a way that an entity's being in no
way in potentiality did not entail that entity's being the same as its
existence and all its attributes, but did entail (and was entailed by) that
entity's being changeless and timeless. On this narrower construal of
potentiality, (3) would turn out to be equivalent to the claim that God
is changeless and timeless. Could this last claim be true? I have tried to
show that two sorts of arguments from God's omniscience and ancillary premises (the existence of change, the openness of the future) to
God's mutability and temporality fail. Since I know of no other good
arguments against the claim that God is changeless and timeless, I'm
inclined to think it could be true, and accordingly that a weakened
version of (3) could be true.

In short, it looks as though at most (1), (2), and (a version of) (3) are
defensible parts of Aquinas' conception of divine simplicity. It is not
clear, though, that the root idea Aquinas takes (1)–(6) to follow
from—*viz.,* that God is not composite in any way—needs to be
abandoned. *Contra* Aquinas, we can admit that God is distinct from
His attributes, His essence, and His existence, and still insist that God
is without (proper) parts of any kind. Naturally, any reconstruction of
Aquinas' thought along these lines will involve sacrificing a great deal
of his metaphysics in order to hold on to his belief in God's absolute
simplicity.

In Part II, I attempt to explicate Aquinas' account of the metaphysics
of the Trinity and the Incarnation; and I ask whether each of these
accounts is internally consistent, and consistent with Aquinas' treatment of divine simplicity. I argue that Aquinas' theory of the Trinity is
internally inconsistent, precisely because of his attempt to make that
account one that could mesh with his account of divine simplicity; and
I argue that Aquinas' account of the Incarnation is inconsistent for the
same reason. Finally, I raise some difficulties about whether a triune
and incarnate God could have even the kinds of simplicity ascribed to
Him by (1), (2), and the weakened version of (3).

[41]If we hold (as Aquinas at least sometimes does) that nothing distinct from its
accidents or its *esse* could be the same as its essence, then given Thomistic assumptions,
each member of (3)–(6) turns out to entail all the others.

PART II

THE GOD OF FAITH

[5]

Is the Doctrine of the Trinity Inconsistent?

In Chapter 6, I provide an exposition of Aquinas' account of the metaphysics of the Trinity, with an eye toward determining whether that account is internally consistent, and consistent with Aquinas' natural theology. But before embarking on that project, I want to confront a certain worry. It may appear the the kind of investigation I have in mind is a nugatory exercise, because the doctrine of the Trinity is a clearly and demonstrably inconsistent one, whose formalization in first-order logic is provably false.

I don't believe this is so. Although a very natural formalization of the doctrine of the Trinity is provably false, there are alternative formalizations that are consistent and not obviously heterodox. In this chapter, I develop and explicate one such alternative formalization, drawing upon some ideas of Anselm.

The Apparent Inconsistency

According to the Athanasian creed, each of these statements is true:

(1) There are exactly three divine persons.

(2) Each divine person is God.

(3) There is exactly one God.[1]

---

[1] "There is one person of the Father, and another of the Son, and another of the Holy Spirit. . . . The Father is God, and the Son is God, and the Holy Spirit is God: and nevertheless there are not three Gods but there is one God" (from the *Quicumque*).

Any number of philosophers and theologians have been aware that (1)–(3) at least resemble an inconsistent set of sentences. And a prima facie case for the inconsistency of (1)–(3) can be made as follows: Suppose we let $P =$ —— is a divine person, and let $G =$ —— is a God. Then a natural way to formalize (1)–(3) in predicate logic with identity is the following (I omit some parentheses for clarity):

(1′) $(\exists x)\,(\exists y)\,(\exists z)\,[(Px \wedge Py \wedge Pz \wedge x \neq y \wedge y \neq z \wedge x \neq z)$
$\wedge\, (u)\,(Pu \rightarrow (u = x \vee u = y \vee u = z))]$

(2′) $(x)\,(Px \rightarrow Gx)$

(3′) $(\exists x)\,[Gx \wedge (y)\,(Gy \rightarrow y = x)]$

In English:

(1′) For some x, y, z: x, y, and z are each divine persons; x is distinct from y, and y from z, and x from z; and if any u is a divine person, then it is either the same as x, or the same as y, or the same as z.

(2′) Any divine person is (a) God.

(3′) There is an x such that x is God, and any y that is a God is the same as x.

(1′)–(3′) are jointly inconsistent: (1′) and (2′) jointly entail that there are at least three Gods—contradicting (3′)—while (2′) and (3′) jointly entail that there is at most one divine person—contradicting (1′). The attempt to formalize a fragment of the doctrine of the Trinity— strangely enough—ends both in Tritheism and something like Modalism.

A defender of the consistency of the doctrine of the Trinity must argue that there is something very wrong with the above formalization of (1)–(3). Ideally, he would do this by offering a consistent, clearly superior formalization of (1)–(3). Short of this, he could try to show that, whatever a good formalization of (1)–(3) would look like, it would not be (1′)–(3′).

It is implausible to deny that (1)–(3)—at least considered in isolation from the rest of the doctrine of the Trinity—*appear* to have the logical structure represented by (1′)–(3′). But there are sets of sentences which, though consistent, seem to have the structure represented in (1′)–(3′); and (1)–(3) may be one such.

Consider, for example, the following triad of sentences:

(A) There are (exactly) three statues here.

(B) Each statue here is gold.

(C) There is just (one) Gold.[2]

(A)–(C) look like a consistent set of sentences.[3] An incautious logic student, though, insensitive to the distinction between being golden and being Gold, might well come up with a formalization of (A)–(C) which had the very structure of (1′)–(3′).

Or, to cite an example discussed by Anil Gupta,[4] there is at least one reading on which these sentences are jointly consistent:

(a) Eighty passengers were carried by U.S. Air in 1980.

(b) Each passenger carried by U.S. Air in 1980 is a person.

(c) (Just) sixty persons were carried in 1980 by U.S. Air.

Here it would be natural to formalize (a)–(c) along the lines of (1′)–(3′), although reflection shows that such a formalization leaves no room for the possibility that different passengers "are" the same person—that possibility in virtue of which (a)–(c) can all be true.

None of this provides much of a defense of the consistency of (1)–(3). It might, if we had reason to think that the structure of (1)–(3) was akin to that of (A)–(C), or of (a)–(c). But it is doubtful that we will get far if we construe the relation of the divine persons to God on the model of the relation of things golden to Gold. And although it looks as if the structure of (a)–(c) has a greater affinity to that of (1)–(3), a good deal more would need to be said about what the structure of (a)–(c) is, and about whether understanding the relation of the different divine persons to the one God on the model of the relation of different passengers to the one man 'they' are can lead to a non-Modalist theory of the Trinity.

Medieval philosophers and theologians—from Augustine to Occam—were not unfamiliar with arguments against the consistency of

---

[2]The example is taken from Augustine, *De trinitate* 7.6.

[3]Someone might hold that (3) is necessarily false, or ill-formed, or some such thing. Since I am only introducing (A)–(C) by way of example, I won't discuss the question of (C)'s truth-value in much detail. Suffice it to say that it can be taken as equivalent to the (true) "Exactly one thing is the metal, Gold."

[4]See Anil Gupta, *The Logic of Common Nouns* (New Haven, Conn.: Yale University Press, 1980).

the doctrine of the Trinity which relied on the claim that (1)–(3) had
the structure of (1')–(3'). Such arguments would appeal both to those
who would "confound the persons" and to those who would "divide
the substance" (to use the language of the Athanasian creed). In opposing those arguments, medieval philosophers and theologians relied on
one (or both) of two approaches.

The first approach might be called 'the way of analysis'. On it, some
technical metaphysical vocabulary is introduced, and (1)–(3) are restated in terms of this vocabulary—one thought to be more perspicuous and more sensitive to distinctions. So (1)–(3) might be restated by
Aquinas as:

(1t) There are (exactly) three relationally distinct divine hypostases.

(2t) Each divine hypostasis subsists in a divine nature.

(3t) There is (exactly) one divine nature.

Then an attempt is made to show—or at least defend—the consistency
of (1t)–(3t). If each member of (1t)–(3t) is related to its counterpart in
(1)–(3) as *analysans* to *analysandum,* and if the attempt succeeds, the
consistency of (1)–(3) has been demonstrated (or at least defended).

The second approach may be called 'the way of analogy'. On this
approach, the attempt is made to show that (1)–(3) are structurally
similar to some other set of sentences which we know to be true (and a
fortiori consistent). To put it in the material mode, the attempt is made
to show that the Trinitarian structure described in (1)–(3) is mirrored—to a greater or lesser degree—in the created order.

The analytic and analogical approaches are complementary, and
indeed are combined by Augustine and Anselm, as well as Aquinas.
Following their lead, I introduce some technical notions in the attempt
to find a reasonably fine-grained, consistent formalization of (1)–(3),
and use an Anselmian analogy to try and specify the content of those
notions. First, however, I want to examine two promising strategies
for formalizing (1)–(3) which ultimately run into problems.

Relative Identity?

It may seem that what we need, in order to get a good formalization
of (1)–(3), is the concept of sortally relativized identity. (Geach has
made just this suggestion.) After all, it is part of the Christian faith that
the Father and the Son are the same God, but not the same person of

the Trinity. (As Aquinas would put it, the Son is *alius* than the Father, but not *aliud*.) If we can make sense of sortally relativized identity, we can give the following analysis of (1)–(3) (where '= $_g$' means 'is the same God as', and '= $_p$' means 'is the same person as', and '*P*' and '*G*' are understood as before):

(1r) $(\exists x)\,(\exists y)\,(\exists z)\,[(Px \wedge Py \wedge Pz \wedge x \neq_p y \wedge y \neq_p z \wedge x \neq_p z)$
$\wedge\,(u)\,(Pu \rightarrow (u =_p x \vee u =_p y \vee u =_p z))]$

(2r) $(x)\,[Px \rightarrow (\exists y)\,(Gy \wedge y =_g x)]$

(3r) $(\exists x)\,[Gx \wedge (y)\,(Gy \rightarrow y =_g x)]$

In English:

(1r) For some *x*, *y*, and *z*: *x*, *y*, and *z* are each divine persons; *x* is not the same person as *y*, *y* is not the same person as *z*, and *x* is not the same person as *z*; and if any *u* is a divine person, then *u* is the same person as *x*, or *u* is the same person as *y*, or *u* is the same person as *z*.

(2r) Any divine person is the same God as some God.

(3r) There is an *x* such that *x* is a God, and any *y* that is a God is the same God as *x*.

My worries about this approach are just the worries expressed by David Wiggins and John Perry about the idea of relative identity.[5] The above formalization presupposes that *a* and *b* can be the same *K* (in this case, God), but different *K**'s (in this case, persons). Wiggins and Perry have argued compellingly that if *a* and *b* are different *K**'s, then they cannot be the same *K*, for any *K*. In outline, the argument goes like this: suppose *a* and *b* are different *K**'s (that is, suppose *a* is a *K**, *b* is a *K**, and *a* is not the same *K** as *b*). Surely, if *a* is a *K**, then *a* could not be a different *K** from *a*; for nothing is a different *K** from itself. In that case, *a* and *b* are discernible, since *b* has, but *a* lacks, the property of being a different *K** from *a*. But if *a* and *b* are discernible, then they cannot be the very same *K*—because they cannot be the very same anything. So, if *a* and *b* are each *K*'s and *K**'s, *a* and *b* are the same *K* if and only if they are the same *K**. Or, as Wiggins puts it, identity is not sortal-relative, but absolute.

[5]See David Wiggins, *Sameness and Substance* (Cambridge, Mass.: Harvard University Press, 1980), and John Perry, "The Same F," *Philosophical Review* 78, no. 2 (1970): 181–201.

This argument is not entirely conclusive: the friend of sortally relative identity may (i) deny that *a* is never a different *K*⋆ from *a*, or (ii) deny that if *b* has a property that *a* doesn't, *a* is not the same *K* as *b*. If (i) is not implausible, nothing is. The trouble with (ii)—as Wiggins has pointed out—is that (on anyone's account) certain inferences of the form "*a* has the property *P*, *a* is the same *K* as *b*, therefore *b* has the property *P*" are valid. Someone who thinks that some but not all inferences having this form are valid owes us an account of just when they are. As Wiggins points out, no such account has been worked out, and it is difficult to see how one would go.

Someone who finds the Wiggins-Perry argument against the relativity of identity compelling may still be attracted to the thesis that identity is sortal-relative, because a good number of English sentences of the form "*a* is the same *K* as *b*, but a different *K*⋆ from *b*" are apparently true. The absoluteness of identity, however, is compatible with the existence of true English sentences of the form just described. For English sentences of the form "*a* is the same *K* as *b*" do not always identify *a* and *b* as the same *K*. (Moreover, as we shall see, English sentences of the form "*a* is a different *K*⋆ from *b*" do not always entail that *a* and *b* are distinct *K*⋆'s.) To take an example of Perry's, "this couch is the same color as this chair" does not identify the couch and the chair as the same color (although it says that the couch and the chair *have* the same color); whatever our views on identity, we shall take that sentence to have a logical form quite different from the statement "the blue of this couch is the same color as the blue of this chair," which *does* identify the blue of this couch and the blue of this chair as the same color. True sentences of the form "*a* is the same *K* as *b*, but a different *K*⋆ from *b*" show that identity is not absolute only if in such sentences *a* and *b* are both identified as the same *K*, and said to be different *K*⋆'s. And Perry and Wiggins have argued convincingly that in all of the cases offered as counterexamples to the absoluteness of identity, this condition fails to be met.

If Perry and Wiggins are right, then (1r)–(3r) is an unsuccessful attempt at finding a defensible formalization of (1)–(3). For—at least as long as we take the predicates '$=_g$' and '$=_p$' at face value—it entails that for some *x* and *y*, *x* and *y* can be identified as the same God, but not as the same person, even though *x* and *y* are both persons. (If those predicates are not to be taken at face value, but in some other way, then (1r)–(3r) are deficient in not specifying how they are to be taken.) At the risk of belaboring the point: the unsatisfactoriness of (1r)–(3r) as a formalization of (1)–(3) does not entail that there is no true reading of the sentence "The Father and the Son are the same God, but different persons of the Trinity." For all we have said, there may be: but if there is, it will not be equivalent to the (necessarily false) assertion that the Father and the Son may be identified as the same God, although they are distinct persons.

Although the notion of sortally relative identity is not the key to providing a formalization of (1)–(3), it still might be that a look at the putative counterexamples to the absoluteness of identity will be helpful in trying to formalize (1)–(3). Because one of them might have a logical form not unlike that of "The Father and the Son are the same God, but different persons," consideration of those (apparent) counterexamples might shed some light on what the logical form of "The Father and the Son are the same God, but different persons" was, and thus shed some light on what a satisfactory formalization of (1)–(3) might be.

Among the statements that have been or might be offered as counterexamples to the absoluteness of identity are the following (I draw heavily on examples discussed by Wiggins and Perry):

(1) The couch and the chair are the same color—but different pieces of furniture.

(2) 'i' and 'i' are the same letter-type—but different letter-tokens.

(3) The ship Theseus sailed in as a youth and the ship his grandchildren gave to the Athenian naval museum are the same ship—but different collections of planks.

(4) The soft clay statue of Pegasus and the (previously formed) soft clay statue of Mercury are the same hunk of stuff—but different statues.

(5) The man I spoke to last week and the man to whom I am currently speaking are the same official—but different men.

(6) The mayor of Lud-in-the-Mist and the high seneschal of Lud-in-the-Mist are the same man—but different officials.

Evidently, this is a rather heterogeneous list. (6) in particular stands apart from (1), (2), (4), and (5); for in (6), the first part of the sentence is straightforwardly equivalent to "The mayor of Lud-in-the-Mist is a man, and the mayor of Lud-in-the-Mist is identical to the high seneschal of Lud-in-the-Mist." Presuming that (6) can be true, in virtue of what can it be true?[6] Just that one and the same man can occupy two different offices. One might think that we had here a claim illuminatingly analogous to the Trinitarian claim that the Father and the Son are the same God, but different persons: mightn't it be that the Father and the Son are the same God, but different persons, by virtue of the difference between the (immanent and economic) roles played by the Son and the Father?

Perhaps. But I tend to think that any theory that takes the structure of the Trinitarian claim at issue to be very much like that of (6) will avoid dividing the substance at the cost of confounding the persons.

Statement (6) is true only if one and the same individual is both the mayor and the high seneschal. (If the individual who is the high seneschal were distinct from the individual who is the mayor, then the first part of (6) would be false, although the second would be uncontroversially true.) Now, if we suppose that "The Father and the Son are the same God, but different persons of the Trinity" has a structure very like that of (6), it will follow that one and the same individual is both the Father and the Son, although the roles (broadly construed) of Fatherhood and Sonship are distinct roles. But this view of the Godhead seems to amount to what Karl Rahner calls "mere monotheism." If one and the same individual is both the mayor of Lud and the high seneschal, then the individual who is the mayor of Lud is (identical to) the individual who is the high seneschal. In that case—since the individual who is the mayor of Lud is (identical to) the mayor of Lud, and the individual who is the high seneschal is (identical to) the high seneschal—the mayor of Lud is identical to the high seneschal. By parity of reasoning, if one and the same individual is both the Father and the Son, and the individual who is the Father is identical to the Father, and the individual who is the Son is identical to the Son, then the Father is the Son. Now, it surely is not part of any orthodox conception of the Trinity that the Father is identical to the Son. How could it be that although there are three persons of the Trinity—the Father, the Son, and the Holy Spirit—the Father is the same as the Son, and the Son is the same as the Holy Spirit?

Since the ship Theseus sailed in as a youth is identical to the ship his

[6]I have some temptation to believe that, although (6) may be used to convey a truth to a listener, it is literally false. If the mayor and the high seneschal are the same man, it is certainly not literally true that they are *two* different officials; and I'm not at all sure it could be true that the mayor and the high seneschal are two officials, unless it was also true that the mayor and the high seneschal are two different officials.

grandchildren gave to the Athenian naval museum, we run into the problems just described if we suppose that the logical structure of (3) is very much like that of the claim that the Father and the Son are the same God, but different divine persons. The moral is that, in attempting to see how it could be true that the Father and the Son are the same God but different persons, it may be better not to look to cases in which one and the same individual (the man who is mayor and high seneschal, the ship that Theseus sailed in and his grandchildren gave to the museum) stands in some relation to two different things (that is, stands in the occupying relation to two different offices, or stands in the *having been composed of or being now composed* of relation to two different sets of planks). It is worth looking instead at cases in which two (distinct) individuals each bear one and the same relation to a third thing. (1), (2,), (4), and (5) are all of this type.

In (1) and (5), two distinct individuals (pieces of furniture, men) are said to share an accidental property (*having such and such a color, being this sort of official*). In (2), two distinct individuals (particular tokens or occurrences of the letter *i*) are held to share a sortal property (*being an i*). None of these helps us much to see what sort of (consistent) logical form "The Father and the Son are the same God, but differnt persons of the Trinity" could have. Intuitively, that is because the individuals in question are related to each other in a way much less intimate than the way in which the Father and the Son are held to be related to each other. This is obvious in the case of (1) and (5), but it also holds for (2). If, in the way that this 'i' and that 'i' are distinct individuals falling under the sortal *being an i,* the Father and the Son are distinct individuals falling under the sortal *being a God,* it would seem that there is more than one God. Nor would it help matters to protest that the Father and the Son share not just the property of *being a God,* but the property of *being God* (that is, of *being this God*); for if that is so, then the logical form of (2) is quite unlike the logical form of the theological statements at issue.

This leaves us with (4), which says that two distinct individuals (in this case, statues) are made of the same stuff. I argue below that (4) is of more use to us than any other member of (1)–(6) in seeing what the logical form of certain Trinitarian statements might be, because two things made of the same stuff may be very intimately related, yet distinct. First, however, I want to look at a different kind of formalization of (1)–(3) which, like the one just considered, deploys more than one identity predicate.

Different Kinds of Difference?

If in the Trinity there are three different persons, but not three different Gods, perhaps this is because the differences in question themselves differ; the sense in which there are three different persons is not the sense in which there are not three different Gods.

This idea could be fleshed out by a quasi-Scotist theory in which substantial identity (and substantial difference) are distinguished from formal identity (and formal difference). The theory would allow for the possibility that two things could be substantially the same and formally distinct, but not for the possibility that two things could be formally the same and substantially different. The persons of the Trinity would turn out to be formally different, but substantially the same.

Suppose we introduce two new predicates '$=_s$' ('is substantially identical to') and '$=_f$' ('is formally identical to'). Then we can symbolize (1)–(3) thus:

(1s) $(\exists x)\,(\exists y)\,(\exists z)\,[(Px \wedge Py \wedge Pz \wedge x \neq_f y \wedge y \neq_f z \wedge x \neq_f z)$
$\wedge\,(u)\,(Pu \rightarrow (u =_f x \vee u =_f y \vee u =_f z))]$

(2s) $(x)\,(Px \rightarrow Gx)$

(3s) $(\exists x)\,[Gx \wedge (y)\,(Gy \rightarrow y =_s x)]$

In English:

(1s) For some x, y, and z: x, y, and z are each divine persons; x is formally distinct from y, y is formally distinct from z, and x is formally distinct from z; and if any u is a divine person, then u is formally identical to x, or u is formally identical to y, or u is formally identical to z.

(2s) Any divine person is (a) God.

(3s) There is an x such that x is a God, and any y that is a God is substantially identical to x.

The crucial question, of course, concerns the nature of formal and substantial identity. Any satisfactory construal thereof must provide us with a consistent and tolerably orthodox reading, not just of (1s)–(3s), but also of the following consequences of (1s)–(3s):

(4s) $(\exists x)\,(\exists y)\,(\exists z)\,(Gx \wedge Gy \wedge Gz \wedge x \neq_f y \wedge y \neq_f z \wedge x \neq_f z)$

(5s) $(x)\,(y)\,[(Px \wedge Py) \rightarrow x =_s y]$

In English:

> (4s) For some x, y, and z, x is a God, and y is a God, and z is a God, and x is formally distinct from y, and y is formally distinct from z, and x is formally distinct from z.

and

> (5s) For any x and any y, if x is a divine person and y is a divine person, then x is substantially identical to y.

Since we want it to turn out that whatever is formally identical to something is substantially identical to it—but not vice versa—we could either (i) take formal identity statements to be logically stronger than identity statements, and take substantial identity statements to be ordinary identity statements; or (ii) take formal identity statements to be ordinary identity statements, and substantial identity statements to be logically weaker than identity statements; or (iii) take formal identity statements to be logically stronger than, and substantial identity statements to be logically weaker than, ordinary statements of identity.

A natural way of following up (i) is to think of formal identity statements as identity statements prefixed by a necessity operator, and of substantial identity statements as ordinary identity statements. We have already seen in a different context the drawback of this strategy: however one cashes out the truth-conditions for statements of formal identity, as long as substantial identity is real identity, we save the unicity of God at the expense of His triune nature. If substantial identity is genuine identity, then (5s)—which is entailed by (2s) and (3s)—is just the claim that any 'two' divine persons are identical (equivalently: there is just one divine person). And this last claim is very like the view that made Sabellius unpopular with medieval theologians.

According to (ii), formal identity is classical identity, and substantial identity is something weaker—but, presumably, not too much weaker. That is, we want a relation that is like identity, in being an equivalence relation, and in conferring indiscernibility with respect to an important range of properties. What sort of relation fills this bill? The first one to come to (my) mind is David Lewis's identity-at-time-t (cf. Lewis, "Survival and Identity," in A. Rorty, ed., *The Identities of Persons*). Two continuants, a and b, are identical-at-time-t if and only if a and b exist at t, and all and only temporal stages of a at t are temporal stages of b at t. As Lewis points out, despite its name, identity-at-time-t is not a restriction of the identity relation: two continuants can be identical-at-time-t without being themselves identical (although identity must hold between some of their stages). Nevertheless, identity-at-time-t resembles identity in interesting ways: it is easy to see that it is an equivalence relation, and that it confers on its relata indiscernibility with respect to an important range of properties. Of course, how important you consider those properties will depend, among other things, on your relation to time t. One might put it this way: from the vantage point of time t, identity-at-time-t is almost as good as real identity. If you are located at time t, and care not at all about anything at any time other than t, then it will not matter to you whether two continuants are identical, or only identical-at-t. Similarly, if you are located at time t, and care only about the present and future, then identity-at-all-times-simultaneous-with-or-later-than-t will be for you as near as makes no matter to real identity.

An interesting feature of identity-at-time-t, according to Lewis, is that we sometimes count by it: that is, we sometimes say at t that there is only one K, when there are distinct K's, all of which are identical-at-t to one another.

Given the formal features of identity-at-time-t, it would be nice if we could construe the substantial identity spoken of in (3s) as identity-at-time-t, or some related notion, such as identity-at-all-times-after-time-t'. We could then understand the claim that there are three different divine persons in the obvious way, and take the claim that something is God, and everything that is God is substantially identical to it, to mean something along the lines of: there is a God, and all the Gods there are are identical-at-now with that God. And we could say that, although there is more than one divine person, and each one is (a) God, it is still true—on one reading—that there is (just) one God, because we count Gods not by identity, but by identity-at-time-t.

That particular construal looks much too weak to capture (3s): it is, for example, compatible with there having been three different Gods who underwent fusion, or with there being a God who will undergo fission in the future. But orthodoxy demands that it never be true that there are two substantially distinct entities, each of which is God. One might respond by taking substantial identity to be identity-at-all-times-t.

This is not an unpromising suggestion. There are two worries about it, however. First, it may be that although identity-at-time-t is not identity, identity-at-all-times-t turns out to be a restriction of the identity relation. In other words, it may be that if two individuals have temporal stages, and have all the same temporal stages, then they are identical.[7] If this is so, then we cannot both suppose that substantial identity is identity-at-all-times-t, and (as strategy (ii) demands) take substantial identity to be a weaker relation than identity. Second, if identity-at-all-times-t holds between distinct persons of the Trinity, and each of those persons is (a) God, then strictly speaking there are three distinct Gods. Note that any way of putting flesh on the bones of strategy (ii) has this result (because of the way (4s) gets interpreted), just as any way of filling out (i) has the consequence that there is actually just one divine person (because of the way (5s) gets interpreted). Perhaps we can live with that result: if we can make out that it is legitimate to count by the relation we take to be substantial identity, then we can say that "There is just one God" has a true reading (even if it also has a straightforward and false one). It is, however, apparently heterodox to suppose that "There are three Gods" is true on any reading—and all the more heterodox to say it is true on that claim's most straightforward reading. Hence we should have recourse to any formalization of (1)–(3) which has this consequence only as a last resort.

Strategy (iii) is clearly no more plausible than either (i) or (ii), since it will entail that there is actually just one divine person, while leaving open the possibility that there is more than one God.

At this point we have a number of options. First, we could go William of Occam's no-analysis analysis one better. In discussing whether the persons of the Trinity differ, Occam tells us that they differ *formaliter a parte rei* (that is, formally, but on the part of the thing—and not merely on the part of the mind thinking about them); but unlike Duns Scotus, he eschews any attempt to explain what differing formally *a parte rei* consists in. For Occam, the *distinctio formalis a parte rei* is a part of the mystery of the Trinity, and not a way of making that mystery any more transparent (cf. Occam, *Summa logicae* II.2). Following Occam's lead, we could take formal and substantial difference (and identity) to be primitive notions, not to be explained in terms of any others.

This move does not defend the consistency of the doctrine of the Trinity; instead it construes that doctrine in such a way that its content becomes ineffable. Indeed, it is not clear why on this line we are

---

[7]For some of the considerations that might make one think this is so, see David Lewis, "Counterparts of Persons and Their Bodies," *Journal of Philosophy* 68 (1971): 203–11, and his "Survival and Identity," in *The Identities of Persons*, ed. A. Rorty (Berkeley: University of California Press, 1976), pp. 17–41.

justified in regarding (1s)–(3s) as an explication of (1)–(3), rather than as a replacement for it. (1)–(3) tell us that there are three divine persons who are just one God; (1s)–(3s) tell us that the divine persons differ formally from one another, and that no two of the Gods there differ substantially from each other. If formal and substantial identity are primitive notions, how are we to connect the first set of claims with the second? (Such difficulties will be encountered, to a lesser extent, if we take one of the pair of notions [substantial identity, formal identity] to be primitive.)

There is a more attractive option. (2s) played a crucial role in undermining our construals of formal and substantial identity; without it, the arguments that give us too many Gods or too few persons do not go through. Might we be able to overcome the problems with our quasi-Scotist formalization if we come up with a less obvious formalization of (2)? Yes. But surprisingly enough, if we come up with the right sort of formalization of (2), we can formalize (1) and (3) in an entirely straightforward way. A fascinating passage in Anselm's "On the Incarnation of the Word" suggests a way of doing this.

Anselm's Nile

In regard to the one God and His three persons, we predicate 'three' of something that is one, and 'one' of something that is three, in such a way that the three are not predicated of one another. Now if my opponent denies that this is possible, on the ground that, since nothing like it is seen in other things, neither can it be understood in God, he will have to endure the fact that there is something in God which his understanding is not able to fathom, and he will have to stop comparing a nature which is above everything, and free from every law of place, time, and composition, with things which are shut up in space and time or are composed of parts. Instead, let him believe that there is something in God's nature which cannot be in created natures, and submit to Christian authority without arguing against it.

However, let us see whether we cannot find what my opponent denies to be the case in God to some extent among created things which are subject to the law of time, place, and composition. Suppose there is a spring from which there originates and flows a river, which later accumulates into a lake. And suppose its name is 'the Nile'. Now we say that the spring, the river, and the lake are different from one another, in such a way that we would not call the spring 'the river', or 'the lake'; nor the river 'the spring' or 'the lake'; nor the lake 'the spring' or 'the river'. And yet the spring is called 'the Nile', the river is called 'the Nile', and the lake is called 'the Nile'. Similarly the spring and the lake together are called 'the Nile', and the river and the lake together are called 'the Nile', and the spring and the river together are called 'the Nile'. And the spring, the river, and the lake, all three together, are called 'the Nile'. But yet, whether the name 'Nile' is applied to them individually, or in combinations of two or three, it is always one and the same Nile—there is not one Nile in this place, and another Nile in that. The spring, the river, and the lake, therefore, are three, and are at the same time one Nile, one stream, one nature, one water. And none of these things can be said to be three. Here is an example, then, in which 'one' is predicated of what is three, and 'three' of what is one, yet the three are not predicated of one another. (Anselm, "Letter on the Incarnation of the Word," in J. Hopkins and H. Richardson, eds., *Anselm of Canterbury: Trinity Incarnation, and Redemption* [New York: Harper Torchbooks, 1970], p. 26)

There is more here than meets the eye. It looks as if Anselm is simply conflating *being the Nile* with *being a part of the Nile*. The spring, the river, and the lake are all parts of the Nile, but none of them is the entire Nile; for the Nile and any of its Nile-features (if I may use this expression to cover the spring, the river, and the lake) are eminently discernible. For instance, each Nile-feature has a different spatial location than the entire Nile. Of course, one could point to the spring, and say truthfully, 'This is the spring', and also point to the spring and say—ostending by metonymy, as it were—'This is the Nile'. But the 'this' in the first utterance has a different referent than the 'this' in the second (hence one could not say truthfully, 'This is both the spring and the Nile').

The continuation of the passage, however, makes it clear that something more interesting than a confusion of 'is z' with 'is a part of z' is going on here; for Anselm is aware that someone might say that different Nile-features are only parts of the Nile:

Now if my opponent objects that neither the spring, the river, nor the lake singularly, nor any two of them, is the complete Nile, but only part of it, let him consider this. The whole Nile, from where it begins to where it comes to an end, exists, as it were, throughout its whole 'lifetime.' It never exists wholly and simultaneously in any time or place, but exists through its parts, and will not be complete until it ceases to exist. For in this respect, it is something like a prayer, which, as long as it is 'pouring forth' as it were, from 'the spring' of the mouth, is not complete; when it is complete, it has already come to an end. Now if anyone were to examine the matter in this way, and to understand it carefully, he would realize that the whole Nile is the spring, the whole Nile is the river, and the whole Nile is the lake, and that the spring is not the river or the lake, the river is not the spring or the lake, and the lake is not the spring or the river. For the spring is not the same as the river or the lake, even though the river and the lake are what the spring is, i.e., the same Nile, the same stream, the same water, the same nature. This is a case, then, in which 'three' is prediated of one complete whole, and 'one complete whole' is predicated of three, and yet the three are not predicated of each other. This situation can certainly exist differently and more perfectly in that most simple of natures which is also completely free from every law of place and time. But yet if it can be seen in some sense in something that is composite, spatial, and temporal, it is not beyond belief that it is also the case in the highest nature which is free and perfect. (p. 27)

Not everything in this passage is easily grasped. But Anselm is at least saying that in some way the whole Nile exists in each of its Nile-features, and that, although for example the spring is not the river, still there is a sense in which *what the spring is* does not differ from *what the river is:* the spring and the river are "one nature, one water." We can perhaps capture some of what Anselm is getting at if we make some idealizing assumptions about the Nile. Let us suppose that the Nile is composed solely of water; that no water enters the Nile except from the spring, and no water leaves the Nile except from the lake; that volumes of water issue from the spring in discrete "pulses," and travel at a constant rate down the Nile; and that volumes of water, upon leaving the lake, either never reenter the Nile or instantaneously return to the spring. We may also assume that any one of the Nile-features, at any moment of its existence, is constituted of just the same number of water molecules as any other is constituted at any moment of its existence. Finally, let us suppose—for reasons that will emerge later—that the ultimate watery constituents of the Nile (water molecules) do not themselves undergo compositional change through time. Then a (partial) picture of the history of the Nile might look like this (where t stands for times, and v for volumes of water):

	Spring Location	River Location	Lake Location
	.	.	.
	.	.	.
t_n	v_n	v_m	v_l
	.	.	.
	.	.	.
t_{2n}	v_{2n}	v_n	v_m
	.	.	.
	.	.	.
t_{3n}	v_{3n}	v_{2n}	v_n
	.	.	.

(A gloss may help. A volume of water v_n constitutes the spring at time t_n, and gradually comes to constitute the river, as the constituents of v_n move from the spring location to the river location. After n units of time, the process is complete, so that at time t_{2n}, the volume of water v_n constitutes the river, and a different volume of water v_{2n}—having no [molecular] constituents in common with volume v_n—constitutes the spring. If we move n units of time farther in to the future, v_n will constitute the lake, and v_{2n} will constitute the river.) The Nile pictured here might either be sempiternal or temporally bounded: in the former case, the picture could be extended upward and downward infinitely. (Why we should want to consider a sempiternal Nile will soon become clear, if it is not already.)

A number of things emerge from this picture. First, we can see that the Nile-features are not identical. The spring has, but neither the river nor the lake has, the property of being composed of volume v_n at time t_n; the river has, but neither the spring nor the lake has, the property of being composed of volume v_n at time t_{2n}; and so on. Second, although the Nile-features are distinct, they are intimately related mereologically: they are built up out of the same parts. Any volume of water that is a constituent of one of the Nile-features at a time will be a constituent part of the other Nile-features (at different times). Third, an intimate mereological relation holds between the Nile and each of its Nile-features: if we consider small enough constituent parts of the Nile, any such part of the Nile at a time will be a constituent part of each Nile feature at some time or other. (Why "small enough"? Well, suppose that v_i and v_j are distinct volumes of water, each of which is big enough alone to constitute a Nile-feature at a time. Now consider the individual $v_i + v_j$, which has as parts anything that is either part of v_i or part of v_j. That individual will be a constituent part of the Nile at t_j, but it will never be a constituent part of any Nile-feature. If we consider volumes of water small enough to fit entirely into any one Nile-feature at a time, this problem does not arise.) Fourth, there is something we may think of as the substance or matter of the Nile, and of each of its Nile-features: and we may think of this as an aggregate of parts shared by all the Nile-features.

We have said that each Nile-feature is made of the same matter, or has the same physical parts. For reasons that soon will become evident, it will be useful to distinguish a number of ways in which individuals may be said to have the same constituent parts, or be co-composite, and in particular to specify the way in which the Nile-features may be said to be co-composite with one another, and co-composite with the water of which the Nile is made.

Types of Co-composition

A pair of individuals may be said to be *weakly co-composite* just in case they are, intuitively speaking, built up out of the same constituents. Suppose, for example, I had a collection of notched popsicle sticks, which I first put together to make a model of the USS *Constitution,* later took apart, and then reassembled to make a model of Chartres Cathedral. We may suppose that the model ship and the model cathedral are built up out of the same parts (notched popsicle sticks, and their constituents in turn). In that case, the two models will be weakly co-composite. Actually, the models almost certainly would not be weakly co-composite, because some (smallish) parts of the popsicle sticks would be lost in the process of disassembling and reassembling them. Also, it might turn out that the models each had evanescent subatomic parts, whose existence failed to cover both the lifetime of the model ship and the lifetime of the model cathedral. In that case, it will not strictly speaking be true that the two models are built up out of all the same parts. (No matter how far down we go, we won't find a level of parts at which the two models have all the same parts.) So, in order to get an example of what I have in mind by weak co-composition, we have to idealize somewhat our models and their constituents. Since I am only using the example for illustrative purposes, nothing hangs on this.

Two features of weak co-composition need to be stressed: weakly co-composite objects need not be built up out of the same parts at the same times, and they need not have all of the same parts (whether at the same or different times). The first point is clear from the example: nothing is a part of the model ship and the model cathedral at the same time, since the lifetimes of those individuals are disjoint. The second point was brought to my attention in conversation by David Kaplan. At least as long as we say that everything is always a (maximal) part of itself, we cannot say that whatever is at any time a part of the model ship is at some time a part of the model cathedral, since the ship is never a part of the cathedral. Similarly, some nonmaximal ('structural') parts of the model ship are never parts of the model cathedral. A model hull is a part of the model ship at any time at which that ship exists; but it is plausible that the model hull is never part of the model cathedral, although all of the popsicle-stick parts of the model hull (and all of their parts) are parts of the model cathedral throughout that cathedral's existence.

Notice that the individuals that are sometimes part of the ship and never part of the cathedral (or sometimes part of the cathedral and never part of the ship) are largeish parts: anything that is at any time an ultimate constituent or ur-part of the model ship is at some time an ur-part of the model cathedral. This suggests that we could define weak co-composition as follows:

> x and y are *weakly co-composite* just in case (i) for some time t, x exists at t; (ii) for any time t, and any part z, if z has no proper parts, and if z is a part of x at t, then there is some t' such that z is a part of y at t'; and (iii) for any time t, and any part z, if z has no proper parts, and if z is part of y at t, then there is some time t' such that z is a part of x at t'.

The idea here is that x and y are weakly co-composite just in case they have all the same smallest parts—though not necessarily at the same times. (Clause (i) is there to prevent any two atemporal objects from being [vacuously] weakly co-composite.)

The trouble with this suggestion is that it only gives the right results for individuals built up (exclusively) out of ur-parts. Thus any two individuals all of whose parts have proper parts will by the above definition be (vacuously) weakly co-composite. Nor would it do any good to define weak co-composition in terms of being built up exclusively from ur-parts, and satisfying the definition offered above: it is clear that, for example, any (temporal) object will be weakly co-composite with itself, whether or not all of its parts have proper parts. What we want is to characterize weak co-composition in terms of having all the same sufficiently small parts, rather than having all the same smallest parts. Before doing this, we need to fill in some background.

Consider a composite object x at a time t. At t, the object will have a finite or infinite number of parts. These parts (which I call x's t-parts) can as it were be stratified into a (finite or infinite) set of layers. The top layer will be a set containing all and only the parts of x at t which are not proper parts of x at t. (We may say that p is a proper part of x [at t] just in case p is a part of x [at t] and x is not a part of p [at t].) Thus the top layer will contain x, since everything is always a maximal part of itself, and whatever else at t both is a part of x and has x as a part.

The next layer of x's t-parts will be the set containing all and only those parts of x which are at t proper parts of some member of the top layer, but are not at t proper parts of any (then) proper part of any member of that top layer. We may call the top layer L_0, and the next layer L_1. We can continue in the obvious way, taking L_n to be the set of parts of x which are at t proper parts of some member of L_{n-1}, but not at t proper parts of any (then) proper part of any member of L_{n-1}.[8]

What emerges from this layering process is a partition of the set of x's t-parts into subsets of same-sized parts. The top layer, for example, contains the largest parts of x at t. If x has finitely many parts, then there will be a bottom layer L_n, containing all and only the smallest parts of x at t. So if x and y have only finitely many parts, then x and y will be weakly co-composite if (i) x exists at some time t; (ii) for any time t at which x exists, there is a time t' and a set of parts P such that P is both the bottom layer of x's t-parts, and the bottom layer of y's t'-parts; and (iii) for any time t at which y exits, there is a time t' and a set of parts P such that P is both the bottom layer of y's t-parts, and the bottom layer of x's t'-parts. We might try to generalize this idea to cover the case of co-composite objects not build up out of ur-parts, as follows:

> x and y are weakly co-composite just in case (i) for some t, x exists at t; (ii) for any time t at which x exists, there is a time t' and a set of parts P such that P is both a layer of x's t-parts, and a layer of y's t'-parts; and (iii) for any time t at which y exists, there is a time t' and a set of parts P such that P is both a layer of y's t-parts, and a layer of x's t'-parts.

In other words: suppose that x and y are weakly co-composite. Then and only then do the following conditions (nonvacuously) hold: (a) for any time t at which x exists, there is a time t' such that if you layer x's t-parts, and layer y's t'-parts, sooner or later (after a finite or infinite number of steps) you'll find a common layer; and (b) for any time t at which y exists, there is a time t' such that if you layer y's t-parts and layer x's t'-parts, sooner or later you'll find a common layer.

To better understand what this definition amounts to, it may help to see that if there is a set of parts P which is both the mth layer of x's t-parts, and the nth layer of y's t'-parts, then for any k, if there are $m + k$ layers, there is a set of parts P' which is both the $m + k$th layer of x's t-parts, and the $n + k$th layer of y's t'-parts. It may not be obvious that this is so: couldn't it be that x at t and x at t' have, say, all the same

---

[8]In line with the idea that we are speaking of constituent parts, and not any old spatial parts, I am assuming here that x has no (non-ur) part p such that every proper part of p is a proper part of some proper part of p. If we don't make this assumption, we have to define the layering process differently—say, by defining a layer in terms of the volume occupied by any of its constituents.

water molecules, but not all the same subatomic particles (because the molecules composing x at t and t' have undergone compositional change between t and t')? Yes, but in that case, it will not be true that the layer that is the set of molecule-sized t-parts of x is the same as the layer that is the set of molecule-sized t'-parts of x. Why not? Well, the set of molecule-sized t-parts of x will include not just molecules, but also (molecule-sized) aggregates of subatomic particles then constituting those molecules. These molecule-sized aggregates of subatomic particles are distinct from the molecules of x they constitute at t, just as the molecule-sized aggregates of subatomic particles constituting the molecules that are part of x at t' are distinct from the molecules they constitute at t'. (If the molecule undergoes compositional change after t, then the molecule and the aggregate of subatomic particles constituting the molecule at t cannot be identical, since they will not be in all of the same places at all of the same times.) And it is clearly not the case that all and only those molecule-sized aggregates of subatomic particles which are t-parts of x are t'-parts of x. So if, say, the set of x's quark-sized t-parts is distinct from the set of y's quark-sized t'-parts, then for any set of larger-sized parts (for example, molecule-sized parts), the set of x's thus-sized t-parts is distinct from the set of y's thus-sized t'-parts. Contraposing and generaliziang, we get that if the set of x's so-big t-parts is the same as the set of y's so-big t'-parts, then the set of x's that-much-smaller t-parts is the same as the set of y's that-much-smaller t'-parts, however much smaller the parts in question are. From this it should be clear that the definition captures the intuitive idea that if two things are weakly co-composite, then—at least if we exclude from consideration parts larger than a certain size—those two things will have the same parts all the way down (although they may have those parts at different times).

Actually, though, the above definition captures more than weak co-composition if (as I intend) weak co-composition is understood just by reference to being built up out of the same (sufficiently small) parts. As we have seen, the sempiternal Nile and the sempiternal spring are built up out of all the same (sufficiently small) parts, and are accordingly weakly co-composite. But they do not satisfy the definition of weak co-composition just provided: if we layer the Nile's parts at any time t, there will be no set of parts P and time t' such that P is both a layer of the Nile at t and a layer of the spring at t'. (The Nile has at any one moment of its existence more molecule-sized, atom-sized, quark-sized . . . parts than the spring has at any one moment of its existence.) Moreover, two things built up out of the same parts can fail to satisfy the above condition even if they are always, as it were, of the same "size." Suppose that in the first third of the lifetimes of x and y, x has as ur-parts just p_1 and p_2, while y has as ur-parts just p_3 and p_4; in the second third of their lifetimes, x has as ur-parts just p_1 and p_3, while y has as ur-parts p_2 and p_4; and in the last third, x has as ur-parts just p_3 and p_4, while y has as ur-parts just p_1 and p_2. Then for some time t, the set $\{p_1, p_3\}$ is a layer of x's ur t-parts, even though for no time t' is it a layer of y's ur t'-parts; and for some time t, the set $\{p_2, p_4\}$ is a layer of y's ur t-parts, although for no time t' is it a layer of x's ur t'-parts: from which it follows that x and y do not satisfy the definition of weak co-composition just provided.

We need, then, to weaken our definition as follows:

> x and y are *weakly co-composite* if and only if (i) for some time t, x exists at t; (ii) for any time t at which x exists, there is a (nonempty) set P such that P is a layer of x's t-parts, and for any z, if z is an element of P, then there is a time t' such that z is a t'-part of y; and (iii) for any time t at which y exists, there is a (nonempty) set P such that P is a layer of y's t-parts, and for any z, if z is an element of P, then there is a time t' such that z is a t'-part of x.

By this definition, the Nile turns out to be weakly co-composite with the spring. Consider the Nile at an arbitrary moment of its existence t. The layer of its molecule-sized t-parts will not be identical to any layer of molecule-sized t'-parts of the spring; but any element of the Nile's layer of molecule-sized t-parts will be a t'-part of the spring, for some t'. (This takes us only halfway to showing that the Nile and the spring are weakly co-composite; but the other half is trivial.)

Weak co-composition is so-called because two things can be weakly co-composite, without being very intimately related. Various other forms of co-composition entail weak co-composition without being entailed by it. One such is the form of co-composition characterized on pages 172–73 in the first, unsuccessful attempt to capture the notion of weak co-composition in a way that allowed for the possibility that individuals were not built up exclusively out of ur-parts. We may call this relation (which holds between any two Nile-features, but not between the Nile and any of its Nile-features) *layer-sharing co-composition*. Another form of co-composition stronger than weak co-composition is *overlap co-composition*, defined thus:

> x and y are *overlap co-composite* just in case (i) x and y are weakly co-composite; and (ii) there is a time t and a set of parts P such that P is both a layer of x's t-parts, and a layer of y's t-parts.

Unless I am mistaken, (ii) could be replaced by

(ii′)   there is a time t and a set of parts P such that P is both the set of x's t-parts and the set of y's t-parts.

The only way in which (ii) could be true, and (ii′) false, would be if x and y had all the same this-small-or-smaller t-parts, but did not have all of the same t-parts. In that case, it would turn out that for some part z, z was a t-part of x but not y, or a t-part of y but not x, even though at some level of smallness, all of z's that-small t-parts were both t-parts of x and t-parts of y. But if all of z's that-small t-parts are t-parts of a thing (whether x or y), it is hard to see what could prevent z itself from being a t-part of that thing. It is of course possible for all of the things that are at (a different) time t' that-small parts of an individual i, to be parts of a thing at time t, without that individual i's being a part of that thing at t. (For example, all of the things that are at some other time the popsicle-stick-sized parts of the nave of my model cathedral could now be parts of my model ship, without the nave itself now being part of my model ship.) But if all the things that are now the that-small parts of an individual are now part of a thing, then that individual must likewise be part of that thing.

An example of a pair of overlap co-composite objects would be a statue and a lump of clay from which the statue was made, if they were also weakly co-composite. (The overlap interval would be the period in which the lump of clay was "statue-formed.")

Although overlap co-composition, like weak co-composition, falls short of identity, it is in one sense a more intimate relation than weak co-composition: individuals that are overlap co-composite are very closely related at some stage in their careers. During the overlap stage, they will be indiscernible with respect to a great many properties— mass, chemical composition, shape, and so on. Indeed, if two objects are overlap co-composite, then there is a set of times t at which those objects are identical-at-time-t (in the sense discussed earlier in this chapter).

A third sort of co-composition is a more intimate relation than either of the two discussed so far. We may say that two individuals are *cohabitant co-composite* just in case they are built up out of all the same (sufficiently small) parts at all the same times. That is:

x and y are *cohabitant co-composite* just in case (i) for some t, x exists at t; and (ii) for every time t at which x exists or y exists, there is a set of parts P such that P is both a layer of x's t-parts and a layer of y's t-parts.

Again, we could replace (ii) by

> (ii') for every time t at which x exists or y exists, there is a set of parts P such that P is the set of x's t-parts and the set of y's t-parts.

Cohabitant individuals are overlap co-composite individuals whose overlap phase coincides with each of their lifetimes. Clearly, cohabitant individuals are very intimately related: any two such individuals will have the same mass, shape, occupy the same region of space-time, and so on. Indeed, for reasons I have laid out elsewhere, I am somewhat inclined to think that cohabitant individuals are identical;[9] but I won't take a stand on this issue here.

Co-composition and the Trinity

We may now—at long last—return to Trinitarian concerns. How are we to understand the claim that the persons of the Trinity are, as the Nicene Creed says, 'of one substance'? If we take it to mean that there is a single substance to which each person of the Trinity is identical, we get two persons too few. If we take it to mean that each person is of like substance (*homoiousios*, rather than *homoousios*), we seem to get two Gods too many. What we want is a relation that links the persons closely, while allowing them to be discernible with respect to a certain range of properties. A natural suggestion here is that a relation holds between the persons which has the structure of the relation *being made of the same stuff as*, or (more cautiously) *being made of the same parts as*. We have seen that there are many different ways in which concrete individuals can be made of the same parts. Two of them offer promising ways of understanding what the consubstantiality relation holding between different persons of the Trinity is. It might be, as Anselm's model suggests, layer-sharing co-composition—or the weaker relation of weak co-composition. Since the former is related to the latter as species to genus, it is safer to identify consubstantiality with weak co-composition. Alternatively, as long as distinct things can be cohabitant co-composite, consubstantiality might be cohabitant co-composition. (In conversation, Richard Gale and Lily Knezevich have defended this approach.) If consubstantiality

[9]In Christopher Hughes, "Is a Thing Just the Sum of Its Parts?" *Proceedings of the Aristotelian Society* 86 (1985–86): 213–35, I argue that considerations of parsimony provide some inducement to identify cohabitant individuals. The inducement, however, is less than irresistible.

is weak co-composition, it is quite clear that the consubstantiality of any two divine persons does not entail their identity (or, for that matter, their identity-at-*t*, for any time *t*). If consubstantiality is cohabitant co-composition, it is at least arguable that the consubstantiality of any two divine persons does not entail their identity.[10] And while we cannot say *how* it is that consubstantial persons of the Trinity are indiscernible with respect to properties such as *being omnipotent, being all-good,* and the like, and at the same time discernible with respect to properties such as *being unbegotten* and *proceeding from the Father and the Son,* nothing about the weak co-composition relation precludes this possibility, and nothing about the cohabitant co-composition relation clearly precludes it.[11]

If the divine persons are either weakly co-composite or cohabitant co-composite with one another, what relation do the divine persons all bear to God? Well, what sort of being is the God who is distinct from each of the divine persons? Anselm's model suggests that we think of God as the substance of which all the divine persons are made, in something like the way some water is the stuff of which all the Nile-features are made. The stuff of which each Nile-feature—and for that matter the Nile—is made, is a portion of water, that is, an aggregate of water molecules. What kind of thing is that? It is a physical object (having mass, spatio-temporal location, and so on) which has exactly the same water molecules as constituents at all the times, and in all the worlds in which it exists. We may think of an aggregate of water molecules as the kind of thing described in Burge's "A Theory of Aggregates" (*Nous* 11 [1977]). On that theory, an aggregate is individuated by reference to its member-components in much the way that a set is individuated by reference to its elements; just as sets are identical if and only if they have all the same elements, so aggregates are identical if and only if they have all the same member-components.

[10]For a putative example of a pair of distinct cohabitant co-composite things, see Tyler Burge, "A Theory of Aggregates," *Nous* 11 (1977): 97–117. (The pair is ⟨a positronium atom, the aggregate of its parts⟩.) The usual argument against supposing that cohabitant co-composition entails identity is that we can do so only if we offer an unstraightforward, unintuitive account of modal predication, according to which contexts like "———— would have existed under such-and-such conditions" are referentially opaque. For attempts to motivate the idea that such contexts are referentially opaque, see Allan Gibbard, "Contingent Identity," *Journal of Philosophical Logic* 4, no. 2 (1975): 187–221, and Lewis, "Counterparts of Persons and Their Bodies."

[11]In supposing that the divine persons are cohabitant co-composite or weakly co-composite with one another, I ignore certain difficulties that arise when we try to put together a co-compositional account of the Trinity with a plausible account of the Incarnation (see Chapter 7, and n. 3 of the Conclusion). For expository reasons, I shall at present ignore these difficulties, which in any case I don't know how to resolve.

So, on Burge's conception the aggregate of water molecules ever in the Nile would be the aggregate having as its member-components all and only those water molecules that are ever parts of the Nile. (Note that on this approach one shall have to distinguish between the parts of an aggregate and its member-components: any part of a part of an aggregate will be a part of that aggregate, but it will not in general be true that any part of a member-component of an aggregate will be a member-component of that aggregate.) There are alternative (mereological) ways of thinking about the aggregate of water molecules ever in the Nile; but we need not go into this matter here.

So, if we take the divine persons to be distinct, weakly co-composite or cohabitant co-composite individuals, we may take God—the substance of each of the divine persons—to be an aggregate whose member-components are parts common to all three divine persons.[12] If we suppose that the divine persons are cohabitant co-composite with one another, then each divine person will also be cohabitant co-composite with God, just as the sempiternal Nile would be cohabitant co-composite with the aggregate of water molecules ever in the Nile if the molecules in that aggregate spent no time outside of the Nile. If we suppose only that the divine persons are weakly co-composite with one another, we should say that any divine person is weakly co-composite with God, just as any Nile-feature is weakly co-composite with the aggregate of the Nile's water molecules. Actually, if the water of the Nile is an aggregate of all the water molecules ever in the Nile, each Nile-feature will stand in a special relation to the Nile which we may call thing-stuff-co-composition:

> x is *thing-stuff-co-composite* with y if and only if x exists at some time t, and (i) for any time t at which x exists, there is a set of

[12]There may be more than one such aggregate. To see this, consider the analogical case of the Nile. There will be an aggregate of all the molecules shared by each of the Nile-features, an aggregate of all the atoms shared by each of the Nile-features, an aggregate of all the quarks shared by each of the Nile-features, and so on. Given that aggregates are individuated in the Burge way, these aggregates will be distinct. Likewise, there might be a hierarchy of aggregates of parts shared by the divine persons. If we suppose that "God" refers to the substance of the divine persons, and that this substance should be construed as an aggregate of parts shared by those persons, which aggregate of shared parts should we take "God" to refer to? In ignorance of what the divine parts are like, there is no obvious answer, although there are lots of possibilities: for example, if the divine persons have ur-parts, "God" could refer to the aggregate of ur-parts shared by the divine persons; or "God" could refer to the union of however many aggregates of parts shared by the divine persons there are. We could circumvent all of these quandaries if we conceived of aggregates mereologically, since that would allow us to identify any 'two' aggregates of parts shared by the divine persons.

parts P such that P is a layer of x's t-parts, and for any z, if z is an element of P, then z is a t'-part of y, for every t' at which y exists; and (ii) for any time t at which y exists, there is a set of parts P such that P is a layer of y's t-parts, and for any z, if z is an element of P, then there is a time t' such that z is a t'-part of x.

Note that this relation is nonsymmetric. Thus the spring is thing-stuff-co-composite with the aggregate of water molecules ever in the Nile: for any time t when the spring exists, there is a layer of the spring's t-parts P such that every member of P is a member of the aggregate at any time that aggregate exists. (Here the idealizing assumption made earlier to the effect that the water molecules in the spring do not have evanescent submolecular parts comes into play.) The aggregate of water molecules in question, however, is not thing-stuff-co-composite with the spring, since, for any time t at which the aggregate exists, and any P that is a layer of that aggregate's t-parts, P will have elements that are not parts of the spring at every time the spring exists.

We may now return to the question of what the logical form of the Trinitarian statements (1)–(3) might be. My suggestion is that it might be something like this (where $T =$ ——— is thing-stuff-co-composite with ———):

(1a) $(\exists x)\,(\exists y)\,(\exists z)\,[(Px \wedge Py \wedge Pz \wedge x \neq y \wedge y \neq z \wedge x \neq z)$
$\wedge\, (u)\,(Pu \rightarrow (u = x \vee u = y \vee u = z))]$

(2a) $(x)\,[Px \rightarrow (\exists y)\,(Gy \wedge Txy)]$

(3a) $(\exists x)\,[Gx \wedge (y)\,(Gy \rightarrow y = x)]$

In English:

(1a) There are exactly three divine persons.

(2a) Each divine person is thing-stuff-co-composite with (a) God.

(3a) There is exactly one God.

Alternatively, it might be just like the above, except that (2a) would be replaced by

(2a★) $(x)\,[Px \rightarrow (\exists y)\,(Gy \wedge Cxy)]$

where $C =$ ——— is cohabitant co-composite with ———.

We leave (1′) and (3′) just as they are, and reconstrue (2) as the claim that each divine person is thing-stuff-co-composite with God. Or we reconstrue (2) as the claim that each divine person is cohabitant co-composite with God.[13]

The advantages of the first formalization are obvious: it is not provably inconsistent; it does not prize identity and indiscernibility apart; and it gives us three divine persons, in a robust sense of 'three', and one God, in a robust sense of 'one'. As a bonus, we get a way of understanding what might (loosely speaking) be called Trinitarian relative identity statements. For instance, the claim that the Father and the Son are the same God, but different persons, is understood to have a logical form reminiscent of "The spring and the river are the same water, but different Nile-features." The advantages of the second formalization are similar, except that there is a question about whether we really do get three divine persons.

Before I discuss further the merits of these formalizations, it may be best to offer an explicit disclaimer: although the formalizations offered here draw on Anselm's model, neither one can be thought of as a formalization of Anselm's view of the Trinity. We have seen that Anselm denies both that any divine person or God exists at any time, and that any divine person or God is in any way composite. Consequently, he could not take (1)–(3) to have the structure of (1a)–(3a), or (1a⋆)–(3a⋆). He would have to say instead that the relation of the divine persons to the one God they are is like the relation of the Nile-features to the water they are made of, except that whereas the latter is to be understood in terms of a co-composition relation holding between distinct composite temporal individuals, the latter is not. To say this is not so much to kick the ladder away after one has climbed up, as to kick it away while one is still standing on it: accordingly, I am suggesting that we take certain features of Anselm's model much more seriously than Anselm himself does.

Of course, someone might object that the conception of the Trinity embodied in the first formalization is heterodox, just because on it the divine persons and God have (proper) parts, or just because on it the divine persons and God are temporal (and subject to [compositional] change). The first of these objections can also be raised against the second formalization, which takes each divine person to be cohabitant co-composite with God.[14]

[13]Again, either formalization will mesh with only certain sorts of accounts of the Incarnation.

[14]If any two divine persons are cohabitant co-composite, then they always have just the same parts. If they always have just the same parts, then they always have each

The first objection looks unmeetable only if one conflates the notion of a part with the notion of a physical (spatially extended) part. If one holds that the divine persons, like the Nile-features, are individuals built up from the same physical parts, one presumably ends up with a heterodox conception of the Trinity. But the notion of a part is—at least on the face of it—broader than the notion of a physical part. (To take just one example, if the only substances were Cartesian *res cogitantes*, there would be no such thing as a physical [spatially extended] part; but we could still speak of parts of the lives of *res cogitantes*, and parts of events in the lives of *res cogitantes*.) Consequently, neither (1a)–(3a) nor (1a*)–(3a*) commit us to the heterodox view that the divine persons and God have physical parts.

Still, isn't the idea that the divine persons and God have a plurality of parts of any kind heterodox? It must be admitted that the idea that they do is a surprising one, which would have been denounced not just by Anselm, but by Augustine, Aquinas, and the whole pantheon of medieval philosophical theology. There is, however a difference between the tenets of medieval Christian philosophers and the tenets of the Christian faith. I know of nothing in any ecclesiastical document which explicitly rules out *all* forms of composition in God, and in arguing that there is no composition in God, both Anselm and

---

other as parts (since they each always have themselves as maximal parts). In that case, each one always has more parts than one (since each one has Himself and the other as a part). The same argument shows that if any divine person and God are cohabitant co-composite, then God has more parts than one.

Notice, though, that we might think of proper parts in two ways. We might suppose that x is a proper part of y just in case x is a part of y, and x is distinct from y. Or we might suppose that x is a proper part of y just in case x is a part of y and y is not a part of x. (If we assume that whenever two individuals have each other as parts, they are identical—as, say, the calculus of individuals does—these characterizations of proper-parthood are obviously equivalent; but if we want to leave room for distinct cohabitant co-composita, we shall not want to make that assumption.) Corresponding to these two characterizations of a proper part, there are two characterizations of incomposition. That is, we might suppose (as Aquinas does) that an individual is incomposite just in case it has no proper parts in the first sense—that is, has no parts other than itself—or we might suppose that an individual is incomposite just in case it has no proper parts in the second sense—that is, has no part of which it is not a part. The argument above shows that no two distinct cohabitant co-composita can be incomposite in the first sense, but it fails to show that no two distinct cohabitant co-composita can be incomposite in the second sense. That is, it fails to show that if x and y are cohabitant co-composite, there is some part z such that z is part of x and x is not a part of z, or z is a part of y and y is not a part of z. Evidently, anything that is incomposite in the first sense is incomposite in the second; but does the converse hold? I lean to the view that it does, in part because—even assuming that distinct things can be cohabitant co-composite—I am at a loss to imagine a case in which something is incomposite in the second sense, but not in the first.

Aquinas rely on metaphysical considerations rather than on orthodoxy.

Similarly, I don't think the view that God and the divine persons are
temporal and mutable is heterodox, even if it was very unpopular with
(Christian) medieval philosophical theologians. In fact, I argue in
Chapter 7 that any theory on which each divine person is outside of
time and beyond change will—for predictable reasons—come to grief
if the attempt is made to give an orthodox (nondocetist) theory of the
Incarnation.

There is, however, a variant of (1a)–(3a) which will be true as long
as (1a)–(3a) is, but does not (obviously) entail that God is temporal or
mutable. We know that in the following sentence,

> Different individuals can be built up out of all the same (small
> enough) parts at different ———.

we can (correctly) fill in "times." There might be other ways of
correctly filling in the blank, however. *Perhaps* there are other undreamt of ways of filling in that blank truthfully; perhaps the divine
persons are different composita having all the same (small enough)
parts at different ?'s, or for that matter different composita having all
the same parts at the same ?'s, where ?'s are not times, or worlds, or
anything dreamt of. Someone who can live with the idea that God and
the divine persons are composite may yet be unwilling to accept that
God, or any of the divine persons, is temporal or mutable. If so, she
may be able to live with a version of (1a)–(3a) which replaces the
reference to times therein by reference to, say, *indices,* where it is left
open whether or not there are, in addition to temporal indices (that is,
times), undreamt of nontemporal indices.

There remain two straightforward theological objections to the
formalizations offered. First, it might be said that neither (2a) nor (2a⋆)
is strong enough to capture what is meant by (2). After all, the
Athanasian creed tells us that "the Father is God, the Son is God, and
the Holy Spirit is God." Mustn't this statement be construed as a
conjunction of identity statements?

I think not. 'The Father is God' looks just like some English sentences that are identity statements. But not all sentences of that form
express identities: for instance, 'Harrison Ford is Han Solo'—on its
natural reading—does not.[15] Moreover, there seem to be sentences of
the grammatical form '*a* is *b*' which have the logical form of co-

---

[15]Harrison Ford played Han Solo in the movie *Star Wars.*

composition statements, and should be formalized as such. Consider an example of Sydney Shoemaker's: my friend, who knows only that I have a statue and a piece of bronze in my study, asks which of the two I shall bring to a party. I reply, "You don't understand—the statue is the piece of bronze." If we construe my reply as an identity statement it will no doubt be false, since the statue and the piece of bronze will be overlap co-composite, without being identical. But we need not so construe it, any more than we need construe "Harrison Ford is Han Solo" as an identity statement; we can suppose that, just as 'is' sometimes works like 'is playing the part of', it sometimes works like 'is made of the same stuff as' or 'is co-composite with'. So we can maintain that (2) only looks like an identity claim, and has the logical form of a co-composition statement. (Which sort of co-composition statement will depend on which formalization is adopted.)

A second objection to either of the suggested formalizations is that on either God turns out not to be a person, but only the stuff of which divine persons are made. Perhaps if both formalizations entailed that 'God is a person' had *no* true reading, this would show that neither captured an orthodox notion of the Trinity. But we may suppose that there is a sense in which God is a person, just as there is a sense in which a certain quantity or portion of water is a lake. True, the logical form of 'God is a person' will not be that of 'The Father is a person', but this is all to the good: from the supposition that it is, one can quickly deduce the claim that either God is a person distinct from the three, so that there are four divine persons; or God is the same person as one of the three, but not the other two; or all the divine persons are identical to one another, so there is just one divine person. (I leave it to the reader to fill in the details of the argument.)

Compositional and Noncompositional Accounts of the Trinity

It may be useful to review here what has and has not been accomplished. Obviously, the actuality of the Trinity has not been demonstrated; nor has puzzlement been banished about how it could be that God is three persons in one Nature. For although we have said that divine parts need not be physical parts, we have said nothing contentful about what kinds of parts they might be.

What we have done is to show that, appearances to the contrary, the doctrine of the Trinity (or at least that fragment of it in (1)–(3) is not demonstrably inconsistent. This is not a trivial result, especially for a Christian: what matters to her is not to have a demonstration of the existence of the Trinity, or even a detailed understanding of how it is possible, but rather to lack a demonstration of its impossibility (and, ideally, to know that no such demonstration could turn up).

Moreover, we have perhaps arrived at some—very limited—understanding of how the divine persons might be related to one another, and to God. They might be compositionally related to one another in the way that the Nile-features are related to one another, and compositionally related to God, in the way that the Nile-features are related to the water that is their substance. Alternatively, they might be compositionally related to one another and to God in the way the sempiternal Nile would be related to the aggregate of water molecules ever in the Nile, if all the water molecules ever in the Nile were always in the Nile.

It may be best to issue another disclaimer here: I am not saying that we can make orthodox sense of the Trinity only along the lines I have suggested. A very different approach to making orthodox sense of the Trinity takes as its starting point the idea that in the Trinity there is just one individual or concrete particular—God—who has three "modes of existing" or "modes of subsisting." On this view—which we may call moderately Sabellian[16]—what it is for there to be three divine persons is for one and the same divine individual to have three modes of subsisting; what it is for there to be one God is for there to be just one divine individual. Naturally, there are all sorts of questions about just what this view amounts to, and how it will enable us to give a consistent and orthodox formalization of (1)–(3). For example, can anything be said about what a mode of subsisting is? Also, on this view of the Trinity, what sort of entity do the singular terms standing for the persons—"the Father" and "the Son" and "the Holy Spirit"—denote? And in virtue of what relation holding between any divine person and God, is it true that each divine person is God? (In other words, given that the moderate Sabellian offers a straightforward formalization of (1) and (3), exactly which unstraightforward formalization of (2) does she give us?) I don't know what the answers to these questions would be, but it is no part of my argument that no satisfactory answers could be given.

Someone might object that no way of developing the moderately Sabellian picture of the Trinity sketched above would allow us to provide an orthodox as well as consistent formalization of (1)–(3). On that picture, because the Trinity involves just one individual in three

---

[16]The moderate Sabellian denies that the divine persons are distinct concrete particulars; the immoderate Sabellian denies that the divine persons are distinct.

modes of subsisting, the plurality of persons in the Trinity is not a plurality of individuals.[17] But, the objection goes, in the robust and interesting sense of "person," a person just is an individual or concrete particular of a certain kind, with the consequence that different persons are different individuals. So, on the view being considered, in the robust and interesting sense, there are not really three persons in the Trinity, even if the view specifies some (ill- or well-understood) Pickwickian sense in which there are.

I have some sympathy for this kind of objection: but there is a symmetrical objection to the co-compositional formalizations adumbrated in this chapter. Someone might say: if there really are three divine individuals (each one omnipotent, omniscient, and so on), then in the robust and interesting sense of "God," there are three Gods. So even if the co-compositional formalizations secure nominal conformity to orthodoxy (by assigning to 'God' an unnatural referent), they fail to secure real conformity thereto.

What this shows is that the doctrine of the Trinity fails to be irremediably inconsistent only if either what it is to be a divine person, or what it is to be a God, turns out to be something rather different than we might have expected. (This is just another way of saying that the doctrine of the Trinity is on the face of it inconsistent.) Unless we revise and stretch our beliefs about what kind of thing a divine person is, or about what kind of thing God is, we won't make room for the Trinity. We can make room in a variety of ways, one of which is captured by the co-compositional formalizations just laid out. Whether that way of making room is (theologically, metaphysically) preferable to the second way considered (or to others not yet canvassed) is an important question that I must leave to another time and place. At present, I want to argue only that co-compositional accounts give us some understanding of *one* kind of structure the Trinity might have, and one way in which (1)–(3) might turn out to be true. As I have already said, our understanding of what that structure would be like is quite partial and schematic.

---

[17]Of course, in one sense of 'individual', 'individual' is a blanket term (like 'thing'): in that sense, every plurality is a plurality of individuals. But when the moderate Sabellian says that the Trinity involves just one individual in three modes of existence, she has in mind a more restrictive sense of 'individual'—one that means something like 'concrete particular'. If a divine person is not a concrete particular, it might, I suppose, be a mode of God's existence or perhaps God-in-a-certain-mode-of-His-existence (as long as "God-in-a-certain-mode-of-His-existence" is *not* thought of as denoting the God who exists in that certain mode). Again, I don't know what either of these sorts of things might be; but this may simply reflect a failure of imagination on my part.

It is probably a mistake to suppose that philosophy could provide more than partial and schematic understanding in this area. For if Christianity is true, the Trinity is a mystery that surpasses human understanding; and if Christianity is false, then there is no determinate, fully fleshed out set of facts about the Trinity to be known. (Fictional objects are notoriously incomplete: that is why they resist reification as *possibilia*.) A passage from Aquinas is apropos here:

> In sacred teaching we can use philosophy in three ways. First, we can use it to demonstrate the preambles of faith . . . for example that God exists, or God is one, or similar propositions that faith presupposes as having been proven in philosophy.
>
> Second, we can use philosophy to make known through certain likenesses what belongs to the faith, as Augustine in his book *De trinitate* uses many likenesses drawn from the teaching of the philosophers to explain the Trinity.
>
> Third, we can use philosophy to oppose what is said against the faith, either by showing that these things are false, or that they are not necessary. (*Expositio super librum Boethii de trinitate* 3.1)

Aquinas is (I would argue) overly optimistic about the prospects for natural theology, but he is well aware of the limitations of philosophical understanding with respect to "what belongs to the faith"—including, of course, the doctrine of the Trinity. I have argued that if we make some very un-Aristotelian, un-Anselmian, and un-Thomistic assumptions about the divine nature, we can use philosophy to carry out what Aquinas would consider its proper task with respect to the doctrine of the Trinity: that is, to show that the Trinity cannot be known a priori to be an impossible object, and to give an inkling of what it might be like should it be real. What if we make Thomistic assumptions about the divine nature? Can we still show that arguments against the possibility of the Trinity are inconclusive? The next chapter provides an answer to this question.

[6]

Identity and the Trinity

Few areas of Aquinas' philosophical theology are more difficult to understand than his treatment of the metaphysics of the Trinity. For one thing, in attempting to give a coherent and orthodox account of the Trinity, Aquinas is wrestling with a notoriously intractable set of problems; for another, in that account, he draws on a set of concepts and distinctions from his metaphysics and philosophy of mind which do not yield easily to the understanding. Before we can begin to grasp what Aquinas has to say about the Trinity, we must be pretty well acquainted with his views on, among other things, the relation of hypostases (or first substances) to quiddities or essences, the difference between identity *secundum rem* and identity *secundum rationem,* the nature of relations, and the metaphysics of thinking-about and willing. Of course, familiarity with the outlines of Aquinas' metaphysics is not a sufficient condition for understanding what he thinks about the Trinity: special difficulties arise when Aristotelian categories are applied to a very un-Aristotelian (Trinitarian) conception of God.

In order to embed his account of the Trinity in a basically Aristotelian metaphysic, Aquinas must recognize certain possibilities that Aristotle never would have envisioned, and might well have wanted to exclude; he must also construe the doctrine of the Trinity in such a way that it ascribes to God a nature that the completely simple God of *Quaestio* 3 of the *Summa theologiae* could have. Precisely because of the obstacles encountered in fitting together a Trinitarian and a (somewhat) Aristotelian conception of God, Aquinas' treatment is of philosophical as well as theological interest: the determined attempt to reconcile two possibly incompatible theories, even if it fails, will usually lead to a better understanding of each theory. In fact, I argue that there is a fundamental incoherence in Aquinas' theory of the Trinity, arising from his desire to eat his cake and have it too—*viz.,* to have a God who is at once triune and free from composition of any kind. First, however, I trace the outlines of Aquinas' theory.

One God and Three Persons

The task of giving an account of the Trinity could be approached in at least two ways. One would be to take as a starting point the existence of three divine persons, and work from there toward an explanation of how the three persons 'are' just one God. Another would be to begin with the unicity of God, and try to get from there to an understanding of how the one God is tripersonal. Following Augustine (and many of Augustine's successors), Aquinas takes the latter approach. For Aquinas, the starting point is that which can be known by unaided reason: that there is just one God, who understands and who wills. Aquinas does not try to show that the God who understands and wills must be tripersonal—this would be tantamount to demonstrating that which, by Aquinas' own lights, surpasses reason. But he does attempt to give some idea of how God's nature as a willing and understanding being gives rise to three distinct but consubstantial persons; and in that attempt, he hopes to show that the idea of a God who is one essence in three persons is not repugnant to (that is, manifestly contrary to) reason.

How do the acts of willing and understanding in God ground a Trinity of divine persons? A crude first approximation to the Thomistic answer to this question would be the following: corresponding to the willing and understanding in God are certain real relations, really distinct from one another. These relations constitute and individuate the divine persons: three relationally distinct persons who are nevertheless of the very same essence. Of course, this answer is compressed enough to be unintelligible to anyone not well acquainted with Aquinas' theory of the Trinity. In trying to say what this answer amounts to, I for the most part draw on discussions of the Trinity in the *Summa theologiae, Summa contra Gentiles,* and "De potentia." My focus is on Aquinas' account of how divine understanding gives rise to a plurality of divine persons, rather than on his account of how the divine will does. This is because Aquinas' account of the understanding is somewhat more accessible than his account of the will, and because the issues that concern me arise equally in connection with the idea that divine understanding is the source of a plurality of divine persons, and the idea that divine will is such a source.

According to Aquinas, our knowledge of divine perfections has its root in our knowledge of creaturely perfections. In order, then, to even partially comprehend how the divine understanding is a source of constitutive and individuating relations in God, we must look to human understanding; just as, in order to see how the divine will is a source of constitutive and individuating relations in God, we need to consider the human will. In what follows, I sketch the outlines of Aquinas' characterization of divine understanding.

Suppose a man is thinking about a rock. On Aquinas' view, a number of things are involved in this event. First there is the *species intelligibilis,* the wherewithal to think about rocks, on account of which a man is able to go from potentially thinking about a rock to actually thinking about a rock. Second, there is the *actio intellectus* or *intelligere,* which is the actuality of thinking about, or state of occurrently thinking about, a rock. Third, there is the *conceptio intellectus,* or *verbum interior* (inner word), which resembles what Franz Brentano calls the intentional object of a thought. The inner word is an entity that can exist only in thought, is the (internal) terminus or goal of the act of thinking, and is a likeness (*similitudo*) of the thing in the world thought about. Finally, there is the *res intellecta,* the ultimate or extramental object of thought—in this case, the rock. Aquinas warns us against confusing the inner word with any of the other items involved in thinking-about:

> A thinker in thinking-about can be related to four things—namely, to the thing that is thought about [*rem quae intelligitur*], to the intelligible species . . . , to his act of thinking [*suum intelligere*], and to the intentional object of his thought [*conceptio intellectus*]. The intentional object certainly differs from the other three items mentioned above. It differs from the thing thought about, because the thing thought about sometimes exists outside the understanding, while the intentional object does not exist except in the understanding; and also the intentional object is related to the thing thought about as to an end. . . . It differs from the intelligible species; for the intelligible species, by which the understanding is made actual, may be thought of as the starting point of the act of thinking. . . . It differs from the act of thinking [*actione intellectus*]: for the intentional object [*conceptio*] may be thought of as the terminus of the act, and as it were something constituted by that act. An intentional object of this kind, or word [*verbum*], by which our understanding thinks about some thing other than itself, proceeds from another, and

represents another . . . it is in truth a likeness of the thing thought about. (DP 8.1, *responsio*)

A recurrent theme of Thomistic theology is that perfections which are manifold and complex in creatures are one and simple in God. So it is no surprise that for Aquinas, the four items discussed above are very intimately related in the divine understanding. To start with, in humans there is a multitude of intelligible species corresponding to a multitude of acts of thinking about different kinds of things. As we go up the chain of being, this multiplicity is pared down, and those species that remain become more closely linked to the essence of the beings having them. Thus the intelligible species of angels are not taken from extramental things, but are connatural; and the higher angels have fewer, higher-powered intelligible species than the lower ones (cf. ST Ia.55.2 and 3). The limit of this series is God, in whom there is just one intelligible species—the divine essence. Aquinas explains this as follows: in humans, the intelligible species of a kind of thing K is needed to actualize the mind's potentiality to think about K's. This holds, even if the being thought about is oneself, or one's own understanding. But in God, there is no potentiality of any kind, and hence no need for an extra factor that reduces potency to act. God does not have (i) a potentiality to think about Himself, and (ii) an entity in Him which actualizes that potentiality; He understands Himself, through Himself, as Aquinas puts it at ST Ia.14.2. And in understanding Himself perfectly, He understands everything else; for in knowing Himself, He knows His power, and in knowing His power, He knows all of the actual and possible objects to which that power extends. Hence God does not need different intelligible species for knowing things other than Himself (and would not, even if—*per impossibile*—He needed an intelligible species distinct from Himself to know Himself). Aquinas tells us that God knows creatures in a way analogous to the way in which a man may know a part of a kind of thing K, by having an intelligible species of a K, or the way in which a man may see a thing, by seeing a mirror in which the thing appears.

Just as there is no intelligible species in God distinct from the divine essence, there is for Aquinas no act of thinking-about, or understanding, or knowing in God distinct from that essence. The (one, complete) divine act of understanding, like every other perfection of God, is just the divine nature. Moreover, Aquinas holds that—because in knowing Himself, God knows everything else—in God's case, the thing thought about is nothing other than God. Finally, he thinks that the intentional object of God's thought is once again God. (For a discussion of these matters, see, e.g., SCG IV.11.)

Setting aside worries about the coherence of this view of divine understanding, we are immediately struck by the following question: on Aquinas' account, divine understanding consists entirely in reflexive relations, since the thinker, His act of thinking, the inner word by which He thinks, and the thing He thinks about are all the divine nature. So how could individuating and constituting relations follow from God's understanding?

There is no straightforward answer to this query. But this much can be said: although in some places (such as SCG IV.11) Aquinas makes it sound as if the God who understands and the inner word (or Word) by which He understands are no different, he also apparently maintains that there is a real distinction between them. A representative passage is again found at SCG IV.11: "Although in God the one understanding, the act of understanding, and the intentional object of the understanding or Word [*intentio intellecta sive Verbum*] are by essence one, and although for this reason each one is necessarily God, there still remains a distinction of relation alone, inasmuch as the Word is related to the one who conceives as to Him from whom It is." And as Aquinas makes clear a number of times (e.g., at DP 9.5), a distinction of relation is a real distinction, and not merely a mental one (arising from our diverse ways of conceiving of one and the same thing). As Aquinas says at SCG IV.14, a distinction arising from relation is the sort of real distinction closest to sameness.

So, when God thinks about Himself, there is an intentional object of God's thought. Just as God's power is not an accident of God, but rather His substance, the intentional object of God's thought is not a *passio* of God's understanding, but the divine substance. But whereas God and His power are entirely the same in reality (although we conceive of them differently), God-as-thinker and God-as-intentional-object-of-His-thought are relationally and really distinct. The natural question here is: 'Whence the relational distinction'? Why not say that in God the understander and that by which He understands are entirely the same?

As best I can see, no compelling answer to this question can be given on purely metaphysical grounds. Had Christianity been a more unequivocally monotheistic religion, Aquinas would have said that the God-who-thinks and the intentional object of His thought are *penitus idem* (completely the same), just as he says that the God who is wise and the wisdom of God are *penitus idem*. Certainly, if there were any way of showing that the structure of divine understanding must give rise to distinction importing relations, we would be on our way to getting what Aquinas thinks we cannot have—natural knowledge of God's triune nature. So the answer to the question 'Why shouldn't the relation between the God-who-thinks and His inner Word be anything other than identity'? is to be found—if anywhere—in Saint John's Gospel, rather than in abstract considerations on the nature of understanding.

None of this answers the following question: how could Aquinas coherently suppose that the divine understanding was the source of really distinct but co-essential entities? Surely if (a) the essence of x = the essence of y, and (b) the essence of $x = x$, and the essence of $y = y$, it follows as the night does the day that $x = y$. And Aquinas maintains both that the divine persons are not distinct from their essences, and that they all have the same essence (cf. DP 8.4; ST Ia.39.2; and ST Ia.40.1). Ultimately I argue that Aquinas lacks the resources to block this argument; but first we must examine Aquinas' views on relations, distinctions, and hypostases and natures.

Three Hypostases of One Essence

So far, we have been stressing the respects in which the procession of the Word is like (and unlike) what goes on when a man thinks about himself. But according to Aquinas, although God's understanding of Himself is in some ways like a man's understanding of himself, divine understanding is in one respect more akin to human generation than to human understanding, in that—like human generation—it gives rise to a distinct hypostasis of the same nature. In human generation, the terminus of the action is a hypostasis, numerically distinct from the generator(s?), but of the same specific nature; in the divine generation of the Word, the result is a relationally distinct hypostasis of (numerically) one and the same nature.

By 'hypostasis', Aquinas takes himself to mean more or less what Aristotle meant by 'first substance' in the *Categories*. As he says at ST Ia.29.1, a hypostasis is an individual of the genus, substance. Hence this man, or Peter, is a hypostasis. A created hypostasis (a) exists in itself, and not in another (unlike, for example, Peter's whiteness, or [on Aquinas' view] Peter's hand); (b) underlies a common nature (in Peter's case, *humanity*); and (c) underlies accidents (whiteness, risibility, and so on). The hypostases of the Trinity, Aquinas holds, satisfy (a) and (b), but not (c) (since whatever satisfies (c) must have the creaturely imperfection of act/potency composition).

If, however, there are three hypostases in the Trinity, each of which underlies the divine nature, it may look as if there are three Gods; after all, if there are three hypostases, each of which underlies the nature humanity, then there are three men. Aquinas' attempt to avoid this consequence turns on a distinction between a real sharing of a nature and a merely conceptual one: "The unity or community of human nature [in different men] is not real, but exists only in the way we conceive of things [*non est secundum rem, sed solum secundum considerationem*]. . . . But the form signified by the name 'God'—that is, the divine essence—is really one and common [*una et communis secundum rem*]" (ST Ia.39.4 *ad* 3; see also SCG IV.11).

So, Aquinas maintains, there are in fact three different humanities in three different men, whereas there is just one divine essence in the three divine persons (ST Ia.39.3, *responsio*). If the different men did in fact have the very same essence, Aquinas notes, they would also have the very same *esse* or existence (since the *esse* of different beings is multiplied only through being received by different essences); but we have already seen in Chapter 1 that for Aquinas the *esse* of Peter is distinct from the *esse* of Paul. By contrast, there is just one *esse* that is both the existence and the essence of each of the three divine persons.

But what *is* this relation of (really) sharing one and the same essence? Aquinas makes it clear that (i) it is metaphysically singular, found nowhere in the realm of created things; and (ii) it is a more intimate relation than merely being the same kind of thing, but less intimate than being the exact same thing. Perhaps (ii) is not the best way to express Aquinas' view: he believes that although there is one kind of thing (*viz.*, God) such that any two hypostases of the Trinity are the very same this kind of thing, there is another kind of thing (*viz.*, hypostasis, or Person) such that any two hypostases are not the very same that kind of thing. So we might put matters this way: to say that two things really share an essence is to say something much stronger than that they fall under the same natural kind; but it is to say something weaker than that they are the very same K, for any kind of thing K that either of them is. This suggests (at least to those of us who think that identity entails indiscernibility) that really sharing an essence will be a relation falling short of identity. Indeed, Aquinas thinks that two hypostases really share an essence if and only if they are distinct from each other, but only relationally distinct from each other. Accordingly, if we can get a grip on what it is for two things to be relationally distinct, we can understand co-essentiality as the relation that, though falling short of identity, precludes any but relational distinction.

Real Relations

I have said that, according to Aquinas, the divine relations that follow upon the divine will and understanding are real, and really distinct from each other. Thus the Father is really related to the Son— by the relation of Paternity—and the Son is really related to the Father—by the relation of Filiation—and those relations are really distinct from each other. One might think that when Aquinas says that the Father is really related to the Son by the relation of Paternity, he means only that it is really true that the Father is the Son's Father. In fact, Aquinas is saying something stronger: to wit, that Paternity is something real in the Father. To explain this, we will need to take a look at Aquinas' general theory of relations.

We have seen that, for Aquinas, individual substances have individual accidents. Most of the accidents we have considered so far have been nonrelational, like whiteness and risibility. Aquinas thinks, however, that individual substances can also have relational accidents. For example, when Abel was conceived, Adam came to have the relational accident *being the father of Abel*. Just as Adam's whiteness was an inherent dependent particular, so was Adam's *being the father of Abel*. But *being the father of Abel* was a doubly dependent being. *Qua* accident, it inhered in Adam, and depended on him. *Qua relational* accident, it related Adam to Abel, and depended on Abel. Relational accidents are peculiar, in depending for their identity and existence not just on their subjects, but also on what they relate their subject to: "Because the proper nature of a relation consists in its being toward another, its proper *esse,* which it adds to a substance, depends not just on the *esse* of the substance, but also on the *esse* of something exterior" (SCG IV.14).

We have seen in Chapter 1 that for Aquinas (even if we assume the truth of "x is F"), not every expression of the form "the F-ness of x" denotes something real in x. For instance, even if Homer was blind, "the blindness of Homer" never denoted anything real in Homer, since for Homer to be blind is not for him to be a certain way, but for him to fail to be a certain way. Similarly, for Aquinas (even if we assume the truth of "x stands in relation R to y") not every expression of the form "x's standing in relation R to y" denotes anything real in x. In the case mentioned above, Aquinas would hold that "Adam's being the father of Abel" denotes something real in Adam—*viz.,* one of his relational accidents—just as "Abel's being the son of Adam" denotes something real in Abel—one of his relational accidents. He would deny, however, that it always works this way. For example, even when it is true that this thing is known by this person, Aquinas would say, "this thing's being known by this person" does not denote anything real in the thing known; and similarly, "God's creating this person" does not denote anything real in God.

Of course, this does not tell us under what conditions Aquinas thinks an expression of the form "*a*'s standing in *R* to *b*" denotes something real in *a*. He clearly supposes that "*a*'s standing in *R* to *b*" denotes something real in *a* only if it is true that *a* stands in *R* to *b*, and that *a* and *b* are distinct, real entities (see ST Ia.13.7). But although this provides us with a necessary condition for "*a*'s standing in *R* to *b*" to denote something real in *a*, Aquinas would deny that it gives us a sufficient condition: as we have just seen, Aquinas denies that "God's creating this creature" denotes anything real in God, and that "this thing's being known by this knower" denotes anything real in the thing. Also, Aquinas appears to hold that "*a*'s standing in *R* to *b*" denotes something real in *a* if *a* came to stand in *R* to *b* by being acted upon by *a*, and that "*a*'s standing in *R* to *b*" denotes something real in *a* if *a* underwent a real change in coming to stand in *R* to *b*. Aquinas would deny, however, that the just mentioned sufficient conditions for "*a*'s standing in *R* to *b*" to denote something real in *a* are also necessary conditions: the Trinitarian relations are real in each of their extremes, although no divine person undergoes change, or is acted upon. What we would want is a statement of necessary and sufficient conditions—that is, a biconditional of the form "*Standing in R to b* is something real in *a* if and only if ———." In fact, Aquinas does provide us with biconditionals of this type in a number of places (see, e.g., SCG IV.14; DP 7.9, *responsio*). But the import of these biconditionals is very obscure, and none of my attempts to explicate them has succeeded, because the attempted explications turn out not to mesh very well with Aquinas' actual examples of real and unreal relations.[1]

---

[1] Sometimes the biconditionals offered by Aquinas are rather open-ended. Thus at SCG IV.14 he says that "every relation that follows from the proper operation of a thing, whether potentiality, or quantity, or anything of that sort, really exists in it, otherwise it would be in that thing only according to our understanding." Given the occurrence of "or anything of that sort," it is not obvious just what biconditional is being asserted here. Because Aquinas says in a number of places that a real relation is one that follows on "quantity, action, or passion" (cf., e.g., DP 8.1), one might think that for Aquinas *standing in R to b* is something real in *a* if and only if *a* stands in *R* to *b* by virtue of having a certain quantity, or by virtue of acting upon *b*, or by virtue of being acted upon by *b*. (Of course, this leaves open the question of what exactly "by virtue of" means.) The suggestion, however, runs into problems with theological cases: although God stands in the creation relation to Adam by virtue of acting upon Adam, (according to Aquinas) *creating Adam* is nothing real in God. Following the suggestion

Since my focus is on Aquinas' theory of the Trinity rather than on his
account of relations, and since it will not be necessary to give a general
account of the conditions under which Aquinas thinks relational predicates denote something real in a subject, in order to evaluate the
cogency of Aquinas' account of the Trinity, I shall not pursue this
matter further here.

We have at least provided enough details of Aquinas' account of
relations to see what he means when he says that the Father is really
related to the Son by the relation of Paternity, and the Son is really
related to the Father by the relation of Filiation. He means that *being the
Father of the Son* is something real in the Father, and that *being the Son of
the Father* is something real in the Son. (What sort of real thing? Not an
accident, Aquinas would say; for the persons of the Trinity could no
more be subject to accidents than God could be. Aquinas concludes
that *being the Father of the Son* is just the Father Himself; and likewise,
being the Son of the Father is just the Son Himself. That is why relations
constitute as well as individuate the divine hypostases. But more on
this later.)

Why does Aquinas think that *being the Father of the Son* is something
real in the Father, while *being the Son of the Father* is something real in
the Son? Aquinas starts from the premiss that, since there are three
divine persons, the divine persons are distinct from one another.
And, he argues, the difference between any two divine persons cannot be grounded in a difference at the level of the essence or nature of
the persons, the way the difference between God and a creature (or
the difference between any two creatures) is, since the divine persons
have numerically one and the same essence or nature. Hence, Aquinas
says, the difference between the persons cannot follow from anything
absolute (that is, nonrelational) in God; for whatever is absolute in
God just is the (shared) divine essence. So, he concludes, the difference between the persons must somehow be grounded in their having
different relational properties: the Father's distinctness from the Son

---

of Geach that real relations are linked in a certain way with real changes, we might
suppose that *standing in R to b* is real in *a* just in case *a* really changed (or came to exist) in
coming to stand in *R* to *b*. But this would entail that *being the Father of the Son* is not real
in God the Father, given the Father's immutability; and Aquinas could not accept this
consequence. Alternatively, we might suppose that *standing in R to b* is real in *a* just in
case *a* could not come to stand in *R* to *b* without either really changing or coming to be.
But this will entail that, even if Cebes is larger than Simmias, *being larger than Simmias* is
nothing real in Cebes, since Cebes could come to stand in the being-larger-than
relation to Simmias without really changing (or coming to be), just because Simmias
shrank. And Aquinas holds that quantitative relational properties (like *being larger than
Simmias*) are always real in their subjects (see, e.g., DP 7.9; SCG IV.14).

is grounded in the fact that the Father has the relational property *being the Father of the Son,* while the Son has the relational property *being the Son of the Father.* Now, the relational property *being the Father of the Son* could not ground the real distinctness of the Father from the Son, unless that relational property were itself something real. And it could not be something real, without being something real in the Father. So *being the Father of the Son* must be something real in the Father. By the same reasoning, Aquinas would say, *being the Son of the Father* must be something real in the Son, and thus something real in God.

Moreover, if the distinctness of the Father from the Son is grounded in the fact that the Father is the Father of the Son, while the Son is the Son of the Father, it cannot be that *being the Father of the Son* and *being the Son of the Father* are really identical, and differ from each other only according to our way of thinking about them. For it could not be that the distinctness of the Father from the Son is grounded in the fact that the Father has a certain relational property, while the Son has that very same relational property. So the relations (that is, the relational properties) which give rise to the Trinity (Paternity, Filiation, and so on) are not only real in their subjects, but also really distinct from one another.

Relations That Individuate?

The heart of Aquinas' theory of the Trinity is the claim that Trinitarian relations "constitute and distinguish" (*constituunt et distinguunt*) the divine persons. How are we to understand this claim? It may be helpful temporarily to put the question of constitution to one side, and work with the idea that relational properties are *distinctionis principia* (principles of distinctness) of the divine persons, since the idea that two substances could be distinct by virtue of certain relational properties they exemplify is perhaps less surprising than the notion that there could be substances that were in some sense constituted by relations.

Aquinas' view that the divine persons are distinguished (from one another) relationally may be better understood in the context of his general conception of how individual substances differ. Any two created substances, Aquinas tells us, differ from each other *per essentiam:* that is, their difference is grounded in the fact that they have different essences (cf., e.g., DP 8.3 *ad* 6). It is important to keep in mind here what we have already noted in another context: that at least some of the time Aquinas thinks of the essence of a thing as something not really shared by more than one member of its species. Otherwise, we would be puzzled about how the difference between, say, Plato and Socrates could be grounded at the level of their shared essence, humanity. (For a discussion of the difference between the [unshared] essence of Socrates and the essence of man, which is not proper to Socrates, see DE 2.)

So any two creatures who differ will for Aquinas differ *per essentiam*. What this consists in will depend on what sort of essences the creatures in question have. If both creatures are immaterial—like the angel Gabriel and the angel Michael—then their essences are likewise immaterial, and for them to differ *per essentiam* is just for them to have (or be) different (subsistent) substantial forms. If both creatures are material, then their essences will be composite—consisting of a substantial form and the matter receiving that substantial form. In such a case, there will always be a difference between the substantial form of the first creature and that of the second, and a difference between the receiving matter of the first creature and that of the second. Sometimes the matter of the first creature will differ from the matter of the second in terms of its potentialities: for example, the matter of an oak tree has a potentiality for losing its current substantial form, and taking on new ones, which potentiality the matter of a heavenly body lacks. Other times, the matter of the first creature will differ from the matter of the second not in any generic way, but in terms of what Aquinas calls "its particular quantitative dimensions" or "dimensive quantity" (see DSC 8, *responsio*). The matter of Socrates differs from the matter of Plato not because they differ with respect to their potentiality to take on substantial form, but just because Socrates' matter is this particular matter, with these quantitative dimensions, and Plato's matter is that particular quantity of matter, with those quantitative dimensions.[2]

So Plato's essence differs from Socrates' in that Plato's essence includes this substantial form received in this matter, while Socrates' includes that substantial form received in that matter. According to Aquinas, however, Plato's substantial form differs from Socrates' because the matter in which the former is received is different from the

---

[2]What exactly are "quantitative dimensions"? If two parcels of matter can have the same quantitative dimensions, then just what individuative work will they do? Won't the distinctness of this matter from that matter be grounded at bottom in nothing besides the fact that this matter is *this* and that matter is *that*? If on the other hand, it is impossible for two parcels of matter to have the same quantitative dimensions, what can quantitative dimensions be? Finally, doesn't supposing that quantitative dimensions are involved in the individuation of different parcels of matter covertly introduce the un-Thomistic idea that accidents after all individuate? To investigate these important questions would take us too far afield.

matter in which the latter is received: as we saw in Chapter 1, the substantial form of humanity is multiplied by being received in different matters (see, e.g., ST Ia.50.4, *responsio;* DSC 8, *responsio*). Hence Aquinas holds that as well as saying that the difference between Plato and Socrates is grounded in the difference between their essences, we may say that it is grounded in the difference between their matters; since the difference between their essences, inasmuch as it does not consist in the difference between their matters, is derivative therefrom. Accordingly, as well as saying that the difference between any two creatures is grounded in the difference between their essences, Aquinas says that the difference between any two creatures results from the differences between their matter(s) or their forms (ST Ia.40.2).

Why does Aquinas suppose that the difference between any two creatures must be grounded in differences at the level of matter, or at the level of substantial form? At SCG Ia.40.2 he links this claim to the idea that whenever two things are distinct, their distinctness must be understood to follow upon something intrinsic to both. This last idea can be understood as follows: distinct things will be discernible with respect to any number of properties—including some properties that Aquinas would count as extrinsic, and having no real existence in their subject. For example, two maritime pines might be discernible with respect to the property *being now sensed by Mara,* whereas we have seen Aquinas would say that *being now sensed by Mara* is nothing real in a maritime pine. If in fact this maritime pine is now being sensed by Mara, and that one is not now being sensed by Mara, it follows that this maritime pine is distinct from that one. So, in one sense, the distinctness of this maritime pine from that one follows upon their discernibility with respect to the property *being now sensed by Mara.* Nevertheless, Aquinas would maintain, there is another sense in which it is wrong (or at least misleading) to say that the distinctness of the first pine from the second follows upon their discernibility with respect to the property of being sensed by Mara. It is possible for this maritime pine and that maritime pine to differ with respect to such unreal relational properties as *being now sensed by Mara,* only because they differ from each other intrinsically. 'Intrinsically' should not be understood here as 'nonrelationally'—on at least one understanding of 'nonrelationally': that the first pine has this matter and the second has that matter is for Aquinas an intrinsic difference between the pines, even though we would want to say that *being made of this matter* (or *having this matter as a constituent*) is a relational property. But although *being made of this matter* (or *having this matter as a constituent*) is a rela-

tional property, it is not an extrinsic one, because it does not link its
subject to anything outside of itself (that is, it fails to link its subject to
anything that is neither the subject nor a part thereof). So we might
express part of Aquinas' view thus: if two things are distinct individuals, then they are not merely discernible, but discernible with respect
to some of their constituents broadly construed (where 'constituent'
covers matter, form, essence, existence, accidents, and so on, but does
not include accidents in the category of relation [which, for Aquinas,
always link a subject to something outside itself]). Moreover, if two
(composite) things are distinct, their distinctness is grounded in, or
explained by reference to, the distinctness of (some of) their constituents. There are difficulties in explicating the notion of 'grounded in'
invoked here, but—however this is to be understood—it is plausible
that, at least for certain sorts of composita and constituents, the distinctness of those composita is grounded in the (metaphysically, if not
temporally) antecedent distinctness of their constituents. For example,
it is natural to suppose that if the set containing only a is distinct from
the set containing only b, the distinctness of $\{a\}$ from $\{b\}$ is grounded in
the metaphysically antecedent distinctness of a from b. (I assume here a
system of set theory according to which singleton sets are not identified with their members.) This example shows that the notion of
grounding resists any straightforward explication in terms of asym-
metrical entailment relations: for we are inclined to say that the distinctness of $\{a\}$ from $\{b\}$ is grounded in the distinctness of a from b, and
not vice versa, even though necessarily, $\{a\}$ is distinct from $\{b\}$ if and
only if a is distinct from b. And I don't know any less straightforward
explication of the grounding relation, so I can only appeal to the
reader's judgment that the notion Aquinas has gotten hold of has some
intuitive content. Of course, even if one grants that sometimes (as in
the case of sets) the distinctness of composite entities is grounded in the
distinctness of their constituents, one may have worries about whether
the distinctness of two (composite) individual substances from each
other is grounded in the distinctness of their constituents (broadly
construed) from each other. I shall in fact voice a worry of this kind
shortly.

   That distinctness is grounded in the intrinsic character of distinct
items does not by itself entail that the distinctness of distinct created
substances is grounded at the level of matter or form: it is, for example, consistent with the view that the distinctness of distinct created
substances is ultimately grounded at the level of accidents, or even at
the level of *esse*. But the supposition that distinct created substances are
different because they have different accidents fits ill with Aquinas'

conception of the metaphysical priority of substance to accidents. As we saw in Chapter 1, on that conception, the fact that an accident is the particular accident it is is derivative from the fact that the substance in which it inheres is the particular substance it is, while the fact that a substance is the particular substance it is is not derivative from the fact that the particular accidents that inhere in it do inhere in it. ("A substance is individuated through itself, but accidents are individuated through their subject, which is a substance; ST Ia.29.1, *responsio*.) It is hard to see how this could be so, if the fact that this substance is distinct from that substance is derived from or grounded in the fact that these accidents inhere in this substance, while those (distinct) accidents inhere in that one. Similarly, Aquinas cannot suppose that the difference between two created substances is grounded at the level of their *esse,* given that he thinks that what makes this created subject's *esse* the particular *esse* that it is is its being received by this particular essence. Consequently, Aquinas ends up with the view that distinct created substances differ because they differ at the level of essence, and hence (for reasons already sketched) at the level of form or matter.

We are now in a position to understand better Aquinas' assertion that the divine persons are distinguished not *per essentiam,* but *per relationes.* It means that while the divine persons are distinct individual substances or *hypostases,* they are indiscernible at the level of essence, since they are neither different subsistent forms nor have different received forms in different matters. Instead, they are discernible (only) with respect to relational properties. Moreover, the fact that the persons are relationally discernible from one another not only entails that they are distinct from one another, but also in some sense gives rise to or grounds their distinctness from one another. As Aquinas says at ST Ia.40.2, rather than presupposing the distinctness of the divine persons, relation grounds it or brings it about: "*[relatio] non praesupponit, sed secum fert distinctionem*" (see also in this connection DP 9.5 *ad* 14). Aquinas believes that only in the case of the Trinity are individual substances distinguished in this way: any (actual or possible) created individual substances that are distinct from one another are distinct *per essentiam.* Is it in fact possible for any individual substances (created or uncreated) to be distinct *per relationes* but not *per essentiam?* It is helpful to break this question down into three subquestions:

(A) Could there be two individual substances that were discernible only with respect to relational properties and haecceitistic properties like *being this?* (I mean to leave open whether or not haecceitistic properties are all themselves relational; however that may be, Aquinas must hold that the divine persons are discernible with respect to properties like *being this very person*.)

(B) Could the distinctness of two individual substances discernible in the way described in (A) be grounded in relation? That is, could the fact that two such individuals are distinct (actual) individuals somehow be grounded in, or follow upon, the fact that those individuals were discernible with respect to relational properties?

(C) Could two individual substances distinct in the way described in (A) and (B) have the very same essence?

None of these questions has an obvious answer—if for no other reason than because there is considerable unclarity about the notions of essence and substance deployed throughout, and about the nature of the grounding relation invoked in (B). (If we assume that the terms in question are to be understood as Aquinas does, this reduces some of the unclarity: but I do not want to make that assumption just yet.)

To start with (A): there are no clear actual cases of individual substances discernible only with respect to relational and haecceitistic properties. On the other hand, there do seem to be pairs of possible individuals which differ only with respect to such properties. Max Black has argued that there is a possible universe containing only two qualitatively indiscernible brass spheres. These spheres will have the same mass, shape, color; be made of the same kind of stuff; and so on. But they will differ with respect to spatial relational properties, such as *being here,* and compositional relational properties involving the haecceity of what they're made of, such as *being made of this matter,* as well as differing with respect to purely haecceitistic properties like *being this* and impurely haecceitistic properties like *being this brass sphere*. If, as seems plausible, there are possible universes of the sort Black envisions, then there are individuals that cannot be distinguished save relationally or haecceitistically.

The bearing of this on question (B) is unclear. If the Black spheres are possible, then there is no illuminating, nonrelational way of completing this sentence: "That this sphere and that sphere are distinct (actual) individuals is grounded in the fact that the first sphere is ————— and the second sphere is —————." We can either say (unilluminatingly) that the fact that the first sphere and the second sphere are distinct individuals is grounded in the fact that the first sphere is *this* sphere and the second is *that* sphere, or we can appeal to relational properties (presumably involving the spheres' compositional properties, or their spatio-temporal relational properties).

This, however, falls well short of showing that the difference between the two spheres is grounded in relation. For there may not be any illuminating way of completing the sentence at issue. Perhaps the fact that the two spheres are different individuals is a primitive fact, not to be explained in terms of any others. To this one might object that, since the spheres are composite, the fact that they are distinct entities must be grounded in facts about their microconstituents. It certainly looks as if the fact that Black's spheres are distinct from each other supervenes on a set of facts concerning the existence, character, and spatio-temporal location of the microconstituents (say, the atoms) of those spheres. (How could two possible worlds differ with respect to whether this sphere was distinct from that sphere, without also differing with respect to facts about the existence, character, or spatio-temporal location of the things that are actually [in the universe Black describes] the microconstituents of those spheres?) To deny that two worlds could so differ, however, is not to say that the distinctness of those spheres is in Aquinas' sense grounded in the microfacts in question. It appears that, on Aquinas' account, if the fact that M and N are distinct K's is grounded in the fact that Q, it could not be that M is distinct from N, unless Q. (Thus Gabriel and Michael could not be distinct archangels, unless they were [these] distinct subsistent forms; Socrates and Plato could not be distinct men, unless their substantial forms were received by [these] different matters; and the Father and the Son could not be distinct persons of the Trinity, unless they stood in opposing relations to each other [*viz.*, Paternity and Filiation].) But it will not be true that Black's first sphere and Black's second sphere could not have been distinct, unless all of their actual constituents had existed, had just the spatio-temporal locations they actually had, and so on. (Those spheres might have existed and been distinct from each other, even if their microconstituents had occupied slightly different regions of space-time; even if one or both of them had had a slightly different batch of microconstituents; and so on.)

But although we can vary the microfacts in question to some degree, while leaving untouched the fact that this sphere and that sphere are different (actual) individuals, it seems that we cannot vary those microfacts too much:[3] if a possible world distinct from the one Black

---

[3]It may be that no amount of tampering with the microfacts affects the truth-value of 'this sphere is distinct from that sphere'—if this last sentence is construed as the negation of 'this sphere is identical to that sphere'—which negation entails neither the actual existence of this sphere nor the actual existence of that sphere. But if we vary the microfacts enough, it will cease to be true that this sphere and that sphere are distinct actual individuals, since it will cease to be true that both this sphere and that sphere

describes has both of Black's spheres in it, there is a limit to how unlike Black's world it can be at the microlevel. So, we might think, there is a (vague) "disjunctive" state of affairs involving the existence, character, and nature of microconstituents, whose obtaining is not only a sufficient condition for Black's first sphere being distinct from Black's second one, but also a necessary condition. (Each "disjunct" state of affairs will represent one way in which the microfacts could entail that Black's first sphere is distinct from Black's second one.) We might then say that the fact that the first sphere and the second sphere are distinct individuals is grounded in the disjunctive state of affairs involving microconstituents just described. As in the set-theoretic case involving the distinctness of $\{a\}$ from $\{b\}$, we will have a two-way entailment: necessarily, the disjunctive state of affairs will hold if and only if the two spheres are distinct (actual) individuals. But, as in the set-theoretic case, there is some intuitive force to the idea that the obtaining of the macrofacts is somehow posterior to, and grounded in, the obtaining of the microfacts.

That Black's two spheres are distinct individuals may then be a grounded, and not a primitive, fact. Moreover, if it is grounded, it is grounded—at least in part—in relation, that is, in relational (as well as intrinsic) facts about microconstituents. Even so, this does not tell in favor of an affirmative answer to (B)—or, at any rate, in favor of the kind of affirmative answer that would be of use to Aquinas. To start with, suppose it is granted that the existence of Black's spheres as distinct individuals is grounded in a (complicated, disjunctive) fact concerning the intrinsic and relational properties of microconstituents. It does not obviously follow that the existence of Black's spheres as distinct is grounded in any facts about the relational properties of the spheres themselves. But if (B) is to be answered affirmatively, it must be possible for the distinctness of two individuals to be grounded in (facts about) the relational properties those very individuals possess. True, there are two disjunctive, compositional properties such that, necessarily, this sphere and that sphere are distinct individuals if and only if this sphere has the first property, and that sphere has the second. (The properties might look something like this: *being made of microconstituents A1 . . . An, arranged in this way*, or *being made of microconstituents A1 . . . An, arranged in that way, . . . , or being made of*

---

actually exist. (Compare: no way of varying the electoral facts will make it false that Reagan is not the same president as Carter; but some way of varying those facts will make it false that Reagan and Carter are different presidents, by making it false that Reagan and Carter are both presidents.)

microconstituents A1 . . . An-1, Aj, arranged in this way . . .) But do we want to say that the distinctness of the spheres is grounded in the fact that the spheres have the disjunctive compositional relational properties just mentioned? I'm unsure about this. (An analogous question: do we want to say not just that the distinctness of {*a*} from {*b*} is grounded in the distinctness of *a* from *b*, but also that the distinctness of {*a*} from {*b*} is grounded in the fact that {*a*} stands in the converse of the membership relation to *a*, and {*b*} stands in the converse of the membership relation to *b*? Are these just two ways of saying the same thing? Not obviously: the first time, we left the facts about membership tacit, and the second time we left the facts about the distinctness of *a* from *b* tacit. Are they different, but both acceptable? I don't have any firm intuitions, and I don't know just what is at issue here.)

However these questions are answered, there is a feature of the example we've been working with which makes it unhelpful in the context of defending Aquinas' views on the Trinity. As we have seen, the fact that Black's spheres are distinct individuals is parasitic upon the fact that other individuals—the microconstituents of the sphere— exist and have certain properties. So, even if we conclude that the spheres' being distinct individuals is grounded in the relational properties of those spheres, this does not show that the distinctness of two individuals *a* and *b* can be grounded in their relational properties, except when the existence of *a* or *b* is parasitic upon the existence of other individuals, distinct from both *a* and *b,* which constitute *a* or *b.* And Aquinas maintains both that relation grounds the distinctness of the divine persons, and that no individuals distinct from the divine persons are constituents of the divine persons.

Isn't there a variant of Black's example in which the qualitatively indiscernible objects have no other individuals as constituents? Apparently: there are possible worlds inhabited only by two qualitatively indiscernible Epicurean atoms. But why should we think that the distinctness of the Epicurean atoms from each other is grounded in the relational properties of those atoms, or indeed grounded in anything at all? Perhaps the fact that this atom is distinct from that one is primitive; perhaps that fact is grounded in a pair of facts about haecceities (to the effect that the first atom is *this* atom, and the second atom is *that* atom). It is just because Black's spheres are composite that we are disinclined to suppose that the distinctness of the one sphere from the other is primitive (or grounded only in haecceitistic facts). Unless we think of the qualitatively indiscernible Epicurean atoms as in some way composite (for example, as bundles of properties, or sets of space-time points), the demand that we be able to say something illuminating not just about how those atoms are discernible, but also about why those atoms are distinct individuals is not a compelling one.

To sum up: Aquinas believes both that

> (i) There can be individual substances discernible only with respect to relational (and haecceitistic) properties.

and that

> (ii) Relation may bring about or ground the distinctness of individual substances discernible only with respect to relational (and haecceitistic) properties.

The plausibility of (i) does not in any obvious way carry over to (ii). Also, thinking about the ways in which (i) could be true does not help us understand what it would be like for (ii) to be true, in the case where the individual substances that are only relationally and haecceitistically discernible are (both) incomposite. Suppose two such substances are discernible only relationally and haecceitistically. What new supposition do we make when we say that the distinctness of those substances is not just entailed by, but also grounded in, their discernibility with respect to relational properties? I don't know. (For the reasons given earlier, explications in terms of entailment relations, or in terms of counterfactuals, will not succeed; by the nature of the case, no explication relying on mereological notions can be given.) I'm not saying: it is necessarily false that relational facts not only entail the distinctness of a pair of incomposite individuals, but also ground that distinctness. But I do think there is a puzzle about what it could be like for the proposition in question to be true.

Be that as it may, it is an open question how crucial it is to Aquinas' theory of the Trinity that (ii) come out true. Consider a pared down version of Aquinas' theory, which does not include (ii), but does say that the divine persons are distinct incomposite individual substances of the very same nature, indiscernible save with respect to relational and haecceitistic properties. Has anything important been lost if we move from Aquinas' original theory to the pared down one? Precisely because it is hard to say what it would be like for (ii) to be true, in addition to (i), it is difficult to see how anything substantial is lost if we hold on to (i), but dispense with (ii). Consequently, we may put (B) to one side, and try to find out whether a modified version of (C) can be answered affirmatively. That version is: can different individuals discernible only relationally and haecceitistically have the very same essence?

Co-essential but Relationally Distinct Individuals?

Manifestly, if we conceive of an essence as something shared by all the members of a particular natural kind, the answer to this question is yes. The Epicurean atoms discussed earlier can be told apart only with respect to relational and haecceitistic properties, and have the very same (specific) essence. We have already seen, though, that Aquinas takes the relation *having the very same essence as* to be a much more intimate one than *belonging to the same (natural or supernatural) kind.* (He must, since he supposes that 'The divine persons [really] have one and the same essence or nature' entails 'The divine persons are not different Gods, but the same God.') So, in the context of evaluating Aquinas' theory of the Trinity, the important question is: if we understand "having the very same essence" more or less Thomistically, can two individual substances, discernible only relationally (and haecceitistically), have the very same essence? (From now on I abbreviate 'discernible only relationally and haecceitistically' as 'H/R discernible'.)

For Aquinas, two individuals have the very same essence if and only if they have (are) the same subsistent substantial form, or have the same received substantial form and the same receiving matter.[4] Consequently, if we can show that two H/R discernible individuals may have the same form and/or matter, we will have shown that two H/R discernible individuals can have the same essence, where 'essence' is construed Thomistically. And we can in fact show that two H/R discernible individuals can have the same form and/or matter (at least as long as we think that any two forms of the same kind in the same matter are identical, and think of matter as what survives substantial change).

Consider a currently existing particular statue of Hermes. It will have a certain form, received in a certain parcel of matter (say, a piece of brass). Suppose that the statue of Hermes is melted down tomorrow, and the brass of the statue is recast in the form of a number of doorknobs, bells, and the like. Suppose, further, that several centuries and numerous recastings later, exactly the brass that was originally in the statue of Hermes comes together again in liquid form, and is cast by a new sculptor in a new mold—which mold happens to be structurally exactly like the mold the statue of Hermes was cast in. (You are

---

[4]If this is to apply to God as well as creatures, we must suppose that God has (and is) a form. At least some of the time, Aquinas is quite happy to make that supposition: for instance, at ST Ia.3.2 *ad* 3 he says explicitly that God is an unreceived, subsistent form. In other contexts, Aquinas avers that it is more perspicuous to describe God as pure *esse* than as pure form. We might then say that what it is for the divine persons to share an essence is for them to have (and be) one and the same (subsistent, unreceived) *esse*.

meant to imagine what is probably physically impossible—that all of the subatomic particles that constituted the brass statue of Hermes at its first moment of existence constitute that statue at every moment until it is melted down, and later constitute the statue cast by the second sculptor from the time it is cast.) What emerges from the casting? Something that has the same matter as the original statue, and something whose matter has the same form as the matter of the original statue (since the second statue not only has all the same subatomic parts as the original statue of Hermes, but also has all those parts put together in exactly the same way). Is the second statue the same statue as the original one? Although I don't know of any knock-down argument to show that it is not, it seems clear to me that it is not. True, the second statue is made of the same stuff as the first statue, put together the same way; but that is no reason to suppose that they are one and the same statue. (I want to add: " . . . , given that the statues have different origins, were made by different sculptors, and so on." But, it might be said, this begs the question against the view I am opposing: someone who thinks the statues are the same would deny that the statues have different origins, and were made by different sculptors, since—he maintains—one and the same statue was made on two occasions by two different sculptors. At the end of the day, I have to appeal to the reader's intuition that there is no good reason to identify the original statue of Hermes with the one cast by the second sculptor.)[5]

Now, if the first statue and the second statue are distinct, they can differ only with respect to relational and haecceitistic properties (*being made by this sculptor, occupying this region of space-time, being this very statue,* and so on). Given that the statues are duplicates built up out of the exact same stuff, there is no room for them to differ in any other way.[6] Consequently, it appears, as long as the statues are distinct

[5]Actually, in the present context it is not necessary to show that we must conceive of the identity conditions of statues in such a way that the first statue is a distinct statue from the second. All that is needed is that there be a permissible way of construing (or tightening up) those identity conditions in such a way that the first statue turns out to be distinct from the second. This could be so, if it were just vague whether or not the first statue was the same statue as the second. For in that case, we could say: let us introduce a precisified sortal 'statue*' that is not vague in the same way as 'statue', in that the first statue* is (definitely) not the same statue* as the second. Now, we can say that the first statue* and the second statue* are different H/R discernible individuals, with the same matter and the same form, and hence the same essence. To block this line, one would have to show that there are no individuals with the identity conditions of statues*: and this would involve much more than showing that it is not (definitely) true that the first statue is a different statue from the second one.

[6]Actually, the statues will also differ with respect to compositional relational proper-ties: they will not have each other as parts, and they will not share certain structural

individuals, they are distinct individuals with the very same substantial form and matter, and hence the very same essence.

Aquinas would object that the statues are not different individual substances with the same matter and form, because to be a statue is not to be an individual substance of any kind. Instead, to be a statue is to have a certain kind of accidental form. *Being a statue,* like any artefactual form, is an accidental form received by an antecedently existing (hylomorphically composite) individual—say, a piece of bronze (see DPN 1). In the same way that a sapling just is (is no different from, is identical to) a youngish tree, a bronze statue just is (is no different from, is identical to) a statuefied piece of bronze (where *being statuefied* is, Aquinas thinks, to be understood in terms of having a shape of a certain sort). If this is so, then the case I have described, instead of involving two hylomorphically indistinguishable substances, involves one enduring substance (a piece of brass), which acquires a certain accidental form—*being statuefied*—loses it, and then reacquires it.

For the usual reasons, I don't find it very plausible that a statue just is a statuefied bit of stuff, in the way that a sapling just is a tree. Because this sapling just is this tree, this sapling and this tree exist at all the same times, in all the same worlds. But it will not in general be true that a statue and the statuefied bit of stuff now constituting it exist at all the same times in all the same worlds. It may perfectly well be true that

> This (now statuefied) bit of stuff will still exist even when this statue no longer does.

or that

> This (now statuefied) bit of stuff existed before this statue did.

Also, in the case of the Hermes statues, we know that the bit of brass that first constituted the first Hermes statue, and then constituted the second, existed at some time at which neither of the Hermes statues existed. (Choose any time in the interval between the time the first Hermes statue was melted down and the second Hermes statue was cast.) So we know that the bit of brass constituting the Hermes statues is not the same as either statue. Consequently, we know that the case of the Hermes statues is not a case involving only one hylomorphically composite individual substance—a piece of brass—

---

parts (for example, they will not have the same torso). That the statues are compositionally discernible in this sense is compatible with their being hylomorphically (and also qualitatively) indiscernible.

which acquires, loses, and then reacquires a statuesque accidental
form. But even if we conceded that the case of the statues does not
involve hylomorphically indiscernible individual substances, it seems
we could construct other cases involving individual substances of this
kind. An oak tree existing ten thousand years ago (or a dog, or a
human) might be made of exactly the same stuff, organized in exactly
the same way, as an oak tree (or a dog, or a human) existing ten
thousand years hence.[7] In these cases, we seem to have shared matter
and shared form. (As long as Aquinas holds that one and the same bit
of matter can receive different substantial forms over time, it is hard to
see how he could deny that the same bit of matter might have constituted an oak tree existing ten thousand years ago, and a duplicate,
co-composite oak tree existing ten thousand years hence. As long as
Aquinas holds substantial forms are individuated by the matter that
receives them, it is hard to see how he could deny that the substantial
form received by the matter of the first oak tree was the same as the
substantial form received by the matter of the second.) Hence, in these
cases we must either suppose that there are H/R discernible but hylomorphically indiscernible individual substances, or suppose that oak
trees, dogs, humans, and so on can have very discontinuous lifetimes.
Again, the former option looks much more attractive. If I learn that in
the twenty-seventh century, a person hylomorphically indiscernible
from me will exist (being made, at its *j*th moment of existence, of
exactly the same stuff, organized in exactly the same way, as I am
made of in the *j*th moment of my existence), I have not thereby found
out that I will be alive in the twenty-seventh century. If, for example,
the processes that led to the generation of this hylomorphically indiscernible person is shot through with randomness, then the person so
generated is not me.

   In short, it looks as though pairs of created individuals can be what
Aquinas thinks only pairs of divine persons can be—H/R discernible,
but hylomorphically indiscernible; distinguishable *per relationes,* but
not *per essentiam* (where essence is construed as form and/or matter).
Of course, in arguing for this, I have relied on a particular understand-

---

[7]To simplify the example, we could suppose that both the oak tree (dog, human) that
existed ten thousand years ago, and the oak tree (dog, human) that will exist ten
thousand years hence, are *very* short-lived, and accordingly undergo no compositional
change throughout their lifetimes. If this were not the case, the oaks (dogs, humans)
could still be hylomorphically indiscernible in the following sense: for any *j,* the ten
thousand years ago oak (dog, human) is at its *j*th moment of existence made of just the
same stuff, organized in just the same way, as the ten thousand years hence oak (dog,
human) is at the *j*th moment of *its* existence.

ing of matter, and a particular understanding of substantial form. I have been supposing that two individuals have the same matter just in case they are, intuitively speaking, made of the same stuff; and that two individuals have the same substantial form just in case they are made of the very same matter, and the substantial form in the matter of one is the same kind of substantial form as the substantial form in the matter of the other. It must be admitted, however, that unless we countenance substances with implausibly discontinuous lifetimes, it cannot be that (a) matter is what survives substantial change; (b) if one substantial form is distinct from another, then those forms must either differ in kind or be in different bits of matter; and (c) matter is what makes a hylomorphically composite substance of a certain kind this substance of that kind. (If (a) and (b) are true, then—unless substances can have weirdly discontinuous lifetimes—distinct material things of the same kind can have the same matter, in which case (c) must be false.) Aquinas, however, clearly wants to endorse (c), as well as (a) and (b). So, one might suppose, although Aquinas says both that matter survives substantial change, and that matter is included in the (individual) essence of a thing, the matter that is included in the (individual) essence of an individual—the matter that makes a material individual of a certain kind this individual of that kind rather than any other—cannot be the matter that survives substantial change. So, even though we can say that the hypothetical oak trees have the very same matter (in one sense of "matter"), and even though the essence of each oak tree is a composite of form and matter (in another sense of "matter"), the two oak trees are not distinct individuals with the same essence. (Unless, of course, one means by "essence" "specific essence.")

Fair enough. Aquinas does hold both that matter is something that (partially) constitutes the individual essence of a material individual, and distinguishes that material individual from others of its kind, and that matter is what survives substantial change. And it seems that no one thing could do both of these jobs. So, if our interest is in interpreting-*cum*-reconstructing Aquinas' theory of matter and form, we probably should suppose that the matter that is included in the essence of a material individual (and grounds its distinctness from other material individuals of the same kind) is not the matter that antedated the generation of that individual, and will survive its corruption. Still, we might want to pose the following question: it seems that there can be distinct individuals with what we might call the same "hylomorphic essence"—that is, the same matter and form, where matter is stuff, and form is that by virtue of which a thing constituted of that stuff falls under a certain natural kind. Will this help us see how a structure like the Trinity might be possible? I will sketch one way in which it might.

By 'matter' we often mean "stuff"—having mass, spatial location, and so on. But although we often use 'matter' in this sense, we can also use it in an extended sense, where talk of parts, wholes, and constitution is appropriate, but talk of stuff is not. For example, we might think of particular notes as the matter of a musical piece; put together in different ways, this matter can as it were constitute different musical individuals. Or, suppose there was an immaterial being equipped with a two-dimensional, colored perceptual field. The perceptual field might be composed of a number of dots of different colors, which could be moved around at will to generate new perceptions (in something like the way that squares can be moved around in a certain kind of puzzle for children). In that case we might speak of the (quite immaterial—that is, nonstuffy) colored dots as the matter of the visual perceptions of the *res percipiens:* put together differently, they constitute different (immanent) objects of perception.

Now, suppose there is matter—in this extended sense—in God. That is, suppose there is a (finite or infinite) bunch of parts which constitutes both God and the three divine persons. As we did in Chapter 5, we can take God to be the matter of the divine persons (that is, an aggregate of divine parts). And we can hold, as we did in Chapter 5, that the sense in which each divine person is God is not (on pain of inconsistency) to be understood in terms of the relation of identity, but rather in terms of some sort of co-composition relation. So far, our account of the Trinity looks just like the one offered in Chapter 5; but we may develop it in such a way as to end up with an account that would in important respects be more attractive to, or at any rate less objectionable to, Aquinas (and, for that matter, Anselm).

We start by assuming, in medieval fashion, that the divine persons and God are timeless. (Perhaps the kind of account that will follow could be developed while leaving it open whether the divine persons and God were atemporal or omnitemporal, but this would complicate matters a good bit.) Co-composition can be defined much more straightforwardly for timeless objects (since whatever parts they have, they have 'always'—that is, once and for all). We may define *atemporal weak co-composition* as follows:

> x and y are *atemporally weakly co-composite* just in case there is a set of parts P such that P is both a layer of the parts x (timelessly) has, and a layer of the parts y (timelessly) has.

Equivalently: x and y are atemporally weakly co-composite just in case they are (timelessly, once and for all) built up out of all the same (sufficiently small) parts.[8]

We now hold that the relation holding between any two divine persons is atemporal weak co-composition, and that the relation holding between any divine person and God is the atemporal analogue of thing-stuff-co-composition. In the Aristotelian-Thomist language of this chapter, this ensures that the divine persons have the same matter as one another, and the same matter as God.

Next, we specify that the matter of the divine persons (that is, the aggregate of divine parts) is essentially (timelessly) put together, or organized, in exactly the same way, in each of the divine persons, and that the divine persons are hylomorphically indiscernible from one another, and hence have all the same sortal properties (that is, fall under all the same natural kinds) [Note that this last condition is guaranteed by none of the forms of co-composition discussed in Chapter 5]. Finally, we suppose that the divine persons have all the same intrinsic qualitative properties. (This last statement might or might not be already entailed by the claim that the divine persons are made of all the same [sufficiently small] parts, put together in the same way, but there is no harm in making it explicitly.)

If the divine persons are hylomorphically indiscernible, and indiscernible with respect to qualitative and sortal properties, with respect to what kind of properties do they differ? Well, the only sort left are relational and haecceitistic properties. What kind of relational properties do the persons of the Trinity differ with respect to (besides compositional ones involving largeish [and perhaps structural] parts)? At this point the account appeals to the idea that the doctrine of the Trinity is a mystery. We admit that (at one level at least) we have no understanding of what kind of relational properties distinguish the divine persons. Nevertheless, we say, reflecting on the statue and oak tree cases makes it clear that two distinct individuals can be hylomorphically and qualitatively indiscernible, as long as they can be told apart with respect to relational properties such as *occupying this region of space-time*. So, as Anselm would put it, it is not beyond belief that there

---

[8]Is this equivalent to saying that x and y are atemporally weakly co-composite just in case they (timelessly) have all the same parts? Not if two timeless objects can have all the same sufficiently small parts, without having all the same parts. Whether this is a real possibility is unclear. I'm inclined to think it is not, but we needn't settle this matter here.

is some other (unknown, undreamt of) set of relational properties with respect to which the divine persons can be told apart, which properties figure in the individuation of the persons in the way that spatio-temporal relational properties figure in the individuation of the statues. Indeed, at one level we can say what relational properties the divine persons are discernible with respect to. Just as the two qualitatively and sortally indiscernible trees would be discernible, in that one was generated by this very oak tree and the other was not, the Father and the Son are discernible, in that the Son is generated by the Father and the Father is not. It would be a mistake, however, to equate in any way our understanding of the first case with our understanding of the second. We know what it would be like for one of the oak trees but not the other to be generated by this very tree, in part because we have a good enough grasp of the system of spatio-temporal relations which, as it were, leaves room for the two individuals to be discernible with respect to properties such as *being generated by this very oak tree*. In our ignorance of the system of Trinitarian relations which is the counterpart of the system of spatio-temporal relations, we have no real understanding of what it could be like for the Son, but not the Father, to have been generated by the Father. So we cannot know how the Trinity is possible, nor even—by unaided reason—that it is possible. (This is what we should expect of a mystery.) We can, however, defend the doctrine of the Trinity against the charge that it is evidently logically inconsistent, and the related charge that the Trinity is a structure whose impossibility can be known a priori. For the account of the Trinity offered here is in no obvious way logically inconsistent, and the Trinity so characterized cannot be known a priori to be impossible, since we cannot know a priori that no other nonspatio-temporal relational properties could figure in the individuation of the (consubstantial, qualitatively indiscernible) divine persons in the way that spatio-temporal relational properties figure in the individuation of the hypothetical statues or oak trees.

At one level, the account just adumbrated is a close relative of the one in Chapter 5: in each case, we avoid Trinitarian inconsistency by taking some form of co-composition, and not identity, to be the relation holding between any divine person and God, and in each case we avoid the existence of a fourth divine person by taking God to be, as it were, the stuff of which the divine persons are all made. The new account, however, places more emphasis on the unity of the divine persons within the divine nature, since (unlike the first one) it entails that the persons are built up out of the same stuff in exactly the same way, and that the divine persons are indiscernible with respect to all

nonrelational and nonhaecceitistic properties. (For this reason, a proponent of the second account may safely assume that, where F is a way
a divine person is qualitatively and noncontingently, the person's
being F is supervenient upon the person's being God—that is, being
made of the divine substance.) Also, the new account meshes nicely
with a conception of God as changeless and timeless. Whether the new
account is not only more medieval than, but preferable to, the Chapter
5 one is too large a question to be answered here. Suffice it to say that a
conception of the divine persons as immutably and atemporally qualitatively indiscernible is not obviously one that leaves room for the
possibility that one person of the Trinity, and no other, was made
man, underwent the passion, died, was resurrected, and so on.

In any case, neither of the accounts of the Trinity developed here
could be called Thomistic (or Anselmian), since each of them presupposes that the divine persons are composite. Someone might wonder
if a third account of the Trinity might not dispense with this presup-
position, and get considerably closer to a Thomistic account of the
Trinity. The Chapter 5 account modeled the relation of consubstantiality on a relation holding between spatially located individuals (the
Nile-features and the Nile), and yet did not presuppose that the relation of consubstantiality could hold only between spatially located
individuals. The new account models the relation of consubstantiality
on a relation holding between temporal individuals, without presupposing that the relation can hold only between temporal individuals.
Couldn't we model the relation of consubstantiality on a relation
holding between composite H/R discernible individuals, without
building into our notion of consubstantiality that it holds between
composite items? Perhaps. But I can't see how this would work. If
heterodoxy is to be avoided, the consubstantiality relation holding
between any two divine persons must be something more than a
relation of likeness, guaranteeing only that its relata are sortally (or for
that matter, qualitatively) indiscernible. If Sabellianism is to be
avoided, consubstantiality must be something less than identity. If the
persons are incomposite, however, it is very hard to see how their
consubstantiality could be at once something more than their being
like, and something less than their being the same.[9]

---

[9]Of course, someone might hold that what it is for any two divine persons to be
consubstantial is for them neither to be of like substance nor to be the very same
substance; instead, it is for them each to be proper parts of the very same substance—
the triune God. If consubstantiality is understood that way, there is no problem about
different divine persons being at once simple and consubstantial with one another. If
consubstantiality is so understood, however, the resulting account of the Trinity is

Just as Aquinas' belief that God has no integral parts makes a compositional account of the Trinity unavailable to him, his belief that the divine persons are entirely incomposite appears to put any kind of (consistent) relational account beyond his reach. According to Aquinas, the Father stands in the relation of Paternity to the Son, and the Son stands in the converse relation of Filiation to the Father. Now, either the relational attribute of Paternity is included in the essence of the Father, and the relational attribute of Filiation is included in the essence of the Son, or neither attribute is included in the essence of either person.[10] Suppose the former is true. If the Father and the Son are discernible with respect to Paternity, and with respect to Filiation, it cannot be that Paternity is both in the essence of the Father and in the essence of the Son, or that Filiation is both in the essence of the Son and in the essence of the Father. It follows that Paternity is in the essence of the Father, but not in the essence of the Son, while Filiation is in the essence of the Son, but not in the essence of the Father. In that case, the Father's essence must be distinct from the Son's, since they have different constituents. Aquinas must deny this, since he holds that the divine persons are persons of the very same essence. On the other hand, if Paternity is not in the essence of the Father, and Filiation is not in the essence of the Son, there are two possibilities. First, it might be that Paternity is nothing real in the Father, and Filiation is nothing real in the Son. Aquinas must reject this option, on pain of Sabellianism. Second, it might be that Paternity is something real in the Father, which does not belong to the Father's essence, and that Filiation is something real in the Son, which does not belong to the Son's essence. But in that case the Father and the Son will both be, by Aquinas' exacting standards, composite, since they will have both essential and extraessential elements. And Aquinas denies that the divine persons are in this or any way composite (see ST Ia.40.2, obj. 1 and *ad* 1). (Could Aquinas meet this dilemmatic argument by supposing that although God [the divine nature] is completely simple, the divine persons are not? The problem is that Aquinas supposes not just that the divine nature is entirely simple, but also that it is incapable of having

---

very un-Thomistic, since it leaves room for the simplicity of the divine persons by precluding the simplicity of God. There are also worries about whether this account is consistent with the truth of "Each divine person is God" (on any orthodox or natural construal).

[10] I use the term 'relational attribute' here, rather than 'relational property', so as not to prejudge whether Paternity and Filiation belong to the category of noninsular property or the category of substance. (As we have seen, Aquinas chooses the second alternative.)

anything added to or combined with it (see ST Ia.3.8). So he could not suppose that the divine persons are constituted partly of the [simple] divine nature, and partly of a relational attribute, and so are more composite than the divine nature itself.)

It begins to look as if Aquinas has gotten things exactly backward. He maintains that uncreated individuals can, and created individuals cannot, differ *per relationes* but not *per essentiam*. We argued earlier that—where essence is construed as form + ("stuff-y") matter—created individuals can differ *per relationes* and not *per essentiam*. And if uncreated individuals are entirely simple, then they are just the sort of things that cannot differ in that way. To put the argument of the previous paragraph more impressionistically: if co-essential individuals differ *per relationes,* then there must be a difference between their relational attributes (with respect to which they differ) and their essence (with respect to which they do not); so for absolutely simple beings, co-essentiality entails identity.

Aquinas considers arguments very like the ones set out here, and claims that they are vitiated by neglect of the difference between two kinds of identity: *identitas secundum rem* and *identitas secundum rationem*. (Provisionally and approximatively, we may translate these respectively as 'sameness in the thing' and 'sameness in concept'.) He reasons as follows: because Paternity and Filiation are distinct from each other *secundum rem,* there is no problem about supposing that Paternity and Filiation ground the real distinctness of the Father from the Son. Because the essence of the Father just is the essence of the Son, there is no bar to supposing that the Father and the Son are not distinct *per essentiam*. And because the divine essence in the Father is the same as His Paternity *secundum rem,* and the divine essence in the Son is the same as His Filiation *secundum rem,* nothing prevents us from supposing that the divine persons lack real composition of essence and relation. The divine persons are distinguished by relations and constituted by the divine essence; but any divine relation is the same as the divine essence *secundum rem,* just as it is the same as the divine person who is its subject *secundum rem* (see ST Ia.28.2, *responsio;* ST Ia.40.1, *responsio*). That is why relations both constitute and distinguish the divine persons: insofar as relations are the divine essence (*secundum rem*), they constitute those persons, and insofar as they are relations with converses, they distinguish those persons.[11]

---

[11]See DP 8.3 *ad* 7: "Relationes autem in divinis etsi constituant hypostases, et sic faciant eas subsistentes: hoc tamen faciunt in quantum sunt essentia divina. . . . Distinguunt vero relationes, in quantum relationes sunt; sic enim oppositionem habent."

Here one naturally objects: if Paternity is the same as the divine
essence *secundum rem*, and Filiation is the same as the divine essence
secundum rem, then Paternity and Filiation must be the same as each
other *secundum rem*, in which case those relations cannot ground the
real distinctness of the divine persons from one another. Aquinas,
however, denies that any two things that are the same as a third
secundum rem must be the same as each other *secundum rem*; he argues
that the belief that this is so results from a confusion between identity
secundum rem and identity *secundum rationem* (or, more precisely, *secundum rem et rationem*). Before evaluating the cogency of this defense, we
must get as clear as possible on *identitas secundum rem* and *identitas
secundum rationem*.

Identitas Secundum Rem and Identitas Secundum Rationem

As far as I know, there is no *Quaestio* in any of Aquinas' writings
entitled "*Quid sit identitas secundum rem*" or "*Quid sit identitas secundum
rationem*." Aquinas assumes that the reader of either *Summa* or the
Quaestiones disputatae will bring at least some understanding of these
notions to his reading of the text. Nevertheless, by looking at the way
Aquinas employs those notions in various contexts, it is possible to get
a pretty good picture of what he means by each.

When Aquinas says that two things are *idem secundum rem* (or *idem re*,
or *idem subjecto*), he appears to mean just that those things are really
identical. *Identitas secundum rem* is just *identitas*. There are various individually inconclusive but jointly compelling bits of evidence for this.
To start with, Aquinas' examples of *idem re* items are either identical,
or were thought to be identical by Aquinas. Thus Aquinas thinks that
a thing and itself are *idem re*, as are the road from Thebes to Athens and
the road from Athens to Thebes, as are the interval from 1 to 2 and the
interval from 2 to 1 (cf. PE III.3, *lect.* 5). In each of these cases, the
items in question are identical (and are recognized by Aquinas as such).
Also, Aquinas thinks that God's power and God's knowledge are *idem
re*, as are God and His essence, and the Father and Paternity (cf. ST
Ia.25.1 *ad* 4; ST Ia.40.1, *responsio*). In each of these cases, Aquinas
supposes that the items in question are identical. Of course, all of this
is consistent with *identitas secundum rem*'s being a weaker relation than
identity; but it is textually implausible that Aquinas thought of *identitas
secundum rem* in that way. To start with, in various places Aquinas uses
idem secundum rem and *idem realiter* (really the same) interchangeably.[12]

---

[12]Thus at ST Ia.39.1 *ad* 1 and DP 9.5, *responsio*, Aquinas says that each of the divine
relations is really (*realiter*) the divine essence; elsewhere (e.g., at DP 8.2, *responsio,* and

The equivalence of *secundum rem* and *realiter* here is also evidenced by Aquinas' use of these qualifiers in other contexts. Thus Aquinas speaks indifferently of relations being in God *realiter* and of their being in God *secundum rem*.[13] Now, in the absence of powerful countervailing evidence, we should translate straightforwardly, and suppose that when Aquinas asserts that two items are *idem realiter*, he is saying nothing more than that they are really the same (just as when Aquinas says that relations are in God *realiter*, he is saying nothing more than that relations really are in God). If being *idem secundum rem* is being *idem realiter*, which in turn is just being really identical, then we should expect Aquinas to describe the very items he takes to be *idem secundum rem* as *idem* (without any qualifier following the *idem*), and to say, when *a* and *b* are *idem re*, that *a* is *b* itself. In fact he does both of these things.[14] Indeed, Aquinas often speaks of items indifferently as either *idem realiter* or *omnino idem* (entirely or completely the same); this again suggests that things that are *idem realiter* or *secundum rem* are, as it were, as identical as you can get—which is to say, identical.[15] There is also a good deal of indirect support for the idea that *identitas secundum rem* is nothing other than identity. At DP 7.1 Aquinas considers an argument (objection 10) to the effect that since there are three persons in God, there must also be composition in Him. He answers that since each of the divine persons is *idem re* with the divine essence, the plurality of persons introduces no form of composition into God. If *identitas secundum rem* is identity, the argument here is a straightforward one, to the

---

ST Ia.39.1, *responsio*) he says that each divine relation is the same as the divine essence *secundum rem*, or that the divine relations do not differ from the essence *re*. Also, Aquinas says at ST Ia.39.1, *responsio*, that no divine person differs from the divine essence *secundum rem*; at ST Ia.39.6, *responsio*, he says that the divine essence is *idem realiter* with all three divine persons. Finally, at DP 9.1, *responsio*, Aquinas says that the essence of an immaterial substance and that substance are the same *secundum rem*; at DUVI 1, *responsio*, he says that in a simple substance *suppositum* and nature are the same *realiter*.

[13]Compare, for example, ST Ia.28.1, *responsio* ("Relationes quaedam sunt in divinis realiter") with SCG IV.14 ("Ex his etiam quae dicta sunt potest esse manifestum quod relationes in Deo sunt secundum rem").

[14]Thus at ST Ia. 39.1 Aquinas says both that in God the person and the nature are the same ("in Deo sit idem essentia et suppositum; quod in substantiis intellectualibus nihil est aliud quam persona"), and that in God the person and the nature are not really distinct ("in Deo non sit aliud essentia quam persona secundum rem"). In that same article, Aquinas says both that in God, relation *non differt re* from essence, and that any divine relation is the divine essence itself ("relationes . . . in Deo sunt ipsa essentia divina"). In reading these passages, and others like it, one nowhere gets the impression that Aquinas takes the statement that *a* and *b* are *idem re* (or *non differunt re*) to have truth conditions any different from the statement that *a* and *b* are *idem*, or that *a* is *b* itself.

[15]See, for instance, DUVI 1, *responsio*.

effect that the presence of *a, b,* and *c* in *x* does not entail the composite-
ness of *x* if each of a–c is the very same thing as *x*. If, on the other hand,
identitas secundum rem were a weaker relation than identity, the rejoinder would not get off the ground. For in that case the fact that each
of the persons was *idem re* with the divine essence would be consistent
with some person's being distinct from that essence; and hence consistent with there being something in God besides the divine essence; and
hence consistent with God's being composite. Consequently, the best
explanation of the fact that Aquinas thinks he has answered objection
10 is that Aquinas thinks of *identity secundum rem* as in no way falling
short of identity *simpliciter*.

More evidence could be adduced for the claim that identity and
identity *secundum rem* (as understood by Aquinas) are one and the
same;[16] but I have already belabored this point. I have done so because—as we shall see—Aquinas ascribes to *identitas secundum rem*
some features quite unlike those had by identity, and because the
relation of *identitas secundum rem* to identity will be crucial to the
coherence of his metaphysics of the Trinity.

If *identitas secundum rem* is classical identity, what is *identitas secundum
rationem?* Well, *secundum rationem* for Aquinas means something like
"according to our understanding" or "according to the way we conceive of it." We may see this in a number of passages. For example, in
his discussion of self-identity at DP 7.11 *ad* 3, Aquinas maintains that
although a thing is the same as itself *realiter*, and not just *secundum
rationem*, the relation of self-identity exists only *secundum rationem*,
because although there is something real in a thing which makes it true
that the thing is self-identical (*viz.*, unity of substance), that thing is
not in fact a relational property, though it is (mis)conceived by us as a

---

[16]On occasion, Aquinas does say things about *identitas secundum rem* which make it
sound rather different from identity. Thus at ST Ia.13.12 he says that in every affirmative proposition the subject and predicate signify one and the same thing *secundum rem*,
and different things *secundum rationem*—so for example, (a) man and white are the same
in subject (*idem subjecto*) and different in *ratio*. Given that Aquinas uses *idem re* and *idem
subjecto* interchangeably, one might conclude from this that *identitas secundum rem*
cannot be identity, because no man is identical to white. Aquinas, however, is not
contending that if a man is white, a form (a whiteness) is *idem re* as a *suppositum* (a man),
but rather that if a man is white, the *suppositum* that is the man is *idem re* as the subject of
the accidental form of whiteness. For after saying that *homo* and *albus* are *idem subjecto*
but *differunt ratione*, he goes on to say that the same point can be made concerning man
and animal, since (if a man is an animal) the very thing that is a man is truly an animal,
on account of the co-presence in him of a rational nature and a sensible nature.
Accordingly, "homo et albus sunt idem subjecto, et differunt ratione" might be
translated more perspicuously: "a man and a white thing are the same in subject, and
differ in *ratio*."

relational property inherent in the thing (namely, self-identity). Also, we have already seen that for Aquinas creature-involving relational properties are not really in God. He expresses the idea that they are not, but are (mis)conceived by us as if they were, by saying that creature-involving relations are in God only *secundum rationem* (see, e.g., ST Ia.13.7). Finally, Aquinas says that the unity or community of human nature is not *secundum rem,* but only *secundum rationem* or (equivalently) *secundum considerationem* (see, e.g., ST Ia.39.4 *ad* 3). By this he means that there is not one human nature really shared by Socrates and Plato, although we conceive of human nature as if it were a one-over-many.

If *secundum rationem* means something like "as conceived by us," then two things are different *secundum rationem* if they are different as conceived by us. There is an ambiguity here: "different as conceived by us" might mean either "conceived by us differently," or "conceived by us as different from each other"—that is, "conceived by us as distinct." If the ambiguity is not clear: suppose someone knew that water existed, and knew that H_2O existed, but was uncertain about whether or not water was H_2O. Such a person could be said to conceive of water and H_2O differently. His H_2O-concept would include having twice as many hydrogen atoms as oxygen atoms, though his water-concept did not; his water-concept might include *being liquid,* though his H_2O-concept did not, and so on. There is, however, at least one sense (the one I intend) in which this person would not conceive of water and H_2O as distinct, since *ex hypothesi* that person would not conceive of water and H_2O as standing in the distinctness relation to each other. Thus if *a* and *b* are conceived of differently, they need not be conceived of as distinct, although if *a* and *b* are conceived of as distinct, they must be conceived of differently.

So, when Aquinas says that *a* and *b* differ *secundum rationem,* he might mean either that *a* and *b* are conceived by us differently, or that as we conceive it, *a* and *b* are distinct items. He appears to mean the former. To be sure, some items that differ *secundum rationem* are also conceived by us as distinct. Socrates' whiteness and Socrates' humanity, which differ both *secundum rem* and *secundum rationem,* are conceived by us as distinct entities. And it may be that (for Aquinas) God's power and God's knowledge, which differ *secundum rationem* though not *secundum rem,* are in some sense conceived by us as distinct, even if we have accepted arguments that they are really the same. (We might be in a position like that of the [knowing] victim of a perceptual illusion, who, in spite of having verified that two lines are of the same length, goes on seeing the lines as being of different lengths.) But in other cases we don't conceive as distinct pairs of items which Aquinas describes as differing *secundum rationem*. Taking his example from Aristotle, Aquinas says that although the road from Thebes to Athens and the road from Athens to Thebes are really the same, they differ *secundum rationem*. Now, we clearly don't conceive of the road from Thebes to Athens and the road from Athens to Thebes as distinct. (If we did, we would conceive of them as distinct roads, and we surely do not.)[17] Moreover, I don't know of any reason to ascribe to Aquinas the (implausible) view that we conceive of the road from Thebes to Athens and the road from Athens to Thebes as distinct. It is better to assume that, when Aquinas says that the road from Thebes to Athens and the road from Athens to Thebes differ *secundum rationem*, he means that we conceive of the road from Thebes to Athens and the road from Athens to Thebes differently. To put this another way, our road-from-Thebes-to-Athens-concept or *ratio* differs from our road-from-Athens-to-Thebes-concept or *ratio;* so that the road from Thebes to Athens and the road from Athens to Thebes, which are really just one thing (*idem secundum rem*), differ with respect to, or according to, their concept (*differunt secundum rationem*).

From these considerations it emerges that neither identity *secundum rationem* nor distinctness *secundum rationem* can be thought of as gen-uine relations between individuals. If *differing secundum rationem* were a relation holding between the individual the road from Thebes to Athens, and the individual the road from Athens to Thebes, it would also be a relation holding between the road from Thebes to Athens and the road from Thebes to Athens (since one and the same individual is the road from Thebes to Athens and the road from Athens to Thebes). But Aquinas would deny that the road from Thebes to Athens and the road from Thebes to Athens differ *secundum rationem*, since, like a tunic and (sleeved) garment, their *ratio* is one. (Aquinas says that a tunic and a garment are the same *secundum rationem*, or have the same *ratio*, at ST Ia.28.3 *ad* 1, and in commenting on *Physics* III.3.) The same consider-ations show that identity *secundum rationem* cannot be a genuine rela-tion holding between individuals.

Of course, when *a* and *b* differ *secundum rationem*, there are two

---

[17]The Oxford English Dictionary says that 'road' can also mean 'journey'. So on one understanding of the terms, we certainly may conceive of the road from Thebes to Athens and the road from Athens to Thebes as distinct roads, since journeys with different starting points and different end points are distinct. But when Aquinas says that the road from Thebes to Athens and the road from Athens to Thebes differ *secundum rationem*, he cannot very well be making a point about roads-as-journeys, since the journey from Thebes to Athens and the journey from Athens to Thebes differ *realiter* as well as *secundum rationem*.

things that genuinely differ: for Aquinas those things are not extra-mental individuals, but things *in intellectu*—the concept or *ratio* of *a*, and the concept or *ratio* of *b*. Likewise, when *a* and *b* are the same *secundum rationem,* the *ratio* of *a* is the same as the *ratio* of *b*. So we could think of *secundum rationem* as playing a different semantic role than we might have thought when it is attached to the end of sentences of the form '*a* and *b* are the same', or '*a* and *b* are different'. It does not, as it were, combine with 'are the same', or 'are different', to form a new relational predicate ('are the same *secundum rationem*', or 'are different *secundum rationem*'), which denotes a new relation said to hold between the original relata by the expanded sentence. Instead, it signals that the denoting expressions linked by the identity or distinctness predicate should not be taken to denote the individuals that are (in ordinary contexts) their referents, but should be taken to denote something like their Fregean sense.

In short: for *a* and *b* to differ *secundum rationem* (or *ratione*) is not for the individuals *a* and *b* to differ in any way, but for our concepts of them to differ. That is why Aquinas, who believes that there are no real distinctions in God, is happy to admit that the divine perfections differ from one another *secundum rationem*. As he sees it, to say that God's goodness and God's wisdom differ *secundum rationem* is to say only that the *rationes* of the names 'good' and 'wise' differ; only to signal a difference between items in our understanding, and not a difference between any items in God. (For an especially clear expression of these views, see DP 7.6, *responsio* and *ad* 3, *ad* 4.)

Identity *Secundum Rem* and Indiscernibility

Given all the evidence that *identitas secundum rem* is just real identity, and that *identitas secundum rationem* is identity between *rationes,* it is surprising to find Aquinas making remarks that make it look as though *identitas secundum rem et rationem* is classical identity, while *identitas secundum rem* is some weaker relation. What Aquinas appears to say is that (i) while two things that are the same *secundum rem et rationem* must have all the same properties, two things that are the same *secundum rem* need not; and (ii) while any two things that are the same *secundum rem et rationem* as a third thing must be the same *secundum rem et rationem* as each other, two things can be the same *secundum rem* as a third thing, without being the same *secundum rem* as each other.

It may look as if Aquinas' assertion of (i) is by itself good enough reason to suppose that he takes *identitas secundum rem* to be something less than identity. In fact, I think the situation here is more complicated than it appears. Aquinas does not clearly commit himself to (i), although he commits himself to something very like it, which he may not have clearly distinguished from (i). We need to look at the contexts in which Aquinas seems to assert (i). At DP 8.2 *ad* 7 Aquinas invokes the authority of Aristotle in maintaining that it is not necessary that all the same things be predicated of those things that are the same, but only that all the same things be predicated of those things that are the same *secundum rem* and *secundum rationem*. He then answers objection 7 by saying that not everything that can be predicated of the divine essence can be predicated of Paternity, even though they are the same *secundum rem*, since they differ *secundum rationem*.

Depending on how we conceive of predication, we might construe this passage in two ways. Aquinas might be saying there that even if two things are the same *secundum rem*, one may not be able to ascribe (truly) exactly the same properties to them. Or he might be saying that even if two things are the same *secundum rem*, one may not be able to say (truly) all the same things about them. The first claim is tantamount to a denial that identity *secundum rem* is an indiscernibility-conferring relation. The second could be understood as a denial that the following conditional always holds: if *a* and *b* are the same *secundum rem*, then all and only open sentences that can be made true by replacing their gaps with '*a*' can be made true by replacing their gaps with '*b*'. We will construe Aquinas as denying the indiscernibility of identicals *secundum rem* if we think that (for Aquinas) to predicate something of *a* is simply to attribute a property to *a;* we shall construe him as denying a version of what Richard Cartwright calls "the principle of substitutivity,"[18] if we think that (for Aquinas) to predicate something of *a* is to wrap an open sentence around the term '*a*'.

What does Aquinas think is involved in predicating something of a subject? Does he think of predication as linking two linguistic items (a predicate term and a subject term), or as linking a linguistic item to something nonlinguistic (a predicate term and the individual of whom the predication is made), or as linking two nonlinguistic items (say, a form and a substance)? A perusal of the texts leads one to answer: none of the above—consistently. Sometimes Aquinas makes it sound as if predication is a relation between nonlinguistic items: at ST Ia.77.1 *ad* 1, for example, he says that no integral whole is predicated of its individual parts; at ST Ia.28.1 *ad* 1 he avers that relation is predicated of God; and at DP 7.2 *ad* 11 he agrees that "God exists" is true because the

[18]See Richard Cartwright, "Identity and Substitutivity," in *Identity and Individuation,* ed. Milton Munitz (New York: New York University Press, 1971), pp. 119–34.

same thing (subsistent existence) is in both the subject and the predicate. Examples of this sort could easily be multiplied. On the other hand, Aquinas sometimes writes as if predication links a name with an individual. At ST Ia.39.3, *responsio,* he argues that "some essential names signify the essence substantivally, and some signify it adjectivally. Those that signify the essence substantivally are predicated of the three persons in the singular only, and not in the plural. Those that signify the essence adjectivally are predicated of the three persons in the plural." Also, at ST Ia.39.6, *responsio,* Aquinas states that although adjectival notional or personal names may not be predicated of the essence, substantival names of this sort may be. Again, examples in which Aquinas appears to conceive of predication as linking a linguistic item with an individual could be multiplied easily (see, e.g., DP 7.5).

In fact, it appears that Aquinas is not in general clear on whether either predicates or subjects are linguistic or nonlinguistic, because his grasp on the distinction between nonlinguistic items and the linguistic items signifying them wavers from time to time. (Or, more charitably, his writing often fails to reflect his grasp of that distinction.) This is evident in various passages in the *Summa theologiae.* At ST Ia.39.5 *ad* 4 he notes that although the divine essence is predicated of the Father *per modum identitatis,* it does not follow that it can stand for the Father, because of its different mode of signification.[19] It certainly looks here as if Aquinas starts by conceiving of what is predicated as something nonlinguistic (the divine essence), and in the same sentence comes to think of it as something linguistic, which has a mode of signification, and stands for the Father. We might think that Aquinas is simply being careless on this occasion; but a similar slide between linguistic and nonlinguistic items can be seen at ST Ia.39.7. The question Aquinas sets himself there is whether essential *names* are to be appropriated to the persons. His answer is that essential *attributes*—such as power (not "power")—are to be appropriated to the persons. Finally, some confusion between linguistic and nonlinguistic items is evident in the very way Aquinas formulates the question of ST Ia.39.6: whether the persons may be predicated of essential names. (Surely one may not predicate a person of any name.)

It does not look, then, as if Aquinas thought that to predicate something of *a* was just to attach a linguistic predicate to '*a*'. But

---

[19]"Essentia divina praedicatur de Patre per modum identitatis, propter divinam simplicitatem: nec tamen sequitur quod possit supponere pro Patre, propter diversum modum significandi."

neither does it look as if he thought that to predicate something of *a* was just to attribute a property to that individual or just to apply a term to that individual. To suppose that Aquinas held any of these views is to attribute to him a uniform and worked-out conception of the predication relation; and it does not look as if he has one. Why doesn't he? Perhaps because, in any ordinary case, all the things we have been distinguishing go together. If in asserting that Socrates is white I predicate whiteness of Socrates, I attach a linguistic predicate ("is white") to a linguistic subject ("Socrates"); I attribute a property or accidental form (whiteness) to a first substance (Socrates); and I apply a general term ("is white") to a first substance (Socrates). So Aquinas might well think that in an ordinary predication, predicate attachment, property attribution, and term application are all involved, and not worry about which of these relations was to be thought of as predication. (After all, for many purposes it does not matter.)

We may conclude that when Aquinas asserts at DP 8.2 *ad* 7 that not all the same things need be predicated of those things that are the same *secundum rem,* he is neither clearly denying the indiscernibility of identicals *secundum rem,* nor clearly denying a substitutivity principle. We ought, however, to construe Aquinas as trying to deny a principle of substitutivity, rather than one of indiscernibility.

We may adduce a number of considerations in favor of this view. For starters, in other contexts Aquinas seems to counter objections rather like objection 7 (put in terms of predicability) by denying the intersubstitutability *salva veritate* of co-referential terms, rather than the indiscernibility of identicals *secundum rem.* For instance, he considers this argument for the distinctness of the persons from their personal properties: "When things are identical, they are so related that whatever is predicated of one is predicated of the other. Not everything that is predicated of a person, however, is predicated of His property: we say that the Father generates, but not that Paternity generates. Therefore property and person are not the same in God" (ST Ia.40.1, obj 3). He replies that "notional participles and verbs signify notional acts, and acts belong to a *suppositum.* The divine properties, however, are not signified as *supposita,* but as forms of *supposita.* So their mode of signification precludes notional participles and verbs from being predicated of the properties" (ST Ia.40.1 *ad* 3).

Aquinas clearly rejects a substitutivity principle here, holding that, even though the Father is Paternity, "the Father" and "Paternity" may not be replaced *salva veritate* in the context " ———— generates." He does *not* seem to say anything that is easily construed as a rejection of the indiscernibility of identicals *secundum rem*. His strategy is to argue that we can say both (i) the Father and Paternity are the same, and (ii) the Father generates, and Paternity does not, once we realize that whether or not a sentence of the form '*a* is *F*' (such as, '*a* generates') is true depends not just on what "*a*" (and "is *F*") refer to, but also on the mode of signification of "*a*."[20] Though this account is incompatible with the principle of substitutivity, it looks compatible with the indiscernibility of identicals *secundum rem*. Indeed, it looks like just the sort of account that would be offered by someone who at some (perhaps unarticulated) level accepted the indiscernibility of identicals. If Aquinas thought that identicals could yet be discernible, he could simply have said (baldly) that the individual that is both the Father and Paternity both has and lacks the property of generating; no ascent to what Rudolf Carnap calls the formal mode would be necessary. If he thought that (true) identicals were indiscernible, but that identicals *secundum rem* were not (because identity *secundum rem* was something less than identity), he could have pointed out that the Father and Paternity are not identical, but only *identical secundum rem*. That he does neither of these things suggests that he accepts the indiscernibility of identicals *secundum rem*, while rejecting the principle that if *a* and *b* are the same *secundum rem*, '*a*' and '*b*' may be truth-preservingly intersubstituted.

A second set of considerations supports the idea that, although Aquinas wants to deny substitutivity, he has no quarrel with the indiscernibility of identicals *secundum rem*. Suppose Aquinas thought that what it was for co-predicability to fail with respect to a pair of identicals *secundum rem* was just for those things to be discernible with respect to some (genuine) property.[21] In that case, he would have to hold that *a* and *b* can be the same *secundum rem*, even though *a* and *b*

---

[20]Compare: we can say both that (i) *b* and the *F* are the same, and that (ii) *b* might not have been the *F*, though *b* could not but have been *b*, once we realize that the truth of a modal sentence may depend not just on its terms' extensions, but also on their intensions. In supposing that the truth of certain sentences depends on more than the reference of the terms in those sentences, Aquinas holds a view not unlike David Lewis' view of modal predication. For Lewis, whether or not a sentence of the form "a might not have been *F*" is true depends not just on what (world-bound) individual "*a*" refers to, but also on which counterpart relation "*a*" selects—so substitutivity fails in modal contexts, even for sortally qualified demonstratives ("this person," "this body"), and for proper names (see "Counterparts of Persons and Their Bodies"). Of course, what makes Aquinas' position much harder to defend than Lewis' is that he denies that certain proper names ("the Father," "Paternity") are intersubstitutable in contexts ("――― generates") which do not look in any recognizable way nonextensional.

[21]'Co-predicability fails for *x* and *y*' is shorthand for 'Not all of the same things may be predicated of *x* and *y*'.

were discernible with respect to some genuine property—where (for Aquinas) this would involve being discernible with respect to some form. (Items discernible with respect to a genuine property might be discernible with respect to accidental form, substantial form, *esse,* essence, or matter, but in each case that would involve being discernible with respect to some form.) In fact, though, I know of no place where Aquinas says that identicals *secundum rem* may have (or be) different forms; and the claim that they could be looks like one Aquinas would reject.[22] In other words: if Aquinas really believed that identicals *secundum rem* can fail to have all of the same properties, he need not have expressed this belief in the ambiguous language of co-predicability. He has the vocabulary to express that belief quite unambiguously, just by saying that identicals *secundum rem* may not have all the same forms. That he never says this, and apparently disbelieves it, is evidence that Aquinas does not reject the indiscernibility of identicals *secundum rem.*

Aquinas does not believe that co-predicability fails only for uncreated identicals *secundum rem;* he cites a number of Aristotelian examples involving created identicals *secundum rem* for which it fails. Those examples reinforce the impression that the failure of co-predicability does not entail discernibility. At DP 7.1 *ad* 5 he notes that, as Aristotle says, contradictories may be predicated of things that are the same *re* and different *ratione,* as is clear in the case of a point that is both the beginning of one length and the end of another. That same point *re,* insofar as it is a beginning, is not an end, and insofar as it is an end, is not a beginning (*idem punctum re . . . est principium et finis; et secundum quod est principium, non est finis et e contrario*). Now, if one and the same point *P* is both the end of length *L* and the beginning of length *L',* then surely the point that is the end of length *L* has all and only the properties that the point that is the beginning of length *L'* has. It is no good objecting that the end of length *L* is, *qua* end, an end (and not a beginning), while the beginning of *L'* is, *qua* beginning, a beginning (and not an end). For it is equally true that the beginning of *L'* is, *qua* end, an end (and not a beginning), while the end of *L* is, *qua* beginning, a beginning (and not an end). *Contra* what Aquinas suggests, we don't get a failure of intersubstitutivity in the *qua* contexts at issue. In what kind of *qua* context does intersubstitutivity fail? Ones in which descriptions as well as properties are brought into the picture. So it may be true that

----

[22]Aquinas would surely deny that one and the same thing *realiter* can both have and lack one and the same form.

(i) The end of length L, *qua* thing satisfying that very description [to wit, "the end of length L"], is an end.

and false that

(ii) The beginning of length L', *qua* thing satisfying that very description [to wit, "the beginning of length L'"], is an end.

just as it is true that

(iii) The beginning of length L', *qua* thing satisfying that very description, is a beginning.

and false that

(iv) The end of length L, *qua* thing satisfying that very description, is a beginning.

But we should not infer from this that the end of length L and the beginning of length L' have different properties, because the expression "that very description" does not refer to the same thing in (i) and (ii), or in (iii) and (iv). Nobody should be tempted to think that a and b fail to have all the same properties, simply on the grounds that a is F *qua* satisfying this description, while it is not the case that b is F *qua* satisfying that (distinct) description.

So in this case, failure of co-predicability is to be understood by reference to nonsubstitutability of terms, rather than discernibility of individuals. The same may be said about various other (nontheological) examples Aquinas provides of the failure of co-predicability with respect to identicals *secundum rem:* the interval from 1 to 2 and the interval from 2 to 1 have all the same properties, as do the road from Thebes to Athens and the road from Athens to Thebes.[23] The point here is not that Aquinas (clearly) understood the failure of co-predicability in these cases in terms of a failure of intersubstitutivity *salva*

---

[23]"But the road from Athens to Thebes is uphill, while the road from Thebes to Athens is not." Suppose we grant that "The road from Athens to Thebes is uphill" is true (being elliptical for "The road from Athens to Thebes is uphill-in-the-Athens-to-Thebes-direction"), while "The road from Thebes to Athens is uphill" is false (being elliptical for "The road from Thebes to Athens is uphill-in-the-Thebes-to-Athens-direction"). Clearly, nothing follows about the discernibility of the road from Athens to Thebes and the road from Thebes to Athens: one and the same road is uphill-in-the-Athens-to-Thebes direction, and downhill in-the-Thebes-to-Athens-direction.

veritate. He did not; but he did think of the failure of co-predicability with respect to identicals *secundum rem* as the kind of phenomenon encountered in the Aristotelian sorts of cases just discussed. And this is evidence that the phenomenon he actually got hold of, and described as failure of co-predicability for identicals *secundum rem,* was in fact referential opacity, even if he did not succeed in clearly seeing or describing it as such.[24]

Identity *Secundum Rem* as a Non-Euclidean Relation?

So Aquinas' remarks about the failure of identity *secundum rem* to entail co-predicability should not lead us to conclude that identity *secundum rem* is a weaker relation than identity (or that identity *secundum rem et rationem* is no stronger than identity). Aquinas' insistence, however, that two things can be the same as a third thing *secundum rem,* without being the same as each other *secundum rem,* seems to support that same conclusion. After all, if we construe identity *secundum rem* as identity, we are forced to say that Aquinas failed to grasp a basic property of the relation of identity. How could a philosopher of Aquinas' acumen deny the evident fact that two things that are the same as a third are the same as each other?

Given all the (already canvassed) evidence that identity *secundum rem* is identity, it is certainly surprising and puzzling that Aquinas denies that identity *secundum rem* is a Euclidean relation.[25] What are his motivations for doing so? One might think they were Aristotelian, because in arguing that identity *secundum rem* is not Euclidean, Aquinas again calls on Aristotle's authority: "According to the Philosopher, this argument (that whatever things are the same as one and the same thing, are the same as each other) holds with respect to those things that are the same *re et ratione* (such as a tunic and a garment), but not with respect to those things that differ *ratione*" (ST Ia.28.3 *ad* 1). He then discusses an example from *Physics* III.3 which (as he sees it) illustrates this point:

[24]As we shall see, there is a striking contrast between Aquinas' nontheological examples of identicals *secundum rem* for which co-predicability fails, and his theological examples of the same. Only in the former case does it look as if failure of co-predicability can be understood as referential opacity. This asymmetry, I argue, results from the fact that the relation between the divine entities that Aquinas takes to be identicals *secundum rem* (Person and Essence, Relation and Essence) is in fact quite different from the relation of the interval from 1 to 2 and the interval from 2 to 1, or the relation of the road from Thebes to Athens to the road from Athens to Thebes.

[25]A relation *R* is Euclidean just in case whenever x stands in R to z and y stands in R to z, x stands in R to y.

Hence he says . . . that although an action is the same as a motion, and likewise a passion, it does not follow that the action and the passion are the same; because action involves being referred to as something from which there is motion in the thing moved [*in actione importatur respectus ut a quo est motus in mobili*], while passion involves being referred to as something that is from another [*in passione vero ut qui est ab alio*]. Similarly, although Paternity, like Filiation, is the same *secundum rem* as the divine essence, nevertheless these two things import opposed relations in their proper *rationes*. Consequently, they are distinct from each other. (ST Ia.28.3 *ad* 1)

A look at *Physics* III.3 reveals that this is at best a questionable interpretation of Aristotle. In that chapter, Aristotle contrasts being the same (or, as he sometimes puts it, being in a way the same) with being the same in definition or account (*en logō*). He says that the interval from 1 to 2 and the interval from 2 to 1, like the steep ascent and steep descent, are one and the same, although they can be described in different ways. And he says that when two things are in a way the same—like the road from Athens to Thebes and the road from Thebes to Athens—they may fail to have all the same attributes; whereas if two things are the same in definition or account, they must share all their attributes. Aristotle brings these distinctions to bear on the question of whether a teaching and a learning (or more generally, an action and a passion) are the same. He appears to answer that—like the road from Athens to Thebes and the road from Thebes to Athens—a teaching and a learning, and an action and (its corresponding) passion, are the same, although they are not the same in the full sense (or properly), since they differ in account: "A teaching is not the same as a learning, or action the same as passion, properly [*kuriōs*], though they belong to the same subject, the motion; for the actualization of X in Y and the actualization of Y through the action of X differ in account" (*Physics* III.3.202b.20; Hardie and Gaye's translation).[26] In context, it is difficult to see in this passage the claim that although an

[26]It is not immediately clear from this passage whether Aristotle has in mind particular teachings and learnings, or the event-types teaching and learning. I think we can make better sense of the passage if we suppose Aristotle has in mind particular teachings and learnings: for whereas the event-types teaching and learning cannot plausibly be thought of as related in the way that the road from Thebes to Athens is related to the road from Athens to Thebes, perhaps a particular teaching and a particular learning can be. That is because, while there is a case for identifying some particular teachings and learnings, there is no case for identifying the event-type teaching with the event-type learning, since people can learn things without being taught. (This was pointed out to me by Richard Spencer-Smith.)

action and passion are each the same as some motion, they are not the same as each other. When Aristotle denies that a teaching is *properly* the same as a learning, or an action properly the same as a passion, and when he says that the actualization of X in Y and the actualization of Y through the action of X (that is, the action and the passion) differ *in account,* he strongly suggests that teaching and learning, action and passion, *are* in a way the same (like the road from Athens to Thebes, and the road from Thebes to Athens). Otherwise, why bother with the qualifiers 'properly' and 'in account'?[27] Now, the distinction between being in a way the same and being the same in account is Aquinas' distinction between being the same *secundum rem* and being the same *secundum rem et rationem* (see PE III, *lect.* 5). So, in Thomistic terms, Aristotle is arguing in III. 3 that a teaching and a learning, an action and a passion, are not the same *secundum rationem,* even though they belong to one and the same subject (the motion). Nothing he says entails that an action and a passion are different *secundum rem,* even though they are each the same *secundum rem* as the motion that is their subject. Indeed, the part of the passage cited above strongly suggests that a teaching and a learning, an action and a passion, are *not* different from each other *secundum rem* but only *secundum rationem.* The idea that a particular teaching and a particular learning are related to each other in the way that the road from Athens to Thebes and the road from Thebes to Athens are is not obviously implausible. For (necessarily) teaching happens only when learning happens; if no learning takes place, teaching was attempted, but not achieved. So we can see why Aristotle might want to say that when a teacher teaches and a learner learns, the teaching and the learning are one and the same thing (involving both the teacher's contribution to the activity and the learner's) described from different points of view, in the way that the road from Athens to Thebes and the road from Thebes to Athens are one and the same thing described from different points of view.[28]

Why does Aquinas give the relevant passages of *Physics* III. 3 such a forced reading? A natural place to look for an answer is Aquinas'

[27]In Gricean terms, the passage of Aristotle just cited implicates that teaching and learning, and action and passion, are in a way the same. The relevant principle of implicature is that, in the absence of special factors, one does not make weaker assertions than one might; thus one does not merely say that teaching and learning are not the same *in account,* if one also believes that teaching and learning are not even in a way the same.

[28]Suppose that, as Lewis suggests, events are identical if and only if they are the same set of regions of spacetime. Then it seems at least arguable that when a teacher T teaches a learner L at a time $t,$ the event that is T's teaching L at t is the same set as the event that is L's learning from T at $t.$

commentary on the *Physics*. There Aquinas again represents Aristotle as denying that if action and passion are one motion, then action and passion are the same (*idem*). He explicates this as follows:

> [Aristotle] says . . . that it does not follow that an action and a passion, or a teaching and a learning, are the same [*idem*]. Instead the motion in which both exist is the same. That motion according to one *ratio* is action and according to another *ratio* is passion. For being an act of this as *in this* differs *secundum rationem* from being an act of this as *from this*. A motion, however, is called an action insofar as it is the act of the agent as *from this*, while it is called a passion inasmuch as it is the act of the patient as *in this*. It should then be clear that although the motion is the same for the mover and the moved, because it abstracts from both *rationes*, nevertheless the action and passion differ because they include in their signification these different *rationes* [*actio et passio differunt propter hoc quod has diversas rationes in sua significatione includunt*]. (PE III, lect. 5)

Oddly enough, much of this passage expresses something very like the view Aristotle appears to actually hold—namely, that a teaching and a learning, and an action and a passion, differ *secundum rationem* but not *secundum rem*. If this is not evident, consider the passage's fourth and fifth sentences: "Being an act of this as *in this* differs *secundum rationem* from being an act of this as *from this*. A motion, however, is called an action insofar as it is the act of the agent as *from this*, while it is called a passion insofar as it is the act of the patient as *in this*." The fourth sentence says that two items differ *secundum rationem*, while the fifth sentence says that a motion is called an action insofar as it is one of those two items, and called a passion insofar as it is the other. If one and the same thing *realiter* (a motion) is called both an action and a passion, then the thing that is called an action is (*realiter*) the thing that is called a passion. But the thing that is called an action is (nothing different from) an action, and the thing that is called a passion is (nothing different from) a passion; so an action is a passion (not *secundum rationem*, but *secundum rem*). It is consequently a very short step from the fourth and fifth sentences of the passage to the conclusion that an action and a passion are the same as each other *secundum rem*, although they differ *secundum rationem*.

So, if the passage just quoted started out, "[Aristotle] says . . . that it does not follow that an action and a passion are the same *secundum rationem*," and ended up, "nevertheless, an action and a passion differ *secundum rationem*, because they include these different *rationes* in their signification," the passage as a whole would hang together better than it does. Why does Aquinas leave these qualifiers out?

Someone might think that Aquinas is simply being elliptical here, and intends to ascribe to Aristotle the belief that action and passion differ *secundum rationem*. This does not seem very likely. For one thing, although Aquinas (as we saw) uses *idem* and *idem secundum rem* interchangeably, I don't know of any place where he uses *idem* to mean *idem secundum rationem*, or uses *differunt* to mean *differunt secundum rationem*. So it would be misleading for Aquinas to leave out the qualifier *secundum rationem* in the relevant sentences of this passage, intending that it be supplied by the reader. For another, when Aquinas discusses the relevant passage of Aristotle in ST Ia.28.3 *ad* 1, he again attributes to Aristotle the belief that action and passion are not the same (*simpliciter*); and it strains belief that Aquinas would be misleadingly elliptical in just the same way in both places. Finally, as we shall see, it is theologically crucial for Aquinas to make out that two things can be the same (*secundum rem*) as a third, while differing from each *secundum rem*, and not just *secundum rationem*, since he will argue that the divine relations are each the same as the divine essence *secundum rem*, although they differ from each other *secundum rem* (cf. ST Ia.28.3 and 39.1). Indeed, Aquinas appeals to *Physics* III.3 precisely to support the claim that the divine relations are really distinct from one another, even though they are each really the same as the divine essence. So it is quite implausible that, as Aquinas understands it, Aristotle is saying nothing more in *Physics* III.3 than that an action and a passion, each of which differs from motion *secundum rationem*, also differ from each other *secundum rationem*.

On the other hand, it is noteworthy that in the passage from Aquinas' commentary just cited, Aquinas does not come right out and say that an action and a passion differ *secundum rem*, although they are each the same as the motion *secundum rem*. Similarly, at ST Ia.28.3 *ad* 1 he does not explicitly deny that an action and a passion are the same *secundum rem*. In each case, Aquinas says only that an action and a passion are not the same. This may indicate a reluctance (perhaps an unarticulated or subliminal reluctance) on the part of Aquinas to attribute to Aristotle, or to hold himself, the belief that an action and its corresponding passion are different from each other *secundum rem*, though they are each the same as some motion *secundum rem*.

It is easy enough to see why Aquinas would have this kind of reluctance. As we have already seen, Aquinas usually thinks of *rationes* as something like concepts associated with terms, rather than as properties inherent in individuals—otherwise the fact that the *rationes* of the divine perfections are many would jeopardize divine simplicity. If *rationes* are understood in this way, we can't get from the premiss that action and passion include in their signification different *rationes,* to the conclusion that action and passion differ *secundum rem* (as well as *secundum rationem*). Indeed, the argument Aquinas himself offers at the end of the passage quoted above is of a form whose instances he rejects in contexts where the compatibility of God's simplicity with His perfection is at issue—namely, *x* and *y* are different, (and not just different *secundum rationem*) because they include different *rationes* in their signification.

Suppose, alternatively, that *rationes* are understood in this context as properties inherent in individuals. That will not help us see how two things can each be the same as a third *secundum rem,* without being the same as each other *secundum rem.* If *rationes* are properties inherent in individuals, and an action and a passion have different *rationes,* then that action and that passion will not have all the same properties, and will accordingly be distinct *secundum rem.* But then, since nothing can have all of the same properties as each of two things that do not have all of the same properties as *each other,* no motion will have all the same properties as that action, and all the same properties as that passion: in which case no motion will be both the same as that action *secundum rem* and the same as that passion *secundum rem.*[29]

So, whether *rationes* are thought of (in more usual Thomistic fashion) as concepts, or thought of as properties, it remains hard to see what reason Aquinas could have had to deny that identity *secundum rem* is Euclidean. Aquinas does, however have a compelling motive to suppose that identity *secundum rem* is non-Euclidean: given the rest of his Trinitarian metaphysic, that supposition is needed to avoid the Sabellian heresy.

Aquinas holds (i) that the essence of an individual is in every case either a proper part of that individual, or identical to that individual *secundum rem;* (ii) that God's essence is the essence of each divine person; and (iii) that neither God nor any divine person is composite. Given that identity *secundum rem* is Euclidean, we may move from

---

[29]One reason Aquinas might find the question of the identity of an action and its corresponding passion, and the identity of either of those and a motion, a particularly difficult one: Aquinas wants to endorse the Aristotelian claim that a teaching and a learning are the same motion, and this claim is most easily understood as an identity-claim concerning particular events. But as we have seen, Aquinas officially has no events in his ontology; for him, every real thing is either a substance or a property inherent in a substance. The reader may verify for herself that it is extremely hard to give an account of "some one thing (motion) is both an action and a passion (for example, both teaching and learning)," if we suppose that the only real things are substances and their properties.

these premisses to the claim that any two divine persons are identical *secundum rem*. Since the Father has God's essence, and is incomposite, the Father must be the same *secundum rem* as God's essence. By the same reasoning, the Son must be the same *secundum rem* as God's essence. So, as long as any two things that are the same *secundum rem* as a third are the same *secundum rem* as each other, the Father and the Son are the same *secundum rem*. This conclusion is for Aquinas theologically out of bounds. As he says at DP 9.5 *ad* 14, if the Father and the Son do not differ from each other *secundum rem*, then the Father is the Son, and the Son is the Father—which is the Sabellian heresy.

If, on the one hand, Aquinas accepts that identity *secundum rem* is Euclidean, and rejects Sabellianism, he must choose between something he thinks is theologically nonnegotiable and something he thinks is philosophically demonstrable. That is, he must give up either the claim that just one (divine) essence is a constituent of each of the three divine persons, or the claim that God and the divine persons are entirely incomposite. If, on the other hand, he denies that identity *secundum rem* is Euclidean, he can block the argument laid out above without renouncing either orthodoxy or divine simplicity. (For the implementation of this strategy, see DP 8.3.) And he can block the similar argument laid out at the end of the last section, insisting that although the constituting divine essence is both the same as the distinguishing relation Paternity *secundum rem*, and the same as the opposed distinguishing relation Filiation *secundum rem*, Paternity and Filiation are not the same as each other *secundum rem*.

On this basis, I conjecture that Trinitarian considerations induce Aquinas to deny that identity *secundum rem* is Euclidean. I don't know whether they provide the only inducement, but they provide a very important one. If this is so, one might expect that when Aquinas is not explicitly worried about reconciling God's simplicity with His triune nature, he slips into thinking of identity *secundum rem* as Euclidean. In fact, there are a number of places in which Aquinas seems to endorse (explicitly or implicitly) the principle that two things that are the same as a third *secundum rem* must be the same as each other *secundum rem*.

For example, at ST Ia.40.1 *ad* 1 Aquinas argues that "because divine simplicity excludes composition of subject and accident, it follows that whatever is attributed to God is His essence: so wisdom and power are the same in God, because they are both in the divine essence." The argument is: the wisdom in God is the same as the divine essence; the power in God is the same as the divine essence; therefore, the wisdom in God is the same as the power in God. The type of sameness Aquinas has in mind here cannot be sameness *secundum rem et rationem*, since (as we have seen) he holds that divine wisdom and divine power differ *secundum rationem*. It must therefore be sameness *secundum rem;* which is to say that in this context Aquinas argues from two things being the same as a third *secundum rem*, to those two things being the same as each other *secundum rem*. In other words, his argument turns on identity *secundum rem*'s being a Euclidean relation.

In that same article, Aquinas offers this argument for the identity of person and essence in God: "Since a relation, inasmuch as it is something real in God, is the divine essence itself, and the essence is the same as a person, as we have already made clear, it must be that a relation is the same as a person" (ST Ia.40.1, *responsio*). The argument goes: a relation is the same as the divine essence; the divine essence is the same as a person; therefore, a relation must be the same as a person. The kind of sameness Aquinas has in mind must once again be sameness *secundum rem*, since on his account person and essence, and relation and essence, differ *secundum rationem*. So Aquinas is arguing here that since a first thing is the same as a second *secundum rem*, and the second is the same as a third *secundum rem*, the first is the same as the third *secundum rem*. In other words, Aquinas appears to rely on the principle that identity *secundum rem* is transitive. It is hard to see how he could have accepted this principle, without (implicitly) accepting that identity *secundum rem* is Euclidean; since the only transitive relations that are non-Euclidean are nonsymmetric, and Aquinas definitely thinks that identity *secundum rem* is symmetric (cf. DP 9.5 *ad* 14).[30]

By way of summary: Aquinas does not deny that identity *secundum rem* is Euclidean because he is thinking of identity *secundum rem* as a relation that, though identitylike, falls short of real identity.[31] (To belabor the point: if he thought of identity *secundum rem* that way, he

---

[30]Someone might object that the arguments in the two passages just cited are enthymemes, and would be recognized as such by Aquinas, so that extra premisses (unspecified there) are needed to get from the premiss that divine wisdom and divine power are the same as the divine essence *secundum rem*, to the conclusion that divine wisdom and divine power are the same as each other *secundum rem* (and likewise for the second argument). This may be so, but I don't see any compelling reason to think it is; it seems at least as likely that in these contexts Aquinas is drawn to the (apparently evident) principle that if each of two things is the same as a third *realiter*, then those two things must be the same as each other *realiter*.

[31]As the reader may verify for herself, it is in any case very difficult to come up with any kind of identitylike relation that is non-Euclidean: any relations I can think of which confer a limited kind of indiscernibility, such as Lewis' identity-at-time-*t*, or *being of the very same matter and the very same form*, are Euclidean. So Aquinas' account of the Trinity does not by any means cease to be logically problematic if we suppose (contratextually) that identity *secundum rem* is an identitylike relation weaker than identity.

could not suppose that divine simplicity is secured by supposing that whatever is in God is God *secundum rem* [though not necessarily *secundum rationem*], and he would not suppose that Sabellianism follows simply from the supposition that the Father and the Son differ *ratione* but not *re*.) Aquinas denies that identity *secundum rem* is Euclidean because (as he sees it) such a move is the only one available to block an argument from premises knowable by natural reason (concerning God's simplicity) to the falsity of the orthodox view of the Trinity, according to which the divine persons are many, but their divine essence is one. Unless he denies that identity *secundum rem* is Euclidean, he must recognize the existence of a sound argument for the impossibility of the Trinity (as conceived by the orthodox), since there are arguments tacitly relying on identity's being a Euclidean relation, whose conclusion is that God is not three persons of one essence, and whose premises are (by his lights) necessary truths about God's incomposition.[32] Aquinas argues that identity *secundum rem* is non-Euclidean because, given his philosophical and theological commitments, there is no other escape route from heterodoxy.

But insisting that identity *secundum rem* is non-Euclidean is no more viable an escape route than any other. The relation Aquinas calls *identitas secundum rem* is just identity, and identity just is a Euclidean relation. To put the point another way: if each of two things is really the same (*idem secundum rem, idem realiter*) as a third thing, those two things cannot really be different things from each other. I shall not argue for these claims because they seem as evident as can be, and at least as evident as anything I could say in their defense.

The moral is that Aquinas' theory of the Trinity is logically flawed at the core. At an impressionistic, intuitive level, we might have been

---

[32]Some arguments of this sort are more streamlined than any yet considered. Start with a premiss that Aquinas certainly regards as necessarily true: that whatever is in God is God (*secundum rem*). Then we may argue:

(1) Whatever is in God, is God (*secundum rem*).
(2) Each divine person is in God.
So (3) each divine person is God (*secundum rem*).
∴   Any one divine person is any other (*secundum rem*).

Aquinas does not take issue with (2), and explicitly endorses (3) (see DP 8.3, *responsio:* "Paternitas enim est ipsa divina essentia . . . et pari ratione Pater est idem quod Deus"). From (3) and the tacit premiss that identity *secundum rem* is Euclidean, we can get to the argument's heretical conclusion. If we substitute 'divine relation' for 'divine person' uniformly in the above argument, we get another argument whose premises Aquinas sees as necessarily true, and whose conclusion Aquinas would again suppose is heretical.

skeptical from the beginning about whether Aquinas could provide a consistent account of the Trinity. For Aquinas, God is the simplest possible being, in whom there is no distinction between person and nature, or part and whole, or subject and attribute. Now, it is on the face of it incredible that such a being could have enough structure to be three persons in one nature. But an impression is not an argument: so I have tried to show exactly how we can move from Aquinas' conception of God and the divine persons as absolutely simple to the Sabellian claim that the divine persons are all the same as one another. Aquinas does have a strategy for blocking this move; but since it depends on denying an evident logical truth about identity, it is unsuccessful.

Divine Simplicity and the Trinity

How might Aquinas' theory of the Trinity be reconstructed? I cannot do justice to so large a question here, but I will make some remarks about a number of ways that a reconstruction might go. First, we might hold Aquinas' conception of divine simplicity fixed, while discarding his view that identity is non-Euclidean. On the resulting theory of the Trinity, the names of the divine persons would all refer to the very same (entirely incomposite) divine individual, which individual would be both God and the one divine person. To go this route is not so much to reconstruct Aquinas' theory of the Trinity as to give up Aquinas' belief that God is triune in order to hold on to his belief that God is completely simple. Alternatively, we might think of the Trinity as involving just one individual (God) who has three "modes of subsisting," where the modes of subsisting are really distinct from one another, and really distinct from the God who is their subject. A theory of this sort (briefly alluded to at the end of Chapter 5) would not be consistent with Aquinas' view that there is no distinction between subject and attribute *in divinis,* and would consequently force us to give up a part of Aquinas' conception of divine simplicity. If the argument of Chapter 1 is sound, however, it is a part we are going to have to give up anyway. Moreover, as I argued in Chapters 1 through 4, the only promising way to defend Aquinas' claim that there is no composition of subject and attribute in God is to argue that the relation holding between subjects and their attributes should not in general be understood compositionally, because attributes are not constituents of their subjects. If a moderately Sabellian theory makes orthodox sense, it may allow us to maintain in Thomistic fashion both that there is a plurality of divine persons, and that God is free from any form of composition. Such a theory would allow us to hold on to a good bit of

Aquinas' conception of divine simplicity, and a fair bit of Aquinas' account of the Trinity. But it appears to leave no room for a claim Aquinas would consider crucial to Trinitarian orthodoxy—*viz.*, the claim that the divine persons are hypostases, or first substances, or complete individual substances. On the moderately Sabellian picture, we get three distinct divine persons (in an attenuated, or at least nonstandard sense of 'person'), but not three first substances. If there were three hypostases or complete individual substances in the Trinity, this would conflict with the moderately Sabellian claim that in the Trinity there is just one divine individual, in three modes of subsisting. At least, a conflict would result if 'hypostasis' or 'complete individual substance' is understood in anything like the Aristotelian way in which Aquinas understands them.

Suppose, on the other hand, we adopt the compositional account of the Trinity sketched earlier in this chapter, according to which the divine persons of the Trinity have a kind of matter, and are as it were relationally discernible but hylomorphically indiscernible composita. Then we can hold on to Aquinas' belief that the different persons of the Trinity are different first substances. Of course, to do so, we have to give up another component of Aquinas' conception of divine simplicity—the claim that neither God nor the divine persons have any integral parts.

What emerges is a tradeoff between holding on to various elements of Aquinas' account of God's simplicity, and holding on to various elements of (what Aquinas considers) Trinitarian orthodoxy. By weakening Aquinas' account of divine simplicity in one way, we can make room for a plurality of persons of God; by weakening it in another way, we can make room for a plurality of first substances in God. I won't examine here the difficult question of what sort of weakening is optimal; at present I want only to underscore that the full-strength account of divine simplicity (the one Aquinas presupposes and deploys in his metaphysics of the Trinity) describes a God who could not possibly be triune.

[7]

Change, Composition, and the Incarnation

The Union of Human and Divine Natures in Christ

We all with one accord teach men to acknowledge one and the same God, our Lord Jesus Christ, at once complete in Godhead and complete in manhood, truly God and truly man, consisting also of a reasonable soul and body; of one substance [*homoousios*] with the Father as regards His Godhead and at the same time of one substance with us as regards His manhood; like us in all respects, apart from sin; as regards His Godhead, begotten of the Father before all ages, but yet as regards His manhood begotten, for us men and for our salvation, of Mary the Virgin, the God-bearer; one and the same Christ, Son, Lord, Only-begotten, recognized *in two natures, without confusion, without change, without division, without separation;* the distinction of natures being in no way annulled by the union, but rather the characteristics of each nature being preserved and coming together to form one person and subsistence [*hypostasis*] not as parted or separated into two persons, but one and the same Son and Only-begotten God the Word, Lord Jesus Christ; even as the prophets from earliest times spoke of Him, and our Lord Jesus Christ himself taught us, and the creed of the Fathers has handed down to us. (The Definition of Chalcedon).[1]

Central to the definition of Chalcedon is the idea that there is a single individual—Jesus Christ—who is at once true God and true man. The Incarnation involves just one person and *hypostasis* (the Word of God, the Lord Jesus Christ); and it involves two complete natures—one

[1]The translation is taken from Henry Bettenson, ed., *Documents of the Christian Church* (London: Oxford University Press, 1967), p. 51.

human, and one divine. By virtue of the union of a human nature with the divine nature in the person of the Word, the Word, who was from eternity God, was made man.

In his treatment of the Incarnation, Aquinas attempts to explicate the notions of hypostasis, nature, and union which figure in the Chalcedonia definition. He also tries to defend the coherence of the idea that, as a result of the union of two natures in the hypostasis of the Word, the Word is true God and true man. Because Aquinas supposes that God is altogether simple and changeless, this defense involves trying to fit together the Incarnation with God's incomposition and immutability. I voice some doubts below about whether this can be done, but first it is necessary to see how Aquinas understands the account of the Incarnation embodied in the Chalcedonian definition. I shall begin by saying something about how Aquinas conceives of the elements of the Chalcedonian definition mentioned above—hypostasis, nature, and union.

As we have seen, by 'hypostasis' Aquinas understands something like an Aristotelian first substance. That is, a hypostasis is for Aquinas an individual that exists in itself and not in another, and underlies a common nature (ST Ia.29.2, *responsio*). Because a particular whiteness or petreity does not exist in itself, but in another, neither a whiteness nor a petreity is a hypostasis. Similarly, Aquinas says, a hand or a foot is not a hypostasis, because, rather than existing in itself, it exists as an integral part of another (ST 3a.2.3 *ad* 2; CT 211). Aquinas accepts that a hand or a foot is an individual or particular, and is even willing to say that a hand or a foot—unlike a whiteness or a petreity—is a particular in the genus of substance, or is a particular substance (cf. ST 3a.2.3, obj. 2 and *ad* 2; DUVI 2, obj. 3 and *ad* 3). Likewise, he is willing to say that a hand or a foot is a subsistent entity (ST Ia.75.2 *ad* 1). He denies, however, that a hand or a foot is a hypostasis, on the grounds that neither a hand nor a foot is a complete substance subsisting *in se*.[2] (As he sometimes says, integral parts do not exist in themselves, but in a whole.) We have seen that Aquinas construes composition broadly enough that an individual may be said to be composed both of integral parts and of received forms. So, construing 'part' in a correspondingly broad sense (so as to cover any of the metaphysical or integral constituents of a thing), we might naturally suppose that for Aquinas a hypostasis is an individual that is not a part of any other individual.[3]

---

[2]"Manus enim, etsi pertineat ad genus substantiae; quia tamen non est substantia completa in se subsistens, non dicitur hypostasis aut suppositum" (DUVI 2, *responsio*).

[3]Here we must be rather strict about what counts as an individual, lest a sheep or a star turn out not to be a hypostasis, on the grounds that it is a part of a flock or a galaxy.

This, however, is not in fact Aquinas' view. As we shall see, for Aquinas' theory of the Incarnation to work, we must suppose that something can fail to be a hypostasis, even though it is a particular substance, and is not a part of any other individual substance.[4]

In the sense of the term relevant to the Chalcedonian definition, Aquinas tells us, a nature is an essence or quiddity—that by which an individual substance falls under its (most determinate) natural kind, or species (cf. ST 3a.2.2, *responsio;* DUVI 1, *responsio*). We saw in Chapter 3 that for Aquinas the nature of a hylomorphically composite individual is itself a composite of matter and form; the nature of an immaterial being 'composed' of essence and existence is a (thin) form; and the nature of a being lacking both composition of form and matter, and composition of essence and existence, is pure existence. Accordingly, Aquinas supposes that the divine nature the Word had from eternity is something entirely simple (pure subsistent *esse*), and that the human nature that the Word assumes in time is composed of a (human) substantial form, and a (parcel of) form–receiving matter.

On Aquinas' account, the divine nature the Word has had from eternity is the very same thing as the Word. By contrast, the human nature the Word assumes in time is distinct from the Word, and comes into union with the divine nature in the person of the Word. What is this union like? Because Aquinas holds that the union of the assumed human nature with the divine nature in the person of the Word is *sui generis,*[5] he thinks that any attempt to render the sort of union found in the Incarnation transparent is bound to fail. Thus at SCG IV.27 he says that of all divine works, the Incarnation most exceeds (our) reason, and in the *Compendium theologiae* he describes the union of human and divine natures in the Incarnation as mysterious, ineffable, and incomprehensible (CT 211).[6] Even so, Aquinas certainly thinks that something can be said about what the union is, and what it is not, and about what does and does not result from it. At a very abstract level of

---

[4]In contexts where the Incarnation is not at issue, Aquinas sometimes appears to accept the principle that whatever is unreceived, and is not a part of anything else, may be said to subsist *per se* ("Proprie et per se subsistens dicitur quod neque est praedicto modo inhaerens, neque est pars" ST Ia.75.2 *ad* 2). In such passages, charity dictates that we intepret Aquinas as ignoring the metaphysically singular case of the Incarnation. For he will say that although the Word's assumed human nature is neither inherent in the Word nor a proper part of the Word, it does not subsist *per se.*

[5]At DUVI 1, *responsio,* Aquinas calls the union of the assumed human nature to the Word an entirely new mode of union, possible only through God's infinite power.

[6]Interestingly, the treatment of the Incarnation in the *Compendium theologiae* appears to stress the mysterious and ineffable nature of the union more strongly than the treatment in either of the *Summas,* or the disputed question "De unione verbi incarnati."

description, the union is a relation holding between a form-matter composite (the assumed human nature) and the divine nature, as they come together in the person of the Word (ST 3a.2.7, *responsio*). By itself, this does not tell us much; but, Aquinas thinks, quite a lot can be said, and defended by appeal to considerations from natural theology or Scripture, about what the relation of union is not.

To begin with, Aquinas holds (in conformity with the definition of Chalcedon) that the union of human and divine natures in the Word is not a union in a nature, or essential union. That is, the human nature and the divine nature in Christ—unlike, say, the form and matter in Christ's assumed nature—did not come together in such a way as to constitute a single nature or essence. Aquinas thinks that this part of Chalcedonian orthodoxy may be demonstrated on philosophical grounds. He argues as follows: complete natures (like the divine nature of the Word, and its assumed human nature) are not the sorts of things that can in their integrity be joined so as to constitute a single nature; it is only the subnatural parts of a thing (*viz.*, matter and form) which can without losing their integrity be so joined (see ST 3a.2.1). ("Subnatural" should be understood here on the model of "subatomic.") Consequently, if the divine and human nature by their union came to constitute a single nature, they did so because one was changed into the other (as food is changed into an eater, or wood is changed into fire), or both were changed into a third thing (as elements combined in a mixture are changed into that mixture). But, Aquinas maintains, anything that can be changed into something else, or can have something else changed into it, is not immutable; so the divine nature cannot have combined with a human nature in such a way that what resulted was a single nature of a single person (cf. CT 206).

Although the union of human and divine natures in the Word is not essential, neither is it for Aquinas an accidental union. The position Aquinas is opposing, in arguing that the human nature in Christ is not united to the Word accidentally, is not—as one might think—the view that the human nature in Christ is an accident of the Word.[7] Rather, it is the view that the human nature assumed by the Word is something accidentally related to the Word, in something like the way a ring on someone's finger is accidentally related to its bearer, or a house is accidentally related to its occupant. Aquinas attributes this

---

[7]Of course, Aquinas also opposes this last view, and thinks it can be refuted on philosophical grounds, since (a) the Word is not the sort of Being who could acquire an accident, and (b) the assumed human nature, as a hylomorphically composite thing, could not be an accident of anything (see SCG IV.41).

view to Nestorius at SCG IV.41, saying that he held that the human nature of Christ was a kind of temple for the Word of God, and that the union was a sort of indwelling by the Word in that nature. Against this view, Aquinas argues that if the human nature in Christ is only accidentally united to the divine nature in the Word, then that human nature, together with its existence and accidents, constitutes a hypostasis, individual, and person distinct from the Word. And the view that the Incarnation involved two persons (one human, and one divine) as well as two natures, he holds, is clearly at variance with Scripture and with the teaching of the Church (for example, in the definition of Chalcedon). To sum up: Aquinas argues on philosophical grounds that the union is not essential, and on theological grounds that it is not accidental.

If the union is neither essential nor accidental, what is it? It is a metaphysically singular relation—in Aquinas' words, "a new mode of union"—which is both like and unlike both an essential and an accidental union. It is like an essential union (and unlike an accidental one) in this way: it results in an individual's having a particular nature. After a particular substantial form—say, a human substantial form—and a particular parcel of form-receiving matter are joined to each other, it thereby becomes true that a particular individual has, or "subsists in," a human nature. Likewise, after the assumed human nature has been joined to the divine nature of the Word, it thereby becomes true that a particular individual (the hypostasis of the Word) has or "subsists in" a human nature. On the other hand, it is unlike an essential union (and like an accidental one) in that, although it presupposes the existence of a nature (indeed, two), it does not result in the existence of a nature. Moreover, it is like an accidental union in that it involves the union of something (the assumed human nature) to something else that is already a complete being, with its own *esse;* it is unlike an accidental union in that it does not make any hypostasis be a certain way accidentally (does not bestow an accidental *esse* on a thing),[8] but rather makes a hypostasis be a certain way substantially (that is, it makes the hypostasis of the Word be a man). For this reason, Aquinas says that the human nature in Christ is united to the Word neither essentially nor accidentally, but substantially (DUVI 1, *responsio*).

[8]In denying that whatever comes into union with something already complete in *esse* is either an accident of it (like whiteness) or accidentally related to it (like a house or a garment), Aquinas appeals to the case of the resurrection of the body. When the body comes into (re)union with the soul, he says, the body is assumed into the *esse* of the preexistent soul, instead of being made an accident of, or something accidentally related to that soul (cf. ST 3a.2.6 *ad* 2).

This substantial union is in certain respects quite unlike either an accidental or an essential union. In any accidental or essential union, the things united become constituents of the same individual; but in the union of the human nature to the divine nature in the Word, this does not take place. Although the assumed nature enters into union with the divine nature in the Word, the human nature and the divine nature do not become parts of the same individual (ST 3a.2.4 *ad* 2); the Word, which is the divine nature, is forever disjoint from the assumed human nature. Because the union involved in the Incarnation does not make anything a part of anything else, and because it does not involve any real change in the Word (which is, by Aquinas' lights, the same as the immutable divine nature), in these respects it resembles a relation like *being created by* more than it resembles either an accidental or an essential union.

In the hope that I have provided some idea of what Aquinas thinks the union of natures in the Word is and is not, I shall go on to discuss what Aquinas thinks follows upon that union. (Actually, I have already said a good deal about this, but there is a good deal more to say.) On Aquinas' account, the union might be said to have both negative and positive results. On the negative side, it precludes the existence of a human person who could have existed, but for the relation of union holding between the assumed form-matter composite and the Word. After all, suppose that God had created the same human nature that the Word in fact assumed, and that neither the Word nor any other divine person had assumed that nature. Then there would have been a human nature (that is, a composite of human form and form-receiving matter) which (together with its accidents and its *esse*) would have constituted a human person, distinct from any of the divine persons. So the relation of union, as it were, prevents the assumed human nature from being its own man. Aquinas appears to accept this consequence. At ST 3a.4.2 *ad* 3 he notes that when Innocent III said that (in the Incarnation) the person of God consumes the person of man, he meant not that the Word of God in the act of assuming destroyed any person, but rather that the Word of God in the act of assuming prevented the existence of one: if the human nature had not been assumed by the divine person, that nature would have had its own (creaturely) personality.[9] Reasoning in the same way, at DUVI 2 *ad* 10 he says that should the assumed nature be separated from the assuming Word, it would then become its own hypostasis and person, and would subsist *per se*.

9"Si enim humana natura non esset assumpta a divina persona, natura humana propriam personalitatem haberet" (ST 3a.4.2 *ad* 3).

After this "disassumption" there would be one more created hypostasis of human nature in the world, even though there would be no more particular substances than there were, and no more natures. Instead, a nature would so to speak have been transferred from one individual to another, newly existing individual: the nature would cease to be that in which the Word subsisted, and come to be that in which a creature subsisted.

We have already seen the central positive result of the union of natures in the Word: it enables the Word to subsist in a human nature, or be a hypostasis of a human nature. Since whatever subsists in a human nature may be said *vere et proprie* to be a man, the union results in the Word's being a man as well as God. True, the way in which God gets to subsist in a human nature, to be a hypostasis of a human nature, is utterly and unimaginably different from the way in which any creature gets to subsist in a human nature, since any creature gets to subsist in a human nature by being composed (inter alia) of a human nature.[10] Nevertheless, the result of the union is that the Word is a man, in just the same sense that any other individual of human nature is; that is, 'man' is applied univocally to the Word and to other men (ST 3a.2.5, *responsio*).

As a result of the union, one and the same hypostasis is both the man Jesus Christ and the Word of God. If the Word and the man Jesus Christ are one and the same person, one and the same individual, then—by the indiscernibility of identicals—the man Jesus Christ and the Word have all the same properties. Aquinas accepts this consequence, and indeed draws attention to it, especially in opposing a Nestorian conception of the Incarnation. Thus he says at ST 3a.9.1 *ad* 3 that because of the union, inasmuch as there is one hypostasis of God and man, those things that belong to God are attributed to that man, and those things that belong to that man are attributed to God.[11] For instance, we may truly say of the man Jesus Christ that He is God, and that He created the stars and everything else (CP 211; SCG IV.34);

---

[10]Admittedly, Aquinas does sometimes speak of the composition of natures in the person of the Word, but he also warns that such talk should not make us think that the natures are different parts of the Word (ST 3a.2.4 *ad* 2). It would be less misleading if Aquinas did not speak of a composition of natures in the Word, and instead spoke only of a plurality of natures in which the Word subsisted.

[11]"Per unionem, secundum quam est eadem hypostasis Dei et hominis, id quod est Dei attribuitur homini, et id quod est hominis attribuitur Deo." Cf. also SCG IV.39 ("Cum enim Scriptura Sacra indistincte quae sunt Dei homini illi attribuat et quae sunt illius hominis Dei . . . oportet unum et eundem esse de quo utraque dicantur") and CT 211.

conversely we may truly say of the Word of God that He was born of the Virgin, suffered, was crucified, died, and was buried (SCG IV.34). So one individual—the Lord Jesus Christ and Word of God—has two sets of attributes: one set whose elements, as Aquinas puts it, "follow upon" or "pertain to" or are "proper to" His human nature, and another (unit) set whose elements are proper to (and identical with) His divine nature.

Although Aquinas insists that we may predicate of Christ the Word both those things that pertain to His human nature and those things that pertain to His divine nature, this insistence is often accompanied by a warning that we must bear in mind that divine attributes are predicated of Christ with respect to His divine nature, while human attributes are predicated with respect to His human nature (see, e.g., CT 211; SCG IV.39). The import and importance of this warning will become clearer in the section "The Incarnation and Change" when we look at certain arguments against the coherence of Aquinas' theory of the Incarnation.

Is Aquinas' account of the Incarnation a workable one? As far as I can see, it is not. As I shall try to show, Aquinas' belief that every divine person is really the same as the divine nature, and his view of the divine nature as absolutely simple and immutable, each prevent him from developing an account of the Incarnation which is both orthodox and consistent.

As we have seen, for Aquinas the union that makes the Incarnation possible is a relation between two natures as they come together in a particular person of the Trinity—the Word. It is *not,* say, a relation between two natures as they come together in the person of the Father. Likewise, assumption is a relation holding between a particular person of the Trinity (the Word) and a human nature: it is not a relation holding between any other person of the Trinity and that human nature.[12] But we saw in the last chapter that for Aquinas, each person

---

[12]"Persona Patris univit naturam humanam Filio, non autem sibi, et ideo dicitur uniens, non assumens" (ST 3a.2.8 *ad* 2). Because the Father unites the human nature to the Son, and not to Himself, He does not assume that nature. There is a complication here: for Aquinas, the Father as well as the Son may be said to assume a human nature to the Son ("Quamvis Pater assumat naturam humanam ad personam Verbi, non tamen propter hoc sumit eam ad se, quia non est idem suppositum Patris et Verbi"; ST 3a.3.2 *ad* 1). The Father, however, may not be said properly (*proprie*) to assume a human nature, since "assuming a human nature," taken properly, means "assuming a human nature to oneself"—that is, to one's hypostasis or *suppositum*—and this the Father does not do. In what follows, by "assuming," I always mean "assuming to oneself"; by the relation of assumption I always understand the relation of assuming-to-oneself, which holds between the Word and Christ's human nature, but not between any other divine person and that nature.

of the Trinity is really identical (*idem realiter, idem secundum rem*) to the divine nature that person has. The trouble is that it cannot be true both that (i) assumption is a relation holding between the Word and a human nature, but not between any other divine person and that human nature, and (ii) each of the persons of the Trinity is really identical to the divine nature, and hence—as we saw in Chapter 6— really identical to any of the others. If the Word is the same as the divine nature, and the Father is the same as the divine nature, then the Word is the same as the Father; and if the Word is the same as the Father, and the Word stands in the relation of assumption to a human nature, then the Father must also stand in the relation of assumption to that nature. If the Father assumed the human nature that the Word assumed, then the Father is a man, just as the Son is.[13] (Indeed, we can reach this last conclusion by a more direct route: if the Father and the Son are really the same as the divine nature, and hence really the same as each other, and if the Son is the man Jesus Christ, then the Father is the man Jesus Christ.) So just as Aquinas' belief that each divine person is really the same as the divine nature leaves no room for the real distinctness of persons upon which he insists, it leaves no room for the Incarnation of the Word and just the Word (upon which he also insists). In short, Aquinas' view of the relation of person to nature in the Godhead is no less antithetical to an orthodox account of the Incarnation than it is to an orthodox account of the Trinity; consequently, Aquinas' account of the Incarnation (which includes that view) is no more internally consistent than his account of the Trinity.

We have already seen how Aquinas would respond to this argument: he would maintain that it depends on conflating *identitas secundum rem* (which holds between any divine person and its nature, does

---

[13]At ST 3a.3.6 Aquinas surprisingly argues that, although only one divine person in fact assumed a human nature, it might have been that all the divine persons (jointly) assumed the same human nature. In that case, he says, it would be true that each of the divine persons would be one and the same man ("verum esset dicere quod tres personae essent unus homo"), just as each divine person is one and the same God. To the obvious objection—that if the divine persons were all one and the same man, then they could not be distinct persons of the Trinity—Aquinas answers that although the three persons would each subsist in one human nature, and would each be one and the same man, they would not be one *simpliciter*, or one hypostasis. But if each of the divine persons was the same man as the Word is actually, then they would each be *this* man— Jesus Christ. (How could it be that the Father and the Son are the same man, but the Son is *this* man, and the Father is not?) And as Aquinas holds against Nestorius, this man Jesus Christ is the eternally existing hypostasis or *suppositum* of the Word. (As he puts it in the formal mode: "Oportet in hoc quod dicitur, 'ille homo', demonstrato Christo, designetur suppositum aeternum" [ST 3a.16.9, *responsio*].) So if each of the divine persons was not just a man, but the same man (*this* man), then each of the divine persons would be the hypostasis of the Word.

not entail co-predicability, and is not an equivalence relation) with
identitas secundum rem et rationem (which does not hold between any
divine person and its nature, although it does entail co-predicability).
Thus Aquinas would say that, although the Word assumes a human
nature, and although the Word is really the same as something (*viz.*,
the divine nature) which is really the same as the Father, nevertheless
the Father does not assume a human nature (see ST 3a.3.2). Since I
have already set out my reasons for supposing that real identity rules
out this possibility, I shall not rehearse them here.

I have been arguing that Aquinas' view of the relation of each divine
person to the divine nature is inconsistent with the Chalcedonian
orthodoxy he wants to uphold. As I shall try to show, there is also a
problem about fitting together Aquinas' characterization of the divine
nature itself with a Chalcedonian account of the Incarnation.

The Hypostatic Union and Composition

In *Quaestio* 75 of the *Prima pars* of the *Summa,* Aquinas argues that
man is a being composed of a human body and a human soul.[14] This
appears to entail that (not just some, but) every man has among his
parts a human body and a human soul. Now, if every man has among
his parts a human body and a human soul, and if the Word is a man,
then the Word has among His parts a human body. Aquinas, however, cannot (consistently) accept this consequence. Whatever has
among its parts a human body is composite (that is, has proper
parts).[15] It follows that if the Word has among its parts a human body,
then something that is God (*viz.*, the Word) is composite; but, Aquinas thinks, nothing that is God is in any way composite (cf., e.g., ST
Ia.3.7).

So, whatever his remarks at ST Ia.75 might suggest, in order to hold
fast to divine incomposition, Aquinas will have to say that in at least
one case, something is a man without (ever) having either a human
body, or any of that body's parts, among its parts. This is indeed the
line Aquinas takes, at least some of the time (see note 17, below). At
ST IIIa.52.3 he maintains that the whole Christ was in Hell after His
death and before His resurrection, and considers the following argu-

---

[14]See, e.g., ST Ia.75.4, *responsio:* "Manifestum est quod homo non est anima tantum, sed aliquid componitur ex anima et corpore." See also ST Ia.76.1, *responsio,*
where Aquinas argues that since man senses, and nothing disjoint from a body can
sense, "oportet corpus aliquam esse hominis partem."

[15]Every human body has proper parts. So whatever has a human body as a part has
proper parts, by virtue of having a part that has proper parts.

ment to the contrary: "The body of Christ is a part of Him. But the body of Christ was not in Hell. Consequently the whole Christ was not in Hell" (ST 3.52.3, obj. 1). He answers: "The body that was then in the tomb is not a part of the uncreated person, but of the assumed nature. Accordingly, the fact that Christ's body was not in Hell does not preclude the whole Christ's being there" (ST 3a.52.3 *ad* 1). If the body in the tomb is not part of the uncreated person of Christ, then the body is not part of Christ, since the uncreated person of Christ is nothing other than Christ Himself. Aquinas' point here is not just that while Christ's body was in the tomb, it was not a part of Christ. (If that were his point, he would say that the body that was then in the tomb *was not* [then] a part of the uncreated person of Christ, rather than that the body then in the tomb *is not* a part of His uncreated person.) For Aquinas, neither Christ's body nor any of its parts are parts of Christ, although they are parts of His assumed nature. I don't, however, see how a being that never has any human bodily parts—a being forever disjoint[16] from every human body—could be a human being; it would be too intrinsically, constitutionally different from ordinary human beings to be a genuine human being.[17] I doubt that anything I could say in defense of this claim would be any more convincing than the claim itself; but to my mind, this is a sign not of the claim's doubtfulness, but rather of its intuitive plausibility.

Someone might think that, even if the argument I've just sketched shows that Aquinas' account of the Incarnation breaks down, it fails to show that Aquinas' conception of divine simplicity is incompatible with Chalcedonian orthodoxy. She might defend this view as follows:

> Aquinas insists that an ordinary man is not his soul, but is instead a composite of body and soul. Suppose, though, that Aquinas is wrong about this, and that a man is "a rational soul using a human body."[18] In other words, suppose that "man"

[16]Again, *A* is disjoint from *B* just in case *A* and *B* have no parts in common.

[17]Surprisingly, Aquinas on at least one occasion directly implies that the Word, like other men, is constituted by a body and soul. At SCG IV.37 he says that we are called men in virtue of being constituted of a rational soul and a body, and that if Christ were not called a man on that account, He would not be univocally a man. Clearly, though, if Christ is constituted of something composite (*viz.*, a body), He must Himself be composite: if the simple can be constituted by the composite, we lose all grip on what constitution might be.

The Definition of Chalcedon lays down that Christ *consists of* a rational soul and body. The claim that Christ or the Word consists of a rational soul and body is surely, on any nontortured reading of "consists of," inconsistent with the claim that the Word is disjoint from every body.

[18]See Augustine, *De moribus ecclesiae* 1.27.52.

is a phase-sortal, applying to a rational soul when and only when that soul is causally hooked up in the right way with a human body. In that case, something will be a man at a time just in case it is at that time a mind or rational soul that is causally related in the right way to a human body; a rational soul will come to be a man (though not necessarily come to be) when it comes to stand in the right sort of causal relations to some human body; and a rational soul will cease to be a man (though not necessarily cease to be), when it ceases to stand in the right sort of causal relations to any human body. If this type of Augustinian-Cartesian account of the metaphysical constitution of man is right, one may after all be able to reconcile the claim that the Word is simple in all the ways laid out in *Quaestio* 3 of the *Summa,* with the Chalcedonian claim that the Word is true man as well as true God. For the intrinsic property of being a rational soul or mind is compatible with the property of being simple in all the relevant ways, and the relational property of being causally hooked up in the right way to a human body is at least not obviously incompatible with the relevant sorts of simplicity. But if a man is just a mind causally related in a certain way to a human body, then a rational soul or mind that is simple in all the relevant ways, and causally related to a human body in the right way, will be both God and a man. So, if the Augustinian-Cartesian account of man is correct, there is no obvious contradiction in the supposition that the Word is at once an altogether simple God and a man. The reason Aquinas cannot hold on both to divine simplicity and to the humanity of the Word is not because these ideas are evidently irreconcilable, but because their conjunction is irreconcilable with Aquinas' more or less Aristotelian, un-Cartesian metaphysic of man.

For the usual reasons, I think that the Augustinian-Cartesian account of what it is to be a man is (necessarily) false.[19] If this is so, and if

---

[19]For an argument to this effect, presupposing a weak and plausible version of functionalism, see Sydney Shoemaker, "On an Argument for Dualism," in *Knowledge and Mind: Philosophical Essays,* ed. C. Ginet and S. Shoemaker (New York: Oxford University Press, 1983), pp. 233–59. To touch on one sort of consideration that makes me think a man could not be an incomposite immaterial substance: I find it highly plausible that although—as Locke argued—there is nothing incoherent about supposing that some purely material things are persons, an incomposite Epicurean atom could not be a person, no matter what causal or relational properties it had. If this is so, it presumably has to do with the incompositeness of Epicurean atoms. If it does, then an incomposite immaterial substance is not the right sort of thing to be a (human) person. I'm also inclined not to believe the non-Augustinian-Cartesian version of dualism—

nothing could be a man without having (or at any rate, having had) some bodily parts, then the Word could not be both incomposite and genuinely human—even if, were the Augustian-Cartesian account (*per impossible*) true, it would be possible for the Word to have both of those properties. Rather than discussing my (not very original) reasons for thinking that nothing forever devoid of bodily parts could be a man, I argue that the Augustinian-Cartesian account does not in any case offer us a way to square the idea that the Word is simple in all the ways laid out in *Quaestio* 3 with Chalcedonian orthodoxy.

The Incarnation and Change

According to *Quaestio* 3, (whatever is) God is simple in all of the following ways: He is not composed of extended parts, or of form and matter; He is not 'composed' of act and potency; and He is not 'composed' of essence and anything extraessential (whether individuating principles, or accidents, or existence). Instead, He is His own essence, and His own (intrinsic) attributes, and His own existence (see (1)–(6) on pages 3–4). From this it follows (for reasons discussed earlier) that whatever is God is immutable and atemporal.

Now, if the Word is God, and if whatever is God is immutable and atemporal, then the Word is immutable and atemporal. In that case, if the Word is the very same hypostasis or individual as Jesus Christ, then Jesus Christ is immutable and atemporal. Now, we know that Jesus Christ "began to fear and be weary" and "to be sad" (Mark 14:33, Matthew 26:37, cited by Aquinas at CT 204; see also ST 3a.15.6 and 7). And we know that when Christ was crucified, He suffered physical pain of increasing intensity (cf. ST 3a.15.5; CT 232). If Christ is immutable and atemporal, and yet grew fearful (or sad, or suffered increasingly intense pain), then it must be that *growing fearful* (or *growing sad,* or *suffering increasingly intense pain*) was a mere Cambridge change in Christ—that Christ did not really change when He grew fearful, or sad, or suffered increasingly intense pain, even if real

---

according to which a man is composed, but not exclusively composed, of an immaterial substance (the soul). My reasons, briefly: nothing is explained by supposing that there are immaterial souls as well as material bodies. Immaterial minds appear to have no more of an explanatory role in, say, cognitive psychology—for example, in explaining vision, or memory, or the sort of divided consciousness we find in split-brain cases—than they do in solid state physics. If immaterial souls do not pull their explanatory weight where one would most expect them to—in psychology—then they are, as Quine puts it, *entia non grata*. For the purposes of the present argument, however, it does not matter whether or not the less Augustinian, more Thomistic version of dualism is true, as long as the Augustinian-Cartesian version is false.

changes took place in something standing in a certain relation to the Word. This is in fact what Aquinas would have to say. When Christ grew fearful, or sad, He remained (really) exactly the same, although the soul He assumed, and the nature He assumed, underwent a real change. Similarly, when Christ suffered physical pain, Christ's body and His soul each underwent a real change, but Christ did not.

But this cannot be right. Someone can grow famous without really changing in any way—for instance, after his demise—but no one can grow fearful, or sad, or pained without really changing. Although you can make an individual more famous than he was, by leaving him (intrinsically) just the way he is, and changing how things disjoint from him are, you can't make an individual more fearful than he was by leaving him (intrinsically) just the way he is, and changing only how things disjoint from him are. If an individual was first less fearful, and then more fearful, or if an individual first suffered less intense pain, and then more intense pain, that individual must be different intrinsically from the way he was—and any individual who is different intrinsically than he was is both temporal and mutable.

In short, any orthodox Chalcedonian account of the Incarnation entails that Christ, the Word of God and God the Word, is temporal and mutable. Hence any orthodox Chalcedonian account of the Incarnation is inconsistent with Aquinas' belief that whatever is God is simple in all the ways set out in *Quaestio* 3. Indeed it is inconsistent with each of (1)–(6), with the possible exception of (1) and (2).[20] And these exceptions can be made out only if we can make a go of the very un-Thomistic and implausible view that a man is an immaterial soul standing in certain causal relations to a human body.

In various places, Aquinas makes an interesting distinction between ways in which incompatibles may and may not be predicated of Christ. Where *F*-ness and *G*-ness are incompatible, he says, it is never the case that Christ or the Word is both *F* and *G* with respect to His divine nature, or both *F* and *G* with respect to His human nature; but it does sometimes happen that He is *F* with respect to His human nature (*secundum naturam humanam*), and *G* with respect to His divine nature (*secundum divinam naturam*).[21] Thus Christ is composite with respect to

---

[20]If, as I have argued, (6) is necessarily false, nothing is consistent with (6). If the Word has some intrinsic attributes only some of the time, then the Word is not the same as all of its intrinsic attributes, so (5) is false. Likewise, the Word has accidents as well as an essence, so (4) is false. Obviously, if the Word really changes, the Word is not free from potentiality, so (3) is false.

[21]I translate *secundum human naturam* as "with respect to His human nature," rather than as "according to His human nature," or "in virtue of His human nature," because

His human nature, and simple with respect to His divine nature; passible with respect to His human nature, and impassible with respect to his divine nature (see, e.g., DUVI 2 *ad* 18; SS 6.2 *ad* 3). Could these qualifying phrases "with respect to His human nature" and "with respect to His divine nature" give us the materials to rebut the arguments just presented, and preserve both divine simplicity and orthodoxy? I don't see how.

The problem is not that something cannot be *F* with respect to one thing, and *G* with respect to something else, where being *F* and being *G* are incompatible. To cite (and slightly vary) some of Aquinas' nontheological examples, an Ethiopian can be white with respect to his teeth and brown with respect to his skin; a man can be incorruptible with respect to his soul and corruptible with respect to his body. And if we think of Christ as one person with a plurality of natures, in something like the way that the Ethiopian is one person with a plurality of bodily parts, or a man is one person with two subnatural parts, we will presumably want to allow that, where *F*-ness and *G*-ness are incompatibles, Christ could be *F* with respect to one of His natures, and *G* with respect to the other. For example, Christ could be spatially bounded with respect to one of His natures, but not so bounded with respect to His other nature. Or Christ could have limited knowledge of God's power with respect to one of His natures, and perfect knowledge of God's power with respect to the other of His natures.

An analogy may make this more plausible. Suppose that a person (call her Viatrix) time-travels not too far back into the past. Then she may, as it were, arrive at a time she already inhabits. That is, she may bring it about that she has two selves at one and the same time—one that got there in the usual way, and one that would not have been there

---

the awkward construction "with respect to" seems to fit Aquinas' use of *secundum* in these contexts better than the just mentioned alternatives. At ST IIIa.16.8 Aquinas avers that while we may say that Christ is a creature *secundum humanam naturam,* we may not say that He is a creature, just as we may say that an Ethiopian is white *secundum dentes,* but may not say that an Ethiopian is white. An Ethiopian is not white according to his teeth, or in virtue of His teeth, but (I think) could be described as white with respect to his teeth. Again, in arguing that incompatibles may in a way be predicated of Christ (with respect to different natures, rather than with respect to the same nature), Aquinas offers us the following analogy: a man is *secundum* his soul incorruptible, and *secundum* his body corruptible (DUVI 3 *ad* 13). Aquinas is saying here that a man (who is a corruptible being, speaking unqualifiedly [cf. QQ 2.1.1]) is incorruptible with respect to his soul, and corruptible with respect to his body. In these two nontheological cases, "The *K* is *F* with respect to its *X*" means "The *K* has an *x* that is *F*." Likewise, "Christ began to exist with respect to His human nature" is equivalent to "Christ has a human nature that began to exist."

but for time travel. Her indigenous self will be her younger self, and her imported self will be her older self. (If you are worried about whether there are enough molecules to go around, suppose complete compositional change in Viatrix over the relevant interval; if you are worried about whether Viatrix can really travel back in time, given the openness of the future and the fixity of the past, suppose Viatrix travels in a Laplacean world, where the future is no more open than the past.) Suppose we ask whether Viatrix has a particular bit of knowledge at one of the times she occupies twice over. The answer may well be that she has the bit of knowledge "in" or with respect to her imported self but not "in" or with respect to her indigenous self (or vice versa). Just as "The Ethiopian is white with respect to his teeth" is equivalent to "The Ethiopian has white teeth," "Viatrix knows with respect to her imported self that Q" is equivalent to "Viatrix has an imported self who knows that Q."

The problem is that, in order to conform to orthodoxy, Aquinas must endorse the truth of such statements as "Christ grew fearful," and not (or at least, not just) of such statements as "Christ grew fearful with respect to His human nature." In fact, he does. For instance, at ST 3a.16.8 he asserts that we may say without further qualification that Christ suffered, died, and was buried. So it is clear enough that Aquinas would also maintain that we can without qualification say that Christ grew fearful, or suffered increasingly intense pain.

But now it looks as if we have not circumvented our original difficulty. Since suffering increasingly just is a real change, if it is true that the Word suffered increasingly, it must also be true that the Word, and something that is God, is temporal and mutable. And this is incompatible with divine simplicity as Aquinas thinks of it.

Perhaps, though, this quick argument overlooks the complexities involved in making predications of an individual that has two natures. Consider Viatrix again, who knows with respect to one of her selves that Q, and is ignorant with respect to her other self of the fact that Q. What should we say about the truth-values of the qualifier-free statements "Viatrix knows that Q" and "Viatrix is ignorant of the fact that Q"? It depends on how we construe those statements. We might construe them as straightforward attributions of the relevant attributes (*knowing that Q, being ignorant of the fact that Q*) to Viatrix. In that case, because *knowing that Q* and *being ignorant of the fact that Q* are incompatible attributes, neither of which (at the relevant time) can be ascribed to the whole Viatrix, "Viatrix knows that Q" and "Viatrix is ignorant of the fact that Q" will each be false, in the way that "*M* is spherical" and "*M* is cubical" are each false, if *M* is an aggregate of a sugar cube and a ball bearing. Perhaps, however, we can construe the statements "Viatrix knows that Q" and "Viatrix is ignorant of the fact that Q" as quite different from straightforward attributions of knowledge that Q and ignorance about Q to Viatrix. That is, perhaps we can take "Viatrix knows that Q" to be equivalent to "Viatrix has a self with respect to which she knows that Q"—that is, "Viatrix has a self who knows that Q"—and take "Viatrix is ignorant of the fact that Q" to be equivalent to "Viatrix has a self with respect to which she is ignorant of the fact that Q"—that is, "Viatrix has a self who is ignorant of the fact that Q." If we can construe the Viatrix statements in this latter way, then even though *knowing that* Q and *being ignorant of the fact that* Q are incompatible attributes, "Viatrix knows that Q" and "Viatrix is ignorant of the fact that Q" will both come out true. So will "Viatrix both knows that and is ignorant of the fact that Q" (on one reading, at least). An analogy: even though *being brown* and *being white* are incompatible attributes, "This spaniel is brown and white" may be true. That is because it is equivalent to something like "This spaniel is brown with respect to some of its (epidermal) parts, and white with respect to some of its (epidermal) parts"—in other words, "This dog has some (epidermal) parts that are brown and some (epidermal) parts that are white."[22]

This suggests that even if *F*-ness and *G*-ness are incompatible, there may be a way of construing the unqualified statements "Christ is *F*" and "Christ is *G*" on which construal they both come out true. So how does Aquinas construe unqualified statements like "Christ grew fearful" and "Christ was born"? It will help to look at Aquinas' explanation of why we may say, without qualification, that Christ was born, suffered, died, was buried, and so on at ST 3a.16.8, *responsio*: "Those things that cannot be suspected of pertaining to the divine person with respect to itself [*secundum seipsam*] may be said simply of Christ by reason of His human nature. Thus we say simply that Christ suffered, died, and was buried." He explicates this as follows:

> It is the same way in the case of human or material things. If doubt could arise about whether attributes pertain to the whole or the part, and if they are in some part, we do not attribute them to the whole *simpliciter,* that is, without qualification. We do not say "The Ethiopian is white," but rather "is white with respect to his teeth." But we do say without

---

[22]Of course, "This spaniel is brown and white" could also be construed as a necessarily false straightforward attribution to this spaniel of the conjunctive property of brown-and-whiteness; but this construal is very unnatural, outside of a special context.

qualification "He is curly" [*crispus*] because this can pertain to him only
with respect to his hair.

There is a linguistic complication here. In Latin, one can say that a man
has curly hair either by saying the man is *crispus,* or by saying that his
hairs (*capilli*) are *crispi.* Similarly, as the Oxford English Dictionary
attests, in English one used to be able to say that a man had curly hair
either by saying that the man was curly, or that his hair was curly.
Once this is seen, Aquinas' point becomes clearer. We cannot say
without qualification "The Ethiopian is white," even if he is white
with respect to his teeth, because "The Ethiopian is white" has different truth-conditions from "The Ethiopian has white teeth." But we
can say without qualification "The Ethiopian is curly," as long as he
has curly hair, because "The Ethiopian is curly" and "The Ethiopian
has curly hair" have the same truth-conditions. What makes each
statement true is the Ethiopian's having the attribute *being curly-haired.*

A different example, at which Aquinas hints at CT 211, can be used
to make the same point. If a brown-skinned Ethiopian is white with
respect to his teeth, we cannot say without qualification that he is
white. But if a man has white skin, we can say without qualification
that he is white (even though he is not white on the inside). That is
because, while "The Ethiopian is white" and "The Ethiopian has
white teeth" have different truth-conditions, "This man is white" and
"This man has white skin" (or, at any rate, "This man has a white
surface") have the same truth-conditions. What makes each statement
true is this man's having the attribute *being white-surfaced.*

Aquinas' idea is that statements like "Christ was born," "Christ
suffered," and "Christ was fearful" are in a certain respect like "This
man is curly." I think the analogy is meant to work like this: just as
"This man is curly" is true because the attribute *being curly* belongs to
this man's hair, "Christ was born" and "Christ was fearful" are true
because the attributes *being born* and *being fearful* belonged to Christ's
assumed nature, or some part thereof. (Some of Aquinas' remarks
suggest that he thinks *being sad* is an attribute of the soul, and "This
man is sad" stands in the same relation to "This man has a soul that is
sad" that "This man is curly" stands in to "This man has curly hair."[23]
On this view "Christ was fearful" will be true because *being fearful* was

---

[23]For instance, at CT 204 he says that because Christ began to be sad, there must
have been another substance in Christ—the soul—which could suffer sadness. This
certainly suggests that *being sad* is—at least in the first instance—an attribute of the
soul. See also Aquinas' treatment of the passions of fear and sadness in the *Prima
secundae* of the *Summa theologiae.*

an attribute of a certain part of Christ's assumed nature (*viz.*, His soul).[24] To put the point another way, just as "This man is curly" is true because this man has the attribute *being curly-haired*, "Christ was fearful" is true because Christ had the attribute of *being fearful-natured* (or perhaps because Christ had the attribute of *being fearful-souled*).[25]

If this is what Aquinas is getting at, he thinks of "Christ was born," "Christ grew fearful," and the like as having truth-conditions akin to those of "Viatrix knows that Q," on the construal of that statement according to which it is compatible with the truth of "Viatrix was ignorant of the fact that Q." (On that construal, "Viatrix knows that Q" is true if and only if Viatrix has the attribute *being knowing-that-Q-selved*). In this connection it is interesting to note that Aquinas holds that "Christ is F" and "Christ is G" can both be true, even if F-ness and G-ness are incompatible attributes. For instance, at SS 21.4 he argues that "Christ is immortal" and "Christ has died" are both true, because whatever belongs to either nature may be affirmed of that person.[26]

The relevance of all this to the argument under consideration should be clear. The gist of that argument is that if, as Aquinas thinks, the Word grew fearful, suffered increasingly, and so on, then the Word cannot also be atemporal and immutable, as Aquinas supposes. But if, as Aquinas maintains, "The Word grew fearful" is true just in case the Word has the attribute of being increasingly fearful-natured (or fearful-souled), it is not immediately evident that "The Word grew fearful" and "The Word is atemporal and immutable" cannot both be true. If the Word is one individual subsisting in two natures, perhaps the Word can have the attribute of *being increasingly fearful-natured*, together with the attributes of *being atemporal-natured* and *being immutable-natured*. Perhaps the Word can even have the attribute of *being increasingly fearful-natured*, together with the attributes of atemporality and immutability.

---

[24]Similarly, "Christ was buried" was true because *being buried* is an attribute of a part of Christ's assumed nature—*viz.*, His body.

[25]Neatly enough, it turns out that "Christ is a man" is true because Christ has the attribute of being human-natured.

[26]"Ad quod in contrarium objicitur, quod Christus dicitur immortalis, dicendum quod hoc verum est, quia ea quae sunt utriusque naturae possunt affirmari de persona: sed tamen haec, Christus non est mortuus, est vera secundum quid, et falsa simpliciter: quia ad veritatem affirmativae sufficit, quod secundum aliquam naturam conveniat, quod dicitur de persona: sed ad veritatem negativae oportet quod secundum neutram." See also SS 6.2, *ad* 3, where Aquinas says that some individual is both passible and impassible, because the *suppositum* of the Word is passible with respect to one nature, and impassible with respect to the other.

Aquinas' ingenious account of the truth-conditions of statements like "Christ grew fearful" may seem to leave room both for Chalcedonian orthodoxy and for divine simplicity as he conceives of it. But I don't think it ultimately does. The root of the problem is this: on the view being considered, "The Word grew fearful" is true because the Word had the attribute *being increasingly fearful-natured,* or maybe *being increasingly fearful-souled.* The Word will have this attribute only if the Word was first less-fearful-natured (or souled), and then more-fearful-natured (or souled). But now we face the old difficulty in a new guise. On the face of it, anything that went from being less-fearful-natured to more-fearful-natured—or less-fearful-souled to more-fearful-souled—would have to undergo a real change thereby. If a soul of a person, and a nature of a person each undergo a real change (as they must, when that person goes from being less-fearful-natured to being more-fearful-natured), then the person who subsists in that nature, and the person who has that soul, cannot remain intrinsically just as he was in every respect. (Compare: if a mind of Viatrix, and a self of Viatrix each undergo a real change, then Viatrix, who "subsists in" two selves, and has two minds, cannot remain intrinsically just as she was.) But if the Word underwent a real change in going from being less-fearful-natured to more-fearful-natured, then (on pain of heterodoxy) it must be conceded that God the Word really changed. More precisely: it must be conceded that, just as God the Word has the attribute *being changing-natured,* He also has the attribute *changing.* This last claim is, I take it, inconsistent with Aquinas' conception of divine simplicity.

Someone might object that, even if it is true that God the Word changes, it still may be true (on the right construal) that God the Word is atemporal and immutable, as Aquinas' view of divine simplicity requires. Granted, it is consistent with everything said so far that "God the Word is atemporal and immutable" has a true reading, because the Word has the attributes *being atemporal-natured* and *being immutable-natured,* in virtue of the atemporality and immutability of His divine nature. But if "God the Word changes" comes out true, because God the Word has the attribute *changing,* and "God the Word is atemporal and immutable" comes out true, because the God the Word's divine nature (but not God the Word) is atemporal and immutable, then God the Word is a changing individual one of whose natures is timeless and unchangeable. This position is substantively anti-Thomistic, even if it secures (partial) verbal conformity to Aquinas by making "God the Word is atemporal and immutable" come out true.

The defender of Aquinas may object that the argument just set out for the mutability of the Word depends on a failure to notice a crucial disanaology between the case of Viatrix and the case of the Incarnate Word. She might put her objection this way:

> If Viatrix goes from being less-fearful-selved to being more-fearful-selved, then Viatrix really changes: for each of Viatrix's selves is a *part* of Viatrix, and any thing changes intrinsically whenever any of its parts change intrinsically. But when the Word goes from being less-fearful-natured to being more-fearful-natured, the Word does not really change, because the assumed nature that undergoes a real change shares no parts with the assuming Word. (More precisely, nothing that is ever a part of the assumed nature is ever a part of the assuming Word.) If we bear in mind the disjointness of the Word's human nature from the Word, we will not boggle at the claim that when the former changes intrinsically, the latter does not.

Fair enough: if the human nature the Word assumes is disjoint from the Word, there is no obvious reason why the one cannot be temporal and changing, while the other is timeless and unchangeable. By the same token, though, if the soul and the human nature the Word assumes are disjoint from the Word, it is more than difficult to see how the assumed soul can be *the Word's* soul, or the assumed nature can be *the Word's* nature. (What Aquinas calls) a human nature is a composite of body and soul, and it cannot be that both a man's soul and a man's body are external to that man.[27] It is no more possible for a man to be disjoint from his body and soul (and from every other body and soul) than it is for a puddle of water to be disjoint from all its hydrogen and oxygen atoms (and from every other hydrogen and oxygen atom). This is so, whether or not the man in question is only a man, or both a man and God. At least, so it seems to me.

Aquinas, of course, would not agree. He would maintain that in the metaphysically singular case of the Incarnation, a soul and a human nature disjoint from Christ are nevertheless Christ's soul, and Christ's nature, in virtue of the hypostatic union of Christ's assumed nature with His simple and immutable person. The nonmereological, asymmetrically real relation of hypostatic union is that whereby Christ's

---

[27]If Augustinian-Cartesian dualism is true, then a man's body is external to a man; but if a man's body is external to him, then he must have a soul or mind that is not.

human nature is *Christ's* nature, and hence that whereby Christ is a man. But the problem is precisely whether the hypostatic union could effect the humanation of the Word, if the Word to whom the human nature is hypostatically united remains immutable, atemporal, and disjoint from every body and every soul.[28] If the Word has all those attributes, then on the face of it, He is not the right sort of thing—constitutionally or intrinsically—to be a man. If He is not constitutionally or intrinsically the right sort of thing to be a man, how can any facts about the relations individuals outside of the Word bear to Him make Him a man?

Aquinas would say that we are confronted here with a mystery rather than an impossibility. Because the hypostatic union effects the humanation of the Word, while leaving Him intrinsically *toto caelo* different from any ordinary (passible, mutable, temporal, hylomorphically composite) man, it "surpasses reason" (SCG IV.39), and is "incomprehensible and indescribable" (CT 211). Aquinas would say, however, although we cannot see how the hypostatic union is possible, neither can we see that it is impossible.

Why does Aquinas think we are faced here with something that is not effably possible, rather than with something that is effably not possible? I take it Aquinas is reasoning along these lines; we have excellent philosophical grounds for supposing that nothing that is God could share any parts with any body or soul, or really change in any way. Also, we have excellent theological grounds for supposing that the Word, who was always God, became a man.[29] So we should conclude that somehow the hypostatic union effects the humanation of the Word while leaving Him just as He always was intrinsically— immutable, atemporal, and disjoint from every body and soul. We should draw this conclusion, even though we do not see how it could be true, and even if untutored intuition tells us it could not be.

Any reader who has won her way through to this chapter will know that I think Aquinas' reasoning should be turned around. Because nothing that is atemporal, immutable, and fails to share parts with any body or soul could be a man, either it is not the case that the God the

[28]More precisely: the problem is whether the hypostatic union could effect the humanation of the Word, if after the assumed nature has come to be united to the Word, it remains true that the Word (timelessly) has the attributes of immutability, atemporality, and disjointness from every body and every soul.

[29]See SCG I.6 for a discussion of the evidence we have for doctrines—like the doctrine of the Trinity, or the doctrine of the Incarnation—which surpass our reason. For Aquinas, this evidence includes the existence of miracles and the conversion of (much of) the world to the Christian faith.

Word became a man, or it is not the case that whatever is God is atemporal, immutable, and disjoint from every body and soul. Aquinas sees that—on pain of heterodoxy—we must give up either

(A) Nothing that is immutable, atemporal, and disjoint from every body and soul could be a man.

or

(B) Necessarily, whatever is God is immutable, atemporal, and disjoint from every body and every soul.

His response is to hang on to (B) and jettison (A). But (A) is much more evident than (B)! If one has to go, the one to go should be (B). A defender of Aquinas might object that, although (B) is not immediately evident—and may look at first blush far less evident than (A)—(B) evidently follows from more immediately evident true propositions (propositions at least as evident as (A)) and so can be shown to be at least as evident as (A). If this were so, then there would be an argument from evidently true propositions to the impossibility of the Incarnation. But I don't thing (B) does follow from any evidently true propositions. I will not go into all of my reasons for thinking this here: that would involve an examination and evaluation of Aquinas' arguments purporting to show that there can be composite, mutable, and temporal beings only if there is a simple, immutable, and atemporal one. (The reader may glean from Chapter 1 some of the reasons I think these arguments do not succeed.)

I have been arguing that Aquinas cannot hold both that the Word is atemporal, immutable, and uncomposed of body or soul, and that the Word was made man. Some readers may wonder again at this point whether Aquinas couldn't get (almost) everything he wants here, if only he had an Augustinian-Cartesian view of what it is to be a man. Suppose a human being = a human soul = a mind causally related in the right way to a human body. Mighn't it be that the Word was an absolutely incomposite, atemporal, and immutable mind that Cambridge-changed into a human soul—and a human being—by coming to stand in the right sort of causal relations to a human body? In that case, couldn't we preserve both the Word's incomposition, immutability, and atemporality and Chalcedonian orthodoxy?

I don't think this will work. If "The Word grew fearful" entails "The Word really changed," immutability or orthodoxy must be abandoned. So anyone who wants to hold that the Word is immutable, and cleave to orthodoxy, must offer an explanation of why this apparent entailment is not a real one. Aquinas' explanation of why it is not is, roughly, that "The Word grew fearful" is true because the Word's assumed but disjoint soul grew fearful (and really changed), leaving the Word intrinsically just as He timelessly is. The proponent of the quasi-Cartesian account of the Incarnation just sketched is in no position to offer this explanation: for him, Christ's soul or mind, far from being disjoint from the Word, just is the Word causally hooked up in the right way to Christ's body. I don't think he has any other workable way of explaining away the apparent entailment at issue; which is to say he cannot after all square the immutability and atemporality of the Word with Chalcedonian orthodoxy.

It may be helpful here to summarize the main results of this chapter. I have argued that Aquinas' account of the relation of each divine person to the divine nature is inconsistent with an orthodox account of the Incarnation, because it precludes the possibility that just one divine person became a man. Also, I have tried to show that Aquinas' belief that whatever has the divine nature is simple, timeless, and unchangeable is inconsistent with an orthodox account of the Incarnation, because it precludes the possibility that even one divine person became a man. As we saw in Chapter 6, it is Aquinas' view of God as absolutely simple which leads him to suppose that each divine person is really the same as the divine nature. So each of the difficulties highlighted in this chapter has as its source Aquinas' conception of divine simplicity. That conception can no more be fit together with an orthodox Christian view of the Incarnation than it can be fit together with an orthodox Christian view of the Trinity.

Alternatives to Aquinas' Account

If Aquinas' account of the Incarnation is unworkable, how might it be reshaped? If we are trying to preserve as much of that account as possible, given the constraints of orthodoxy, perhaps the most natural way to reconstruct it would be to hold on to Aquinas' idea that the Word's assumed human nature is a created particular composed of body and soul, and to give up Aquinas' idea that the Word's assumed nature is disjoint from the Word. On the resulting account the Incarnation will turn out to resemble the case of Viatrix in a number of interesting ways. The assumed human nature will be a proper part of the Word, just as Viatrix's imported self is a proper part of Viatrix. The person who has the assumed human nature as a part—the Word— will be identical to the person who has the divine nature as a part, just

as the person who has the imported self as a part—Viatrix—is the
person who (simultaneously) has the indigenous self as a part. In other
words, the Word will be one person having or 'subsisting in' two
natures, just as Viatrix is one person having or 'subsisting in' two
selves. The Word will be a man, but He will be unlike ordinary men,
in having an extra nature, over and above His human nature. Likewise, throughout the interval in which Viatrix is two-selved, Viatrix
will be a human being, but will be unlike ordinary (non-time-travel-
ing) humans, in having an extra self, over and above her indigenous
self.[30] Finally, because the Word has two natures, He (unlike one-
natured beings) will be able to be one way with respect to one of His
natures, and an incompatible way with respect to the other—for
instance, impassible and immortal with respect to His divine nature,
and passible and mortal with respect to His human nature. Again, as
we have seen, there is an analogy with Viatrix: because Viatrix has two
selves, she (unlike one-selved persons) can be one way with respect to
one of her selves, and an incompatible way with respect to the other—
say, fearless with respect to her indigenous self, and fearful with
respect to her imported self.

Naturally, even if we think of the assumed human nature as a part of
the Word, the case of the Incarnation will not be in every respect
analogous to the case of Viatrix.[31] Even so, the Viatrix case is enough

[30]Note that Viatrix is not a human being simply by virtue of having some self or
other of the right kind among its parts. If that were enough to be a human being, then
the aggregate of Viatrix's indigenous self and, say, the Matterhorn would be a human
being. Similarly, the Word could not be a man simply by virtue of having a human
nature among His parts. The relation of hypostatic union, whose holding between the
assumed human nature and the Word makes the Word a man, could not hold between
disjoint entities: but this does not mean that the relation of hypostatic union is just the
part-whole relation. (A parallel: someone who thinks of properties as constituents of
their subjects will deny that a property can be disjoint from its subject; but she will not
want to identify the inherence relation with the part-whole relation, lest it turn out that
whatever is a property of a part of a subject is also a property of that subject.)

[31]One disanalogy: although Viatrix has more selves than an ordinary human being,
she is, like ordinary human beings and unlike the Word, only human. I think we can
imagine a variant of the Viatrix example in which this is not so. Suppose that—through
some natural or artificial process—Viatrix mutated into a creature of another species.
(We can apparently imagine the very individual who was once a member of the species
Homo sapiens surviving a mutation into a creature of a different but quite similar
species.) Suppose that after Viatrix has finished mutating, she steps into the time
machine and set the dials for one second before she began to mutate. It turns out that
what began to mutate was not after all (the whole) Viatrix, but Viatrix's indigenous
self. At the time Viatrix's indigenous self began to mutate, Viatrix had two selves, only
one of whom was a human self—just as, after the Incarnation, the Word has two
natures, only one of which is a human nature.

like the Incarnation on the reconstructed account that thinking about the Viatrix case helps us see what it would be like for the reconstructed account to be true, and helps us see that the reconstructed account (unlike the original Thomistic account) is not obviously unworkable.

There are all sorts of interesting questions about how the reconstructed picture compares to quite different pictures of the Incarnation—for example, the kenotic picture.[32] I shall, however, leave the question of the relative merits of the reconstructed account and its (un-Thomistic) competitors to another time and place.[33]

A last word: it is important to distinguish particular accounts of the metaphysics of the Incarnation from the doctrine of the Incarnation

[32]On the kenotic picture, in the Incarnation the Word becomes a man by losing those attributes incompossible with human nature, and gaining those attributes entailed by it; this process does not involve anything analogous to the doubling of selves in the Viatrix example, and is more analogous—though only remotely so—to what happens when a caterpillar becomes a butterfly. Accordingly, even though the Word subsists in a human and a divine nature, there is no room on the kenotic picture for the Word's being one way with respect to His divine nature, and an incompatible way with respect to His human nature. For a very helpful discussion of kenoticism, see Thomas V. Morris, *The Logic of God Incarnate* (Ithaca: Cornell University Press, 1984). The view of the Incarnation Morris himself advances appears to be quite like the reconstructed Thomistic account. In fact, some of Morris' remarks suggest that he thinks that what I have been calling the reconstructed Thomistic account is Aquinas' actual account. (In describing Aquinas' position, he says: "Not being an independent whole, but only a part of that greater whole which was God Incarnate, they [Christ's soul and body] did not alone constitute a person or characterize a suppositum distinct from the single person who was the Christ, or from that single eternal suppositum dwelling in both divine and human natures" [p. 157].) Although Aquinas sometimes speaks as though the assumed human nature were a part of God Incarnate, for reasons already adduced I don't think that really is his view—although perhaps it should have been.

[33]The reconstructed Thomistic picture has one clear disadvantage in comparison with the kenotic one: it commits one to the doubtful view that an individual with a mind utterly unlike any human mind can be a man. Sometimes, this view seems very implausible to me. A being with an utterly inhuman sort of mind seems intrinsically too unlike ordinary men to be a man, even if that being also has a garden-variety human mind (and body). If Aquinas' simple and immutable Word, as it were, has not enough structure to be a man, a being with an utterly inhuman sort of mind in addition to the ordinary mind and body appears to have too much. (Compare: if [as in our embellished example] Viatrix has an inhuman self, isn't she intrinsically too unlike ordinary human beings to be a human being, even if she has a human self?) The defender of the reconstructed account might respond, in Thomistic fashion, as follows: "The Word is a man" is true, by virtue of the fact that one of the Word's natures is a human nature. To put this another way, "The Word is a man" is true, because the Word has the attribute of being human-natured; just as "Socrates is a man" is true, because Socrates has the attribute of being human-natured; and just as "The Word was fearful" is true, because the Word has the attribute of being fearful-souled. Two worries about this response: is there a reading of "The Word is a man" which has the same truth-conditions as "The Word is human-natured"? And if there is, does that reading capture the orthodox belief that the Word was a man? I'm not sure.

itself. If Aquinas' view (or for that matter the reconstructed Thomistic view) of the metaphysics of the Incarnation is incoherent, that does not show that the doctrine itself is incoherent. If it is, it is not obviously so. There is no patent incoherence in supposing that the man Jesus Christ is the very same person as God the Word. It is interesting to compare the doctrine of the Trinity and the doctrine of the Incarnation on this score. On the most straightforward construal of the doctrine of the Trinity, it is the manifestly incoherent doctrine that there are three different beings (the divine persons), each one of whom is the same as one and the same being (God). (Indeed, at the end of the day that is the way Aquinas construes the doctrine, since the relation he calls *identitas secundum rem* is identity.) Because the doctrine of the Trinity is, on its most straightforward construal, clearly necessarily false, something needs to be said about why that construal is not the only one or the best one available. (That was the aim of Chapter 5.) By contrast, the assertion that the same person who is now the man Jesus Christ has always been God the Word, straightforwardly construed, does not look in any obvious way self-contradictory; if someone thinks it is incoherent, the burden of proof is on him to bring this unobvious incoherence to light. This will not be an easy task. It might be thought that if one and the same person were God the Word and the man Jesus Christ, then that person would have to have each of a pair of incompatible attributes. But which pair? ⟨*Having no material parts, having some material parts*⟩, perhaps? This contestably assumes that God the Word (always) has the attribute of having no material parts.[34] ⟨Omniscience, nescience⟩? Someone who favors a "two-selves" or two-minds account of the Incarnation can reply that the pair of attributes the Word has is the compatible pair ⟨*being omniscient-minded, being nescient-minded*⟩; someone who favors a kenotic account of the Incarnation can say that when He becomes incarnate, the Word loses the property of being omniscient (while retaining the property of being God). Because the point should be clear, I won't multiply examples. I'm not arguing

[34]Of course, it might be argued for, and not just assumed, that God the Word always has the attribute of having no material parts. One argument to that effect would go: before the Word was made man, He had no material parts. But as Descartes maintains, anything without material parts is essentially without material parts, and hence incapable of acquiring any. So the Word never has material parts. It is easy enough to get from here to the impossibility of the Incarnation—given, of course, the un-Cartesian view that whatever is a man must have some material parts. The idea that anything immaterial is essentially immaterial is a plausible one; but for the sort of reasons adduced by Shoemaker, I think that if we concede the possibility of immaterial thinking substances, we should also concede the possibility of such substances becoming material (see Shoemaker, "On an Argument for Dualism").

that the Incarnation can be seen to be possible; I'm not even saying that there is no decisive argument against its possibility. But if there is such an argument, it is not an obvious one—or at least, it is not obvious to me.[35]

[35] For a careful discussion of the incogency of arguments for the impossibility of the Incarnation, see Morris, *Logic,* esp. chaps. 1–4.

Conclusion

In Aquinas' philosophical theology we find two incompossible Gods. The first is the altogether simple God of *Quaestio 3*—a God identical with His (intrinsic) attributes, essence, and existence. The second is the triune and incarnate God of Christianity. Since at most one of these Gods is actual, we might think reconstructing Aquinas' philosophical theology would involve choosing between two *possibilia*—the altogether simple God of Aquinas' natural theology, and the Christian one. This is not so. If the arguments of the first three chapters are sound, the completely simple God of *Quaestio 3* is an *impossibile*. Nothing could be an insular existence, an insular wisdom, an insular goodness, or the like. Also, as long as what God knows varies from one possible history or world to another, nothing that is God could be the same as its essence, any more than it could be the same as all of its intrinsic attributes.

We shouldn't conclude straightaway that there could not be an absolutely simple God. At least, we shouldn't conclude this if by "God is absolutely simple," we mean "God is absolutely incomposite"—that is, "Nothing distinct from God is a part of God." Aquinas thinks that "Nothing distinct from God is a part of God" entails "God is the same as His intrinsic attributes, essence, and existence," because he thinks the intrinsic attributes, essence, and existence of an individual are all—in a broad sense—parts or constituents of that individual. We needn't make this assumption; if we don't, nothing stands in the way of our supposing that although God is not the same as (all) of His intrinsic attributes, or His essence, or His existence, neither they nor anything else are both a part of God and distinct from God. In this way, we can save Aquinas' view that God is altogether simple, at the price of abandoning his compositional account of subject and attribute, essence and existence. God will be absolutely simple, though absolute simplicity will not amount to as much as Aquinas thought. Perhaps some of what is missing can be captured by supposing that all of God's perfections share a supernatural supervenience base in God.

Could an absolutely simple God be the triune and incarnate God of Christianity? Aquinas fails to make this possibility out. The triune and incarnate God He describes is once again an *impossibile*—a being really identical to each of three persons really distinct from one another; a being who is incarnate (since He is really identical to a divine person who is incarnate), and not incarnate (since He is really identical to a divine person who is not incarnate); a being one of whose persons suffers, dies, and is resurrected without undergoing any real changes.

This does not settle the question of whether anything absolutely simple—that is, anything identical with all of its parts—could be either triune or incarnate. On any view according to which the divine persons are parts of God, a triune God will not be absolutely simple. (This is so, whether or not the persons of the Trinity are their only parts.)[1] But the proponent of a moderately Sabellian account of the Trinity may deny that the divine persons are parts of God. For him, the divine persons and God are individuals in different senses: a divine person, unlike God, is not a concrete particular. If this is so, it is not obvious that the divine persons will be parts of God. More generally, if God's being triune is a matter of His being one individual subsisting in three modes, there is no evident reason to suppose that a proper-partless being could not be triune.

Whether or not a being that was its only part could be triune, I doubt that such a being could be a God one of whose persons was incarnate. I think Aquinas is right to suppose that, necessarily, anything that is an ordinary man is composed of bodily parts. For reasons set out in Chapter 7, I think that if this is true, it is also true that, necessarily, anything that is a man is composed of bodily parts. In that case, if the Word is both God and man, then something that is God is composed of bodily parts. But if something that is God is composed of bodily parts, how can God Himself be absolutely simple, and hence not composed of bodily parts? I don't have a knockdown argument to

---

[1]As we have seen, the divine persons cannot all be the same as God, lest they all be the same as one another. So, if each divine person is part of God, something distinct from God is a part of God, in which case He is not absolutely simple. (He has more parts than one.)

show that this is an impossibility. That is because it is an open question what relation (weaker than identity) holds between the person of the Word and God, in virtue of which the Word may be said to be God. It might be a co-composition relation, and it might be some quite different relation. All the same, whatever the relation is, it is plausible that if the Word of God is God, then the Word is not composed of bodily parts none of whose parts is ever a part of God. If the Word of God is partly constituted of bodily parts none of whose parts are ever parts of God, then on any remotely natural construal of "The Word of God is God" I can think of, that statement comes out false. So, even if we can tailor-make a construal of "The Word of God is God" on which it is consistent with the Word's having integral parts forever disjoint from God, it is doubtful whether doing so secures more than verbal conformity with orthodoxy.[2] Taking the Incarnation seriously appears to involve giving up divine simplicity and—as I have argued in Chapter 7—divine changelessness as well. If this is so, we cannot "compossibilize" the God of Aquinas' natural theology and the God of Christianity by weakening Aquinas' conception of divine simplicity in the way suggested in Part I. By weakening the Thomistic conception of divine simplicity that way, we may end up with a possible God, but not—as best I can see—a God compossible with the Christian one.

[2]It is natural to suppose that the bodily parts the Word acquires, although they are parts of God, are never parts of the un-Incarnate persons (the Father and the Holy Spirit). But if they are not, then the Father and God will not be cohabitant co-composite, or thing-stuff-co-composite, or even weakly co-composite. (No matter how small the parts get, there will be now-parts of God which never have been and never will be parts of the Father.) So, unless we can live with the idea that the bodily parts of the Word are parts even of the divine persons to whom the assumed nature is not hypostatically united, the Incarnation means trouble for co-compositional accounts of the Trinity. Perhaps the moderate Sabellian is better placed to get round these difficulties, since in his view, the assumed parts *in divinis* are not parts of just one of the three divine persons, but rather parts of the one concrete individual who is God. Perhaps a non-co-compositional, nonmoderately Sabellian account of the Trinity is needed here—although I can't see offhand how such an account would work.

Selected Bibliography

Anselm, Saint. "Letter on the Incarnation of the Word." In *Anselm of Canterbury*. Vol. 3. Edited and translated by J. Hopkins and H. Richardson, pp. 7–39. Toronto: Edwin Mellen Press, 1976.

Aquinas, Saint Thomas. *Compendium theologiae*. Edited by P. Frette. Paris: Vivès, 1939.

——. *De ente et essentia*. Edited by M.-D. Roland-Gosselin, O.P. Paris: Librairie Philosophique J. Vrin, 1948.

——. "De potentia." In *Quaestiones disputatae*. vol. 2. Edited by P. M. Pession. Turin: Marietti, 1965.

——. *De principiis naturae*. In *Opuscula omnia*. Edited by R. Perrier. Paris: Lethielleux, 1949.

——. "De spiritualibus creaturis. In *Quaestiones disputatae*. vol. 2. Edited by M. Calcaterra and T. S. Centi. Turin: Marietti, 1965.

——. "De unione verbi incarnati." In *Quaestiones disputatae*. vol. 2. Edited by M. Calcaterra and T. S. Centi. Turin: Marietti, 1965.

——. "De veritate." In *Quaestiones disputatae*. vol. 1. Edited by P. Spiazzi. Turin: Marietti, 1964.

——. *Exposito super librum boethii de trinitate*. Edited by Bruno Decker. Leiden: E. J. Brill, 1955.

——. *In duodecim libros metaphysicorum expositio*. Edited by R. Cathala and R. M. Spiazzi. Turin: Marietti, 1964.

——. *In octo libros physicorum expositio*. Edited by M. Maggiolo. Turin: Marietti, 1964.

——. *In peri hermeneias*. In *In peri hermeneias et posteriorum analyticorum expositio*. Edited by R. Spiazzi. Turin: Marietti, 1955.

——. *Quaestiones quodlibetales*. Edited by R. Spiazzi. Turin: Marietti, 1949.

——. *Scriptum super libros sententiarum*. 4 vols. Edited by R. P. Mandonnet. Paris: Lethielleux, 1929.

——. *Summa contra Gentiles*. Leonine Edition. Rome: Desclee and Herder, 1934.

——. *Summa theologiae*. 3 vols. Edited by P. Caramello. Turin: Marietti, 1952.

Aristotle, *Physics*. Translated by R. P. Hardie and R. K. Gaye. In *Basic Works of Aristotle*. Edited by R. McKeon, pp. 218–394. New York: Random House, 1941.

Armstrong, D. M. *A Theory of Universals*. 2 vols. Cambridge: Cambridge University Press, 1978.

Augustine. *De trinitate*. In *Basic Writings of St. Augustine*. Edited by Robert P. Goodwin, pp. 667–879. New York: Random House, 1948.

Bettenson, Henry, ed. *Documents of the Christian Church*. London: Oxford University Press, 1967.

Burge, Tyler. "Individualism and the Mental." *Midwest Studies in Philosophy* 4 (1979): 31–51.

——. "Mass Terms, Count Nouns, and Change." In *Mass Terms: Some Philosophical Problems*. Edited by F. J. Pelletier, pp. 199–219. Dordrecht: D. Reidel, 1979.

——. "Other Bodies." In *Thought and Object: Essays in Intentionality*. Edited by A. Woodfield, pp. 97–121. Oxford: Oxford University Press, 1982.

——. "A Theory of Aggregates." *Nous* 11 (1977): 97–117.

Burgess, John. "The Unreal Future." *Theoria* 4 (1978): 157–74.

Geach, Peter. "Aquinas." In *Three Philosophers*. Edited by G. E. M. Anscombe and P. Geach. Ithaca: Cornell University Press, 1962.

——. "Form and Existence." In *God and the Soul*, pp. 42–65. London: Routledge and Kegan Paul, 1969.

——. "God's Relation to the World." In *Logic Matters*, pp. 318–27. Berkeley: University of California Press, 1972.

——. "What Actually Exists." In *God and the Soul*, pp. 65–75. London: Routledge and Kegan Paul, 1969.

Gibbard, Alan. "Contingent Identity." *Journal of Philosophical Logic* 4, no. 2 (1975): 187–221.

Gupta, Anil. *The Logic of Common Nouns*. New Haven, Conn.: Yale University Press, 1980.

Hughes, Christopher. "Is a Thing Just the Sum of Its Parts?" *Proceedings of the Aristotelian Society* 86 (1985–86): 213–35.

Kenny, Anthony. *Aquinas*. New York: Hill and Wang, 1980.

Kim, Jaegwon. "Causality, Identity and Supervenience in the Mind-Body Problem." *Midwest Studies in Philosophy* 4 (1979): 31–51.

——. "Concepts of Supervenience." *Philosophy and Phenomenological Research* 3 (1984): 151–63.

Kretzmann, Norman. "Omniscience and Immutability." In *Readings in the Philosophy of Religion*. Edited by B. Brody, pp. 366–77. Englewood Cliffs, N.J.: Prentice-Hall, 1974.

Lewis, David. "Attitudes De Dicto and De Se." *Philosophical Review* 88 (1979): 513–43.

——. *Counterfactuals*. Cambridge, Mass.: Harvard University Press, 1973.

——. "Counterparts of Persons and Their Bodies." *Journal of Philosophy* 68 (1971): 203–11.

——. "Extrinsic Properties." *Philosophical Studies* 44 (1983): 197–200.

——. "General Semantics." In *Montague Grammar.* Edited by B. H. Partee, pp. 1–51. New York: Academic Press 1976.

——. "New Work for a Theory of Universals." *Australasian Journal of Philosophy* 61, no. 4 (1983): 343–77.

——. *On the Plurality of Worlds.* Oxford: Basil Blackwell, 1984.

——. "The Paradoxes of Time Travel." *American Philosophical Quarterly* 13, no. 2 (1976): 145–52.

——. "Survival and Identity." In *The Identities of Persons.* Edited by A. Rorty, pp. 17–41. Berkeley: University of California Press, 1976.

Massey, Gerald. "The Eternity of the World: Maimonides and Aquinas." Unpublished manuscript.

Morris, Thomas. *The Logic of God Incarnate.* Ithaca: Cornell University Press, 1984.

Occam, William. *Summa logicae.* Edited by P. Boehner, G. Gal, and S. Brown. St. Bonaventure, N.Y.: Franciscan Institute, 1974.

Perry, John. "The Problem of the Essential Indexical." *Nous* 13 (1979): 3–23.

——. "The Same F." *Philosophical Review* 78, no. 2 (1970): 181–201.

Prior, Arthur. "The Formalities of Omniscience." In *Papers on Time and Tense,* pp. 26–44. London: Oxford University Press, 1968.

Quine, W.V.O. *Set Theory and Its Logic.* Cambridge, Mass.: Harvard University Press, 1963.

Shoemaker, Sydney. "On an Argument for Dualism." In *Knowledge and Mind: Philosophical Essays.* Edited by C. Ginet and S. Shoemaker, pp. 233–59. New York: Oxford University Press, 1983.

Sorabji, Richard. "Closed Space and Closed Time." In *Oxford Studies in Ancient Philosophy,* 4:215–31. Oxford: Clarendon Press, 1986.

——. *Time, Creation, and the Continuum.* London: Duckworth, 1983.

Stump, Eleonore, and Norman Kretzmann. "Absolute Simplicity." *Faith and Philosophy* 2, no. 4 (1985): 353–81.

——. "Eternity." *Journal of Philosophy* 78, no. 8 (1981): 429–58.

Thomason, Richmond. "Indeterminist Time and Truth-Value Gaps." *Theoria* 36 (1970): 23–42.

Wiggins, David. *Sameness and Substance.* Cambridge, Mass.: Harvard University Press, 1980.

Wippel, John F. *Metaphysical Themes in Thomas Aquinas.* Washington, D.C.: Catholic University of America Press, 1984.

Index

Library of Congress Cataloging-in-Publication Data

Hughes, Christopher M.
  On a complex theory of a simple God: an investigation in Aquinas'
philosophical theology / Christopher M. Hughes.
    p. cm.—(Cornell studies in the philosophy of religion)
  Bibliography: p.
  Includes index.
  ISBN 0-8014-1759-7 (alk. paper)
    1. Thomas, Aquinas, Saint, 1225?-1274—Contributions in concept of God. 2. God—
History of doctrines—Middle Ages, 600–1500. 3. Trinity—History of doctrines—
Middle Ages, 600–1500. 4. Incarnation—History of doctrines—Middle Ages, 600–1500.
I. Title. II. Series.
BT100.T4H83 1989
231—dc20   89-42877